FLEET TACTICS AND NAVAL OPERATIONS

THIRD EDITION

FLEET TACTICS AND NAVAL OPERATIONS

THIRD EDITION

CAPT Wayne P. Hughes Jr., USN (Ret.)
and RADM Robert P. Girrier, USN (Ret.)
Foreword by ADM John Richardson, USN

NAVAL INSTITUTE PRESS
Annapolis, Maryland

The views presented are those of the authors and do not
necessarily represent the views of DoD or its components.

Naval Institute Press
291 Wood Road
Annapolis, MD 21402

Library of Congress Cataloging-in-Publication Data
Names: Hughes, Wayne P., date, author. | Girrier, Robert, date, author.
Title: Fleet tactics and naval operations / CAPT Wayne P. Hughes Jr., USN
    (Ret.) and RADM Robert Girrier, USN (Ret.) ; foreword by ADM John
    Richardson, USN.
Other titles: Fleet tactics.
Description: 3rd edition. | Annapolis, Maryland : Naval Institute Press, [2018] |
    Series: The U.S. Naval Institute blue & gold professional library |
    Includes bibliographical references and index.
Identifiers: LCCN 2018004418 | ISBN 9781682473375 (hardcover : alk.paper)
Subjects: LCSH: Naval tactics—History.
Classification: LCC V167 .H84 2018 | DDC 359.4/2—dc23
    LC record available at https://lccn.loc.gov/2018004418

♾ This paper meets the requirements of ANSI/NISO z39.48-1992
(Permanence of Paper).
Printed in the United States of America.

26 25 24 23 22   9 8 7 6 5

To CAPT Hugh G. Nott, USN (Ret.)

Contents

Figures and Tables

Foreword to the Third Edition

When considering a revision to a work that is without question a classic, one should approach with caution and deliberation. I am sure that I am not alone when I say that my copy of *Fleet Tactics* is one of the most consulted, most dog-eared, most underlined, most marked-up books in my library. So why a third edition? A review of the history can inform us.

The first edition was published in 1986, at a time when technology had made major advances. The book filled an important void, providing an up-to-date treatise on the importance and execution of tactics in modern naval warfare. At that time, we were focused on the Soviet Union as our peer competitor. ADM Thomas B. Hayward, USN, the former Chief of Naval Operations and a consummate Cold War leader, wrote in his foreword: "Phenomenal advances in technology over the last few decades have affected virtually every aspect of naval warfare in ways that have not been easy to anticipate." True enough. Naval warfare has always been strongly linked to technology. Which navy has the best equipment? Which navy can operate and employ its gear most effectively? These are critical questions for any practitioner of war at sea. The first edition of *Fleet Tactics* became an instant addition to the canon, and its six cornerstones provided a solid common foundation for understanding throughout the U.S. Navy.

The second edition, published in 2000, was again inspired in part by the introduction of new technologies—in particular cruise missiles—and in part by the fact that the Cold War had ended. The U.S. Navy had no blue-water peer competitor in 2000. As a result, we turned our attention to littoral combat—*From the Sea.* The United States became very good at projecting power and influencing activities ashore. Again, *Fleet Tactics* informed our way. VADM Arthur K. Cebrowski, USN, wrote the foreword to the second edition, and highlighted an emerging intellectual tension that was becoming more acute with advances in technology. If, as Nelson said, "a ship's a fool that fights a fort," and the effectiveness of coastal defense cruise missiles was quickly extending the effective range of a "fort," what did that have to say about the role of the Navy? How could we best contribute to the "seat of purpose on the land?" These developments further reinforced the importance of mastering tactics. For indeed, as Captain Hughes has emphasized since the beginning, tactics are inextricably linked to strategy and policy.

Each edition of *Fleet Tactics* addressed how technological advances affected tactics, and, by extension, strategy and policy. There is one additional thread through the first two editions that presaged the fundamental importance of this third edition. In the foreword to the first edition, Admiral Hayward wrote, "All tactical elements must fight as a cohesive team, must integrate into the whole the best that can be brought to bear by individual units. These, in the future, will most likely include land- and space-based assets."

And in the second edition, it was very fitting that Vice Admiral Cebrowski, one of the founding fathers of Network Centric Warfare, wrote: "The importance of scouting (information-gaining activities) and missiles reflects the dominant characteristics of the information age—access and speed. . . . Hence, the modern-day practitioner fights first for information superiority, indicating the technical and tactical choices that must be made. Put another way, we must buy the forces and develop the tactics necessary to ensure information superiority."

As successive editions of *Fleet Tactics* addressed the impending information age, in 2000 it was still a bit early to talk about the implications in detail. But now, in 2018, there can be no doubt. The information age is upon us and has dramatically changed everything, including naval warfare and fleet tactics.

In this third edition the topic of information warfare is addressed in full— and none too soon. Although the U.S. Navy has not had a peer competitor for decades, that time is over; that window is closing. Enabled in large part by advances in technology and shifts in the global economy, the U.S. Navy now faces significant blue-water competition. It is no longer possible to ignore fleet-to-fleet engagements as naval forces seek to influence events ashore; navies will have to fight their way in from far out at sea. The sea-control game is back on, and we need to get moving—and new tactics will lead the way.

Technological change has unfolded in ways that have been difficult to anticipate.

- Once the technological train got moving, it moved faster than most people thought. The pace has been exponential to date, with effectiveness doubling every few years.
- And as the rate of *introduction* of new information technology into the environment has been exponential, the rate of *adoption* by users has also grown steadily faster. People are becoming proficient users of these tools more quickly than before. For example, it took about thirty years for people to begin using Alexander Graham Bell's telephone, but only about three years for the smartphone to gain wide acceptance—and that doesn't address the fact that the smartphone brings infinitely more capability than our old rotary dial phones.
- The pace of technology has, to date, outstripped our military acquisition system's ability to keep up. The military-industrial base cannot field technology as fast as it is being invented, introduced, and adopted in the private sector.
- This has led to a shift of sorts, from a time when the military was a leader of inventing and introducing cutting-edge technology to now, when the military is a technological "follower" in many important areas.

But there is more than just the technology. As with all revolutions, the technological advances have fueled systemic change across a wide spectrum. Since the second edition, two new warfighting domains have been formally recognized—space and cyberwarfare. The emergence and importance of these domains largely stem from the need to create and move information.

And there is more still. These advances have also disrupted the way naval forces operate in the traditional domains—undersea, on the surface, in the air, and over land in the littorals. Information and networks surpassing the vision of Vice Admiral Cebrowski now bring near-ubiquitous and highly accurate sensing information. Precision is available on demand, not just to militaries, but to almost anyone, anywhere. This has shifted the competition from *information* superiority to *decision* superiority. How does one make best use of the avalanche of information available to the operator and commander? How does the fleet commander leverage the physical and virtual domains to greatest effect? When all information is available to any who seek it, how do strategic and operational commanders suppress the impulse to reach down to the tactical level of warfare? What will it mean when the networks come under attack and are degraded? We are just beginning to explore these questions in earnest, and this third edition pushes us further to think about these problems.

What has emerged is a much more challenging scenario, where the first considerations for fleet action must account for maneuver—not only in the physical world on, under, and over the sea, but also in the virtual world—the electromagnetic spectrum, space, and cyberspace. When naval forces do get moving in the physical world, they will be made more capable when networked together, and their success will depend very much on achieving and maintaining decision superiority.

The introduction of information warfare into fleet tactics is an important development that demands critical analysis and thought. The imperative that we update our tactics to account for this new reality is here. And as Captain Hughes has taught us best, updated tactics will inform new thinking in strategy and policy. In an era where "firing effectively first" may now mandate that the first salvos will be non-kinetic, this update is a timely "kick" to remind us to rig for sea and get under way.

—ADM John M. Richardson, USN

Foreword to the Second Edition

// "Fire effectively first!"

The young officer deals in tactics. That is what he cares about most. While he chafes against other duties, his first focus is meant to be the development of skills to bring combat power to bear on an enemy in circumstances of mortal danger. Later in life, the much older officer returns to tactics after wandering through the fuzzy landscapes of operations, strategy, and policy. He returns to tactics, first, because it is what animates his profession. It is where the transactions are made and the payoffs, for better or worse, are harvested. Second, he returns there for consistency, almost as a matter of aesthetics.

At the height of the Cold War, the then–Chief of Naval Operations was reported to have said the U.S. Navy had lost its thin margin of superiority over the Soviet Navy. That was a complex, carefully considered, and grave judgment. One of the principal technical ingredients in that calculus was the threat of air-, submarine-, and ship-launched cruise missiles. Fortunately, that judgment was never tested. In this second edition, Captain Hughes, using actual combat data not available to the CNO at the time, indicates that the CNO's concerns were justified. This called for action at all levels. At the time, young officers turned to tactics as the only tool available to them, technology being fixed in the near term. Once again, tactics informed operations and strategy.

Captain Hughes opens the introduction to this second edition with Admiral Fiske's caution that wise naval policy must take into careful account the tactics to be used. Later, he takes up Admiral Nelson's admonition that "a ship's a fool that fights a fort." Yet, in the 1994 vision statement, "Forward from the Sea," the U.S.

Navy and Marine Corps leadership state that "the new direction for the Naval Service is projecting power from the sea in the critical littoral regions." More recently, the CNO has envisioned "a 21st Century Navy capable of influencing events ashore—directly and decisively—anytime, anywhere." For both Admiral Nelson and the modern-day U.S. Navy and Marine Corps, this resolves to the fundamental mission of the Navy of controlling and exploiting command of the seas. This is classic Navy. Do our tactics and our technologies support these policy statements? If not, then Nelson continues to be right. This present-day example of tactics animating policy indicates the focus required of tacticians young and old and profound changes in our technology choices.

Our present information age illustrates the close coupling between tactics and technology and portends a sharply increased power of tactics in effecting operations and strategy. While strategy may seek to control the scope, pace, and intensity of a conflict, tactics controls the very powerful second derivative, that is, the rates of change that affect men's minds where wars are won and lost. The importance of scouting (information-gaining activities) and missiles reflects the dominant characteristics of the information age—access and speed. Long-range high-speed weapons have power only insofar as they are informed. High levels of shared awareness among forces have been shown to dramatically increase speed to scout, to decide, and to execute. Hence, the modern-day practitioner fights first for information superiority, indicating the technical and tactical choices that must be made. Put another way, we must buy the forces and develop the tactics necessary to ensure information superiority. Captain Hughes would argue this isn't new, only that the importance and complexity of the choices may be greater.

Similarly, access must be ensured, indicating technologies and tactics that we do not now have. Pressures impeding their acquisition abound. Among them is the wistful belief that combat can be conducted from sanctuary. Much to the contrary, everything in harm's way, whether placed intentionally or by chance, is a combat consumable. This is why again the Naval War College at Newport has returned to the task of developing a Navy based on the tactics and technologies necessary to win. This requires a focus on the constants and long period trends that Captain Hughes illuminates so well.

My fear is that, thinking tactics subordinate to their interests, officials who are involved in strategy and policy will not read this book. The result will be the further neglect of the bloody lessons of history and the failure to position appropriately for the opportunities and significant risks in this high-speed information age. Events and developments between the two editions of this book have revealed the accuracy of Captain Hughes' analysis and insights. In this second edition, he once again uses the lamp of history in artful and compelling ways to light the future, its pitfalls and its opportunities, for Navy leadership.

Why study tactics? It is the sum of the art and science of the actual application of combat power. It is the soul of our profession.

—VADM Arthur K. Cebrowski, USN

Foreword to the First Edition

As a naval aviator—harboring all the biases that term connotes, forged from years of exhilaration at the reassuring sensation of a hot cat shot and the welcomed tug of the arresting gear on a dark blustery night—I am often asked, "How much longer will carriers be the centerpiece of the U.S. Navy's tactics?" It seems as if the question of the carrier as sitting duck just won't go away. A responsible answer must revolve around technology and tactics, and the pages that follow, which treat these topics extensively, are relevant to the whole issue. The book you are about to read does a masterful job of blending technology and tactics in a historical context. Indeed, it is the most comprehensive and comprehensible of any book on tactics yet written.

Fleet Tactics appears on the scene none too soon. Phenomenal advances in technology over the last few decades have affected virtually every aspect of naval warfare in ways that have not been easy to anticipate. Technological innovations make some systems obsolescent while they are yet in the development stage, before they reach the fleet in significant numbers. This, in addition to the fact that for decades the Soviet Union has been out-investing the United States in naval forces and defense commitment, has created in our Navy a need, unrivaled by that of any time in our history, for the study and mastery of tactics.

When a naval aviator raises the gear on his flying machine he is being catapulted into another dimension, the realm of tactics, one in which he must function until his return to the carrier. Likewise, a submarine skipper passing the harbor entrance outbound sails into a realm that demands a finely honed tactical sense—in his case, as an underwater sailor conducting independent operations, intimate knowledge of his combat systems, the capabilities and limitations of his crew, and the tactical doctrine specified for his ship.

But it is not enough for an individual pilot or commander to be tactically proficient. Today, as in Nelson's time, all tactical elements must fight as a cohesive team, and tactics must integrate into the whole the best that can be brought to bear by individual units. These, in the future, will most likely include land- and space-based assets. Neither have yet achieved their full potential in the maritime environment. Space systems exist only in embryo: if and when they are developed, it will require of naval professionals tactical skills even more sophisticated than those they yield now.

The demand on today's naval tactician to be competent in the multiplatform operations of the battle force might be challenged by some who would point out that since World War II we have seen no scenario in which a major naval battle was fought or in which the use of battle force tactics was critical. Some say that the British experience in the Falklands was merely a small-scale test of tacticians' skills, and that the Arab-Israeli encounters and the U.S. bombing of Libya provide but glimpses into the broad spectrum of naval warfare. However these operations are viewed, we should guard against the insidious tendency to limit our tactical horizons to peacetime evolutions; we should instead seek to understand the ordeal of tomorrow's technological war at sea, in all its ramifications.

Regrettably, I would contend that we fall prey to the pressures of peacetime priorities, and thus over tactical excellence favor program management, systems acquisition, and—in the absorbing struggle to keep our complex weapon systems ready for action—ship maintenance. While it would be foolhardy to neglect these important areas, it is risky and not in keeping with the lessons of history to permit tactical excellence to play second fiddle to any other needs, however essential. After all, what is the naval profession about if not tactics, tactics, and more tactics? Nothing inspires more excitement in the sailor than the opportunity to exercise his knowledge of his ship and her weapon systems—to demonstrate their full combat potential.

Fleet Tactics is a treasure house of commonsensical guidelines and stimulating ideas. It is not just easy to read, but a joy as well. Captain Hughes, with his literary wand, has transformed what can be a dry topic into a fascinating treatise that will leave the reader with a desire to read it again and again. The five cornerstones—to mention only one set of principles among many in these pages—should be committed to memory and beyond; they should become instinct.

Nor has Captain Hughes failed to accentuate the most vital ingredient of tactics: leadership. At sea, as nowhere else, "men go where their leaders take them." They survive to fight yet another day and to taste the fruit of victory, or fail, together. Thus they had better learn quickly and well how to operate as a unit. War is the unexpected; and beyond a certain point, war is unimagined violence. Only the best team can cope.

Absorbed study of *Fleet Tactics* will inspire every dyed-in-the-wool sailor who has not already done so to put tactics in its proper place—first and foremost.

And now to the reader, you have a treat in store. Best wishes for the voyage ahead!

—ADM Thomas B. Hayward, USN

Preface

··

No naval policy can be wise unless it takes into very careful
account the tactics that ought to be used in war.

—*CDR Bradley A. Fiske, USN, 1905*[1]

I am writing this overview as the author of the first and second editions of *Fleet Tactics*. In the body of the book I am joined by co-author RADM Robert Girrier, USN (Ret.). Admiral Girrier has the advantages of more recent operational experience afloat and in the Pacific, Mediterranean, and Middle Eastern theaters, as well as a keen knowledge of new technological advances and their applications in the maritime domain. At the Pentagon, he stood up and headed the office under the Chief of Naval Operations that was charged with expanding the Navy's use of unmanned vehicles, both in the air, on and under the water. He has been invaluable in improving the new book throughout in many ways, and especially instrumental in drafting chapter 6, on new kinds of naval operations.

In 1986, when the first edition, *Fleet Tactics: Theory and Practice*, was published, my intent was to write a timeless description of fleet tactics, chronicle their evolution, and describe current practices. In 1989, after the collapse of the Soviet Union, it became apparent how much the book had been influenced by the Cold War threat and a single set of strategic circumstances. It is a well-known aphorism that technology forces changes in tactics and that new technology

---

1   Fiske, "American Naval Policy," U.S. Naval Institute *Proceedings*, January 1905.

cannot be exploited fully unless it is accompanied by the development of new tactics that enable users to take best advantage of it. I was surprised to see how much *geopolitical* changes could affect tactics as well.

After 1990 the U.S. Navy was devoted to the projection of power and influence around the world. At the same time, the focus of that effort was shifting to coastal regions. Appropriately, the second edition, published in 1999, reflected both those developments. Now, in this third edition, we seek to make explicit the kinds of refocusing that the U.S. Navy—or any navy—undergoes periodically, and how international relationships inevitably affect tactical readiness. The new chapter on naval operations reviews the conjunction between the operational level of war and the tactical level at sea. It would take an entire book to discuss the campaign planning and peacetime operations of a dominant navy. Our goal is a modest one—to describe the interrelationships of tactics, logistics, and operations in historical campaigns.

As it has turned out, the U.S. Navy was so successful in maintaining command of the seas peacefully that it never has had to put into practice the tactical advice that was offered in the first edition. Yes, the Navy suffered some losses from unexpected missile attacks and from mines. In October 2000, for example, terrorists successfully attacked the USS *Cole* (DDG 67) in Yemen's Aden harbor. That aside, the Navy has not had to fight a fleet action or even a regional action in a land-versus-sea battle since World War II. All its experience has been vicarious, learned from battles fought by other countries.

The second edition also added factual details on the missile age of warfare that began in the late 1960s, and on the effects it has had on tactics. Other nations have recognized and exploited the capabilities of missiles of many kinds. To an extent, so has the U.S. Navy—first with defensive surface-to-air missiles and later with Harpoon and Tomahawk offensive missiles. Now Navy leaders have become more fully aware of the dangers of fighting in confined coastal waters. A major purpose of the third edition is to describe littoral combat and to explore how recent trends in information warfare are affecting tactical planning and execution.

Much has been written on maritime strategy in seemingly every corner of the globe and in every age, but scarcely any of these books and doctrinal publications are devoted to modern naval tactics. Yet there is much to be said about information warfare, cyberoperations, unmanned vehicles, and a growing certainty that ever-more-capable antiship missiles will lead to new modes of scouting, commanding, and fighting. The missile age is now almost fifty years old. Seventeen years ago the second edition predicted that the next era of naval warfare would be the robotics age—the age of unmanned and autonomous vehicles. The transition from the missile era to the era of robotics and cyberwarfare is now upon us, and it demands more study and application. In this edition we focus on how to exploit these new technologies to fight in dangerous littoral waters.

Missile attacks to and from the sea add to the already prevalent strikes by aircraft, blurring the longstanding tactical distinction between sea and land combat. The engagements that have been fought for the control of coastal regions have been most effective when land, sea, and air forces have acted in concert, using missiles as the principal weapons. Perhaps the navies of the world should no longer refer to *naval* tactics at all, but instead should think in terms of *littoral* tactics, which include warships.

Both the first and second editions of this book were written for an international audience. The Naval Institute Press sanctioned translations into Spanish, Portuguese, Italian, and Chinese. Although the Soviet Union did not obtain permission to translate and distribute the first edition, there is no doubt that it was studied closely by the Kremlin. A lengthy policy brief for the Indian navy refers to the second edition's salvo equations and applies them extensively to make force-on-force comparisons with Chinese naval elements that might operate in the Indian Ocean.[2] There are many other indications that *Fleet Tactics* has been influential worldwide.

Yet the most important reader of his volume has always been the American naval officer. Despite our effort to avoid tailoring the exposition of modern tactics exclusively for naval officers in the United States, both previous books give the most attention to the U.S. Fleet. The disconcerting truth, however, is that Navy officers today are buried in reports, inspections, and lectures on the social issues of the day that deal with everything except how to fight. The objective here is to provide them with a book that can compete with these many peacetime distractions. The U.S. Navy ended World War II with battle-tested tactics that had been formulated in fleet doctrine and embedded in the minds of leaders who had participated in sea battles. Both the doctrine and those leaders are no more. More than seventy years have passed since the U.S. Navy fought a fleet action. Close to an enemy coastline the Navy may face competent air, sea, and land opposition that is fully capable of giving it a bloody nose. Does the United States have

---

2   J. Sankaran, "The Tactical Reach and Requirement of the Indian Navy," S. Rajarantnam School of International Studies, October 2013.

the right ships and the right combat doctrine to take on a battle fleet that has trained assiduously to fight in its own home waters? Or will it be like the U.S. Pacific Fleet of 1942, which had become accustomed to thinking that its superior numbers would prevail, only to be shocked again and again by the Japanese navy's superior tactics throughout the first year of fighting?

Since World War II, the Navy has had to learn its tactics and combat doctrine by observing and examining the naval conflicts of other nations. The fighting ships in the Arab-Israeli wars, the South Atlantic War, and the Indo-Pakistani War were relatively small, but the stakes of the battles they fought were large, and the tactical outcomes were deadly and decisive.

C. S. Lewis, the late scholar and writer, referred to himself as a layman when it came to theological matters. Similarly, there is a layman in naval matters, and he or she is our third category of reader. A layman often speaks with more eloquence than the Navy's blue-uniformed theologians, and is capable of wise and detached insights. Yet if an outsider is going to play a constructive role in maritime affairs, then he or she needs a better grounding in naval tactics than is often the case today. Competent amateurs discuss current strategy as aims or ends, often forgetting that a strategy comprises ends, ways, and means. The means are the forces and tactics that achieve the strategic ends. This book is not a comprehensive guide to all the lessons of twenty-first-century naval warfare, but anyone who reads it will be better equipped to reach sound conclusions about modern combat at sea. For example, journalists who observed British and Argentine ships being sunk during the South Atlantic War of 1982 predicted there would be a dire future for surface warships because they had no knowledge of how deadly naval battles have been in the past. In chapter 7 we have juxtaposed ill-founded amateur opinions side by side with the lessons that would have been drawn by someone who had had a better understanding of naval tactics and operations.

The fourth and last reader for whom this book is intended is a youngster of about thirteen, which is the age at which the future commander at Jutland, John Jellicoe, all four feet, six inches of him, entered the Royal Navy and reported aboard the old wooden line-of-battle ship *Britannia*. In many cases, genius in mathematics, music, and other disciplines blossoms early, and we want to fill the present void in the literature of naval tactics in order to help stimulate interested young readers. Since there are now so many competent computer battlefield games, there ought to be at least one *book* that helps explain to some Nelson or Nimitz of the future why his or her tactics succeeded or failed.

Today's youth, with its captivating apps and other electronic devices, seems more fortunate and sophisticated than earlier generations were with the toy ship-models they pushed along to explore naval tactics on the living-room floor. Lest the cyber generation grow cocky with its advantages, however, here is a warning: the formulation of good tactics on home video screens today is no more the measure of battlefield prowess than what emerges from the war-game rooms of the Naval War College. Tactical theory deals with things that are necessary but not sufficient. The execution of tactics on the battlefield is a matter of leadership that captures the hearts and minds of officers and sailors. What Thomas Edison said about inventive genius—that it comprises 1 percent inspiration and 99 percent perspiration—is just as true of success on the battlefield.

—CAPT Wayne P. Hughes Jr., USN (Ret.)

Acknowledgments

....

CAPT Hugh G. Nott, USN, would have co-authored the first edition of this book had he lived. His contribution at the outset is beyond expression. We agreed that tactics was a worthy discipline within the broader study of naval warfare; that the foundations of this discipline needed to be brought up to date; that the study of principles was inadequate because trends, constants, and contexts were fundamental in staying abreast of the ever-changing activities of combat at sea; and that tactics are *actions* to take before and during a battle. An abiding success has been our adoption of the inelegant turn-of-phrase as our central maxim of naval tactics, "Attack effectively first." It has proven to be accurate, enduring, and much quoted. After thirty years Hugh's influence still abides.

RADM Robert Girrier, USN (Ret.), joins me in the authorship of this, the third edition of *Fleet Tactics*. Bob has provided many complementary perceptions and contributions. But these acknowledgments stem from the original author.

My dear friend ADM A. J. Whittle, USN (Ret.), was the first to read every word of the original draft, and he probably had the greatest effect on the modes of expression. Frank Uhlig and Frank Snyder of the Naval War College suggested detailed improvements that were almost as important. Among many others who sharpened the material were VADM Thomas Weschler, USN (Ret.), and RADM C. E. Armstrong, USN (Ret.), on operations; professors John Hattendorf and Thomas Hone on naval history; LTG Philip Shutler, USMC (Ret.), on littoral warfare; and Drs. Joel Lawson, John Wozencraft, and Michael Sovereign on command-and-control. For this third edition, the research and personal advice of chairmen Peter Denning and John Arquilla were valuable in bringing information warfare up to date.

Much credit goes to the Military Conflict Institute, which served as an early sounding board and helped me to sharpen the distinctions between the processes of land and sea battle. Among its leadership, Dr. Donald Marshall, COL Trevor Dupuy, USA (Ret.), and Lawrence Low were unstinting of their time and advice.

Special thanks go to Mehmet Ayik, who sharpened "The Battle of the Aegean" in chapter 15 while he was a doctoral student at the Naval Postgraduate School. Having an extraordinary seagoing background in the Turkish navy, Mehmet kept my vivid imagination in bounds with technical advice—after I persuaded him that my aim was to illustrate tactics, not geopolitics.

Many others provided material, ideas, and inspiration, including VADM Joseph Metcalf III, USN; VADM John A. Baldwin, USN (Ret.), Dr. Wilbur Payne, Dr. J. J. Martin, Professor Neville Kirk, and CAPT Stuart D. Landersman and CAPT E. M. Baldwin, USN. At the Naval Postgraduate School, Dr. Richard Rosenthal and Dr. Alan Washburn were especially generous with their encouragement.

Ideas not communicated are seeds cast on rocks. Readers should join me in saluting those who contributed not to the substance but to the form and expression of that substance: in Monterey, Ellen Saunders, Sherie Gibbons, and Ruthanne Lowe, and at the Naval Institute Press, Paul Wilderson, Tom Cutler, Jim Dolbow, Therese Boyd, and Connie Buchahan. My wife, Joan, gave a double measure through these editions. Forbearance without untoward jealousy of The Book was one thing; serving as foil and grammarian was to walk the second mile.

ADM Thomas Hayward, USN (Ret.), has my thanks for his advice and encouragement while he was serving as Chief of Naval Operations; he also deserves the appreciation of the Navy for reemphasizing tactical competency in the fleet. Another close friend, VADM Arthur Cebrowski, kept the flame burning with his foreword to the second edition. Our serving Chief of Naval Operations, ADM John H. Richardson, deserves double-barreled thanks, first for writing the current foreword, and second for encouraging us to take on this third edition, with its special emphasis on the growing importance of information warfare.

—CAPT Wayne P. Hughes Jr., USN (Ret.)

INTRODUCTION

A Third Edition for the Cyber and Robotics Age

For a study of tactics by American authors one must go back almost to the start of the twentieth century, when tactics was *the* subject debated by naval officers.[1] In an essay that won the Naval Institute Prize Essay of 1905, then-commander Bradley A. Fiske devoted twenty-three out of eighty pages exclusively to tactics. It was a time when naval officers aggressively asserted that policy and strategy were not merely wishes, but were well-founded plans derived from a calculated capacity for tactical success. As one French officer, frustrated by the irresolution of his government toward the German kaiser's naval buildup, wrote, "Let us be economical but let us be honest. . . . It is by *objectivity*—that is, with reference to the possible opponent—that we proportion our arms. . . . If we cannot have the navy estimates of our policy, then let us have the policy of our estimates."[2] These are watchwords for the twenty-first-century American Navy. After fifty years of uncontested maritime superiority during which Americans have become accustomed to a Navy that can do everything asked of it, having a basic understanding of modern tactics and how fleets win battles will help avoid the careless assumption that the seagoing forces have more capabilities than they do.

The onset of the twentieth century also was a time when tacticians governed the direction of warship technology—so much so that at least one American and one Russian author incorporated technology into their *definitions* of tactics. Factors

---

1   In 1942 RADM Samuel S. Robison, USN, assisted by his wife, Mary, updated *A History of Naval Tactics from 1530 to 1930.* It is an excellent history from which we have drawn extensively, but its subject is history, not tactics.
2   Baudry, pp. 16–17.

such as the size and placement of guns, the location and thickness of armor, and location of the conning station and signal bridge were central concerns of tacticians. Issues of U.S. Naval Institute *Proceedings* at the time abounded in prize-winning essays, dominated by those dealing with tactics. In the 1920s the Navy's General Board of senior officers fused strategy, tactics, and the characteristics of new warships in its deliberations and used the war-gaming facilities of the Naval War College as a principal tool for resolving design disputes. A comprehensive book by Tom Hone, Norman Friedman, and Mark Mandeles, entitled *American and British Aircraft Carrier Development, 1919–1941,* illustrated in detail how war games, fleet exercises, the General Board, and the Bureau of Aeronautics all collaborated in the development of Navy airpower just in time for World War II. Read together with Mark R. Peattie's *Sunburst: The Rise of Japanese Naval Air Power, 1909–1941,* it provides the background that the reader should have in order to understand how the well-conceived and determined development of technology during peacetime resulted in the tactics of two superb navies that fought in the Pacific in World War II. Today U.S. Navy tacticians should have a similar reference work to help them develop the competency to fight in littoral waters against the forces of Russia, China, or Iran should that mission ever be required. To succeed, it must treat tactics and technology as two sides of the same coin.

Fleet Tactics: A Definition

The etymological root of the word *tactics* is the Greek *taktika,* meaning "matters pertaining to arrangement." Tactics are not studies, but techniques—not an art or a science, but the very actions of warriors in battle. Thus, strategists *plan*, while tacticians *do*. The traditional definition of tactics is the art or science of distributing or maneuvering forces in relation to each other and to the enemy and of employing them in battle. In this book, "tactics" refers to the *handling of forces in battle*. The definition is deliberately fuzzy. The key words are *handling, forces,* and *battle*. Specifically and contextually, the book will seek to clarify these terms. Some say tactics are deployments to win battles, but this may be too much to expect from tactics designed for an inferior force. Moreover, not all naval missions are narrowly directed at battlefield victory. Sound tactics seek to help the forces committed to combat achieve their full potential.

In many studies, the phrase *fleet tactics* is synonymous with *naval tactics*. The term fleet tactics deals with operations involving the coordination of multiple ships and aircraft, manned and unmanned, and of the sensors that support them. Sometimes single-unit techniques and procedures are discussed, but such instances come only in contexts that are incidental to fleet battles. In the nomenclature of ground combat, fleet tactics are similar to *combined-arms tactics, grand tactics,* and *air-land battle tactics.*

Perhaps naval officers stopped writing about tactics after World War II because they associated tactics with maneuvers. In the 1950s junior officers were bemused by what were termed "tactics drills." Although corpens and turns at five hundred yards were exciting, they were by then no more related to sea warfare than a parade ground drill was related to land warfare. When leaders scheduled "tactics," the term meant seamanship maneuvers, not battle practice. The evolutions were a vestige of the day when maneuvers of warships *were* at the very heart of a battle. In 1972 John Creswell, in his preface to *British Admirals of the Eighteenth Century,* wrote: "The era of fleet tactics, the period during which the major results in sea warfare were influenced by the maneuvering in battle by rival fleets of big ships, lasted for something under two centuries."[3] Creswell marks the end of the era with the Battle of Jutland. But since tactics are the employment of forces in battle, then tactics exist whether or not ships are maneuvered. Although Creswell is correct that maneuvers have lost the central function that they once served for weapon delivery, the position of a naval force in relation to the enemy is still a vital element of tactics, and maneuvering before the shooting starts is still a tool used by the commander to establish positions for effective attack.

Another source of confusion is that substantial portions of modern "fleets" are land based. Much of the Soviet navy was made up of long-range bombers and missiles tasked with sinking American warships and shipping. The Chinese navy increasingly relies on those weapons as well. Now many navies have land-to-sea missiles. Fleet tactics concern combat in which maritime security is at stake—in other words, with battles that are fought either for command of the seas worldwide or to deny the enemy command of its home seas. The sensors and weapons of some coastal states may be so predominantly shore-based that the true strength of such a fleet is literally and metaphorically invisible. The ships of a seagoing navy enter their coastal battle space only at great peril.

More Terminology

Prominent among the terms used here is *scouting,* which means reconnaissance, surveillance, code-breaking, and all other ways to obtain and report combat information to commanders and their forces. For all practical purposes the Russian

---

3   Creswell, p. 7.

word *razvedka* means the same thing. *Screening,* another navy word of distinguished lineage, is very similar to *antiscouting,* but screening includes the possibility of attacking a threatening enemy.

Antiscouting refers to all measures used to frustrate the enemy's scouting effort. *Escorting* means acts of ships and aircraft that accompany and defend valued units from enemy weapons. Escorting is a form of *counterforce.* An antisubmarine screen defends a convoy or formation of warships that have few if any means to defend themselves. By threatening enemy submarines and complicating their attempts to close and target the escorted force, the escorting ships and aircraft also perform two antiscouting functions—to inhibit a submarine's own search efforts and to warn the screened units to turn away when and if a submarine is detected.

Command-and-control (C^2) is the term used for the functions variously referred to as command, control, and communications (C^3); C^3 and Intelligence (C^3I); and so on. Beyond a clear delineation of authority and reporting responsibilities at the macro level, there is a fundamental function that C^2 performs. Specifically, C^2 refers to the correlation of information received from scouting, the commanders' decisions, and, finally, the dissemination of commands to their forces. The term command-and-control encompasses all information-based decision-support systems, including artificial intelligence and various means of communicating orders. (This book excludes scouting systems and the scouting process from command-and-control and treats scouting as a distinct and extensive process of its own.)

C^2 countermeasures (C^2CM) are actions taken to inhibit effective enemy C^2. The term *signals warfare* embraces scouting, antiscouting, C^2, and C^2CM.

The definition of C^2 used here is not universally accepted, but it is becoming more common. It has many advantages. One is to ensure that C^2 denotes not only the use of scouting information but also the influence over the allocation of scouting resources. Thus, the C^2 process focuses the search effort—its direction, depth, intensity, and duration. Since a great constant of tactics is that there is never enough scouting capacity, these are some of a tactical commander's most critical decisions. In recent times tactical commanders have come to know that the task of directing their search efforts and culling the vital observations and data from a large amount of information can consume staff attention.

This volume uses the word *littorals* to describe "where the clutter is"—first, the sea side of the littoral, where islands and inlets, shoals and shallows, oil drilling rigs, commercial air traffic, coastal shipping and fishing, and electronic transmissions of many kinds abound to complicate combat tactics; and, second, the land side, where airfields, missile-launch sites, electronic detection systems, and dense populations complicate coastal warfare. Technological advances have extended the lethal ranges of missiles, aircraft, and unmanned systems; and satellites or over-the-horizon radars now extend detection well beyond the clutter into blue water. In narrow waterways such as the Skagerrak Strait, Taiwan Strait, Dardanelles, Strait of Hormuz, and the Bab el Mandeb, the littoral extends from coast to coast. To seaward of the North and South American coasts, the littoral region extends perhaps only fifty miles from the shoreline. In *cul de sacs* such as the Baltic Sea, Eastern Mediterranean Sea, Gulf of Aden, and Yellow Sea, the "clutter," for operational planning, extends from coast to coast. The commercial airways of sea and land and radio broadcasts add to the clutter. Shoals and shallows affect underwater operations. A major factor in planning is the existence of so-called "moving clutter," such as commercial ships and aircraft that are either transiting or operating in the region. In July 1988 the USS *Vincennes* (CG 49) mistakenly shot down an Iranian airliner in the belief that the plane was an attacking jet fighter. Again, in the confined Arabian Gulf during operations preparatory to Desert Storm, Iraqi ground forces fired two Silkworm missiles at the USS *Missouri* (BB 63), which was shooting 16-inch shells at Iraqi coastal emplacements. Although the *Missouri* was eighteen miles to seaward no U.S. escort vessel got off a shot, partly because in the coastal clutter that filled the area the Navy ships wanted to be sure they were not shooting at an innocent aircraft.

One term, *strategic weapons,* is deliberately missing in these pages. The concepts of strategic warfare, strategic bombing, and strategic defense—and the transfer of those concepts into the realm of intercontinental ballistic missiles (ICBMs)—are understandable, but not entirely consistent. The text discusses the *tactical* considerations in the use of long-range nuclear weapons. When and if such weapons are used, handling them on a world-girdling, intercontinental battlefield will involve special tactical skills. In such a ghastly battle, the National Command Authority would become a tactical commander with the problem of coordinating the use of air-, land-, and sea-based weapons. Even though the prospect of a general nuclear war now seems remote, military planners should remember that the local use of weapons of mass destruction, or WMD, is a growing possibility. The paradigm of sea combat, emphasizing destruction, lends itself much more to understanding the tactics of WMD than that of land combat, which emphasizes position and maneuver.

A Pre-Underway Tour

Chapter 1 of this edition retains a description of the Battle of the Nile seen through the eyes of Vice Admiral Francois Paul Brueys d'Aiguilliers, the operational and tactical commander of the defeated French fleet, who could not overcome the tactical genius of British Rear Admiral Horatio Nelson and his captains. Vice Admiral Brueys did not lack physical courage—he went down with his ship—and he had taken a reasonable defensive position. Yet, he had neither the acumen to anticipate how the battle would flow nor the willpower to resist General Napoleon Bonaparte, whose army he had just delivered to Egypt and who was overwhelming a weak opposition ashore. Fought in 1798, toward the end of the age of fighting sail, the Battle of the Nile is still relevant as an example of littoral warfare. The rest of the chapter names six cornerstones that all successful commanders must engrave on their souls, as Nelson had done before the Battle of the Nile.

Chapters 2 through 5 seek to build a historical foundation for the material that follows. They contrast the roles of maneuver, control, tactical scouting, and, above all, of concentrating force as practiced over the years first by ships of the line, then by battleships, and next by aircraft carriers. Three simple but clear models of battle help the reader visualize the dynamics of naval actions and the changes that took place in three successive eras of fleet combat. The commanders' roles are given special emphasis. Rather than searching for errors on the losing side, as is common among some historians, we identify the skills of the victors. One may infer what it takes to win a battle from ADM Arleigh Burke's often quoted words: "The difference between a good officer and a poor one is about ten seconds." In the Battle of Midway in June 1942, Admiral Isoroku Yamamoto and Vice Admiral Chūichi Nagumo fought with the skill and tenacity that they had acquired during an unblemished record of tactical successes before Midway. Their mistakes and misfortunes at Midway were less important than the extraordinary skill and courage of ADM Chester W. Nimitz, RADM Frank Jack Fletcher, RADM Raymond A. Spruance, and their aviators.

The descriptions of the night surface battles off Guadalcanal in 1942 contrast the fighting experience and night training of the Japanese navy with that of the constantly changing U.S. Navy ships and commanders who had been trained to fight daytime gunnery duels and had no time to learn in 1942. Then, early in 1943, there was a pause in the remorseless flow of action that gave Arleigh Burke and his superiors time to reflect on how to defeat Japanese warships by combining scouting with radar and with firing salvoes of torpedoes instead of shooting their guns. The 1942–43 Solomon Islands campaign also is worth studying today because it was the acme of successful joint American military operations, blending mutually reinforcing air, sea, and ground fighting into a unified campaign.

Chapter 6, After World War II, has been added to emphasize that since World War II the U.S. Navy has conducted continual operations around the world, but has fought no sea battles. It collects in one chapter the bits and pieces describing naval operations scattered through two previous editions of *Fleet Tactics* and also draws heavily from an essay published in the *Naval War College Review*.[4]

Chapter 7 covers fleet tactics in the age of missile warfare, describing how naval battles have been fought in the eastern Mediterranean and Middle East since World War II (with a natural emphasis on the sea-land interface) and telling how victory came to the side best prepared and equipped to conduct joint littoral operations, especially regarding the Falkland Islands (South Atlantic) War between the United Kingdom and Argentina in 1982.

Chapters 8 through 11 synthesize the various historical perspectives, eschewing the traditional discussion of the "principles of war" in favor of identifying the constants, trends, and contexts (or variables) of past and present tactics. We draw from all four eras of naval combat to describe and understand the key processes of naval action—maneuver, scouting, command, control, and firepower.

Chapter 12 recognizes the dominant current trend in military combat—the rise to prominence of information warfare (IW). The chapter looks beyond the influence on naval tactics of IW and its related elements, such as electronic warfare, unmanned vehicles, cyberoperations, artificial intelligence, new techniques for spying on an enemy, and the expanding potential for deception and distraction. Broadly understood, the term *information warfare* applies in peace and war, as well as in commercial, financial, and geopolitical endeavors. Its many facets are surveyed concisely before shifting to the impending influence of IW on combat at sea.

Chapter 13 assimilates previous material to focus on today's *littoral* combat operations and the demanding training under new fleet doctrine that will be necessary to win in confined waters against enemies fighting in their own land and proximate seas. The new role of information warfare is applied explicitly to wartime campaigns and tactics.

---

4   "A Close Look at the Operational Level of War at Sea," *Naval War College Review,* Summer 2012, p. 23.

Chapter 14 recaps some of the fundamental lessons in tactics that this book has presented and highlights some insights that readers should draw from the material.

Chapter 15 details an imaginary "Battle of the Aegean," which occurs more than two centuries after the Battle of the Nile and compares and contrasts the tactical lessons in this book with those learned from that time. The text is written from the point of view of the American operational and tactical commander, who is challenged to the utmost by a foe who is fighting in his own home waters and with superior numbers. The concluding recapitulation is a discussion of the relationship between a campaign and the fleet tactics within it. The same vignette appeared in the second edition, but the ship composition and basing have been updated.

1

SIX CORNERSTONES

Commentary from Aboukir Bay

I magine this running commentary by a senior French naval officer describing the Battle of the Nile as it unfolds:

We are with Vice Admiral François Paul Brueys d'Aiguilliers in his flagship, *L'Orient*, anchored at Aboukir Bay, Egypt. Less than 10 years ago, when our revolutionaries decapitated the leadership of the King's navy, Brueys was a mere lieutenant. Now he is a protégé of General Bonaparte. Our admiral is good at organization, having accomplished the prodigious feat of escorting 400 troop transports carrying 36,000 French infantry, cavalry, and artillery to Egypt. Still, if there were any serious danger today, 1 August 1798, we would be ill at ease.

Brueys, having attained our Napoleon's confidence, is now having trouble living up to that trust. One feels the tension of his inexperience: he has refused to enter Alexandria, just ten miles away, for fear of grounding a ship, and for weeks now, while Napoleon has swept aside all opposition and become master of Egypt, Brueys has vacillated between fighting his thirteen ships of the line under way or here at anchor in the western crescent of the flat Aboukir coastline. There will be a fight in the end. This *diabolique* Nelson is running pell-mell all over the Mediter-ranean looking for us. Brueys has (we think) made a decision of sorts: he will fight at anchor. *Bien.* But why not get on with the plans to fortify Aboukir Island to our north? Half a dozen six-pounders in place are nothing. When one fights pinched against a coast, one builds up the shore batteries. In our position, shore batteries employed to strengthen the van are no luxury, because our admiral (sound though we know his plan to be, *mon ami*) has put his strongest ships in the rear of his column. Or rather, we should say, at the southern end of this line of ships riding at anchor. It involves something about the British aim to double on the rear—an argument that we do not grasp because we are immobile. Or has it something to do with the prevailing wind—at this hottest season of the year, an onshore breeze to push the ships of Nelson toward the rearmost, southern end of the column?

And there are the other things that have been agreed upon, but never accomplished: using stern anchors to keep the starboard batteries all in line to seaward; running cables between ships to prevent the enemy from breaking through our line and raking us fore and aft in the passing; and tightening up the anchorage, for we are 150 meters apart, not much closer than a column under way—a distance that is safe for swinging with the tide and convenient for boating, but too far apart for ships that will be fought at anchor. Ganteaume, our chief of staff, worries about food and water, and we are grateful, but we have so many men ashore foraging—three thousand, we have heard—that there is no one left with the energy (the heat, it is so oppressive!) to make these preparations. In the end we may yet get under way. Brueys himself says nothing is certain in war—we are *toujours flexible*—and how much longer before we must up anchor and seek a place with more food? If we did, we could practice shiphandling under way. How did we get in this mess? Vice Admiral [Armand Blanquet] Du Chayla, who knows more about seamanship than any of us, says we should fight under way.

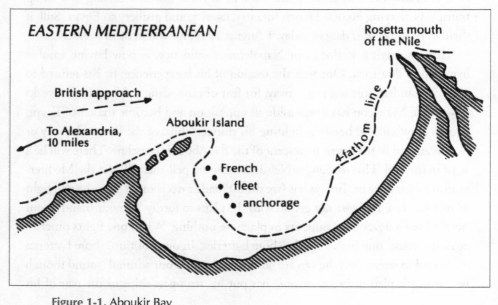

Figure 1-1. Aboukir Bay

But the captains resist: the men are too raw and untrained, they say. So what do we do—atrophy at anchor for a month and forget more and more of our training in everything but stealing Egyptian camel meat?

Stop grousing? *Oui,* it is the heat! Nelson's fleet will be inferior. *L'Orient,* beneath our feet, has 120 guns. She is a monster. Not one English ship can stand up to us by itself for 15 minutes. Just ahead is Du Chayla's *Franklin* of 80 guns (who was this Franklin—*un citoyen?*), and astern is *Le Tonnant,* of eighty. Nelson has only seventy-fours, and fewer of them at that.

Attention! The *Heureux* has signaled the sighting of a dozen sail! It is the English, coasting just east of Alexandria. We see the sails now, above the flats to the northwest. *Eh bien.* We will find out now about this battle. We are galvanized. Up goes the signal for the general recall of our foragers ashore; most will be back by morning. Clear for action! One side only? It is because of all those sailors ashore. Clear to starboard, you idiot—larboard is toward the land! We may not be able to sail with the shopkeepers, but we will out-fight them. When? Tomorrow, at first light, a day-long fight, and it will be hard.

Brueys paces the quarterdeck. Six bells in the afternoon watch, and they have not cleared Aboukir Island. Why do they not haul off? The afternoon breeze is brisk, and a sailor wants sea room before dark. Signal in the air from their *Vanguard.* The madman Nelson has seen our impregnable column and will stand clear now. An ounce of sense and he would blockade. That would be a pretty pickle for Brueys. In time we would have to sail out and fight and we sail like lubbers. But Nelson, he has no patience. Tomorrow we fight. There will be little sleep tonight.

Mais écoutez! The *Zealous* in the lead is wearing round into the bay! A man in the chains—they are sounding. Nelson is coming in *now,* standing before the afternoon sea breeze. We look to Brueys. *"Impossible!"* he cries. He is a fighter, but he has not *le sang-froid.* How many men are back from the abominable desert? Where are the cables? The stern anchors? *Now* the pitiful batteries on Aboukir Island finally fire. They are a great nothing.

So we will have a night action. No one fights at night. It will be mass confusion for ships under way. We are at anchor. Night action is crazy, but it is crazier for the English madman. Nelson's line wears around the point, starboard tack now, sailing almost west. The van! Nelson is aiming for our van, not the rear. The weak van. And he will not wait; the wind is with him. Why don't the English fall into disarray? They can sail, these sea demons of Nelson. Closed up two hundred meters between ships, yellow stripes outlining the gunports, two and three tiers of them, thirty-five muzzles from each of their black hulls. Closer, closer they come, and the hairs stand on the back of the neck and the hot sea breeze of the late afternoon has a cold chill in it. Shouts drift across three miles of bay water. The shopkeepers are cheering. Another signal from the *Vanguard.* The *Goliath* passes the *Zealous* to windward, her mainsails gathered up and then her topgallants, battle canvas only for the last rush, which she now leads.

The *Guerrier* and the *Conquerant* let go their starboard broadsides! *C'est magnifique!* A raking position, but at half a mile? We glance at Brueys, his hands gripping the bulwark, chest high. He is shaking his head. *"Non, non*—too soon, too soon!" he cries out.

Closer, closer sail the *Goliath* and the *Zealous* and the ten other English ships of the line. In our van, activity will cool the passion of fear. No place to hide in ships: where the captain fights, you fight. Back here we must stand and tremble a little, for the pall of death is staring at us. How beautiful, how relentless, how awful! Why do they not waver? Our line outguns them. Ah! Now I see why. Our line is out of the action, all but the first half-dozen ships. Nelson is doing the impossible; he masses on the van. It is his stupid luck, nothing but luck, to have this sea breeze catch us within only hours of our being ready.

The *Goliath* is almost upon the *Guerrier.* The Englishman must wear his ship to larboard now, to return fire with her first (starboard) broadside. Nelson's line will pass down our line front to rear exchanging broadsides. In the dark what else can he do? One broadside each, twelve ships. Heavy, but *L'Orient,* with a sixty-gun broadside, will pulverize them. Stupid Nelson. He plays our game.

Mais qu'est-ce que c'est que cela? We do not look at the *Goliath's* starboard battery; it is her larboard battery that stares at us! Can this be so? We look at Brueys. He is chalk-white. He grips the rail, his eyes aflame, aghast. This terrible fighter has fear? *"Merde!"* he murmurs, in the voice of our doom. The *Goliath* passes in front of the *Guerrier,* inshore of her, raking at twenty yards. The *Goliath* fires with her larboard battery! The British will double on the van and destroy us ship by ship. We feel the screams, the blood, a sickening desperation in the van, and now we see death creep down the line, ship after ship . . .

Before he dies Brueys will suffer further tactical humiliation. Nelson's ships do not remain under way. Each anchors by the stern alongside the enemy, two of the Royal Navy for every one of the French Marine Nationale. Successive ships from the rear will pass on the disengaged side of the British ships ahead and anchor alongside the next French ship astern to the south along the French column, four altogether finding their way to the landward side, where the French are without preparation and defenseless. As the northern French ships are smashed, the British will make their way down the line, always with the firepower of two or more against one.

The French fought at the Nile with the passion that Napoleon inspired. The French flagship, *L'Orient*, handled the English *Bellerophen* and *Majestic* so brutally that the *Bellerophen* cut her anchor cable to drift clear, and the *Majestic* was dismasted and her captain was killed. Meanwhile, the *Alexander* slipped cannily between *L'Orient* and *Le Tonnant*, which at anchor in Aboukir Bay were too much separated to provide fire support or prevent penetration of their line. The *Alexander* then devastated *L'Orient* from landward side, almost unopposed. *L'Orient* caught fire, and the flames spread to the magazines. At ten that night the French flagship blew up. No one who saw it ever forgot the stunning, soul-searing terror of it.

The southern French ships, five of them, were frozen at anchor, out of the action. To this day it is not known whether this was because they were awaiting a signal sent from Brueys to join the action, which was never seen amid the smoke and in the darkness, or whether it was because the rear admiral, Pierre de Villeneuve, had no time to cut cables, reach painfully to windward, and join the action. We only know what he wrote in his report later, asking how his own ships, "moored by two large anchors, a small one and four cables, [could] have weighed and tacked to get within range of the fighting before the ships engaged had been disabled ten times over." Far from being destroyed professionally by this debacle, Villeneuve would command the combined French and Spanish fleet at Trafalgar. But it is said that his spirit was broken at the "Horror of the Nile," and that he and his fleet, in facing Horatio Nelson a second time, were morally beaten before the first broadside was fired.

Of paramount importance, Nelson had done what Brueys had not: he had spent his two months at sea not merely drilling his force but discussing and planning the battle. His captains all knew his plans for concentrating firepower by doubling. Exactly how would depend on circumstances: whether the French were at anchor or at sea and, if they were at sea, whether they were to windward or leeward. He was to write before the Battle of Trafalgar that "something must be left to chance," but nothing was left undone that could have been foreseen. His fleet would attack at once. At the Nile it was fortuitous for him that Brueys had three thousand or four thousand men ashore. Nelson did not know this; he could not know *what* profit he would extract by a readiness to go in on arrival, but all of his forces were inculcated with the belief that in battle time is precious.

At the Nile the payoff was tremendous. Besides being short-handed and there-fore desperately having to fight with only their starboard batteries, many of the French ships were at anchor only by the bow. It is not certain whether it was Nel-son or Captain Thomas Foley in the *Goliath* who first saw that a ship anchored only at the bows must have space to swing and therefore must leave sailing room ahead to pass across to its landward side. Either way, it was Nelson's emphasis on concentration that inspired the move. His original plan for fighting ships at anchor envisioned one ship on the bow and one on the quarter of each unit of the engaged enemy. It was the temper of his captains to implement his intent by doubling in the more conventional manner of ships under way—by placing ves-sels on either side of each ship of the French van.

We may also believe that Nelson attacked at once because he had an after-noon sea breeze and he recognized that the wind would die toward evening. He had to accept a night action in exchange for a speedy attack and a favorable wind. That Nelson contemplated night action is plain from the provision for a series of horizontal lanterns in the rigging that would distinguish friend from foe, and from his plan to anchor from the stern instead of remaining under way. The final, masterful touch was his plan, well-drilled in the mind of every captain, to reverse the order of ships—the first two British ships would engage the northernmost French ship at anchor, the next two taking the second, and so on—in shrewd recog-nition of the fact that coming down on an enemy at anchor was entirely different from closing when he was under sail and in motion. Some of Nelson's captains thought his plan could not be executed. They argued that if one ship had two ships concentrating on it, the two would mask each other's fire. Yet, it was a risk that Nelson accepted and drilled to overcome. And with his own towering knowl-edge of seamanship he could talk down all reluctance.

As figure 1-2 (below) shows, Nelson's plan was distorted beyond superficial rec-ognition in the execution. So it is with battle. But Nelson's captains never wavered from his intent. A good battle plan is a simple plan. It will leave room for subtle and complex considerations, for variations, and for both error and initiative at the moment of execution.

The imaginary Frenchman who described the battle's onset at the beginning of this chapter was not exaggerating his armada's capacity and will to fight. At the Nile the French fought with the fervor of men unaccustomed to losing. They were weak on seamanship, but they could pour out broadsides. Against first-class fighting men, which the French crews certainly were in 1798, tactics established the circumstances of victory, while willpower and skill translated the potential into reality. The battle raged—and that is the appropriate word—all night and into the dawn. The British incurred almost one thousand casualties. The French suffered more than three thousand killed or wounded, and they lost another three thousand prisoners.

Six Cornerstones

The Battle of the Nile illustrates six crucial points, or cornerstones, about maritime warfare that have affected naval tactics ever since:

- Leadership, morale, training, physical and mental conditioning, willpower, and endurance are the most important elements in warfare. To be sure, one cannot win without the quantitative and qualitative sufficiency of material and sound tactics that are needed to bring one's weapons down upon the enemy. Yet—and this is especially important in regard to an enemy with competitive means—*sailors matter most.* At the Nile, Nelson established tactical ascendancy at the outset, but his force also had to win

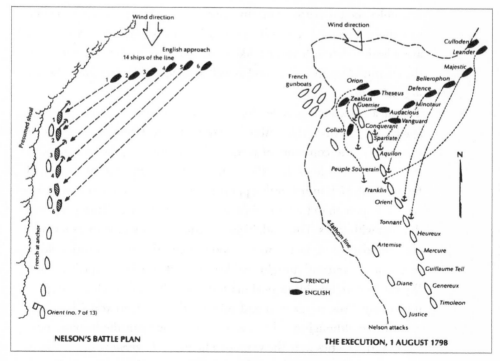

Figure 1-2. Royal Navy Maneuvers at the Battle of the Nile

a very hard battle. Sound tactics, extensive training, and careful planning will win a great victory when they are accompanied by an unwavering determination to inflict—and accept—losses.

- Doctrine is the companion and instrument of good leadership. It is the basis of training and all that that implies—cohesion, reliability in battle, and mutual understanding and support. It also is the springboard and benchmark of all tactical improvement. Formally, doctrine is standard battle methodology. But it is not dogma. No one is esteemed more than Nelson for his readiness to unfetter the Royal Navy from the doctrinaire rigidity of its Permanent Fighting Instructions. At the same time, Nelson always had a plan of action, a comprehensive one. He always transmitted it to his captains and practiced it so that they were of one mind about what was wanted. On a fundamental level, there can be no better definition of battle doctrine than a comprehensive and practiced plan of action. Sound doctrine will establish and maintain unity amid chaos. So, while in one sense the Battle of the Nile did not go as planned at all (you can search figure 1-2 in vain for an execution pattern that resembles the pre-battle plan), in a deeper sense it was the epitome of a sound plan executed flawlessly in spirit. The nineteenth-century Prussian army leader Helmuth von Moltke said, "No plan survives contact with the enemy." Nelson understood as well as anyone that *doctrine is the glue of good tactics.*

- Tactical and technological developments are so intertwined as to be inseparable. That is why ADM Alfred Thayer Mahan, USN, rejected (rather too readily) the constants of tactics while promoting the principles of strategy. The Battle of the Nile occurred close to the end of the age of fighting sail. Nelson had little opportunity to adopt tactics to new material, as Napoleon did with mobile artillery and the great Panzer captains did later with tanks. That said, Nelson's achievement is even more remarkable: he adapted his tactics to a weapon system that was centuries old in its essentials, and with insight that has rarely, if ever, been equaled at sea. We can believe that his tactical mastery was achieved by a lifetime spent under way. Prussian general and military theorist Carl von Clausewitz argued that although good strategy could come from the inspired novice, effective tactics were the work of a lifetime. *To know tactics, you must know weapons.*

- While it is proper to think of the destruction of the enemy's fleet as the fleet's foremost objective, beyond that immediate quest is always some higher goal. *The seat of purpose is on the land.* That is another reason the Battle of the Nile is so appropriate as an example. It was fought inshore, as so many decisive battles have been—almost in the harbor, with one side at anchor and the other partly so, and with shore batteries playing a part that could and should have been greater. The battle shattered Napoleon's ambitions and would have destroyed a lesser man. The battle that nearly obliterated a fleet also, and more significantly, destroyed an army's sea line of communications.

- Although Nelson probably was not the first to think so, he is credited with having expressed the great cornerstone of all fleet operations, that *"A ship's a fool to fight a fort."* The thought may have crossed his mind on 1 August 1798 as he brought his fleet around Aboukir Island, where land batteries would have lurked had Brueys been more perspicacious. Nelson must have relaxed when he saw that his fleet would not have to run past a substantial emplacement, and he probably sighed with relief when he knew that the *Cullodin* would not be pounded to pieces after she ran hard aground in front of that very spot. A battery would not have deterred Nelson, however, for no defense of Aboukir Bay could have compared with the fortification at Calvi, where he lost an eye in 1794; or with the defenses of Santa Cruz in the Canary Islands, where he lost an arm in July 1797 while trying to cut out a Spanish treasure ship; or with the great Trekoner fort at the entrance to Copenhagen, where he won his second great victory over anchored ships of the line in 1801. Nelson's victory at Copenhagen—he said later it was his toughest fight—was achieved with his usual blend of preparation and boldness. In part he won by getting at the anchored Danish fleet by circumventing the great fortress. Nelson fought inshore again and again, and his style gets to the heart of his own aphorism—that ships may do all they can to avoid a slugfest with fortifications ashore, but they cannot operate in coastal waters without dealing with weapons that have been directed toward the sea from the land.

- The tactical maxim of all naval battles is: *attack effectively first.* This means that the first objective in battle is to bring the enemy forces under concentrated firepower while forestalling their response. Later chapters will deal with this greatest imperative of sea warfare more fully, but suffice it to say about Nelson's tactical plan that with the readiness of his force, and his instant decision to bore in at once and exploit the lack of preparedness of the French fleet, he clearly was adhering to this maxim. As we shall see, however, doing so embodies much more than the element of surprise, more than mental and material preparedness for immediate action, or even more than the spirit of the offensive.

Sailors Matter Most

Warfare is deadly conflict. Tactics, as the devices by which battles are waged, are conceived and executed at the center of this violence. They are more visceral in the execution than policy, strategy, operational art, or logistics. For more than two centuries, a debate over whether warfare is a science or an art has continued. Yet, both science and art are activities of the mind. As far as the battle itself is concerned, neither transcends the importance and role of the mystique or charisma of leadership—the matter of will and endurance and, among combat leaders, the ability to inculcate these qualities in their forces. Except in the earliest literature on warfare, both sides consistently have understated this role.

This book is not about the inspirational qualities of leadership; it treats tactics as a matter of the mind. Beneath the veneer of reason, however, lie passion and mortal danger. Nothing about battle can be understood without grasping the impact of its violence. Poetic imagination is not a quality with which military leaders are heavily endowed; if it were, they might all be mad. It was said of C. S. Forester's great fictional hero, Horatio Hornblower, that had he really lived he would have been put ashore with ulcers. Patrick O'Brian's bluff, tough sea dog Jack Aubrey is a truer image of an archetypal warship captain in the age of fighting sail or any other era. Hopefully, our opening vignette of the Battle of the Nile has evoked a picture of the human element of warfare, of emotion elevated to fevered pitch, and of the way that tactical plans and battlefield decisions are influenced by an environment of controlled violence and directed chaos.

There is no way to judge Napoleon's assertion that "the morale is to the material as three is to one." Although that may be true in ground combat, the ratio in naval warfare is probably narrower because in ships at sea the crews *must* go where the leaders go. In planning naval tactics it is best to assume that there will be equal acumen, valor, and perseverance on both sides. This is an important assumption. Sun Tzu, who wrote *The Art of War* three centuries before the birth of Christ, argued that the greatest of commanders win by outwitting the enemy force, by outmaneuvering it, and even by leaving open a line of retreat so that its members will be encouraged to break and run from the battlefield. Liddell Hart, the prolific champion of maneuver warfare after the bloody stalemate on the western front in World War I, believed that the best tactics involve ingenuity and avoid head-to-head battles of attrition. But his famous philosophy of the indirect approach applies almost entirely to battles on land; it has a hollow ring to a commander at sea. Naval battles are hard fought and destructive. Nevertheless, it is possible to overstate the significance of courage and high morale in combat, which is dependent upon machines. This the Frenchman Ambroise Baudry did in his treatise on naval tactics at the turn of the century. He was doubtless influenced by his compatriots in the army, who maintained a zealous commitment to élan until they found in World War I that in a ground war an offensive mindset can be overdone. At sea, the greater danger is from a misplaced faith in tactical cleverness. If the enemy's morale or intellect is inferior, so much the better, but to base tactical success on outwitting, outmaneuvering, or outfighting a first-class enemy often turns out to be the height of folly. Tacticians undertake what they can to position their forces in the best circumstances for battle, but they risk the stark possibility that the tables may be turned on them. On the contrary, on land, officers such as U.S. General Ulysses S. Grant and British General Douglas Haig, both of whom had been accused of military butchery, recognized that the enemy—the Confederates in the first instance and the Germans in the second—was composed of determined soldiers who were led by officers of great tactical skill. Such forces are not defeated without a bloody battle. Superior tactics may tip the balance, but in the latter stages of a long war the wit and ingenuity required for such tactics ultimately are overshadowed by sheer grit.

At sea the predominance of attrition over maneuver is a theme so basic that it runs throughout this book. Forces at sea are not broken by encirclement; they are broken by destruction. Over the years naval strategists have been careful about committing their forces to battle at sea because of its awesome destructiveness. Compared with land warfare, major sea battles have been few and far between. Partly this is because the estimation of material superiority is relatively easier to gauge at sea than ashore, and strategists in an inferior navy have tended to avoid battle until the jugular vein was threatened. As a result, a superior navy with a modest force advantage often has been able to contain and neutralize a strong enemy and carry out many strategic objectives without fighting—up to a point. Considering the death and destruction wrought by naval warfare, it may be that the very decisiveness of battle at sea, which so often leads tacticians to try to avoid it, is actually a virtue for which the civilized world can be grateful.

Doctrine: The Glue of Tactics

The second cornerstone of naval tactics is doctrine. Doctrine is the commanders' way of controlling their forces in writing before military action. Doctrine enunciates policies and procedures that govern action. In its broad sense, doctrine is what is taught as "right behavior"—"rules upon which we act spontaneously and without orders for the accomplishment of the mission," wrote the late ADM Harry E. Yarnell, USN.[1] In its most stringent sense, doctrine enjoins the "right" behavior; its success depends on obedience, except when obedience leads to the failure of the fleet. Either way, high levels of command seek coherence of policy to strengthen their control, while tactical levels demand procedures for cooperative effort. Yet, these are merely matters of emphasis. Two points about doctrine must be remembered—that it is vital and that it must not become dogmatic.

Fleet doctrine may be thought of as the commanders' comprehensive battle plan—their standing operation order. (Nelson's plan of action is an exemplar.) Every echelon of combat command has its battle plan. One of the anomalies of modern American organization is that the Chief of Naval Operations prescribes a comprehensive doctrine—the Naval Warfare Publications—although the CNO is not actually in the operational chain of command.

Doctrine also can be defined as every action that contributes to unity of purpose. Doctrine is not what is written in the books; it is what warriors believe in and act upon. Clausewitz called it "a sort of *manual* for action."[2] Doctrine is greater than tactics in that it encompasses command structure and communication. It is less than tactics in that it can establish no more than procedures that enable and enhance the execution of tactical choice on the battlefield.

There is always tension between conformity and initiative in the execution of good doctrine. Ask any good naval leader senior or junior, about his or her experience in naval operations, and it will quickly emerge that the tactical plan imposed by those senior was too rigid. These officers maneuvered more cleverly and fired weapons more effectively than doctrine prescribed. When they were in command, all units moved together like clockwork. The captains knew exactly what each teammate would do as instinctively as a basketball player knows from

---

1   Quoted in Robison and Robison, p. 827.
2   Clausewitz, p. 141.

body language which way a teammate will cut.[3] It will never occur to the speaker that there is the slightest inconsistency in this account. To a person, strong military leaders want freedom for initiative from their seniors and reliability from their juniors. Doctrine in the hands of able commanders will, at its most sublime, allow the achievement of both these things. There is a measure of entropy in all doctrine. With too little entropy there is order and understanding but no initiative. With too much entropy there is creativity and change but no order.

Since the sublime rarely is possible, if one must err it is better to do so on the side of too much rather than too little doctrine. Too little doctrine indicates laziness, indecisiveness, or uncertainty. The clearest evidence of doctrinal deficiency is too much communication—reams of orders and directives that in the planning stage are little more than generalities and exhortations, and which defer too much to the moment of decision. Good doctrine reduces the number of command decisions in the heat of battle, for even a cool head will be gripped by passion and, very quickly, by emotional and physical exhaustion.

American naval officers today are wary of doctrine. This is nothing new. The excessiveness, rightness, or meagerness of doctrine is so much a part of tactical discourse that the Robisons' *History of Naval Tactics* might well have been entitled *The History of Naval Doctrine;* their stress is very much on systems or orders, commands, and signals. They recount the active debate that began when the U.S. Fleet was big enough to make controlling it in battle an important matter. Then, as now, doctrine tended to mean what the user wanted it to mean. Rear Admiral Robison attempts to referee and interpret the various viewpoints rather than declaim his own, but at one point he expresses his attitude in this way: "It [the term *doctrine*] gradually fell into disuse [about 1915]. It is probable that 'doctrine' would not have been offered as a naval term if 'Fighting Instructions' had been in existence, separate from signal books."[4] In 1981, when he was commander of the Second Fleet, ADM James A. Lyons promulgated fighting instructions

---

3   The immediate source of this analogy is LTG John Cushman, USA (Ret.), one of the ablest of our writers in C[2]. But many have used sports analogies. The first person I know of to relate sports to tactics (not to esprit, which goes back to the Iron Duke and his playing fields of Eton) was RADM William S. Sims, USN, who likened drilling for war to practicing plays for a football game.

4   Robison and Robison, p. 827.

for his fleet. His successor, VADM Joseph Metcalf, was deeply interested in developing them further. During the 1920s and 1930s the fleet tactical publications expanded into combat doctrine. Little analysis has been published of the documents' effectiveness in World War II. Most commentary is critical of their flaws, as one might expect of observations after the fact, but it is evident that the publications were believed in and acted on, the *sine qua non* of doctrine. They provided the foundation of training, gave the fleet standard operating procedures, and served as the point of departure for tactical developments.[5] In recent years the U.S. Navy's wariness of doctrine has been simultaneously subverted and magnified by the introduction of the Joint Publication series issued by the Joint Staff. Partly in response, the Navy established a Naval Doctrine Command to try its hand at doctrine, which it did with modest success. Most naval officers were unimpressed, however. One might observe that when a service makes the attempt from a standing start it is bound to be rusty. But neither the Joint Publication series nor that of the Naval Doctrine Command has created tactical doctrine suitable to unite a fleet in combat. It is fair to ask what useful tactical doctrine should achieve.

Doctrine is the basis for training and for measuring what training standards should achieve. On one hand, it is the tactical commander's assurance that when a new combat unit reports to a fighting force, it comes already equipped with certain combat skills needed by the commander. On the other hand, doctrine is the assurance to the captain of the new unit that the ship will fit into the new fighting force quickly and that her crew will not have to adapt to a bewildering set of new signals and procedures on the eve of battle. Doctrine provides continuity of operations when captains are transferred or killed.

Doctrine also provides the commander's staff with a basis for comparison of its own force with that of the enemy. Force evaluation requires the association of weapons with tactics. Any evaluation is a good deal more than the comparison

---

5 One well-researched evaluation of fleet tactical publications and their effectiveness in World War II is by then-lieutenant Terrance McKearney. In a master's thesis, McKearney reviewed the many battles of the Solomons Islands campaign of 1942–43 and concluded that our pre-war tactical doctrine for long-range daytime gun duels had been inappropriately adapted for short-range night battles against the Japanese in the fall of 1942. They were fought by pickup forces under tactical commanders who were constantly changing. The results were unsatisfactory. Then, in 1943, under stable leadership, including CDR Arleigh Burke, who developed new tactics exploiting our radar advantage and employing torpedo salvoes as the decisive weapon, we started winning the night battles consistently and effectively.

of orders of battle, but if the comparison—in Soviet parlance, the correlation of forces—cannot be made, battle outcomes cannot be estimated, and without them no strategy can be drafted, and without that, defense policy is built on sand.[6]

Tactical doctrine is the standard operating procedure that the creative commander adapts to the exigencies of battle. It is the procedure from which a ship's captain knowingly departs to exploit an opportunity, fully confident that fellow commanders will act in a predictable way; indeed, in the best of worlds with the best of captains, even the departures seem predictable in the circumstances. Paradoxically, doctrine generates initiative: a trained subordinate can see from it not only what will be done but what will not be done and will know—as Nelson did at Cape St. Vincent—how to save the battle.

Doctrine is the procedure to which the tactician may propose a change, and it also is the standard that the tactical analyst uses to evaluate the new against the old. It describes the way existing weapons are employed so that their effectiveness can be compared with that of a new weapon. It is the basis for understanding the new tactics that accompany new weapons—that is, for understanding the reward of prospectively greater effectiveness, the challenge of training in new techniques, and the burden of undergoing the transition from an old weapon doctrine to a new one.

In sum, doctrine must be whole and firm, but not dogmatic. It must leave room for leaders of freewheeling genius, for they will be the aces of the next war. But doctrine must never surrender control, because control is the prerequisite of concerted action. Although the creator of doctrine may find that control alone will not be enough to win in the most difficult circumstances, control still comes first and will count for more than inspiration in the midst of battle.

To Know Tactics, Know Technology

These two facts are universally recognized: that continual advances in technology keep weapons in a state of change, and that tactics must be designed to fit the capabilities of contemporary weapons. The U.S. Navy in particular has been fascinated with hardware, esteems technical competence, and is prone to trying to overcome its tactical deficiencies with engineering improvements. Indeed, there are officers in peacetime who regard the official statement of a requirement for

---

6 Some experts talk as though the national policy determines national defense policy, which in turn determines strategy and tactics. This scheme is a rational way to approach force procurements for a *future* strategy, but present policy, like wartime aims, depends on current means.

a new piece of hardware as the end of their responsibility in correcting a current operational deficiency. This is a trap. Former Atlantic Fleet commander ADM Isaac Kidd Jr. was always a champion of the need to be prepared to fight with what you have. And no wonder: his father died fighting in the USS *Arizona* (BB 39) at Pearl Harbor.

The tactician stays ready by knowing the available weapons systems. Technical facility, like good leadership and sound doctrine, is the third cornerstone of this book because the effects of a new technology usually must be exploited by new tactics to achieve its full advantage. To illustrate, the many recent changes in information technologies, such as artificial intelligence, and also unmanned systems can be expected to change radically the way fleets fight in the future.

Our ablest naval officers were tacticians who knew their technology. RADM William S. Sims, with his continuous-aim fire; RADM Bradley A. Fiske, with his host of patents, including one for aerial-torpedo-release gear, before aircraft were even capable of lifting a torpedo payload; and RADM William A. Moffett and other early aviators who foresaw the day when naval aircraft would be potent ship-killers and who helped develop bigger engines, better navigating equipment, and carrier arresting gear—all machinery to fulfill their visions.

The great historian of the Civil War, Douglas Southall Freeman, condensed the ten commandments of warfare into three: "Know your stuff; be a man; and look after your men."[7] His first commandment dealt in large part with competency in battle tactics and field equipment. But what is true in ground combat, where machines serve human beings, is magnified at sea, where human beings serve machines.

The Seat of Purpose Is on the Land

In the classical manner, this book centers attention on fleet actions. Command of the sea, which today includes the air and space above the surface and the water beneath it, is still the requisite of the effective employment of sea power. We live in an era in which the U.S. Navy no longer can take sea control largely for granted and concentrate solely on how to exercise that control with operations that project naval influence ashore. Although the purpose of this volume is to examine and highlight the tactics of fleet-on-fleet action, it is important to say at the outset that sea battles are not fought for their own sake.

---

7 Freeman's speech of 11 May 1949 is reprinted in the *Naval War College Review* (March–April 1979): 3–10.

For one thing, the study of maritime history shows that fleet battles have been rare; once again, the most common use of navies has been for the landing of ground forces, the support of operations ashore, and the protection of shipping at sea. It is worth pointing out that conducting an amphibious operation, clearing a minefield, or escorting a convoy never were easy propositions, and each demands special tactical skills. The recent emphasis on irregular warfare at sea is another example of how events at sea can yield rewards on the land.

Indeed, the great decisive sea battles between fleets have always been connected with events on land, usually in an immediate, direct, and obvious way. These connections are matters of strategy, and therefore are outside the purview of this book. Later chapters, however, shall link tactics with mission and strategic purposes to show that peacetime tactical development derives from anticipated wartime roles. The only certainty about the Navy's wartime role is the uncertainty of predicting in peacetime what site, enemy, and mission will be involved. This makes the problem of developing tactics acute. The modern means of achieving direct naval influence include

- Using submarine-launched ballistic missiles, nuclear or conventional cruise missiles, aerial bombs, or naval gunfire in attacking the enemy.
- Augmenting land combat operations with air and missile strikes, naval gunfire, and riverine warfare.
- Isolating an enemy with a naval blockade, attacks on shipping, or offensive mining operations.
- Initiating land operations with expeditionary operations.
- Protecting military reinforcements and resupply.
- Protecting economic sea lines of communication.
- Protecting shipping (which is as important in peacetime as in wartime). If a major war occurs, the existing trade routes will be distorted beyond recognition, most likely never to resume their prewar structure.
- Maintaining a peacekeeping presence or "deterrence." Presence is only as effective as the apparent willingness to exercise force. Presence should be appreciated not only for its military and political value but also for its economic value in fostering favorable trade and investment.

It has long been axiomatic that naval influence cannot be exercised before "sufficient" control of the sea is secured. The classic way of securing control is to defeat the enemy's means to contest that control—its main force or "fleet." Today the potential is greater for tactical interaction between land and sea elements, including aircraft, land-to-sea missiles, and long-range sensors. A naval force-on-force action need no longer be ship-on-ship. The threat of land-based aircraft and missiles now extends hundreds of miles out to sea if it is aided by long-range detection and targeting methods. Clear thinking is required to determine whether the purpose of an intended battle, over a continent or an ocean or both, is continental or oceanic—that is, whether it is projecting force from the sea (implying a measure of control over the land) or controlling the sea (implying the threat of attacks from the land).

"A Ship's a Fool to Fight a Fort"

The reason a fleet did not choose to fight protected land batteries toe-to-toe was well expressed by a man who ought to have known—John Ericsson, the designer of the armored Civil War ship *Monitor*. "A single shot can sink a ship," he said, "while a hundred salvos cannot silence a fort." Today a "fort" can be an airfield or the launch site for a missile battery. Either of these can be repaired or rebuilt quickly, but a warship cannot.

Since the potential is so much greater now for interaction between land and sea, how do we interpret this cornerstone of naval operations, knowing that we must enter and fight in the enemy's coastal regions? Since tactical commanders, including Nelson, historically have sought to avoid having to fight in front of fortifications, evidently the goal is to maneuver so that the immobile fort cannot prevent the operation or make it too costly. In a modern campaign, naval officers are interested in either winning a conflict without having to confront the forts or in defeating them by finding an Achilles' heel. To do this, they must exploit both the fleet's mobility and the fort's inability to move, for even a mobile missile launcher is much more constrained in its motion than a warship. History can provide some clues on how warships must contend with land-based air and missile attacks, guns, minefields, and coastal submarines.

When guns had far shorter ranges than they do today, a fleet could risk a run past to get beyond them. The gauntlet of fire usually was short enough to endure—if the reward were worth the price. The American Civil War is full of examples of subtlety and brute force, of success and failure. The many Union fleet engagements with fortifications along the Confederate coast and western rivers show that victory was difficult to achieve, and that it depended on preparation, choice of the moment, and well-coordinated execution, often in cooperation with land forces.

Strange to say, after the range of cannon had increased substantially, large guns ashore were no longer the sort of "forts" that frightened battleship captains the most. In World War I torpedo boats, minefields, and submarines held the Royal Navy at bay. In that conflict and again in World War II, the narrow waterways of the English Channel and North Sea were the domain of a flotilla of many small combatants. The flotilla threatened (yet could not stop) coastal shipping, dropped off spies and raiders, and rescued pilots who bailed out over water.

In missions involving an attack on a fleet that was anchored in a protected port, many commanders chose to approach from the rear. That was the tactical plan at Port Arthur in the Russo-Japanese War, Santiago in the Spanish-American War, and Singapore in World War II. The attackers landed ground troops against weak opposition and away from the center of gravity—the harbor—so that it could be overwhelmed by land, though sometimes at considerable cost, lives and time required. At Guadalcanal, where the airfield was still under construction and not yet operating, the American Navy was able to put the Marines so close to land that the leathernecks could walk ashore. Only after the landing did the Japanese navy's fireworks explode. In the battle over the Falklands, when the British were planning for their own amphibious landing, they saw that the islands covered enough real estate to ensure that their ground forces could get ashore at San Carlos Sound, remote from Stanley, banking on the navy's mobility to help surprise the Argentine forces.

In each of these cases, the mobility offered by the navy ships provided a sufficient element of surprise for the attacking force to gain a foothold. What happened next would depend on the talents of the commanders ashore. The Gallipoli operation was one of the worst failures, with Anzio running close behind, but American soldiers did well enough in North Africa, Sicily, Salerno, southern France, and in the greatest landing of them all—at the Normandy beaches.

Still, on the theme that ships don't want to fight forts, the Marines' amphibious assaults in the Pacific contrasted in two ways during their magnificent sweep from the Gilbert Islands to the Marianas and Iwo Jima. When they attacked their little atoll island targets they had no choice but to dive into the teeth of enemy fire. In the few times when the opposition was weak and Marine Corps losses light, Nimitz used the Navy's mobility to strike across vast distances before the Japanese could prepare a fortified response. A second advantage—and offsetting the punishment to an opposed assault—was that the tactic isolated the defenders so they could not be reinforced. Thus, Navy ships were not at risk and their bombs and shellfire were crucial in weakening Japanese resistance. That changed when the Navy had to beat off a determined counterattack during the Marianas Islands landings in June 1944. Later, at Okinawa, the Navy lost more than a ship a day to kamikazes and was vulnerable to the land-based repelling forces as long as it was compelled to support the soldiers and Marines ashore.

GEN Douglas MacArthur's long strides up the New Guinea coast are often cited for skill at maneuver warfare and his landing against weak opposition at Inchon is regarded as a masterpiece almost without parallel. This is the essence of *operational maneuver* from the sea and its latest Marine Corps manifestation, *ship-to-objective* maneuver. In Operation Desert Storm, the Kuwaiti coast of one hundred miles was not long enough for an amphibious maneuver to gain a lodgment without the possibility of needless casualties. Shore bombardment by the battleship *Missouri* and the well-publicized Marine amphibious force afloat served as the best and safest ways to draw Iraqi defenders away from the primary coalition thrust through the desert.

As for strikes, raids, or hit-and-run attacks, the common denominators of success are stealth, swiftness, and surprise. Failure to achieve all three bodes ill for the attacking ships. In World War I the German navy contemplated using battlecruisers to shell English ports—and occasionally succeeded. In World War II, carrier air strikes greatly increased the Navy's potency from the sea. The British attack on the Italian fleet at Taranto in 1940 and the Japanese destruction of American battleships at Pearl Harbor a year later were precursors of crushing attacks by American airmen during the remainder of the war. U.S. carrier strikes against the air bases and ships at Pacific islands such as Truk and Rabaul were spectacular successes because a fleet of aircraft carriers could run in at twenty-five knots under cover of darkness to surprise the unalerted—and immobile—defenders. But it was not until October 1944 that the American Third Fleet and Fifth Fleet were strong and supple enough to begin in-and-out raids against the large airfield complexes of Formosa and Japan. These were land bastions indeed. When the fleet came and stayed—in support of the landing and of extensive ground campaigns in the Philippines and Okinawa—it relearned the hard lesson that when ships fight forts (in this case "forts" in the form of kamikazes), the ships will suffer again as they have in the past.

Something similar happens to a landing force when there is no alternative to a direct assault in which the reward outweighs the punishment. Two early, brilliant examples were the capture of Louisbourg in July 1758 and in Quebec the following summer. In the first, after a bloody direct assault under heavy fire, a few thousand British regulars gained a winning foothold. In the second, the brilliant British General James Wolfe lost his life but, with the capitulation of Quebec, won half of North America. The supporting fleets numbered 157 sail at Louis-bourg and about as many at Quebec.[8] In World War II, U.S. forces decided on bitter, brutal, direct assaults on Tarawa, Peleliu, Saipan, and Iwo Jima because the islands were too small to provide opportunities for the Americans to deceive and surprise the defenders. The opposed landings succeeded because *operational maneuver* on a grand scale enabled the United States to launch attacks in which the Japanese enemy, though deeply entrenched, was vastly outnumbered.

How does a modern campaign planner beat a "fort" that comprises land-based aircraft and missiles supported by space- or land-based sensors reaching far out to sea? How can a fleet continue to perform its tasks in a littoral campaign, defeating the enemy forces without getting into a slugfest? The solution must exploit the longstanding advantage of *operational maneuver* from the sea by for-mulating a campaign in a way that the forces ashore will be a day late and a salvo short. This is as much a campaign problem as it is a matter of tactics, but either way it is a major concern in joint littoral warfare.

The rule for ships is to move and hit from a place where a fort cannot hit back. If a "fort" is weak—whatever its composition—then crush it; if it is strong, avoid it. If a fortification itself is the center of gravity and is too resilient to be put permanently out of action from the sea—for instance, enemy bases, sensors, and a command-and-control system—then commanders should use the operational mobility that ships provide to gain a foothold ashore and then deploy Marines or special forces to attack the fortification from its metaphorical rear. If all these choices are foreclosed and the reward is worth the punishment, then mass against it in overwhelming numbers, assault it, and face the bloody consequences. Play the fool and fight the fort!

Attack Effectively First

The first five cornerstones of maritime warfare (as distinct from naval tactics) have been introduced in part to obviate the need for a running apology.

Yes, sailors will dominate battle.

Yes, doctrine, though not the same as tactics, must be sound to facilitate tactics.

Yes, weapons influence tactics deeply.

Yes, the decisive sea battle is a means and not an end in itself.

---

8   Strategy is not our subject in this volume, but these two battles were won in the Seven Years' War, 1756–63, in which William Pitt, the English prime minister, conceived a strategy so masterful that Sir Julian Corbett, Mahan, Vice Admiral Philip Colomb, Major General Sir Charles Callwell, and most later naval historians regard it as the model of a perfectly executed worldwide maritime war—the more so because Britain carried it out against quite competent French opposition.

Yes, fleet tactics are complicated by the advantages land based forces have when attacking warships.

The sixth cornerstone is different: it is the tactical theme running throughout this book. The great naval maxim of tactics—"attack effectively first"—should be thought of as more than the principle of the offensive; it should be considered the very essence of tactical action for success in naval combat.

Fifty years ago the Robisons ended their long history of tactics by observing that the most important tactical maxim is "attack." It is a strange conclusion; most everyone else regards the fundamental tactical goal to be the concentration of force. We have seen the disaster for the French of a blind faith in élan and the offensive in land battle. We know also of Clausewitz's great respect for defensive positions. Let us agree that there is wisdom underlying the Robison conclusion, note that we are dealing with fleet tactics and nothing more, acknowledge that selecting the time and place of battle bestows an obvious advantage on the attacker, but for the moment defer consideration of the Robison enjoinder: attack.

Lanchester's Equations

In 1914 British automotive engineer Frederick W. Lanchester introduced his celebrated equations to show the impact of concentration of force in the modern era.[9] The narrow physical consequences, expressed quantitatively, yielded a square law of effectiveness. Lanchester compared these results with a linear law (refined later by other authors) governing two forces constrained in their ability to concentrate firepower.

The physical effect of concentration was phenomenal. Lanchester said that "ancient conditions" (that is, linear law conditions) of limited weapon range and mobility pitted individual against individual in what was equivalent to a series of duels. If the fighting value of individual combatants were the same on both sides, 1,000 fighting men meeting 1,000 enemies would result in a draw; but if 1,000 men were concentrated against 750 in a battle of annihilation, 250 of the larger force would be left when the smaller force was eliminated. Superior concentration would lead to victory, but barring psychological effects, the larger force would suffer casualties equal to those of the smaller. Under modern conditions, however, a new advantage favors the side with larger numbers. When both sides can aim their fire, there is an expanding, cumulative advantage for the larger force. At any

---

9   Lanchester was a successful British engineer with an intellectual curiosity that swept over aerodynamics, economics, fiscal and industrial policies, the theory of relativity, and military science.

instant, the rate of casualties imposed is proportionate to the numbers of forces remaining, and the ratio of forces continuously increases in favor of the stronger initial force. In simplest form, if the attrition rate of force A is proportionate to the remaining strength of B and vice versa, we have attrition equations

$$\frac{dA}{dt} = -B$$

and

$$\frac{dB}{dt} = -A$$

omitting for clarity the killing rate parameters for both sides, so that in these equations the fighting effectiveness of individuals on both sides is the same. The solution to these coupled equations is

$$A^2_{o} - A^2_{t} = B^2_{o} - B^2_{t}$$

where Ao and Bo are the initial force strengths and At and Bt are the strengths later, at time t. If A has 1,000 fighters, each of whom can fire at any enemy, and B has 750 fighters with the same capability, when the battle is fought to the annihilation of B, about 660 of the A side will survive, rather than the 250 that would be left under linear law conditions.

Lanchester then asked what would happen if the fighting quality of one side's forces were superior to that of the other side. He showed that for aimed fire, numbers of fighting units are more valuable than fighting quality. A commander is better off with twice as many units of force than with units with twice the rate of effective firepower.[10]

Uninformed writers have carried the application of Lanchester's equation further than he intended. With reason, critics have taken some of these extensions as too literal or too ephemeral. There is irony in this, because the square law treats only the dynamic physical effects of homogeneous firepower. Lanchester wholly set aside the possibility of the enhanced effectiveness of synergism.[11] Lanchester

---

10 Lanchester's ingenuity was in recognizing the simpler form that could be used to express the mathematical effects of concentration previously quantified by Bradley Fiske and others. Fiske also saw that collective fighting strength was more important than individual fighting value. A contemporary of Lanchester's, the Russian M. Osipov, published similar equations in 1915 and explored their applicability to ground combat.

11 That is, of using combinations of weapons in such a way that the effectiveness of the whole is greater than the sum of the parts, or mathematically, the set $[A + B]$ is greater than set $[A]$ + set $[B]$.

did not dabble in this, nor did he deal with the comfortable psychological advantage that numerical superiority usually bestows.

Adaptations of Lanchester's equations have been applied commonly in ground combat analysis but infrequently in naval combat. This is because land battle has been fought by larger numbers of forces, which are very difficult to analyze except in some simplified and aggregate form. This book suggests that, with suitable modification to allow for ships that can take hits and continue to fight, his exposition of cumulative advantage is more relevant to sea than land, because the opportunity to concentrate firepower in the manner that he specified is more likely to occur at sea. Ground combat is characterized by position, movement, and ultimate considerations of territory. Rather than attack effectively first, perhaps the best maxim for ground commanders would be the statement by Confederate general Nathan Bedford Forrest: ". . . make it a rule to get there first with the most men." The subtle distinction is the same as that in chess between pawn-takes-pawn and pawn-to-king-four.

The potential to *effect* this concentration is greater at sea than on land. At sea there is no high ground, no river barrier, no concealment in forests that requires what is often used as a rule of thumb on land, a three-to-one preponderance of force to attack a prepared position. As others have said, battle at sea and conflict in the open desert have much in common. Sun, wind, and sea state all affect naval tactics, but not to the extent that terrain affects ground combat. It is because of this that attacking has not carried the penalty at sea that is imposed ashore. Over the course of history, the central problem of naval tactics has been to attack effectively—that is to say, to bring the firepower of the whole force into battle simultaneously.

A second and subordinate objective of naval tactics has been to try to concentrate one's entire force on a portion of the enemy's in order to defeat him in detail. For the inferior force, this was a necessity. For either side, superior or inferior, massing in the face of an enemy who could *see* the opposition was so tricky that the superior commander usually declined to try and the inferior commander vastly preferred (mission aside) to decline battle or cripple his enemy so that he could withdraw. But it was evident that a concentrated first strike by one force against a part of the enemy's was at once an opportunity to exploit and a hazard to avoid.

In the days of fighting sail and the rifled gun, tacticians sought ways to achieve "decisive first attack" by maneuver and technologists sought ways to achieve it by weapon range and ship maneuverability. In World War II the necessity of attacking first became more important. During daylight hours, aircraft were more valued than guns because they outranged them by an order of magnitude. The importance of timing reached a new peak. Since the range of action of carrier-based aircraft on both sides was comparable in 1942, the side with superior reconnaissance and intelligence—in other words, better scouting—was the one that launched the first effective attack. Land-based assets for scouting and attack also played a key role. In the great Pacific carrier battles, what was foremost in the carrier fleet commander's thinking was the paramount advantage of initiating the first concerted attack.

The essential foundation of all naval tactics has been to attack effectively by means of superior concentration, and to do so first, either with longer-range weapons, an advantage of maneuver, or shrewd timing based on good scouting. Everything else—movement, cover and deception, plans, and command, control, and communications (C^3)—has been aimed at achieving such an attack. We can now understand why the Robisons chose to distill their wisdom into the one word *attack*, even as we reject it and consider our own maxim with great care.

Like all general truths, "attack effectively first" is not very helpful in specific circumstances. As a maxim of naval tactics, it is most useful not for what it says, but for what it excludes and leaves unsaid. All fleet operations based on defensive tactics (but not all defensive forces) are conceptually deficient. A successful defensive naval strategy entails a concentration of force and a successful tactical attack.[12] Effective fusion of reconnaissance, surveillance, and intelligence information is so important that it must receive the same emphasis as the delivery of firepower. Contrarily, obstructing the enemy's scouting by cover, deception, confusion, or distraction merits enormous attention, for successful scouting and screening are relative to each other and are a matter of timeliness.

Nothing about naval combat is understood if its two-sided nature is not grasped. Each side is simultaneously stalking the other. Weapon range is relative to the enemy's weapon range. The weapon range that matters is the productive range—that is, the range at which a telling number of weapons may be expected to hit their targets. For a battle force, the weapon range that matters is the range at which enough weapons can be aimed to hit with great effectiveness.

---

12 Excluded as inappropriate here is the strategy of a maritime *guerre de course* (commerce-raiding), which is discussed in chapter 10.

The maxim cannot be reduced to the principle of the offensive. Defensive *forces* and *operations* are very much a part of operational plans. Mere ambition to attack does not preclude the enemy's success. Indeed, the first responsibility of a fleet that has achieved sea control is to defend its sea space while extending its influence on land. At times the enemy tactical commander will have the means to attack at longer range. If so, the aim should be to see that the enemy cannot attack so well that a counterattack will fail.

Left to itself, the spirit of attacking first will fritter away weapons piecemeal; left to itself, the spirit of the offensive will marshal great magazines of weapons to serve as a funeral pyre. The warfighter who believes that the quicker rapier will always win will lose to the opponent who wields a battle ax and carries a strong shield.

The warrior with the quickest aim and the farthest-seeing vision will teach the wrong tactics to one who is less skilled and gifted. The enemy will have its own Sir Francis Drake, André de Suffren, or Raizo Tanaka, and tactical theory must teach steady leadership first because genius will take care of itself.

2

TACTICAL DEVELOPMENT, 1650–1815

The Age of Fighting Sail

The 165-year period of sea warfare known as "the Age of Fighting Sail" marked a slow and hobbled beginning in the development of naval tactics. On one hand, it was a time when sailors could use the entire ocean as a battlefield laboratory for developing and testing tactics. Yet, the process frequently encountered serious headwinds. This chapter discusses a strange phenomenon of the age—the ossification of British tactics for almost a century—and tells how hard-headed naval fighters often became handcuffed by the entire system of command-and-control called the Permanent Fighting Instructions. More than merely a first attempt at promulgating doctrine, these detailed directives created a rigid interlocking system of tactics, doctrine, and communication that frustrated British admirals of that period at almost every turn.

In eighteenth-century battles, the ship of the line was the primary means of delivering concentrated naval firepower, and the line-ahead formation was the most practical means of unleashing that firepower in a coordinated way. Since it was natural for sailing ships to fire abeam, the practice of positioning ships in a straight line in order to fight an enemy was entirely logical for that day. At the same time, because the admiral's signal flags—then the only effective way of communicating orders within a squadron or fleet—were difficult to see for vessels arrayed in a single line, command-and-control was more reliable if the admiral placed his flagship in the center of the column. With that combination, he could maneuver a large number of ships with a minimum of confusion and with fewer communication problems. The direction and force of the wind and the bearing and distance of the enemy still effectively determined the commander's maneuvers. He deployed his ships in full view of the enemy. His objective was to bring all of his force against the enemy, "well ordered, well knit, and simultaneously," and with no unengaged reserve.[1] Training at sea improved captains' seamanship skills, enabling fleet commanders to place a tightly spaced column alongside a raggedly disposed enemy line—a step that could significantly bolster the squadron's collective firepower, especially in cases where enemy ships were spread thinly or where they overlapped and masked each other's fire.

The Ship of the Line: Massing Firepower

Indeed, it took skillful seamanship to bring the firepower of even two ships simultaneously against a single enemy. To be fully effective, guns had to be well within three hundred yards of the enemy, firing essentially at point-blank range. The maximum significant range for naval guns was eight hundred or nine hundred yards; beyond this the probability of hitting the enemy was remote and roundshot would barely be able to penetrate a hull. The firing arcs of broadsides were limited to about 25 degrees forward and aft of the beam. Training a gun was a slow and awkward process, so that, by and large, it was easier to train a ship's guns by maneuvering the ship herself than by trying to turn her cannon to one side or another. As a result, it was rare for two consecutive ships in a column to enjoy the advantage of directing fully effective fire at a single enemy simultaneously. Figure 2-1 illustrates how, at the outer limits of effective range—about five hundred yards—it was barely possible for two ships closely spaced in column to direct broadsides against an enemy unless those in his column also were closed up.

The most effective method of massing force and increasing the density of firepower was to stack cannon vertically—hence the logic of building two-deckers and three-deckers. By the late seventeenth century three-deckers were common, and naval leaders knew well their great practical value. In 1697 the highly respected Jesuit priest and French naval tactician Paul Hoste would write that the size of vessels contributed more than numbers to the strength of the fleet. Hoste cited two reasons—first, that larger ships had more and heavier guns, and, second, that a fleet of large ships would bring more and larger guns to bear in the same length as a column made up of smaller ships that were spaced more closely together.[2] In fact, single-deck ships diluted the density of firepower too much to warrant a

---

1 The felicitous words of Creswell, p. 178.
2 Robison and Robison, p. 220.

place in the line, and by the latter part of the eighteenth century even two-deckers were being used in the line only with reluctance.

From combat experience the two-decker was known to have more than a two-to-one advantage over a single-decker (which later would be known as a frigate). It was the firepower advantage that mattered most: Hoste spoke of the defensive strength of a larger ship's timbers, but he understood that this was a lesser advantage. Two ships fighting each other at sea were much the same as two stockades on wheels, with wooden walls protecting the guns and gunners—at least somewhat. Barring a lucky shot that landed in a magazine, ships were not often sunk by gunfire (although they later sank from hull damage, which is a separate issue). Ships were defeated by what today we would refer to as a firepower kill—by knocking out their guns and gunners and crushing the ships' morale and their will to fight. As many ships were captured as were sunk. Since British seamen fought better and French ships had excellent sailing qualities, many of the ships sailing in the Royal Navy were rehabilitated French vessels.

If two vessels were armed with the same number and quality of men and guns, the winner would be decided by the rates of fire, accuracies of fire, and shot

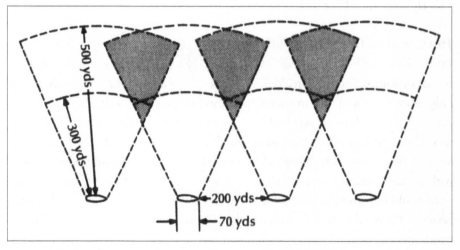

Figure 2-1. Effective and Point-Blank Range of Ships in Column

1. Ships are at two-hundred-yard intervals, extremely tight.
2. At point-blank range, three hundred yards, ships in column are just able to present a solid front of broadsides to ships trying to break through the column.
3. At a reasonably effective range of destructiveness, about five hundred yards, adjacent ships have some power of concentration (shaded areas), but not much.

penetration. On the other hand, if a two-decked seventy-four (capable of firing a thirty-six-gun broadside) were to meet a frigate of thirty-eight guns (which could fire an eighteen-gun broadside), the "square-law effect" would result in the frigate's suffering far more cumulative damage than the seventy-four. No amount of prowess could be expected to save the frigate in a stand-up fight. According to the computation, with simple continuous fire on both sides and no hull strength advantage for either, the two-decker would lose only five guns, at the same time destroying the frigate's entire broadside of eighteen. If the frigate's captain had surrendered sometime before his entire broadside had been destroyed, his force of thirty-eight guns and three hundred seamen would have been lost at a cost to the two-decker of no more than five guns, with similarly light casualties and structural damage.

If a two-decked seventy-four were matched against a three-decker rated at one hundred guns, then, using the same model and assumptions as before, the two-decker would be forced to capitulate before the three-decker had lost twenty guns. This cumulative advantage of a modest edge in initial firepower was displayed in actions in the North Sea and the English Channel. Quite likely many excessively critical courts-martial of two-decker captains transpired, as well as scarcely warranted knightings of three-decker captains.

The Column: The Means of Control

By the latter half of the seventeenth century, the column served primarily as a means of controlling the force that was inherent in an admiral's larger ships and only secondarily as a way to concentrate their firepower. In fact, the use of two-decked fighting ships already had become widespread in the first half of the century, when the concept of the commanded column was instituted. Admirals also learned, however, that keeping a close interval between ships could provide them with increased mutual support, so the distance specified in their Fighting Instructions could be almost unattainably short—as little as three ship lengths between vessels.[3] It took skillful seamanship to keep even a short line of a dozen ships at close interval, especially when each vessel had to avoid overtaking and masking the fire of those ahead. Keeping station was difficult at best, but it was made easier in one respect: ships under "fighting sails" (that is, using only their middle

---

3   Distance was specified in cables (each 240 yards long). In the Anglo-Dutch wars, when ships were 50 yards long, a distance of half a cable was specified in at least 1 set of instructions. Later a prescribed interval of 2 cables was common (Robison and Robison, pp. 153, 361).

sails, known as topsails) typically advanced at bare steerageway—stately speeds of about three hundred feet a minute. Cohesion and control in action as well as firepower were valued more highly than speed. Crews were needed at the guns.

A second reason for tight spacing was to prevent an enemy from breaking through the column and raking ships on either side with entire broadsides at point-blank range, and from an angle where the target ship was unable to return the fire. It also prevented "doubling"—a process under which ships that had broken through the column (usually at the rear, which was to windward) could envelop that portion of the column on both sides, making it easier for them to destroy it (see figure 2-2).

Finally, a closely spaced column afforded more protection in case the enemy, by design or accident, came against a portion of the line with his entire force. Unengaged ships that were not part of the line or were positioned downwind, which was usually in the van, would have to beat upwind as quickly as possible to get into action, and for them distance meant time.

As a result, the tactician's primary problem during this era was to concentrate firepower at sea at a time when effective gun range was very short—less than five hundred yards. The command-and-control solution was to form a firing line to keep the closest possible interval between ships without risk of overlap and to stack firepower vertically. A look at how these tactics evolved makes it easier to understand why British naval leaders were reluctant to tamper with the great tactical strength of line.

The Creative Phase

The formal beginning of the commanded column as a naval tactic came in the latter half of the seventeenth century, when it became commonly incorporated into the Fighting Instructions issued to English fleet admirals. We take as our starting point the incorporation of the commanded column into the English fleet admirals' fighting instructions. Trade frictions between England and Holland sparked three Anglo-Dutch wars during that period. In the first of these conflicts, from 1652 to 1653, the opposing sides fought six major sea battles over two years.

Because warships cruised in haphazardly positioned clusters, the actions often ended in tactical indecision. Ships were polyglots in size, shape, and sailing qualities, and their captains, who frequently doubled as tradesmen, were undisciplined in formation sailing. At the outset there were too many ships and there was too little control. The measure of victory in such battles was whether the enemy fled

The aim of doubling was to achieve one of these positions:

Both fleets were moving, at about the same speed when well handled, so it was difficult to attain the positions without splitting a fleet temporarily and risking the enemy's closing on one half or the other and counterconcentrating. Nelson successfully doubled on the French at the Battle of the Nile because they were at anchor and other circumstances were fortuitous:

The plan to double on the rear, depicted below, illustrates the difficulties. In the first sketch victim fleet *B* is sailing close hauled on the starboard tack. Doubling fleet *A* is squared off, ship for ship, just outside of effective range to windward.

In the next sketch the ships of fleet *A* have backed sail until the half in the van are abreast of the rear half of *B*'s line. As *A*'s van closes to engage, the rear of *A*'s fleet falls off the wind to sail in echelon under the sterns of *B*'s passive column.

With *A*'s van now closely engaged with *B*'s rear, the rear of *A*'s line now to leeward, hauls up close to the wind. *B*'s engaged rear is presumed to be moving slowly, allowing *A*'s leeward ships to move up into doubling position. *B*'s unengaged van must wear around, and if it takes too long it won't gain the battle.

It doesn't take an 18th-century seaman to appreciate that even a lethargic fleet *B* could itself back its sails and spoil the plan, or fall off downwind to disengage from *A*'s windward ships and frustrate those attempting to get to leeward. Doubling on the van would be less propitious still, because *B*'s unengaged ships in the rear would automatically sail forward and enter the fray, even in the absence of orders to do so.

Figure 2-2. Doubling

from the scene, not how many ships were sunk or captured. Evidence suggests that when the enemy was sighted, commanders tried to form loose columns, each of them under a flag officer, but that once the battle was joined it became a back-alley brawl. After an indecisive third battle near Portland, Lord Protector Oliver Cromwell sent three of his generals, Robert Blake, Richard Deane, and George Monck, to sea. Accustomed to order and discipline, they jointly issued new instructions that made columns the basic formation for the English fleet, with orders that ships form on each flagship separately, in several lines.

There is no evidence that concentration of firepower was the initial motivation for these orders. Indeed, the ships began the war as armed merchantmen, with captains who were patriotic and piratical but unschooled in naval discipline, fighting under flag officers who were land soldiers and new to the sea. Given those realities, the columns probably were conceived as the simplest way to control the fleet. Then, as now, it was considered folly to devise a battle plan that the force had not been trained to execute, and keeping station under sail—even in a short column of ships—was no mean accomplishment. Yet, to the extent that the formation was maintained, the tactic succeeded. It achieved four things:

- Enabled each admiral to control his column, using only a few signals, each of them keyed to an article of the commander's own Fighting Instructions and appropriate to the level of skill and training of the squadron.
- Eliminated the danger that ships would inadvertently fire on vessels in their own squadrons—a frequent and terrifying problem in the smoke and confusion of a melee. Merely the confidence that this possibility had been removed would have been as important as the fact. A warship captain would not have wanted to take time for the gun smoke to clear to be sure that he had an enemy in his sights.
- Effectively ended the serious problem with shirkers. Article seven of the Fighting Instructions sternly warned potential recalcitrants that the most severe punishment awaited captains whose ships failed to join a column as directed. It is clear that this was not a parade-ground injunction.
- Offered, through the system of at least three commanded columns, the promise of getting all ships into action and under control in the shortest time. There was to be no reserve. A ship at a distance was not viewed as a reinforcement that could be thrown in at a critical time or place; a ship that was out of range was considered wasted firepower.

The Fighting Instructions Mature

The admirals understood quite early in the age of fighting sail that the close column also concentrated a fleet's firepower. As the Royal Navy sailed, drilled, and fought, it became a professional force of fighting seamen. Firepower was improved by increasing the rate of fire and by keeping station at close intervals—a maneuver that demanded superb seamanship. By the sixth and last battle of the First Anglo-Dutch War, the Dutch were forced to form columns as well. Because the Dutch came determined to fight, the Battle of Scheveningen in 1653 was bloody and decisive. Although the English won a tactical victory, the Dutch achieved their strategic goal—forcing the English to lift their blockade of Dutch ports—and the war ended.

In the second and third Anglo-Dutch wars, the single column became the standard formation for the fleets of both sides, but maneuvering could be adapted to circumstance. Since both sides were aggressive and skillful, the English admiral could be content with a single column and devote his fleet's skills to gaining the weather gauge, upwind; the line to windward could come down and fight or stand off and decline battle. While the English were putting more and more faith in the single line, the potential of the windward fleet to mass or double on the enemy was not lost on the combatants.

But for the English, the single column, or *fleet* line ahead, would soon be too much of a good thing: designed for beginners, the formation became a rigid doctrine before the new breed of naval professionals could develop and exploit the full command-and-control potential of the Fighting Instructions. It was indisputable that a tightly knit column maneuvered by its admiral was the best way to achieve concentration of firepower in a small squadron. But when the entire fleet—as many as one hundred ships—was formed and maneuvered as a unit, the result was a thin ribbon of firepower, miles long but less than five hundred yards deep on its sides. It took an hour for the aft-most ship to arrive at the spot where the forward-most had been. Worse yet, depending on the wind, the van might not be able to succor the rear at all.

English Tactics Ossified

At the start of the eighteenth century, fleets were so large that it was almost impossible to position a single long line, that thin ribbon of destruction, squarely alongside a reluctant enemy, van to van, center to center, and rear to rear. The eighteenth-century French were such a reluctant enemy. Seeking to avoid a decisive action, they concentrated on improving their accuracy instead of on increasing the volume of their fire, arming their ships with more long-range guns, positioning themselves to leeward, and firing high into the rigging to cripple English ships, forcing them to slow, drop back, and weaken the line. But the main reason the French succeeded was the result of a change in English tactics. By 1740 the English admirals' own individual fighting instructions had been supplanted by what came to be called the Admiralty's "Permanent Fighting Instructions." Although commanders in chief were permitted to supplement the Admiralty's instructions, they undoubtedly thought they must comply without substantial changes or possibly face pain of death.

As Professor John Hattendorf of the Naval War College points out, John Creswell offers recent evidence that until 1799 the Fighting Instructions were not, in fact, Admiralty instructions—contrary to the belief expressed by Mahan and Corbett. Indeed, Creswell contends that there was nothing basically wrong with Royal Navy tactics. If this is true, it reinforces the argument for coherent, practical doctrine. But whether the "Sailing and Fighting Instructions for His Majesty's Fleet" were issued by the Admiralty or merely noted by that body hardly seems to have mattered; the concept of the line, preferably positioned to windward, was drummed into the minds of the fleet commanders in chief. And by using the coterminous line as a standard, the Royal Navy suffered almost a century of inconclusive battles and frustration.

Part of the problem was that the Fighting Instructions were not only doctrine, but had become dogma. Besides being the approved means of controlling the fleet, they prescribed all the signals that commanders would use to control maneuver. The fleet could hardly conceive of, much less comply with, any sort of creativity in devising tactics: the instructions were thought not to allow it, and what could not be practiced could not be executed in battle. Therefore, the admirals could not exploit—or even see—ways to concentrate firepower on the enemy's flank, break up its line, or double on the rear. As the eighteenth century wore on, this albatross not only stifled tactics but squelched tactical imagination as well.

Naval Tactics Restored

We venerate Horatio Nelson not for breaking free from the rigid formalism of the Admiralty's Permanent Fighting Instructions—Admiral George Rodney in 1782, Admiral Richard Howe in 1794, and Admiral Adam Duncan in 1797 did that, and John Jervis shares the glory for appreciating the significance of Nelson's tactical genius at the Battle of Cape St. Vincent (1797). Nelson is our peerless tactician because he knew how to exploit the Royal Navy's new-found freedom. Corbett gives credit to English Rear Admiral Richard Kempenfelt for drawing up new orders and signals that permitted more flexible maneuvering as early as 1780. Robison implies that even then the problem of too much formalism was widely understood, and that the ideas for how to solve it were already fermenting. As usual, the French were well ahead of the British in developing tactical theory, and their writings were thought to have inspired a better understanding by the British. For sound practice and aggressiveness, rare in Frenchmen of that time, the skillful tactics of Admiral Pierre André de Suffren are still admired two centuries after his actions in the Indian Ocean. Even so, the person who implements a new tactic is rarely the inventor. We honor the former because that person has the vision to pluck a kernel of wisdom from a barn floor of ideas and has the courage and skill to make it grow.

Nelson stands out in memory because the Battle of Trafalgar, fought on 21 October 1805, was the last big fleet action for more than a century. Yet, his fame does not rest on an accident of history. The reason that there were no more fleet actions was that Nelson did what no one else had been able to do: he eliminated the enemy fleet, ending the need for further fleet actions and setting the stage for a hundred years of British naval dominance. It is clear that Trafalgar was not a lucky stroke; Nelson, with his experience at the Nile and at Copenhagen, understood concentration and timing. We also know the instructions he issued to his captains before the battle. They are often quoted, but no one has analyzed them better than the Frenchman Ambroise Baudry.[4] Baudry directly addresses the time-and-motion elements and Nelson's contingency plans. He points out that French Rear Admiral Villeneuve knew in advance almost everything that Nelson would do, and yet did not know how to stop him. Villeneuve could not conceive a counterinitiative.

Nelson need get little credit for winning, even though he did so against the numerical odds; he had twenty-seven ships against Villeneuve's thirty-three. That he would seek to win as much of the battle as he could was a foregone conclusion. His real accomplishment was to destroy both the French and Spanish fleets, which had been the primary British strategic objective for the previous ten years. He succeeded as no other admiral had for a hundred years.

His problem was to close and grip the enemy, so his captains would destroy it if they got within that deadly three-hundred-yard range. He chose the right

---

4 Baudry, pp. 218–36.

tactics to defeat a particular enemy and thereby achieve his country's particular strategic objective. He had a plan, he communicated it, and as events proved it was demonstrably adaptable even as he executed it. His commanders were trained to carry out his plan—to unleash a high rate of close-range fire—and his plan fit their training. His captains knew what to do because he talked to them at every opportunity and because the plan in its essence could not be misconstrued. Last, his plan could be executed almost without signal from beginning to end. The order of sailing will be the order of battle, he said. This notion, now a pertinent watchword for a modern fleet, was a stunning innovation in 1805.

One can learn the wrong lesson from Trafalgar. Had Nelson used his Trafalgar tactics against, say, Dutch Admirals Maarten H. Tromp or Michiel de Ruyter or France's de Suffren, the result would have been disastrous. Every one of his ships in those light winds of October had to run a gauntlet of three or four unanswered broadsides, which would have guaranteed his defeat had his opponent been first-rate. His ships would have been half-crippled before they fired their first effective shot, and Nelson would have known this. To argue that Nelson won simply because he attacked boldly would be a shallow interpretation. A lesser commander who has not measured his enemy carefully will destroy his fleet by parroting Nelson's charge into the enemy's fire. No one knows how Nelson would have fought the Dutch in 1688 or the Germans in 1916, but almost certainly his tactics would have been right for the strategic objective, the weapons, and the forces assembled.

The Influence of Strategy

A brief comment on national policy and strategy is necessary in order to understand the tactics of the British, the Dutch, and especially the French. Tactics influence strategy and in turn are influenced by it as well. Tactical commanders must never forget their aim in battle, and that aim often will extend beyond the destruction of the enemy fleet.

In the three Anglo-Dutch wars, both countries' wartime objectives were centered on the oceans, and as a result, many battles were fought. The strategic issues could have been summed up in Monck's characteristically blunt reply when he was asked the cause of the second of these wars: "The Dutch have too much trade . . . and the English are resolved to take it from them."[5] There was no question of a land invasion; trade was the issue, and it was appropriately fought over at sea. For

---

5   Quoted in Lewis (1948), p. 89.

the Dutch, commerce via the English Channel was survival. With it they would prosper; without it they would wither into nothing. Neither side could decline battle and still achieve its purpose in the war. It either built up its navy and fought, or made peace and lost its objective. The wars had limited objectives, so the winner could indeed anticipate a net financial gain and the loser could anticipate financial and national ruin. As a result, the motivation to fight and fight to win was strong. Both sides knew that the decisive battle would settle the war until a new fleet was constructed, at which time there would be a new battle.

British advantage lay in winning a decisive battle and then exercising command of the sea. But the Royal Navy had learned its tactical lesson too well in opposing the aggressive Dutch. Similar tactics had failed when used against the reluctant French. It suited France's strategic objectives to decline to engage in a decisive battle. For the French, the ocean was a flank to be held while the decision was fought out on land. Whenever they believed their war aim would be determined on land, they adopted one of two naval strategies: they either would maintain a substantial fleet to divert the British navy (not always successfully) and look for opportunities to do so, or they would conduct a *guerre de course*, raiding commerce in hopes of achieving a moderate gain at little cost.

Whether France's naval strategy was wise is not an issue for this discussion. But concerning its tactics, there are several valuable observations:

- France's tactics were, on the whole, more successful in implementing French strategy than Britain's tactics were in implementing British strategy—at least before Nelson.
- When great benefits would have accrued to the French by aggressive, decisive battle, the possibility was virtually out of reach. Long-practiced tactical habits ran deep.
- When the Royal Navy learned how to close and fight a decisive battle, the French, who wished to avoid fighting, were devastated tactically and therefore were severely hampered strategically.

Summary

Because decisive weapon range was very short, tactics in the age of fighting sail were always dominated by ship-on-ship combat. Until almost the end of the era, improvements in the concentration of firepower came primarily from building up the weight of the broadside on each ship, or the rate of fire, or the accuracy of fire. The British built up the rate of their fire; the French, increased the accuracy of their fire.

The commanded line was invented in the 1650s to achieve coordination (rapid maneuvers in formation with minimal communications) and cooperation (movement at close quarters without shooting at one's own ships and without permitting shirkers). Very quickly the commanders saw that multiple columns also afforded tactical concentration of firepower: ships could be brought into action together and in mutual support, so that the opening firepower of the whole force could be massed.

The single-fleet line-ahead had the appeal of simplicity, but in the early eighteenth century British naval doctrine became frozen into dogma. With rare exception, the commander was required to maintain a single rigid line, inhibiting the possibility of tactical surprise or of achieving fleet concentration by doubling on part of the enemy. Worst of all, the Fighting Instructions limited the ability of a commander to close and defeat a reluctant enemy, even when enemy firepower was distinctly inferior or when strategic circumstances demanded that he take tactical risks to force the action. For the admirals of the Royal Navy, the last fifty years of the era of fighting sail were dominated by an effort to escape their doctrinal straitjacket and bring about a decisive engagement against an enemy who was inferior in close action.

When the fleet commanders finally freed themselves of the stricture of the single line ahead, they had still to rediscover a means of fleet concentration that prevented enemy escape. Nelson did so, and in one final stroke—Trafalgar—he eliminated the enemy at sea. His successful tactics involved

- Operating in mutual support by column and by ship-in-column until the battle was joined and the inevitable melee occurred.
- Devising a simple and unequivocal plan that still allowed flexibility of execution.
- Using minimal signals because, from experience, Nelson's captains knew his mind.
- Seizing the initiative of the windward position, but with due regard for the possibility that contact might be made when his fleet was to leeward.
- Acquiring a full understanding of motion and distance relationships at sea, resulting (remarkably) in the achievement of tactical surprise and concentration of force in full view of the enemy.

- Training the way he intended to fight and fighting the way he had trained.
- Recognizing high risk in cases where his foe was strong and competent, but knowing there would be little risk in the event, because his foe's gunnery and control of formation were known to be poor.

The tactical objective of the Royal Navy—usually to destroy the enemy fleet—fitted Britain's strategic objective. France's tactics also fitted its own strategic objectives and the relative inferiority of its forces, which did not have the size or training to win a decisive head-to-head battle. France, too, often enjoyed success. The predictable consequence, however, was long-term corrosion of its fleet's tactics, competence, and will to fight.

3

TACTICAL DEVELOPMENT IN PEACETIME

The Golden Age of Tactical Thought, 1865–1914

For the world's navies, the years from 1865 to 1914 marked a golden age of tactical thought, without parallel before or since. Bolstered by the industrial revolution, the period saw a surge of technological advances that rivaled even the present age for peacetime development. Dramatic improvements in armament, armor, and mobility demanded out-of-the-box thinking about the tactics that would be needed to use these innovations effectively.

The explosion of tactical thought also was sparked by another phenomenon—*Pax Britannica*, the peace that resulted from the domination of the seas by the Royal Navy. While tactical development during the age of fighting sail had been spawned by experimentation during fleet actions, the order imposed by *Pax Brittanica* left few such battles in which navies could test and improve their tactics. As a result, the tactical implications of the new steam propulsion, its effects on maneuverability, countervailing advances in armor and armaments, torpedoes and big ships versus smaller vessels, and, toward the end, the wireless and aircraft, all became the subjects of great debate.

By 1900 the weaker tactical concepts had generally been discarded and a compatible marriage of new tactics and new warships had emerged. In World War I there were few surprises either in naval tactics or in the performance of warships, and post-war assessments of tactics and leadership more often confirmed rather than challenged prewar analyses. It was the triumph of much hard thinking.

The tactical discourse of the period reveals the tremendous thought and energy devoted to the application of mathematics to tactics. The logic of engineering skill spilled over from the design of war machines and influenced tactics tremendously. One cannot read letters and papers of naval officers such as Ambroise Baudry, Bradley Fiske, Romeo Bernotti, William Bainbridge-Hoff, and Stepan O. Makarov, and naval journals around 1900 without being inspired by the tremendous outpouring of technical and tactical creativity.[1] True, there was some outlandish speculation during the early years of the technological revolution, but naval officers quickly tamped down the more extreme tactical concepts that could not be implemented. In the end, tactical analysis erred in only two significant respects: it too often overvalued the impact that greater speed would have on fleet actions, and it failed to foresee the limitations that poor visibility would continue to impose.

Precursors

The impact of the industrial revolution was quickly felt in the navies of Europe. With the exception of modern methods of fire control and the self-propelled torpedo, all of the elements for the transition from sail to steam warships were conceived between the Napoleonic Wars and the American Civil War. The list included steam propulsion and screw propellers; iron hulls and armor; bigger guns with greater muzzle velocity and more penetrating power; breech-loading guns; effective shells and their necessary companions, fusing and rifled gun barrels; and gun turrets. (Initially these guns had more range, with greater size to smash through armor, but the range was not much more effective.)

The spate of technological advances sparked a vigorous debate over how rapidly the inventions should be adopted, but one thing was clear: they would quickly make the wooden ship of the line and its single line of battle obsolete. The British, slow as they were to adopt iron hulls, never built another wooden-hulled ship after they launched the formidable nine-thousand-ton HMS *Warrior* in 1860; instead, the Royal Navy was replaced from scratch. Strategy, too, was overturned. The advent of reliable steam propulsion set off a worldwide race to provide for coaling stations—a move made necessary by the spread of colonialism; in turn,

---

1 Some of the notable Naval Institute *Proceedings* prize essays of this period are LCDR Richard Wainwright, "Tactical Problems in Naval Warfare" (January 1895); LT R. A. Niblack, "The Tactics of Ships in the Line of Battle" (January 1896); LT R. H. Jackson, "Torpedo Craft: Types and Employment" (January 1900); Professor R. Alger, "Gunnery in Our Navy" (January 1903); CDR Bradley Fiske, "American Naval Policy" (January 1905); and LT W. S. Pye Jr., "The Elements of Fleet Tactics" (January 1906). Clark Reynolds, whose characterization of the period as a golden age is more sweeping than ours, highlights strategy. He points out that the Russians were the first to publish a professional naval journal, the fine *Morskoi Sbornik*, dating from 1848, and that Italy's *Rivista Marittima* came to be the best of all the journals in the years before World War I.

the construction of more coaling stations made it easier for countries to support still more colonies. The push to fortify harbors, once considered an effective way to protect naval bases, no longer was necessary; the construction of repair facilities to service engines and guns reduced the necessity of maintaining large numbers of fleet sites. The shift from sail to steam would limit the range and endurance of battle fleets, profoundly affecting the way a naval power would conduct a blockade. Such strategic limitations delayed the transition from sail—a fact that did not go unnoticed by Europe's admiralties. The so-called modern British navy was still building ships with sails in the 1880s, ostensibly to provide it with strategic mobility.

At the same time, the opportunities opened by steam propulsion had tacticians fairly aglow with anticipation. Not only could a superior fleet now attack directly into the wind, but it could close an enemy in the lightest wind and run the gauntlet of opponents' fire at double or triple the former speed. While these advantages were not fully appreciated until after the Battle of Lissa in 1866, the tactical discussions of the 1840s already had centered on the end of the coterminous column and the potential effectiveness of ram-bows.[2] At this stage armor was ahead of armaments in the race for technological superiority, so the attractiveness of the ram was linked to tactical mobility, kinetic energy, and the ability to close an enemy whose effective range and rate of fire had not kept pace with ship speed.

One combat laboratory for testing the rudimentary technology was the Crimean War. Although logistics and strategic mobility, not tactics, drew preeminent consideration in that war, participants became convinced of the value of steam power for close-in work. Ironclads, not very seaworthy, nonetheless demonstrated their ability to stand up to forts and land batteries—a capability that hastened their development over the next several years and in the U.S. Civil War. In 1853 the Battle of Sinope was seen as the proving ground for the explosive shell. Six large Russian ships descended out of the haze on 7 hapless Turkish frigates and smashed them all, killing or wounding nearly 3,000 Turks with the loss of only 266 Russians.[3] Three of the Russian ships of the line carried new "shell guns" into the battle, and the navies of Europe marveled at how effective they were. The battle may have been just as influential in fostering improvements in armor and the iron-hulled ship as it was in hastening the development of shells, which suddenly became perceived as the nemesis of wooden warships.

---

2 See Robison and Robison, pp. 579–90.
3 Woodward (1965), p. 99.

Still, it is fair to speculate how much the use of shell guns at the Battle of Sinope merely promoted a conclusion that was preordained without them. A simple Lanchester-like model shows an outcome almost as overwhelming. If an analyst credits each of the six Russian ships of the line with an average broadside of fifty-five guns and both of the frigates with fifteen, and then pits them against the seven Turkish frigates, which had fifteen broadsides each, then by the time the Turkish broadsides were reduced to zero, the eight Russian ships would have lost only two guns each.[4] Such was the power of Russian numbers, independent of the supposed quality of their materiel. In addition, the Russians probably achieved some advantage from surprise.

After the Civil War, 1865–85

The U.S. Civil War was almost devoid of fleet-on-fleet battles. Almost all fleet actions were what we call today littoral operations—inshore work—undertaken to control seaports, harbors, and rivers. The military targets that they sought to neutralize were forts. "Fleet" actions occurred when the Confederates supplemented batteries ashore with ironclads—ships that in effect were mobile forts, heavily armored and armed. These inshore Confederate warships were effective everywhere, but not for very long, because the Union could always concentrate overwhelming numbers against them. The Confederates had no hope of assembling a fleet to challenge the Union at sea; their aim could never be any more ambitious than to conduct a *guerre de course* against Union shipping, to break the Union blockade locally, and to hope for the intervention of the Royal Navy.

Consequently, the Battle of Lissa in 1866 served as the sole reference point for the study of fleet action. The following tactical lessons can be drawn from that battle:

- Steam propulsion gave the offensive fleet new options.
- The ram was an effective weapon of naval combat.
- The single column would fail as a method of concentrating firepower.

It is noteworthy how quickly naval tacticians embraced the study of hypothetical fleet actions. The ascendancy of armor plate over gunshot and early shells was so fleeting that some analysts are prone to make light of the ram. But writings

---

4 The three ships carrying the sixty-eight-pound shell guns each were 120-gun three-deckers. For simplicity we ignore the fact that one Turkish frigate escaped.

of the 1870s and 1880s extolled the ram. For some twenty-five years the mobility of steamships enabled them to "charge"—a common description at the time— through a gauntlet of effective fire that was short, only a half mile deep at most. A fleet of rams could run eight hundred yards in three minutes or less and (it was thought) devastate a column that was armed with guns. And it could steam right into the wind. The more a defensive column closed up to concentrate its fire, the more vulnerable it was to ramming. The bigger the fleet was in single column, the longer the column and the easier it was for a ramming fleet to concentrate on a single segment. Figure 3-1, a schematic of the Battle of Lissa, illustrates this.

After 1866 the tactical debate threw the traditional column overboard, and chaos reigned amid wide-ranging speculation about the best tactical course to take. Some advocated breaking the long column into small components. Others argued for short mutually supporting columns; still others for short lines abreast; and yet others for units of two to five mutually supporting warships that could turn together as the unit commander dictated. (The last of these looked very much like what would become a World War II circular formation—or, on land, the British infantry square.) The logical consequence of each scheme was a melee, and tacticians despaired of finding any solution that would give the fleet com-mander in a well-drilled navy anything but the briefest advantage during his approach. Many plans of action were based on strong analogies with land com-bat. Some were so amateurish that they envisioned the attacker maneuvering against a defending fleet that would be fixed in a stationary line, much as defend-ing troops were in the ground battles of the era.

Happily for the tacticians, as well as for the fleet commanders who would have employed those tactics, technology came to the rescue before any such a fleet battle was fought. No doubt the results of such exercises would have been chaotic. The new proposals, inadequate at best, were designed to concentrate all forces without a reserve, took advantage of the newly available power of maneuver that steam propulsion would provide, and sought to exploit the effectiveness of the fleetingly ascendant ram. Their signals and concepts were designed to provide a commander with an initial advantage. They assumed that the battle itself would be shrouded in gun smoke, and won by a combination of chance and the courage of individual captains.

Between 1877 and 1879, just before the end of the ram's perceived domi-nance, there were some engagements on the west coast of South America that indicate what might have happened had major fleets engaged in battle. In four

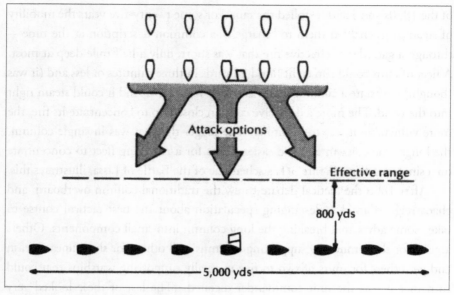

Figure 3-1. Employment of the Ram

drawn-out fights between one or two ironclads and other warships, there were several attempts to ram the opposition force, and nearly all of them were unsuccessful. The performance showed that it had been underestimated how difficult it would be to hit a moving target, especially in engagements where ships were freer to move than they would have been in larger fleet actions.

The *Huascar*, controlled by Peruvian revolutionaries, was a central participant in all four battles, fighting first against Britain and later against the Chilean navy. She took an enormous number of hits at close range—sixty in her first battle—few of which penetrated; she participated in bombarding a fort; and she survived the war intact. The tacticians were right about one thing, however: the effectiveness of the naval gun had been eclipsed, and for a brief period defensive technology was dominant.

The Battle of the Yalu River (between Chinese and Japanese forces) in September 1894 should have confirmed the end of ram tactics. According to a contemporary account, the Chinese fought in line abreast with every intention of using their two battleships—which were the heart of their fighting power—to ram their Japanese opponents.[5] As it turned out, however, they were unable to carry out their plan; ramming played no part. The Japanese stayed in two columns

5 Marble, pp. 479–99.

and literally steamed circles around the Chinese. The firing range was very short. Most of the damage appears to have been done by medium-caliber guns at ranges of about two thousand yards. An enormous number of rounds were fired, and the cumulative effect of the gunfire was devastating. The two Chinese battleships showed evidence of together having taken 320 shell hits. Both, however, survived with their armor unpierced. Never did more heterogeneous forces fight with such different tactics, and never was a battlefield more difficult to analyze. Although the ram remained unused, its utility was not laid to rest, and only in retrospect is it clear that the great tactical debate had begun to take form.

Triumph of the Big Gun, 1900–1916

It is widely thought now that gunnery usurped the ram, or that the ram was never an effective weapon at all. A better conclusion is that the torpedo superseded the ram. The Whitehead torpedo was a ram with reach: if it hit, it was almost as lethal and was a lot safer to use. As a result, the study of gunnery became as obsessed with countering torpedo boats as it had been with regard to penetrating armor. Thus, as the nineteenth century drew to a close, guns of many calibers, torpedoes, and rams were the weapons of interest, with the ram rapidly fading into oblivion.

The reemergence of naval guns as the central weapon at the beginning of the twentieth century and the confirmation of the armored battleship as the backbone of the fleet make for a complex, fascinating, and often told story. Naval tacticians influenced the direction of these developments. The Spanish-American War proved that even when gun shells had the potential to penetrate iron and steel plates, in at least two navies the gun could seldom hit a target in motion. Naval officers led by the brilliant British Admiral Sir Percy Scott and ADM William S. Sims, USN, who played key roles in the push for gunnery accuracy, put their minds to improving fire control.[6] It was high time, because the thirty-knot torpedo boat and torpedo boat destroyer threatened to dash through the short gauntlet of secondary battery gunfire and wreak havoc on the battleships. In tacticians' thinking, a balanced fleet comprised more and more torpedo craft. In theory, destroyers could be forestalled with rapid-fire short-range weapons. To do so, however, required accurate gunfire, and commanders at sea shuddered at the thought of having their battleships caught unprotected by their destroyer and light cruiser screen.

---

6   In one gunnery test observed by Assistant Secretary of the Navy Theodore Roosevelt, battleships fired two hundred shots at a condemned lightship at a range of 2,800 yards and obtained two hits (Mitchell, p. 148).

Here is how one tactician evaluated weapon effectiveness as a function of range in 1910:

Extreme range	10,000–8,000 meters	Heavy-caliber guns within range
Long range	8,000–5,000 meters	Heavy- and medium-caliber guns effective, the latter against personnel and unarmored parts
Medium range	5,000–3,000 meters	Medium guns worth a "special value"—having the same as big guns plus higher rates of fire.
Close range	3,000–2,000 meters	Torpedoes a hazard, depending upon relative ship positions
Close quarters	Inside 2,000 meters	Collisions possible (but no attention to ramming)[7]

The advocates of more and bigger guns in all-big-gun ships (the *Dreadnought* concept) could not yet make their case. Medium- and small-caliber guns had the same accuracy and higher rates of fire. Admiral Fiske presented three rules of thumb:

- A 6-inch gun fired eight times as fast as a 12-inch gun.
- A 12-inch projectile carried eight times the energy of a 6-inch-gun projectile.
- A 12-inch-gun system weighed eight times as much as a 6-inch gun.[8]

Therefore, on equal ship displacements, 6-inch guns delivered eight times the projectile energy of 12-inch guns. Muzzle energy, the product of projectile weight and muzzle velocity, was the quantitative measure of a gun. Extensive computations of armor penetrability were made as a function of range, target angle, and plunging angle of shell. Tacticians also sought a high rate of fire. A significant break point occurred at the 6-inch gun, because its 100-pound projectile was the heaviest that sailors could handle. In 1910 a 6-inch gun had a nominal firing rate of twelve rounds per minute, which seems very fast indeed. If accuracy of the big long-range guns could not be improved, their greater ability to penetrate armor would not count for much. Small- and medium-caliber gunfire could inundate an enemy at short range, as the Japanese amply demonstrated at Tsushima in the Russo-Japanese War (1905), where their gunnery ranges were maintained at four thousand

---

7   From Bernotti, p. 50.
8   Fiske (1905), p. 25. Despite these data, Fiske became an advocate of the all-big-gun battleship with better fire control.

to six thousand yards. To dominate the battle, big (10- or 12-inch) guns needed accurate fire control at ranges beyond the reach of medium (4- or 6-inch) guns.

Still, the final outcome was predictable. One of the great trends in warfare has been the increasing range of effective weapon delivery, and during this period the change transpired with stunning speed. Around 1910, when continuous-aim fire and director control replaced local gunlaying, the all-big-gun ship was certain to dominate. The USS *Michigan* (BB 27) already had been built, so close on the heels of HMS *Dreadnought* that American xenophobes were able to claim prior sponsorship of all-big-gun battleships, including a superior arrangement of turret.[9] All arguments pointed toward bigger and bigger battleships. Between 1906, when the construction of the *Michigan* was begun, and 1913, when the keel of the USS *Pennsylvania* (BB 38) was laid, displacements doubled. The debate still had not settled on turret arrangements and the proper allocation of displacement between armor, speed, and endurance. Some extreme solutions were evident in the battle cruisers HMS *Invincible* and *Repulse*, which had great firepower, high speed, and very little protection.

By World War I, a mere ten years after Tsushima, big guns of the 12- to 15-inch class were *the* weapon, hitting repeatedly on a clear day after a few ranging salvoes out to eight miles and more. Behind the scenes and scarcely noticed, crucial developments were under way to improve the fire-control computers that gave guns their accuracy on these longer ranges. Secondary batteries of five- and six-inch guns were installed to ward off torpedo attacks, but admirals wanted to avoid having to use them for that purpose because even though the weapon debate was settled, the torpedo was still a threat to be reckoned with. As Admiral Makarov, the great Russian tactician, wrote, with droll insight:

Up to the present this [command of the sea] has been understood to mean that the fleet commanding the sea openly plies upon it and the beaten antagonist does not dare to leave his ports. Would this be so today? Instructions bearing on the subject counsel the victor to avoid night attack from the torpedo-boats of his antagonist. . . . Some seamen have

---

9   Mitchell, p. 139, says dispensing with intermediate-caliber guns had been urged by progressive naval officers since 1901. Sims was the officer most effective in selling the all-big-gun battleship while destroying the contrary arguments of Mahan, who had lost touch with the fleet. For Sims' arguments, see "The Inherent Qualities of All-Big-Gun, One-Caliber Battleships of High Speed, Large Displacement, and Gun Power." For a more popular perspective on guns and gunnery, there is also E. E. Morison, *Admiral Sims*.

become reconciled to this abnormality, yet if the matter were represented to a stranger he would be astonished. He would probably ask whether he properly understood that a victorious fleet should protect itself from the remnant of a vanquished enemy.[10]

Makarov the tactician was explicitly challenging the authority of Mahan and Corbett, the strategists. The gun was in thought and fact the principal naval weapon in a fleet action, but the more perceptive tacticians were aware that the strategists' overly neat concept of command of the sea was too big a bite to be swallowed whole.

Reemergence of the Fighting Column

At this point, with the exception of how to meet the threat from torpedoes, all of the pieces of a tactical concept for fleet actions were in place and agreed upon. The ram was out of the picture. The battleship with the big gun was the decisive weapon. The bigger, more stable, better armed and more heavily armored the battleship, the better. Battleships did not defend themselves against torpedoes; light cruisers and destroyers were built for that purpose, and they would be responsible for fending off enemy destroyers and torpedo boats. Scouting cruisers were the eyes of the fleet and would remain so until airplanes or dirigibles were sufficiently advanced to do the job. Battle cruisers, a vestige of the late nineteenth-century influence of land combat on naval thinking, would be a heavy cavalry in support of the scouting cruisers and able in theory to outrange or outrun any opposition. Mines were a wicked and ungentlemanly threat in shallow water, but they were largely defensive and had to be planted by surface ships. Submarines, like mines that had a deep-water offensive potential, were worse—an instrument of the devil. The wireless radio was a new tool of command, above all useful tactically to speed the results of scouting.

The tactical formation was the column, now restored to respectability for reasons shown in figure 3-2. Using 15,000 yards as the range of effective fire in good visibility, a column of, say, sixteen battleships could engage anything with every centerline gun bearing over the full length of its nine-thousand-yard-long column. More than half the guns would bear at least within thirty degrees of the beam of the first or last ship in column. For comparison, figure 3-2 depicts (on the same scale) the narrow ribbon of death for a column of thirty-one eighteenth-century ships of the line.

---

10 Makarov, p. 20.

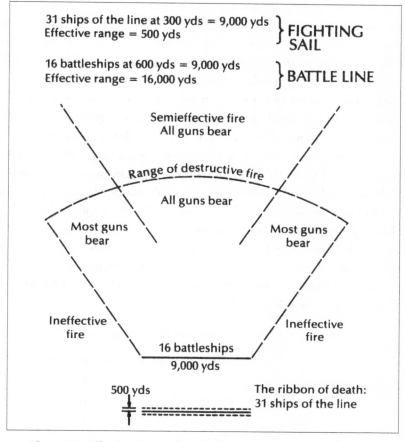

31 ships of the line at 300 yds = 9,000 yds } FIGHTING
Effective range = 500 yds   SAIL

16 battleships at 600 yds = 9,000 yds   } BATTLE LINE
Effective range = 16,000 yds

Semieffective fire
All guns bear

Range of destructive fire

All guns bear

Most guns   Most guns
bear   bear

Ineffective   Ineffective
fire   fire

16 battleships
9,000 yds

500 yds   The ribbon of death:
                   31 ships of the line

Figure 3-2. Effective Range of Gunfire Compared, 1750 and 1910

Basic (but by no means ultimate) force-on-force correlations of the day began with opposing columns abreast. At least three tactical writers, J. V. Chase, Bradley Fiske, and Ambroise Baudry, described the cumulative effects of a superior concentration of firepower in the following way.[11] Assume that opposing warships each have a staying power of twenty minutes under the enemy's unopposed effective

---

11 Anticipating Frederick W. Lanchester and his celebrated equations, the three naval writers explained their analyses using discrete time periods, which may be thought of as the time to exchange salvos. The engineer Lanchester used coupled differential equations, which were a cleaner and quicker way to make essentially the same points. Today the modern digital computer operates on discrete time differentials, the periods of which may be as small as desired. The authors wanted to illustrate that firepower effectiveness was not in simple direct proportion to weapon effectiveness (as, for instance, accuracy or rate of fire) but in proportion to the square of the number of weapons engaged. Robison and Robison refer to the latter as the N-square law, as an effect well understood in the fleet.

fire. Let the remaining offensive capacity—that is, surviving guns and fire-control systems—be proportionate to the remaining staying power. (In modern parlance we are speaking in terms of firepower kills.) If all other things are equal, the battle will be a draw. It will also last a very long time because both sides' offensive capacities are reduced simultaneously.

But let side *A* fire for four minutes in advance of side *B*, as Baudry does, and then table 3-1, which shows remaining firepower and staying power for both sides, suggests that what had been an even battle now leads to the destruction of the side that was four minutes slow to open fire; being late, it lost a seemingly modest 20 percent of its fighting power.[12] Side *A* takes twenty-six minutes to reduce the tardy side to impotence. That is only six minutes longer than it would take if *B* had not returned fire at all. Also observe that the winner retains 57 percent of his fighting power at the end of the battle.

Fiske built similarly simple tables to show the cumulative effect of preponderance of force. Let *A* now have two warships to concentrate on one of *B*. Under the same conditions of firepower and staying power as before, the table of surviving fighting power looks like table 3-2.

Table 3-1. Remaining Firepower and Staying Power

	Units of Residual Firepower and Staying Power	
End of Minute	Side A	Side B
0	10.00	10.00
2	10.00	9.00
4	10.00	8.00
6	9.20	7.00
8	8.50	6.08
10	7.89	5.23
12	7.37	4.44
14	6.93	3.70
16	6.56	3.01
18	6.26	2.35
20	6.00	1.72
22	5.83	1.12
24	5.72	0.54
26	5.67	0.00

---

12 Baudry, pp. 1161–17.

Table 3-2. Surviving Firepower

End of Minute	Superior Force A			Force B	Ratio of Fighting Values*
	Ship A_1	Ship A_2	$A_1 + A_2$	Ship B	
0.00	10.00	10.00	20.00	10.00	4.0
2.00	9.50	9.50	19.00	8.00	5.6
4.00	9.10	9.10	18.20	6.10	8.9
6.00	8.79	8.79	17.58	4.28	16.9
8.00	8.58	8.58	17.16	2.52	46.0
10.00	8.45	8.45	16.90	0.80	446.0
11.0	8.25	8.25	16.50	0.00	—

* Fighting values are defined as the square of the fighting power, and they indicate just that: the force's relative fighting value when concentrated.

Having been introduced to the Lanchester form of these calculations in chapter 1, the reader should not be surprised that after the inferior force is reduced to impotence, the superior force still retains 16.5 units (83 percent) of its strength. If a "continuous-fire" Lanchester form is used, the surviving fighting power of the stronger force is slightly greater, 17.3 instead of 16.5. The difference is that, in the salvo model above, the weaker force's attrition does not begin until after it has fired without damage for two minutes.

All four of these theorists were successful, practical men. Chase, Fiske, and Baudry were naval officers, and Lanchester was a prominent automotive engineer. They were working out different combinations of effects for a situation in which the conditions held. Fiske described quantitatively such factors as the effect of more armor (a 10 percent increase in firepower is worth more than a 10 percent increase in staying power), better fire control, and a smaller effective target area (to compensate for a firepower inferiority of 50 percent, the effective number of hits taken must be reduced by 75 percent), and whether concentrating first on the greater or lesser force affects the theoretical battle outcome (it does not).

Fiske regarded such tactical parameters as the proper basis for determining ship design. In 1905, the year the all-big-gun USS *Michigan* was authorized, he calculated his way to the conclusion that such a ship was unequivocally the battleship of the future. While Mahan was saying there were few principles of tactics because technology would always be changing them, Fiske was using abstract tactical models to guide the adaptation of technology and improve tactics.

Crossing the T

The similarity in the form of equations used in the age of fighting sail and the age of the big gun can conceal the major change in the way concentration of force was achieved. Although the column was the accepted tactical formation during both periods, in sailing ships firepower had to be concentrated in the ship because gun range was so short, while in battleships firepower of an entire column—the firepower of every ship—could be concentrated. When the big gun dominated, it was weapon range that made "crossing the T" so advantageous; instead of a single ship of the line in raking position, the whole fleet could concentrate fire on the enemy van.

The column was finally acknowledged (unequivocally after Tsushima) as the best offensive formation for simplicity of control and effective concentration of gunfire. As everyone knew, the column was vulnerable ahead or astern, and, because of its motion, especially ahead. Tactical discussions centered on how to cross the T. In tabletop tactical studies, the only means of achieving this concentration by maneuver was speed, and speed along with armor and armament was in every tactical and technological discussion.[13] As events transpired, the tabletop would prove to be misleading.

The decision in favor of the column simplified tactical thinking, and until World War II, which ended the relevance of the battle line, tactical discussions centered on these elements:

- How to distribute gunfire: doing both what was best in theory (e.g., leaving no ship free from fire) and tackling the knottier problem of how to achieve the distribution. The fleet commander would be unable to *order* the solution in battle; the method had to be a part of doctrine or communicated with the simplest of signals. In practice, undistributed fire was to be a major tactical defect until the end of the surface gunnery era.
- How to cross the T against a maneuvering enemy, and whether partial success had much value.
- How to achieve or forestall torpedo attacks by a swarm of destroyers.
- Where in the line to place the flagships.
- How to shift from cruising formation to battle formation.
- The new importance of scouting and measures to safeguard the scouting line.

---

13 The U.S. Navy, after a lengthy and lively debate much influenced by Mahan, opted for heavy armor and armament at the expense of speed.

Cruising Formation and Tactical Scouting

Greatly increasing weapon range and effectiveness was also having a profound influence on the need for reconnaissance. The commander of a large fleet in World War I had to have information about the enemy's force well before he could see it. Nelson's plan for Trafalgar, according to which the order of sailing was the order of battle, no longer was feasible. For cohesion, communication, station-keeping under cruising conditions, antisubmarine screenings, and rapid deployment in any direction, the cruising formation had to be a series of short columns, each abreast of the others. Shifting to a single column for battle was a major and irrevocable commitment. The distance between columns had to be such that each column fitted exactly into the battle line, as depicted in figure 3-3. Battleship divisions were organized with the final sequence of ships in mind. It was important to maintain a close interval before and after the maneuver. All possible speed was also important, relatively more so than in the age of sail, when "fighting sail" meant minimum sail for steerageway. Still, the new battle fleet speed could be no more than two or three knots less than the slowest ships in the column, about a 20 percent margin, to allow the rearward ships a chance to keep station. It was observed that both seamanship and drills were imperative if the line were to be closed up and ships were to avoid colliding and masking one another's batteries. Although the column was the simplest formation, the challenges of forming it quickly, keeping it closed up, and orienting it properly with respect to the enemy, the wind (gun smoke was blinding), and the seas (rolling ships could not lay guns well) required skills derived from a lifetime at sea.

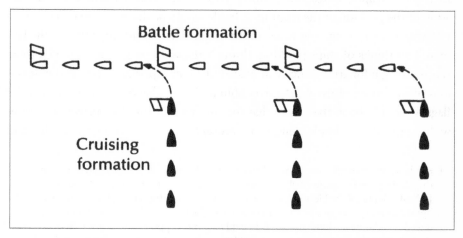

Figure 3-3. Deployment of the Battle Line from Cruising Formation to Battle Formation

What looked simple on paper required consummate skill on the ocean. Captains and flag officers received approbation or opprobrium based on their proficiency in close-order drills. One of the most famous of all maritime disasters— and a wonder of its day—was the collision in 1893 between HMS *Victoria* and HMS *Camperdown,* flagships of the Royal Navy's Mediterranean squadron. It occurred because the officer in tactical command, famous for tactical infallibility, ordered an impossible maneuver that went unchallenged.

The scouting plan received much emphasis, and considerable fleet resources were devoted to it. At Jutland both the British Grand Fleet and the German High Seas Fleet committed 20 to 25 percent of their heavy firepower and 35 to 45 percent of their supporting cruisers and destroyers to scouting forces. The disposition is shown in figure 3-4. To give ships in the scouting line a measure of safety, they were permitted to fall back on the fast battle cruiser support group when the enemy was sighted and threatening. The entire scouting force would attempt to join the main body and augment it as the battle line went into action. But no one was sure that this could actually be done. The scouting line, which covered about 35 degrees on either bow of the battle fleet, was sufficient to sweep out a wide swath of ocean and protect against an undetected approach. No enemy could make an end run past the scouting line as long as the fleet was steaming ahead smartly. Reorienting the axis of advance of such a disposition was a tense and prolonged experience for every flag officer and ship captain.[14]

Command-and-Control

Increasing weapon range and gunnery effectiveness also demanded reconsideration of the position of the flagship. A battle would be decided very quickly once effective gunnery range was reached. Although it may seem surprising to the layman who thinks of ships plodding through the water at seventeen knots, there was no margin for error or delay in maneuver. After experimentation and observation of the battles of the Yalu and Tsushima, the sensible conclusion was that the flagship should be in the van so that the commander could maneuver a column without signals—a simple "follow me" procedure. In contrast, turns together had

---

14 Airplanes and dirigibles already were being equipped with wireless radios and were seen as the scouts of the future. Justifiably, however, aircraft were not yet considered reliable. At Jutland Admiral of the Fleet David Beatty launched a scout from the seaplane carrier *Engadine* immediately after the first scout cruiser's contact. The flimsy seaplane flew off in the wrong direction, eventually found some of Admiral Franz von Hipper's ships as it was flying beneath the low overcast, and reported what it could see to the *Engadine.* But nothing useful to Beatty or Jellicoe came of this first tactical experiment with aerial navy reconnaissance.

to be executed precisely and therefore required the flagship to signal orders, which would take up valuable time. Simplicity and speed were everything. In the battle cruiser chase and counter-chase that preceded the Battle of Jutland it took only a couple of minutes' delay in the receipt of a signal from David Beatty to Admiral Hugh Evan-Thomas for the latter to fall hopelessly behind while the former was losing two battle cruisers.

Still, Admiral John Jellicoe and Admiral Reinhard Scheer at Jutland had battle lines of twenty-eight and twenty-two battleships, respectively, which were simply too long to lead from the van. A fleet commander in the leading ship could not hope to know what was happening at the rear of his column six or eight miles away. He was better placed in the center. That position, although it was held at the expense of maneuverability, was the best for maintaining cohesiveness and control and visualizing the scene of action. Jellicoe knew that if his forces were concentrated his numerical advantage in firepower should compensate for any temporary loss of positional advantage. Scheer's concept of fleet management was similar. He had expected to entrap a weaker British element at Jutland. He had no desire to fight the entire Grand Fleet.

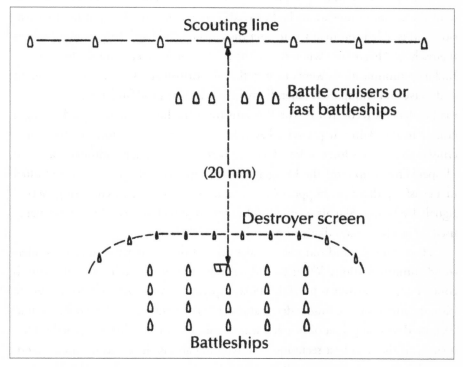

Figure 3-4. Cruising Disposition, Showing the Scouting Line and Support Force

The dilemma of the commander of a large fleet is illustrated by Scheer's tactical position at Jutland: if he had been at the head of his column he might have foreseen and avoided the extreme misadventure of twice having his T crossed. On the other hand, if he had been in the van he might not have succeeded in executing the famous simultaneous turns that allowed him to disappear into the haze two times and extricate his fleet from disaster.

Much progress had been made in formulating commands. Signals were not keyed to the fighting instructions, the combat doctrine itself, as they had been during the days of sail. Instead, they were commanders' way of communicating what was in their minds. Through continuing practice, the signal book was to become a compact, unambiguous vehicle by which desired actions could be transmitted precisely. That this was so is inferred from the absence of discussion about the *system* of signals. By the end of World War II the signal book used by the U.S. Navy was a tactical instrument of collective genius, as reliable and thoroughly tested as the laws of physics. It was a treasure of efficiency, conciseness, and clarity—one that needs to be rediscovered by naval commanders at all levels today.

The signal book was only one component of the tactical communications system. Radio communications had arrived. The wireless made scouting lines feasible and enabled commanders to alter the cruising and battle dispositions of fleets themselves. Already the wireless was the subject of intercept and traffic analysis. Radio communications were one way that the British and German navies sought to deceive and entrap each other. Early in World War I the British received a German codebook recovered by the Russians from the hulk of a grounded German cruiser in the Baltic. It played a key role in leading Beatty's force of five battle cruisers to a weaker force of four German battle cruisers under Admiral Franz von Hipper. That action, off the Dogger Bank in January 1915, might have resulted in a crushing defeat of Hipper's force had it not been for two confusing tactical signals by Beatty. Signals warfare and cryptology had arrived. Both were being used tactically in ways that had never been seen before.

History books and old sailors' tales are full of lost, delayed, and misunderstood communications. What should we think of this? As far as tactical theory is concerned, the answer is fourfold. First, experience is the best way for a crew to learn the intent of its commander; teamwork is the result of a lot of work as a unit. Second, developing a set of simple, clear signals, used navy-wide and practiced frequently, is the next best technique for avoiding ambiguities and misunderstandings. Third, some messages will be lost, delayed, and misunderstood anyway; no human system can eliminate communication errors—they are to be expected and as far as possible hedged against in tactical doctrine. Finally, the more commanders plan in advance, doctrinally and operationally, and the simpler the plan, the fewer the communication gaffes will be and the more smoothly the action will flow. As twenty-first-century capabilities expand—in communications bandwidth and computing power, for example—and as concepts for expanded C^2 such as network-centric warfare grow more ambitious, tacticians should remember to apply these abiding lessons of the past.

That said, it is remarkable how few tactical communication errors occurred in World War I. A useful study would be to compare the total volume of tactical signals transmitted with the number of vital signals—those of grave consequence—and of signals that were lost, delayed, or misunderstood. In World War I the total as a percentage of the whole was probably microscopic, serious though the recorded consequences of communication failures such as Beatty's were.

The Destroyer Screen and Torpedo Threat

The planned stations for destroyers and flotilla leaders were generally ahead of the van and abaft the rear on the engaged side.[15] The purpose of these ships was to influence the main action: to force the enemy to turn or, if he did not, to cripple him with torpedoes. In battle, destroyers were treated as mad dogs on the leash of the destroyer flotilla commander. The fleet commander's practical control of them was limited to commands like "go" and "come." Their role was to rush in a tight pack and seize a battleship's throat if they could or, as was more likely, to leap and claw and growl at the enemy's own mad dogs, which had also charged into the fray at a single word from their master. If a destroyer were impaled on a battleship's bow and sunk, it was a scarcely mourned impediment to the battleship's effectiveness. If one were caught in the crossfire between battle lines, it may as well have been invisible. But a squadron of destroyers, bows-on with a bone in their teeth, was a very visible and chilling threat indeed. A destroyer squadron commander fought for a semblance of order, living in the chaos of neglect by friends and spreading chaos among enemies as he was able.

---

15 For his book about the Solomons fighting, *Night Work*, Fletcher Pratt drew little diagrams of Japanese and American cruiser destroyer formations with the destroyers forming such bow screens. He was a great student of tactics before World War II, and he and his friends played his naval war game on his New York apartment floor. But, sad to relate, his sketches rarely resemble the facts. Although his book paints vivid word pictures of what command in the dark of night was like in 1942 and 1943, it is useless on the subject of tactics.

The peacetime tactician's picture of the destroyers is represented in figure 3-5, and the wartime tactician's picture is in figure 3-6. Even the latter is really more like a spectator's view from the grandstand than a player's view, which is besmeared with smoke, confusion, noise, and fear.

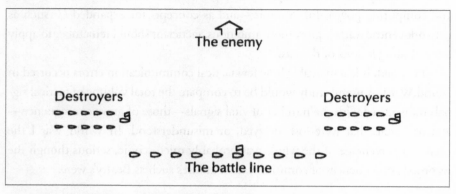

Figure 3-5. Peacetime Plans: A Battle Formation

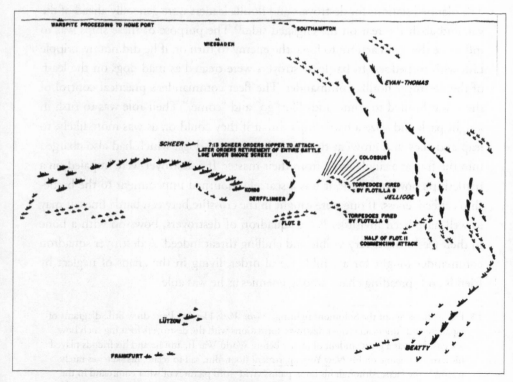

Figure 3-6. Wartime Reality: The Battle of Jutland, Crisis at 1915

Turn-of-the-Century Theory and Practice

If all this disorder was inevitable, what good were precise mathematical calculations about weapon effectiveness? The answer hinged on what the fleet commander needed to know—some rough relationships between range and hitting effectiveness (e.g., when a torpedo-launching vehicle was a threat to the force) and *how the range was figured.* Some of the finest analytical thinking of the time on this subject seems to have been done at the Italian naval academy, judging from the writing of Romeo Bernotti and Guiseppe Fioravanzo. Bernotti's calculations of torpedo effectiveness in battle are a good single example of how astutely tactical quantitative theory and practical considerations were blended from 1890 to 1915. Bernotti treated in detail a thirty-one-knot torpedo with a running range of 6,500 meters and a maximum speed of fifty knots.[16] To dispense with the simple-minded notion that raw running range was a significant tactical parameter, Bernotti ran through twelve pages of precise, concise, analytical, geometric, and probabilistic calculations of torpedo effectiveness, footnoting as he was able with Russian experimental results. Having calculated the effective range of a single torpedo against a non-maneuvering two-hundred-meter target from different directions, he showed the mathematical advantage of firing from off the target's bow. Next he calculated the threat of a spread of five aimed torpedoes against a single target and of an unaimed spread against a battle line. He concluded that from the defense's point of view, outside of 3,500 meters—that is, half the running range—"there is no occasion to trouble oneself very much about it" even though there was a perceptible risk; and from the offense's perspective, it was "well not to sacrifice, even to a minimum degree, the [effective] employment of the gun" (p. 25). On torpedo-boat tactics, Bernotti argued for attacks by successive squadrons of three and demonstrated both the power of simultaneous torpedo launch and how to achieve it. He conceded that a coordinated attack is difficult in battle, but he showed that single-ship attacks in sequence brought with them scant probability of individual success. Bernotti's derivation of what seems today like point-blank range stemmed from a tactical philosophy that returns to haunt every commander planning a modern missile attack: "A weapon, the action of which cannot be repeated except at considerable intervals of time, and of which the supply is very limited, must be employed only under conditions that assure notable probability of hitting" (p. 14). Today's missile battle will center on keeping

---

16 Bernotti, pp. 13–25 and 161–71. Lieutenant (later Admiral) Bernotti was then an instructor at the Royal Italian Naval Academy.

the enemy uncertain of his target and its position. Once launched, missiles cannot be recalled, and empty magazines can quickly become a terrible reality.

Will effective missile-firing ranges be shorter than their maximum ranges? Finding out is essential, judging from the Israeli and Egyptian experience in the 1973 war. The missiles of the Egyptian warships outranged those of the Israeli warships. But the Israelis induced the Egyptians to fire all their missiles ineffectually—and then closed in for a devastating finale.

Jutland

Like the combat data of all complicated battles, that for Jutland is difficult to assess. Ranges, gunnery accuracies, relative motion and position, speed of communication transmission and reception, and timeliness of execution—the meat and potatoes of tacticians—all are hard to trace among 250 warships. Those data, when they come from smaller actions, are more easily sifted and compared with the data from controlled tests and experiments.

Even so, there has been no shortage of second-guessing Jellicoe, the British tactical commander. A river of ink has been undammed in analyses of the battle he fought at Jutland. It was not only the last big battle of a war, but under slightly altered circumstances it also might have been, like Trafalgar, the decisive battle envisioned by Mahan and Sir Julian Corbett. As a result, it was the centerpiece of analysis in all navies until World War II. Jellicoe was unable to destroy the German High Seas Fleet, and the postmortems had to decide the reason. He failed where Nelson had triumphed. The controversy boiled down to why Jellicoe, with a superior fleet that had taken Scheer by surprise, had not been more aggressive. His famous turn away from the desperate German destroyer attack, his tenacious faith in the single column, and his other conservative measures may all be explained on purely tactical grounds—the self-imposed demand for control. But the heart of the matter was that battle tactics on both sides were governed by the two national maritime strategies.

It does not do simply to dismiss Jellicoe as lacking the Nelsonian will to win. The analyses that reach this conclusion also compare the quality and gunnery of his fleet unfavorably with that of the German fleet; some authors went so far as to say that Scheer had a chance to win.[17] Yet, one cannot have it both ways. Either Jellicoe retained sole power to destroy, provided he exercised no imprudence, or else his caution was justified because he in fact might have lost, in which case the

---

17 For example, see Fioravanzo, p. 154, or Hough (1983), p. 122.

consequences were incalculable. There is no question that Jellicoe had the forces to win. Scheer fled the field. But at what odds? That is the key question.

If we accept for examination the common presumption that strategically it was more important for Jellicoe not to lose a decisive battle than to win one, then it is reasonable to say that he faced a situation where he could fulfill that goal only if he maintained offensive concentration through fleet cohesion. His three-to-two numerical advantage in dreadnoughts guaranteed that. Better German gunnery and ship staying power could not redress the numerical advantage of the Grand Fleet. However, with quality taken into account, the force-on-force comparison might have been as narrow as four to three or even five to four. That would have been close enough to permit the High Seas Fleet to win with a brief ten-minute advantage in concentrated fire—if the tactical positions had been reversed and it had been the British fleet's T that was crossed.

With the fleets positioned as they were on that late May afternoon, Jellicoe's biggest danger lay in an effective enemy destroyer attack. Perhaps the danger was less severe than Jellicoe envisioned it.[18] But we must remember that he had announced what he would do in the circumstances, not only to the Admiralty but also to his captains, and he had to fight his fleet as he had trained it. A signal to turn toward rather than away from the torpedoes at that moment was an invitation to pandemonium. Given the circumstances, if and when Jellicoe ordered a turn, he was bound to turn away.

As far as an attack by the British destroyers was concerned, no such opportunity came to Jellicoe. His best tactic was to use his battleships for firepower and his destroyers to screen. A destroyer attack is an equalizing tactic, one to be risked by the weaker force, and his fleet was not in that category. Moreover, his tactical position was ideal for the battle line and questionable for a destroyer attack.

There was no opportunity for Jellicoe to adopt the kind of tactical initiative that would have reflected the offensive spirit of Nelson. Given the weapon characteristics of 1916, it is difficult to imagine one even in theory. When Beatty assumed command from Jellicoe eighteen months after the battle, all possible lessons had been assimilated. Yet, the changes in tactics that he introduced were insignificant. Nor do we see any Nelsonian changes to fighting by squadrons or anything at all radical in the battle tactics of the 1920s and 1930s. And as for the execution of some theoretical tactical initiative on the spot, it would have been

---

18 Contrary to H. H. Frost and many other critics, Jellicoe's assessment of the situation was accurate. This conclusion resulted from study of the devastating effects of large torpedo spreads in the night actions around Guadalcanal.

impossible. Only today's game-players, who have the magical power to move whole fleets on video screens with buttons, can carry out such unpracticed maneuvers. An admiral of a fleet does not expect to exploit opportunities with tactics that have not been inculcated.

It is reasonable to believe that Jellicoe and Scheer knew this. If so, the explanation for Jellicoe's actions is one he could never offer in public—that ship for ship Scheer's warships were better, and Jellicoe's superiority rested narrowly on maintaining unity and mass. Any concentration without massing was unmanageable. Jellicoe could not fight like Nelson because he was not fighting a fleet like Villeneuve's. Jellicoe was opposed by superb weapon systems that were skillfully handled.

Concept versus Reality

If tactical theorists had underestimated the smoke and confusion of big battle, it is evident from Jellicoe's handling of Jutland that he had not. Tactically he executed what he conceived to be his mission—to bottle up the High Seas Fleet, make his numbers count, win as he could, and avoid loss due to carelessness, enemy wit, or bad luck. His so-called mistake—a preference for risk-avoidance over aggressiveness—was a calculated, preprogrammed, doctrinal, and totally predictable appreciation of Britain's maritime strategy. In fact, the refusal of the High Seas Fleet to come out and submit to its calculated fate was only the first of several unanticipated *strategic* surprises; just as significant were the threat of the submarine to the British sea lines of communication, the snail-paced impact of the strategic blockade, and the effect of mine warfare on all kinds of naval operations. The new weapons not only changed tactics but altered strategic and logistic planning as well.

Tactical plans served well, owing to the great deal of preliminary thinking and writing that had been done and to the debate that had been carried on by the naval officers who executed them. A handful of tactical surprises, however, did arise. Prominent among them was an almost total disregard before World War I of the importance of deception. Every major engagement in the North Sea, the cockpit of the naval war, was part of an effort at seduction. Both sides knew the advantage of numbers and the N-square law (described in footnote 11). Neither fought voluntarily when it was outnumbered ever so slightly; as a result, trap and counter-trap became the method of war, and more often than not the schemes backfired—even at the Battle of Jutland.

If planned surprise through traps did not work very well, unplanned surprise resulting from failures in scouting abounded. Beatty, Jellicoe, Scheer, and Graf Maximilian von Spee (at the Falklands in 1914) all suffered rude surprises from accidents stemming from scouting deficiencies. A dominant feature of Jutland was poor visibility, caused by the gun and engine smoke of 250 warships. There is something about the game floor or video screen that deludes the tactical planner, who may forget that circumstances can drastically foreshorten opening ranges and change the whole nature of the battle. Certainly that is what happened to the Americans in the night actions around Solomons Island in 1942–43, when, unlike the rehearsals of the 1930s, the battles often opened at point-blank range. The American Navy of today, used to the wide sweep of the oceans, can easily forget that inshore work now extends many miles out of sight of land. Submarines aside, there may be many opportunities for hide-and-seek in the narrow seas. If history is any guide, a fleet can achieve a planned surprise, and unintended surprise is always near at hand.

That leads to a consideration of speed. Prewar writers thought, correctly, that gunfire would work very quickly once forces were within effective range. As a result, they envisioned elaborate maneuvers beyond effective range to achieve an advantageous position. In practice, however, it usually was futile to use engineering speed to achieve tactical advantage. The practical speed of a fleet was the speed of the slowest ship in formation. The lesson of the Japanese advantage at Tsushima—that small- and medium-caliber gunfire would inundate an enemy at short range—was learned too well. The trend from the period of the ram through that of short-range gunnery and into that of director-controlled long-range gunnery amounted to a steady erosion of the advantage that had been predicted for warship speed. In addition, some prewar writers omitted from practical consideration the problem faced by the commander whose force included damaged ships that had to slow down. Mahan wisely said that "the true speed of war is . . . the unremitting energy which wastes no time."[19] Failures to consummate opportunities were failures to communicate and comprehend clearly. The speed that mattered was in the realm of decision-making: decisions had to be made quickly and transformed into simple, correct maneuvers.

---

19 Quoted in Hughes (1953), p. 193. In that essay, the Mahan quote was preceded by these timeless words: "The great end of a war fleet . . . is not to chase, nor to fly, but to control the seas. . . . Not speed, but power of offensive action, is the dominant factor in war. . . . Force does not exist for mobility, but mobility for force. It is of no use to get there first unless, when the enemy in turn arrives, you also have the most men, the greater force. . . . The true speed of war is not headlong precipitancy, but the unremitting energy which wastes no time."

And what then of simplicity? When the chips were down, the fleet commander opted for simple formations to maintain control. Echelons, boxes, anything that gave more theoretical superiority was set aside. To achieve his astute maneuvers, Admiral Heihichiro Togo took the lead and guided his own column, using the simplest mode of control. We may believe that he knew that by leading his single simple column he could make his twelve-ship battle-line maneuver with one mind.

Summary

Until the start of World War I there were few opportunities to see the effects of the many technological advances in battle, and so the period between 1865 and 1916 is a case study of the relationship between theory and practice. It was a time of extravagant speculation, but it culminated in superb tactical thought, incorporating what today we call operations analysis. Most of the tactical hypotheses were advanced by naval officers and debated in professional journals.

These tactical studies succeeded admirably in preparing wartime leaders. The battle fleets fought as they had been expected to. The rigorous debate had not overlooked the importance of the column, scouting, concentrated firepower, torpedo salvoes, leadership, training, morale, or C^2. Only deception, accidental surprise, and the limited payoff of ship speed were underestimated or erroneously called.

By the end of this period everything was aimed at concentration of long-range, big-gun firepower. Commanders achieved superior concentration through massing and maneuver. For most of the period, fleets saw one another and maneuvered before they were within effective range, but by the beginning of World War I they needed to deploy for battle while still out of sight, and so tactical scouting assumed prominence and consumed resources. Command was keyed to a faster pace. Simplicity and doctrine dominated tactical procedures.

Other trends emerged as well:

- An increase in the range and destructiveness of weapons
- Oscillation between the dominance of armaments and the dominance of armor
- An increase in the speed and maneuverability of weapon systems in battle (although tactical maneuverability afforded by steam propulsion came at the expense of *strategic* mobility)
- An increase in the importance of tactical scouting as weapon ranges and ship speeds increased

Most surprises were strategic, even if they were generated by technology. The tactical roles of guns, torpedoes, mines, and every class of ship had been anticipated. But either one or both sides failed to predict the end of close blockade, the strategic success of submarine warfare, and the pitfalls of amphibious warfare. All of these were major changes.

4

WORLD WAR II:
THE REVOLUTION
IN WEAPONRY

Surprise or Upheaval?

The phenomenal shift in tactics during World War II took almost everyone by surprise. Even the airpower zealots, who professed to have foreseen the tactical revolution, had been too conservative in their predictions. The attack on Pearl Harbor and the Battle of the Coral Sea were the culmination of events that had occurred during the peacetime of the 1920s and 1930s. In discussing the tactics of carrier warfare, it is worth remembering that everyone was learning on the job. One only needs to read Bernard Brodie's 1942 edition of *A Layman's Guide to Naval Strategy* to appreciate the turmoil in many minds three years after fighting broke out.[1]

Brodie need have had no cause for chagrin. Naval operations off the northern European coast and in the Mediterranean confirmed that the ascendancy of airpower had not been obvious and revealed that the competition between gun and airplane was far closer than anyone had realized. To illustrate: in 1940 two German battleships caught the British aircraft carrier HMS *Glorious* in the open sea and sank it; by 1944 U.S. Fleet anti-air warfare (AAW) defenses were so impregnable that Japan had to abandon bombing attacks and instead resort to kamikaze missions. Land-based horizontal-bomber attacks against warships—the original mission of the B-17—proved not to be effective.[2] The torpedo bomber,

---

1   Brodie, *A Layman's Guide to Naval Strategy.* See chapters 8 and 9 of that book. Brodie's *Sea Power in the Machine Age* (1943) is also insightful.
2   It was easy to explain geometrically why. For an elementary analysis, see Fioravanzo, pp. 177–78. It should also be added that high-level bombers coordinated with simultaneous low-level attacks could be effective against poorly defended merchant ships. The remarkable Battle of the Bismarck Sea in 1943 proved that.

while scoring successes, came to be a kind of unintentional kamikaze. In the end only the dive-bomber spelled the difference. As usual, strategic vision played its part in the rise of naval airpower, but it was the pragmatic tactician and the technologist, working arm-in-arm, who hammered out the details.

The "battleship admirals" were not as important as has been thought. For one thing, aerial bombing tests in the early 1920s against the old U.S. battleships *Indiana* (BB 1), *New Jersey* (BB 62), and *Virginia* (BB 13), and the new but uncompleted *Washington* (BB 47), along with Billy Mitchell's rigged attacks on the *Ostfriesland,* proved not so much that heavy bombs could sink warships as that the aircraft of that day would have great difficulty sinking a moving, well-defended, buttoned-up warship. For another, the 1920s were a time when the Navy was vigorously supporting measures to expand the use of naval airpower. Between 1922 and 1925 the budget for naval aviation held steady at 14.5 million dollars while that for the Navy as a whole shrank 25 percent. From 1923 to 1929 the naval air arm increased by 6,750 men, while Navy manning overall decreased by 1,500—and those figures do not include the crews of the manpower-intensive USS *Lexington* (CV 2) and USS *Saratoga* (CV 3).[3]

In an astonishing sleight-of-hand, all five major signatories of the Washington Disarmament Treaty of 1921 were permitted to maintain substantial total carrier tonnage—135,000 each for the United States and Great Britain; 81,000 for Japan; and 60,000 each for France and Italy—at a time when "no naval power . . . possessed a single ship that could be applied against the allowed carrier tonnage." All carriers in service or still under construction were classified as experimental and were not included in the total. "Drastic as were its reductions in capital ships, the conference clearly determined that there would be no statutory interference with the development of aircraft carriers."[4] From 1921 to 1935, the treaty years, there could be up to about one-third as much carrier tonnage as battleship tonnage. Both Japan and the United States built every ton allowed for carriers. In sum, the Washington Treaty and those that followed it over the next several years did not impose a *constraint* on airpower, but rather provided an *incentive* for expanding it.

William Sims, Bradley Fiske, William Moffett, Ernest King, Joseph Reeves, and Thomas Hart were among the American surface officers who appreciated the importance of naval air very early and encouraged aviators such as Henry Mustin,

3   Melhorn, pp. 93, 94, and 154.
4   Melhorn, p. 83.

Kenneth Whiting, John Towers, and Marc Mitscher to hasten its development. The United States led the way, eyeing the broad Pacific, followed closely by Japan. Britain's naval air arm, backward in some ways, would prove to be the best in the Mediterranean. Still, no naval power could have predicted the dominance of naval aircraft. Technology that had lain dormant like a sleeping giant between the wars was prodded awake by combat in 1939. Even then, the issue remained unsettled. Consider one of Charles Allen's perceptive illustrations of the connection between technology and tactics:

> In the delicate balance of interactions it is noteworthy that the greatest swing factor in the battleship versus carrier issue may have been the actual performance of the newly introduced technology of radar. If [radar] had proven more effective in directing heavy AA guns [or if, as others have said, the proximity fuze had come along a few years sooner], the effectiveness of tactical strike aircraft might have been largely neutralized. If it had been markedly less effective for early warning and fighter direction, carrier vulnerability might have been too great to bear. In either case, the fleet would have been dramatically different in 1945.[5]

All the powers foresaw that aircraft would have *some* vital role. Aircraft were essential as scouts and—not to be overlooked—acted as spotters for gunfire in those days before radar. They were useful enough that the battle force deplored the possibility of losing its air cover. But if carriers were positioned too closely to the battle line, they would be exposed to attack. As early as 1930, the commander of aircraft squadrons for the scouting fleet wrote, "Opposing carriers within a strategical area are like blindfolded men armed with daggers in a ring. There is apt to be sudden destruction to one or both."[6] In developing their interwar plans, inferior navies—the Japanese when fighting the United States, and the United States when fighting the British—expected to use aircraft to soften up and slow the enemy battle line. Whether airpower should be land- or sea-based was debated everywhere, but the need to command the air space over the fleet was acknowledged by all but the least perceptive, and fighter aircraft were seen as key players in this effort. By the 1930s U.S. and Japanese carrier aviators knew their own potency and used every chance they had to experiment—although such

5 Allen, p. 77.
6 May 1984 letter to author Wayne P. Hughes from Dr. Thomas C. Hone, then of the Naval War College faculty, who has studied the surviving documentation from the U.S. Navy fleet problems, 1929–39.

opportunities were infrequent. The Japanese navy already had begun practicing leading with carrier strikes, and insight into what U.S. naval officers regarded as the paramount threat was evident in the intensity with which naval intelligence tried—and failed—to track Japanese carriers, rather than battleships, just before Japan's raid on Pearl Harbor. Yet, the questions of how battles would be fought and what tactics would be used were still unresolved in 1941, even after two years of fighting in the North Sea, the Atlantic, and the Mediterranean.

Indeed, the state of naval tactics just before the United States entered World War II was sharply different from the situation on the eve of the previous World War. By 1917 most of that era's technological advances already had been assimilated and fleet tactics had been set in place. At the onset of World War II, however, technology was in ferment and tactics had not yet caught up with its potential. The dreams of those who envisioned aircraft sweeping the oceans clean of surface warships were so patently premature that they only served to bolster the case made by conservatives, who asserted that the line of battleships would remain the primary weapon of naval warfare. In large measure the fleet tactics anticipated for World War II were similar to those that had been used in the previous war, except that aircraft, the new mad dogs of their day, would finally fight one another in the air. This outlook prevailed in all navies. After the war actually broke out, tacticians had to adapt so extensively that by the end of the war every major category of warship that the U.S. Navy was deploying—except for minecraft—was being used for a different purpose from the one for which it had been built. The striking and supporting roles of battleships and aircraft carriers were reversed; heavy cruisers, designed in part for fleet scouting, did almost everything but that; light cruisers, designed as destroyer-leaders, became AAW escorts for carriers; destroyers, conceived for defending the van and rear of the battle line against torpedo attacks from other destroyers, were adapted to function as antisubmarine warfare (ASW) and AAW escorts; and submarines, designed for forward reconnaissance and attacks on warships, were diverted to attack merchant ships and the sea lines of communication. By the end of World War II the upheaval of tactics, hastened by technology, was complete. Along the way tactical problems had to be solved.

This book discusses the evolution of sea-based airpower solely within the U.S. Navy. Recent research, using Japanese sources, has comprehensively appraised Japanese preparations during the same interwar period. The definitive book on the subject is by David Evans and Mark Peattie: *Kaigun: Strategy, Tactics, and Technology in the Imperial Japanese Navy, 1887–1941*. It describes in detail the Japanese navy's struggle with the difficult task of competing with the U.S. Navy under the constraint of the Washington Naval Treaty, which relegated it to a three-to-five ratio numerical inferiority in capital ships. The Japanese solution was three-fold—to seek qualitative superiority in battleships, naval aircraft, and submarines; to outnumber the U.S. Navy in cruisers and destroyers; and to develop complicated but coherent tactics that would whittle down the American battle line before the decisive battle, which would then be fought in the western Pacific. Above all, the Imperial Japanese Navy believed in *bushido*, the elan of the individual warrior, and infused it in the men of its fighting ships and aircraft.

The technological evolution of Japanese carriers and carrier aircraft is different in detail from that of the U.S. Navy, but equally astute and devoted to success. Evans and Peattie show that, overall, the American struggle to achieve viable carrier tactics was similar to that experienced by the Japanese side. The several works of Thomas Hone affirm these appraisals. He concludes that both the U.S. and Japanese navies brought along carrier aviation with full vigor, intensity, and financial commitment; by contrast, Britain's Royal Navy lost an early lead due to fiscal stringency and a decision to build up the Royal Air Force, which sapped funds from the naval aviation program.[7]

In the fleet exercises of 1929 the *Saratoga* made a night run around the defending fleet and conducted a successful air strike against the Panama Canal. The attack is often celebrated as the symbolic arrival of carrier aviation as a force to be reckoned with. Yet, it had mixed ramifications. After launching the strike, the *Saratoga* was found and "sunk" three times—by surface ships, by a submarine, and by aircraft from the *Lexington*. That proved to be prophetic. During World War II, the center of concern for Navy tacticians was the vulnerability of warships of every description to attacks by naval aircraft—foremost among them the carrier of the aircraft itself.

Five New Tactical Problems

Among the many tactical problems facing U.S. and Japanese naval commanders in the Pacific, five were prominent—and interrelated.

The tactical formation. Thanks to prewar experimentation, both U.S. and Japanese naval aviators understood the advantages of the circular formation for the

---

7 Hone is an authority on the evolution of the principal navies between the world wars. Two short and excellent articles are "Spending Patterns of the United States Navy, 1921–1941," *Armed Forces and Society* (Spring 1982), and (with Mark Mandeles) "Interwar Innovation in Three Navies: U.S. Navy, Royal Navy, Imperial Japanese Navy," *Naval War College Review* (Spring 1987). A comprehensive comparison of American and British aircraft-carrier development is Hone, Friedman, and Mandeles (1999).

defense of a carrier. For the United States, the introduction of the many-faceted radar system made station-keeping easy. Offensively the formation could be maneuvered by simultaneous turns to maintain unity under radio silence during flight operations. Defensively, a circle was best because it guarded against the possibility that enemy aircraft might discover a gap in the screen of escorts and try to exploit it. The major question was whether each carrier should have its own screen to maximize its flexibility or whether two or three carriers should be surrounded by a single, stronger ring of escorts. Protection against torpedoes from slow-moving, submerged diesel submarines was also a consideration. A "bent-line" screen would do better for that, but it was generally incompatible with carrier operations. Instead, speed was the carriers' best security, along with avoiding having to steam through the same waters repeatedly.

The effectiveness of air offense and defense was the issue. At the outset, the Japanese established separate carrier formations; they changed only when forced to do so by a shortage of escorts. For the U.S. Navy the issue was less clear-cut. The debate among senior aviators began to peak after the Battle of the Eastern Solomons, when one commanding officer added a new wrinkle by contending that the *Saratoga* had escaped attack and survived because of her ten- or fifteen-mile separation from the *Enterprise,* which had been heavily damaged. Would it not be better to lose one carrier and save the other than to lose two carriers to a concentrated attack, he asked? Which should take precedence—passive defense through physical separation with concomitant flexibility for air operations, or better AAW defense through more compact positioning?

Dispersal or massing? The increasing maximum range of attack aircraft opened up the possibility of mounting joint sorties from two or more carrier formations that were physically separated by hundreds of miles. In practice, the need for radio silence hampered—perhaps even spoiled—this possibility, and the United States never entertained it. Instead, American tacticians argued over the use of separate formations, but kept the formations close enough for the fighter air defense—the combat air patrol (CAP)—to protect the entire carrier force. For the U.S. Navy, concentration and massing were synonymous.

The Japanese had a penchant for separating their carriers during fleet actions, and they have been much criticized for it. E. B. Potter, for one, takes Vice Admiral Takeo Takagi to task for doing so in the Battle of the Coral Sea in 1942 in an attempt to "catch the American carriers in a sort of pincer-movement."[8] Later,

---

8   Potter, p. 664.

Admiral Isoroku Yamamoto's plan for the Eastern Solomons battle placed the light carrier *Ryujo* in front of his two larger carriers as a decoy. She was sunk, and the Japanese have since been called out for dividing their forces. As an explanation for such complicated Japanese tactics, U.S. critics have called Japan "sneaky" and pointed to its history of surprise attack. No doubt surprise attack—an effort to attack effectively first—was the basis of Japanese planning, but why did they separate their carriers? At the Coral Sea the main striking fleet took advantage of a weather front and approached from a direction toward which land-based U.S. aircraft could not search and carrier aircraft were less likely to approach. A pincer movement is an absurdity for someone as astute and familiar with carrier airpower as Yamamoto was. Was there not a better rationale for these strange Japanese dispositions? The answer is yes, and it reflects the Japanese faith in the dominance of successful air strikes.

Offensive vs. defensive firepower. Although tactical commanders must fight with the forces at their disposal, they have choices. They can emphasize fighter escort for their strikes, or they can emphasize their fighter CAP. They can add fighters to their flight decks for defense and carry fewer bombers and torpedo aircraft, or vice versa. They can use most of their scout bombers for scouting, or they can take calculated risks in scouting and then husband the bombers for a stronger attack. They can integrate their battleships in the carrier screen for AAW defense, as the U.S. Navy did in the Pacific, or they can keep their battleships separate for offensive follow-up attack, as the Japanese did. These decisions hang much on the estimate of the power of the offense. Like many commentators, Clark G. Reynolds was disappointed at Raymond Spruance's failure to use his carriers more offensively in 1944.[9] Were not the enemy carriers simultaneously Japan's most potent threat and America's most important objective? Spruance was the best U.S. naval tactician in World War II. Then why did he not act as the Japanese had— leave a small force to cover the amphibious assault and use his fast carriers to go after the Japanese carriers and hit them first?

Daytime vs. nighttime tactics. Carriers dominated the daylight hours, but they were sitting ducks for gunfire at night. Detaching before darkness, a battleship or heavy cruiser formation could travel two hundred nautical miles at night, a distance engraved in the mind of every tactical commander. Since air strikes were mounted at ranges of around two hundred nautical miles, the attacking force could not close the distance to the target carrier(s) unless the enemy was crippled

9 Reynolds (1968), pp. 181–205.

and presumably retreating. Because of the damage to the U.S. battle line at Pearl Harbor, there would be no need for a command decision in 1942 about whether to send gunships against gunships halfway between two opposing carrier forces two hundred nautical miles apart.[10] Yet, the Japanese, who were the aggressors in 1942, three times sent their surface ships hunting for carriers. The U.S. tactical problem in 1942 was whether to pursue the enemy after dark and risk an encounter with Japanese gunships or stand clear and let the Imperial warships or invasion force steam safely away. In 1944, however, the problem was whether to employ fast battleships as a unit for offensive action, in the Japanese fashion, or else keep them with the carriers for defense. What was the basis for tactical decision?

Dual objectives. Typical American planning before the war would have held that the U.S. battle fleet steaming west to relieve Guam and the Philippines would be met by the Japanese battle fleet and a great decisive action would take place. It is true that as logistical considerations intruded, this simple tactical paradigm was complicated by the need for bases and the fleet train. But guarding the train or an invasion force was not yet a mission about which fleet tacticians worried much.

The airplane changed that. Until there was a threat of invasion by the navy on the strategic offensive, a weaker battle fleet on the defensive could not be induced to fight. But an invasion force had the responsibility of protecting amphibious assault ships, and with aircraft in the offing this presented new and complicated problems. Aircraft had to cover the transports as well as attack the enemy. In all six of the Pacific carrier battles the attacker had a primary or secondary mission to attack and destroy the enemy fleet. In each instance an amphibious operation was involved. Obviously the attacker did not want to expose its transports. This dual objective was inescapable for the Japanese in 1942 and for the Americans in 1944. Tactical plans and decisions also had to deal with the new problem that strategic offensive brought: how to dispose forces while protecting transports. In the era of aircraft, tactical commanders had to solve the unprecedented problem of enemy attack from a long range.

A Tactical Model of Carrier Warfare

The five new problems facing Pacific carrier tacticians can be illuminated in a simple model that also will foreshadow understanding of modern missile warfare, which will be discussed later. In several ways, the model of carrier warfare contrasts

---

10 Such a night action was a real possibility at the Battle of the Coral Sea and a remote possibility at the Battle of the Marianas. Under rather different circumstances, it occurred in the Battle for Leyte Gulf.

with the Lanchester-Fiske model of gunnery. Fiske envisioned a mutual exchange of salvoes that would erode the residual strengths of both sides simultaneously. His aim was to show the cumulative effectiveness of superior firepower; how a small advantage could dominate the action if it could be exploited with coherent maneuvers; and how the inferior force would inflict disproportionately scant damage no matter how well the battle was handled tactically. Gun range was a matter of indifference to Fiske because both sides faced essentially the same range. He felt free to disregard (at least for purposes of illustration) the possibility that one side could out-range the other and maintain a significant advantage. In effect, the pace of the battle would accelerate as the range closed, but the final ratio of losses would not change. His model took into account the "staying power"— that is, warship survivability—in accordance with the assessments of his day: a modern battleship would be reduced to impotence in about twenty minutes by unopposed big guns within effective range.

The gunfire model of simultaneous erosive attrition does not work for the World War II carrier offensive force. That force is best represented as one large pulse of firepower unleashed upon the arrival of the air wing at the target. If, as was common, the second carrier force also located the first and launched its own strike, simultaneous pulses of firepower would be delivered from both fleets. If the second carrier fleet did not find the first in time, it would have to accept the first blow. By then it would probably have located the first force, and if any attack capacity remained, it would strike back.

To calculate damage from an air attack it is necessary to figure the defender's counterforce as the combination of both active defense (fighters and AAW strength) and passive defense (formation maneuverability and carrier survivability). In the Pacific, effective carrier-based air-attack ranges were comparable, 200 to 250 nautical miles, and neither side could out-range the enemy's carrier aircraft. So in carrier battles, the crucial ingredients were *scouting effectiveness* and *net striking power.* Scouting effectiveness came from many sources: raw search capability, including organic and land-based air reconnaissance; submarine pickets; intelligence of every kind; all enemy efforts to evade detection; and, not to be overlooked, the planning skill of the commander and supporting staff. Net striking power was made up of raw numbers of attacking bombers and fighter escorts, reduced by the active and passive defenses and the relative quality of material and personnel on both sides.

In this example, *scouting* effectiveness can be determined simply by asking who attacked first or whether the attacks were simultaneous. As for *striking* effectiveness—that is, the amount of damage inflicted—the crucial question there is the value of a carrier air wing's strike capacity. There is much room to examine trade-offs in practice between attack aircraft used for scouting or attacking and the fighters that are used for escort or CAP. These were problems with which air staffs had to deal.

For the moment, assume that in 1942 one air wing could on balance sink or inflict crippling damage on one carrier and that cumulative striking power was linear—that is, two carriers were about twice as effective as one and so could sink or cripple two. A very rudimentary table of outcomes after the first strike can be constructed for three cases below: (1) the equal or superior force A attacks first; (2) the inferior force B attacks first; or (3) A and B attack together.

If we permit the survivors of the initially superior but surprised force A to counterattack, the final outcome is:

Initial force (A/B)	2/2	4/3	3/2	2/1	3/1
B strikes first	0/2	1/3	1/2	1/1	2/1
Survivors (A/B) after A counterattacks	0/2	1/2	1/1	1/0	2/0

It may be inferred from reading the views of naval aviators at the time that they believed a carrier air wing would sink more than one enemy carrier on average. It is pretty clear that U.S. aviators thought the thirty-six dive-bombers and eighteen torpedo bombers that constituted an air wing at the outset of the war could sink or put out of action (i.e., achieve a "firepower kill" on) several carriers with a single cohesive strike. They estimated that the enemy could do the same. They were obsessed with the need to get at the enemy first, and we need not accept their optimism to see the enormous advantage of striking first.

Table 4-1. First Strike Survivors*

	Initial Number of Carriers (A/B)				
	2/2	4/3	3/2	2/1	3/1
(1) A strikes first	2/0	4/0	3/0	2/0	3/0
(2) B strikes first	0/2	1/3	1/2	1/1	2/1
(3) A and B strike simultaneously	0/0	1/0	1/0	1/0	2/0

* It is immaterial here whether the nonsurvivors are sunk or out of action. But later we will take the survivors to mean carriers with operational flight decks and viable air wings.

The picture gets interesting when the results for *B*, the inferior force, are presented. If both sides attack together, *B* cannot win. Compared with its performance in the Fiske model of continuous fire, *B* does well; although the enemy may be winning, it can suffer severely. Even more instructive are the numbers when *B* successfully strikes first. Unlike *B* in Fiske's continuous-fire model, here *B* can be outnumbered 1:2 and still establish the basis of future equality if it can attack and withdraw safely. *B* can be outnumbered 2:3 and establish the same after-action equality even if *A* is able to counterattack after absorbing the first blow. Evident as all this may seem, it still is crucial, since it is the basis for understanding much about the five interrelated tactical problems just introduced.

Before proceeding we should roughly calibrate attacker effectiveness by reviewing the four carrier battles of 1942 and then comparing them with the Battle of the Marianas, fought in June 1944.

Reviewing the battles of 1942 (not later) we will assume that

- The carrier-air-wing effectiveness of every carrier on either side was equivalent.
- The defensive features of every carrier and its escorts on either side were equivalent.
- Japanese carriers that are physically separated should be counted. Whether deliberately or inadvertently, they served as decoys and absorbed U.S. attention and air assets.

The numbers show who attacked the enemy main force first. To compute theoretical results the table shows the results of all attacks, including diversionary actions, in the proper sequence. Although they do not enter into the calculations, initial and surviving carrier *aircraft* strengths are also shown.

The Coral Sea, May 1942

On 7 May the U.S. force (the *Lexington* and the USS *Yorktown* [CV 5]) launched a major strike against the little Japanese force that was covering the invasion force (the small carrier *Shoho)* and sank the carrier. On 8 May the U.S. force and the Japanese striking force (the *Shokaku* and the *Zuikaku*) struck simultaneously. The *Lexington* was sunk; the *Yorktown* suffered minor damage. The *Shokaku* suffered heavy damage; the *Zuikaku,* not found by U.S. aircraft, survived undamaged. This battle was marred tactically by very poor scouting on both sides.

Theoretical Survivors		
	After 7 May	After 8 May
A *Japan*	2	0
B *United States*	2	0

Battle Synopsis				
	Initial Forces		Actual Survivors	
	CV	Aircraft	CV	Aircraft
A *Japan*	2½[a]	146	1[b]	66
B *United States*	2	143	1[c]	77

[a] The small Japanese carrier *Shoho* is counted as one-half.
[b] The *Shokaku* suffered heavy damage and is not counted as a survivor.
[c] The *Yorktown*, though damaged, is counted as surviving. She fought at Midway.

Midway, June 1942

The U.S. force—the USS *Yorktown*, USS *Hornet* (CV 8), and USS *Enterprise* (CV 6)—successfully surprised the Japanese striking force (the *Kaga, Akagi, Soryu,* and *Hiryu*) on 4 June. Most of the circumstances are well known, but many have not noted that the island of Midway served in effect as a highly significant decoy. After the successful U.S. surprise attack, the Japanese counterattacked, and then the surviving U.S. force re-attacked.

Theoretical Survivors			
	After U.S. attack	After Japanese counterattack	After U.S. re-attack
A *Japan*	1	1	0
B *United States*	3	2	2

Battle Synopsis				
	Initial Forces		Actual Survivors	
	CV	Aircraft	CV	Aircraft
A *Japan*	4	272	0	0
B *United States*	3	233	2	126

The Eastern Solomons, August 1942

On 24 August the U.S. force (the *Enterprise* and the *Saratoga*) attacked the small carrier *Ryujo* with its three escorts, which were exposed in front of the Japanese striking force. The *Ryujo* was sunk. Once the Americans had taken the bait, the Japanese striking force (the *Shokaku* and the *Zuikaku*) surprised the U.S. force. The U.S. striking force never pinpointed the Japanese force for a counterattack.

Theoretical Survivors		
	After U.S. Attack	After Japanese Attack
A *Japan*	2	2
B *United States*	2	0

Battle Synopsis				
	Initial Forces		Actual Survivors	
	CV	*Aircraft*	CV	*Aircraft*
A *Japan*	2½[a]	168	2	107
B *United States*	2	174	1[b]	157[c]

[a] The *Ryujo* with her thirty-seven aircraft is counted as one-half.

[b] The *Enterprise* was heavily damaged and is not counted as a survivor.

[c] Though surprised and unable to find and counterattack the Japanese, the United States had fifty-three fighters in the air, warned by air-search radar. U.S. aircraft losses were light because the aircraft from the *Enterprise* were able to land at Henderson Field, Guadalcanal.

The ascendancy of the attacker is starting to wane. Although the survival of the U.S. carriers under surprise attack can be explained by many details of battle training and leadership, the capabilities of U.S. defenses clearly had improved.[11]

The Santa Cruz Islands, October 1942

On 26 October the U.S. force (the *Hornet* and the restored *Enterprise*) and the Japanese striking force (the *Shokaku*, *Zuikaku*, and small *Zuiho*) struck each other simultaneously. The small *Junyo* (fifty-five aircraft), although detached in a support unit covering reinforcements for Guadalcanal, also was able to attack the American carriers. The *Hornet* was sunk and the *Shokaku* and the *Zuiho* were heavily damaged.

Theoretical Survivors	
	After 26 Oct
A *Japan*	1
B *United States*	0

---

11 Polmar (p. 253) goes so far as to call the battle a U.S. victory.

The Revolution in Weaponry 89

Battle Synopsis				
	Initial Forces		Actual Survivors	
	CV	Aircraft	CV	Aircraft
A *Japan*	3[a]	212	1½	112
B *United States*	2	171	1[b]	97[c]

[a] Two small Japanese carriers are counted as one-half each.

[b] The *Enterprise* suffered three bomb hits but was able to recover the *Hornet*'s and her own aircraft. She is counted as a survivor.

[c] The continuing terrible aircraft attrition—174 aircraft collectively for the Japanese and U.S. air wings—and the greater-than-theoretical survival rate for carriers indicate strengthened defenses. This is the battle in which the USS *South Dakota* (BB 57) is credited with twenty-six aircraft kills.

After the Battle of the Santa Cruz Islands both sides were reduced to a single operational carrier. Their respective air wings had suffered grievously. In 1943 both forces husbanded their new and repaired carriers while the Solomons campaign continued to rage. The Japanese, however, were too quick in employing their naval aircraft from airfields in the Solomons and Rabaul, and they suffered accordingly. Unavoidable as the Japanese commitment probably was, the loss of naval aviators established the basis for the air disaster that overtook them in 1944.

Meanwhile, the U.S. carrier navy sorted out its air tactics, added AAW ships and AAW weapons, and built up its fast-carrier task force to fifteen carriers—more than double the number at the war's outset. The Japanese succeeded only in building their carrier force back to nine (they had had ten carriers in January 1942). Qualitatively the Japanese were even more outmatched.

The Philippine Sea, June 1944

On 19 June Admiral Jisaburo Ozawa's fleet, built around all 9 of Japan's carriers, attacked the U.S. Fleet of 15 carriers from 400 nautical miles away. His plan was for Japanese aircraft to attack from beyond the range of U.S. aircraft and then continue on and land at Guam. Admiral Spruance could not simultaneously stay close to Saipan, where he was supporting the amphibious assault, and reach the Japanese. He chose to stay near the beach and concede the initiative of first attack to the Japanese. Their air attack was crushed. That evening Spruance allowed VADM Marc Mitscher to attack at very long range—almost 300 nautical miles—with 216 aircraft. Meanwhile, U.S. submarines sank 2 large carriers. The U.S. air attack, in part because of the long range, succeeded only in sinking the small *Hiyo* and heavily damaging the *Zuikaku*. In this attack the United States suffered the only significant aircraft losses of the battle; they were mostly operational, occurring on the long return flight at night.

Theoretical Survivors			
	After Japanese strikes	*After U.S. sub attack*	*After U.S. counterattacks*
A *Japan*	9	7	4
B *United States*	6	6	6

Battle Synopsis				
	Initial Forces		Actual Survivors	
	CV	Aircraft	CV	Aircraft
A *Japan*	9	450	5[a]	34[b]
B *United States*	15[c]	704	15	575[d]

[a] Mitscher's evening attack with 216 aircraft is the equivalent of three carrier deckloads. According to our rule of thumb, they should have sunk or incapacitated three carriers. In fact, they knocked out two. Subs sank the other two.

[b] In addition to overwhelming Japanese carrier aircraft losses there were a few losses among scout planes aboard Japanese battleships and cruisers, and many more losses among Japanese planes based at Guam.

[c] Not all the carriers were large carriers. But putting the carriers in tables without distinguishing them does no violence to the comparisons and displays more familiar numbers.

[d] Of the 129 U.S. aircraft lost, Mitscher's late-evening counterattack accounts for 100.

The Battle of the Philippine Sea was no longer a battle of scouting and attack. The defense had overtaken the offense. Years later, in a rare public statement, Spruance said he would have preferred to move away from the beach and attack, but his mission was to defend the beachhead. Through either wisdom or inadvertence, his defensive tactics worked. Ozawa's plan hinged on combining sea- and land-based air. By waiting near Saipan for the Japanese fleet, Spruance was able to destroy the land-based air threat, achieving numerical superiority for the carrier battle. Ozawa's shuttle tactics were foredoomed, because U.S. fighters pounced on most of the Japanese aircraft at or en route to Guam. By staying nearby, Spruance continued to command the airfields in the Mariana Islands. By waiting for the Japanese, the U.S. Fleet could devote all fighters to CAP. And *two-thirds* of Spruance's aircraft—470 of them in 15 carriers—were fighters. The United States had more fighters than the Japanese had carrier aircraft.

The slaughter of Japanese aircraft was due to a combination of U.S. defensive strength, its highly effective fighter direction, and superior American pilots. How much the result should be attributed to one factor or the other matters little. They were sufficient to guarantee an American victory as long as the U.S. Fleet maintained effective tactical concentration, which had become so much a Spruance trademark that even Ozawa expected it.

Had the year been 1942, Spruance should have gone after the Japanese fleet just as he had at Midway. In that year offense still dominated defense, and the first strike could have been expected to be an effective one. Three-quarters of a U.S. air wing comprised attack aircraft. But in 1944 circumstances were different. The concentrated U.S. carrier battle fleet had great potential to defend itself effectively. To strengthen that defense, the proportion of fighters in the air wings had been increased to 65 percent, from 25 percent before. The decks of the Japanese carriers, however, were still heavy with attack aircraft: two-thirds were dive-bombers and torpedo bombers. We must surmise that until the Battle of the Marianas the Imperial Navy clung to the misplaced hope of surprise and a forlorn faith in the offensive. After that battle and until the end of the war Japanese carriers were impotent, used only as decoys at the Battle for Leyte Gulf.

Many more fighters escorted a strike in 1944. What had been a battle to sink carriers in 1942 had become a battle to destroy aircraft. From June 1944 on, battles were between Japanese land-based aircraft and American carrier aircraft.

This shift of emphasis is not fully appreciated by naval critics. On the written record even Spruance only grasped the shift instinctively. ADM William F. Halsey did not see it at all. Nimitz, disappointed at Spruance's failure to sink ships (although Spruance's mission actually was to guard the beach), revised priorities at Leyte Gulf and made the destruction of the Japanese fleet Halsey's primary mission. For his part, Halsey was overly eager to be thrown into that briar patch. In the Battle for Leyte Gulf he ran north—chasing carriers and a battleship that had been planted by the Japanese to draw him away from the main action around the Leyte beachhead.

Resolution of Tactical Problems

What insight do these rough-and-ready comparisons yield with regard to the five main tactical problems?

The tactical formation. The first problem was whether to give each carrier its own screen or to place two or more carriers inside a common screen of escorts. The Japanese used single-carrier formations at the Coral Sea.[12] At Midway, however, they were forced by a scarcity of escorts to double up (in 1942 Yamamoto still believed that carriers would protect battleships, not the converse). In 1944 the Japanese doubled up, having lost too many cruisers and destroyers to continue their previous tactics. By then the question was decided for the United States by numbers of a different kind. The fifteen fast carriers were combined in groups of three and four—for cohesion, control, and AAW firepower.

---

12 Wilmott, p. 260.

The wisest conclusion is probably that in 1942 single-carrier screens were best because defenses were poor, aircraft could be launched and landed more efficiently when carriers had their own screens, and attacking first was the primary objective. Single carriers separated by even as little as ten or twenty miles might escape attack, as the carriers *Zuikaku* in the Coral Sea and *Saratoga* in the eastern Solomons did.[13] By 1944, however, U.S. tacticians had concluded that they could give up something in offensive efficiency to exploit the potentially withering defenses of the tight AAW circle. U.S. formations enclosed three or four carriers, and the entire disposition was kept close enough so that the entire fleet could be protected by a massed CAP. For them, the decision to put two or more carriers in one formation properly rested on the effectiveness of the defense.

Dispersal or massing? The second tactical question was whether to divide the forces to the extent that mutual support was lost or significantly weakened. In 1942 that question confronted the Japanese commanders, who were required to cover an invasion or reinforcement in all four of the big carrier battles. Their objectives were mixed, for the Japanese also sought to draw out and defeat the U.S. Fleet. Admiral Nimitz, aware that his forces were inferior, was not going to risk his fleet unless forced to do so. Each of the four battles had its own peculiar circumstances, but based on Yamamoto's otherwise incomprehensible practice of spreading his forces and, at least in the Eastern Solomons, of baiting a trap, there seems to be only one conclusion: as a leading exponent of naval aviation himself, Yamamoto must have believed—as American and Japanese naval aviators did— that a successful surprise attack by two big carrier air wings would destroy *more* than an equal number of the opposition. Airpower proponents thought that one carrier's aircraft could sink two or three carriers clustered together, and therefore massing two or three units against one risked three units and gained nothing. If this was Yamamoto's rationale, it fell short on three counts. Code-breaking was providing the United States with significant amounts of strategic intelligence. Air-search radar provided unparalleled warning on tactical developments. And, from the evidence, the destructive power of a carrier air wing was not sufficient to justify expectations of a two-for-one effectiveness potential.

There are two points to infer from this experience: first, that concentration of *offensive* firepower sufficient to win at one blow is *always* desirable, and can be

---

13 At the Coral Sea the *Lexington* and the *Yorktown* were placed in formation by Frank Jack Fletcher to receive the Japanese air attack of 8 May inside a single screen of twelve cruisers and destroyers. They separated during evasive maneuvering (at thirty knots) into separately screened task groups.

achieved in principle by using modern long-range aircraft or missiles, without physically massing ships; and second, that the decision to mass rests on whether it would enhance defense or else help in coordinating a concentrated first attack. If massing fails on either count, dispersal may be better than massing. Still, some thoughtful analysis of the scouting process is in order before one jumps to the obvious conclusion—that since modern missiles provide a many-for-one offensive punch, both stealth and dispersal are appropriate.

Offensive vs. defensive firepower. As for the third tactical problem, whether to optimize the formation for offense or defense, the solution developed in World War II can be inferred from the tacticians' responses to the first two problems. As the war progressed, the U.S. Navy strengthened its carrier defenses. First, it increased the number of fighters at the expense of bomber totals. Second, it steadily added AAW batteries, it began using the *Atlanta*-class AAW cruisers, and, starting with the Battle of the Eastern Solomons, it integrated fast battleships into carrier screens. Third, it emphasized and improved damage-control procedures and equipment on its warships. As a result, defensive considerations came to dominate and ultimately the destruction of aircraft became more significant than the destruction of carriers.

By 1944 the simple but elegant model of the carrier battles in use for the two previous years was beginning to fail. It asserted that one carrier air wing would, throughout 1942, sink one enemy carrier if and when it found a carrier:

CVs out of action = Attacking airwings

In the Battle of the Philippine Sea the defensive component also must be taken into account for the model to work. This is because the simple 1942 model inputs must be adjusted to give the correct results. That can be done adding a defense component, with the following equation:

CVs out of action = [Attacking airwings] −
　　　　　　　　　[Airwings defeated by defending CVs]

Unlike the situation in 1942, the numbers are statistically meaningless because we must fit too many parameters and we have but one battle. However, with realistic inputs the new model will give results that fit the outcome of the Battle of the Philippine Sea:

USN CVs out of action = [7 IJN airwings] –

[15 USN CVs x ½ IJN airwings/USN CV]

= less than 0 (in other words, no losses)

IJN CVs out of action = [3 USN airwings] –

[7 IJN CVs x 1/7 USN airwing/IJN CV]

= 2 IJN CVs

The American defense was very strong—amounting to half of each carrier's aircraft. First, *all* fighters were used for the defense of the Fifth Fleet; second, by 1944 U.S. cruiser and destroyer AAW defenses were very effective. The Japanese defense was much weaker—constituting only about 14 percent of each carrier's aircraft complement—and less potent in reducing the effectiveness of U.S. forces. Imperial Navy fighter strength had been severely depleted during the previous Japanese air strike, and Japan's surface escort defenses were not as good as those of the Americans.

Daytime vs. nighttime tactics. The fourth tactical problem was the dominance of the gunship at night. As early as the Battle of the Coral Sea the Japanese tried a night air attack, but it was night surface action that they continually sought. In three of the four 1942 carrier battles, the Japanese detached gunships to find U.S. carriers. Owing to American prudence or merely to luck, the Japanese never succeeded in forcing an engagement. Judging from their performance in the 1942 night battles in the Solomons, it was best for the United States that they failed. Later, when the U.S. Navy began taking the offensive it set up an ingenious task organization that permitted commanders to detach fast battleships from their carrier screening role and to form a battle line for surface action. That guns still dominated after dark is clearly seen in the climactic action in the Battle for Leyte Gulf. That huge battle is best thought of as a final and desperate Japanese effort to bring gunships within range of their targets. The last and very effective line of American defense was surface warship guns.

Dual objectives. Finally, there was the unanticipated tactical problem of split objectives for the attacker. In 1944, when the U.S. Fleet swept across the Pacific from Pearl Harbor to the Philippines in less than twelve months, it was so strong that it could accompany the landing force and dare the Japanese to come out. It had a two-to-one numerical advantage in carriers, decisive in itself, and an even greater advantage when the quality of pilots and screening ships was factored in. Moreover, it no longer was necessary for U.S. forces to attack first. Mass and unity of action were the keys to effective application of force. Battle victory was not the problem. The issue was simply how to accomplish the objective with minimum losses and in minimum time.

The Japanese tactical problem was not so simple in 1942. Strategic imperatives drove Yamamoto's tactics. Why were the Japanese caught at the Battle of the Coral Sea with a striking force of merely two carriers? It was because Yamamoto was in a hurry. His carriers were all busy. As figure 4-1 shows, in just four months he had spread Japanese outposts like tentacles of an octopus out to the south, where his oil supply lay; to the southwest, so he could seize Singapore and safeguard the East Indies to the west; and to the southeast, so he could seize Rabaul and safeguard the Indies to the east. He had already secured his line of communications to the East Indies by taking the Philippines and Guam in December and January. He had eliminated Wake Island as a threat and now he wanted Midway. Unlike U.S. commanders, he had always envisioned supplementing sea-based aircraft with land-based aircraft.

Yamamoto proceeded unchecked until the Battle of the Coral Sea. Then he paid a price, albeit a modest one, for overconfidence. His alternative was to concentrate the Imperial Fleet's entire carrier striking power of ten carriers—a step

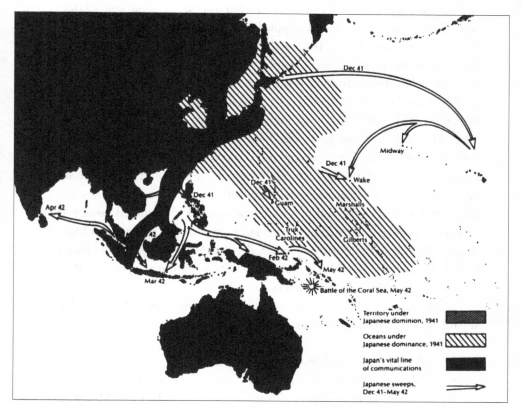

Figure 4-1. Japanese Maritime Expansion, December 1941–May 1942

that would have resulted in a glacial move southward that would have been too slow. Indeed, the United States force had seven big carriers, flying as many air-craft as his ten did, and the Americans would be coming soon.

At the same time, while Yamamoto consolidated his network of air bases, he desperately needed to entice the U.S. Fleet into battle—an objective that he could only achieve with the threat of an invasion—just as the United States later planned to do with the Japanese fleet in 1944. The Battle of the Coral Sea illustrates his priorities. The April operation was intended for the establishment of Japanese outposts at Tulagi and Port Moresby to screen Rabaul and threaten the U.S. link to Australia. Yet when the two U.S. carriers appeared and fought back, Yamamoto blasted Vice Admiral Shigeyoshi Inouye, who was in tactical command—not for pulling back the invasion force headed for Port Moresby, but for failing to pursue the surviving carrier. He ordered the *Zuikaku* to go plunging fruitlessly in pursuit of Fletcher in the *Yorktown*. At this stage of the war American naval leaders were no wiser than Yamamoto. The U.S. Navy had two carriers tied up in the Doolittle raid against Tokyo, which is why the *Lexington* and the *Yorktown* were all that was available (the *Saratoga* had been crippled by torpedoes from a submarine).

Yamamoto split his carriers for the Midway operation because he was in a hurry and he faced competing demands. With two widely spaced objectives, Mid-way and Kiska-Attu, he had to cover two invasion forces. But the Kiska-Attu force was being used to attract the U.S. Fleet and divert it from the Battle of Midway. Yamamoto had wanted to launch the carrier striking force ahead of the invasion force. That was well and good, but he still thought of the battleships as final arbiters, there primarily to mop up and too precious to expose until Japan had gained command of the air space. He need not—and should not—have squan-dered effort in the Aleutian sideshow, which drew away two small carriers. On the other hand, he was correct not to wait for the repair of his damaged carriers. By all reasonable estimates he could have been facing two carriers at most plus Midway's aircraft. Had he waited thirty days more, the *Yorktown*'s wounds would have been healed, the *Saratoga* would have joined up, and in another thirty days the USS *Wasp* (CV 7) would have arrived from the Atlantic.

Yet, history has been too eager to second-guess Yamamoto's decisions. He lost at Midway for all of these reasons:

- The U.S. Navy had strategic intelligence.
- Vice Admiral Chūichi Nagumo had no air-search radar.
- Japanese scouting was mediocre. Nagumo launched a feeble air recon-naissance effort, and the Japanese were beyond help from land-based air

reconnaissance—a rare thing for the Imperial Fleet. And Yamamoto's subs arrived too late on picket stations.

- The American air wings were brave.
- The American air wings were lucky.
- Midway Island served as a fourth—and unsinkable—aircraft carrier.

Take away any of these seven conditions and it is more than likely that the Japanese would have destroyed the American fleet and captured Midway. If good luck influences battle results, then results are not a perfect indicator of the soundness of the planning involved. Historians must not evaluate a tactician's acumen solely on the outcome of the battle.

Still, the Battle of the Coral Sea was Yamamoto's clue that it was time to proceed more carefully—to make sure that his operational plan was designed to achieve its objective. At the Battle of Midway the foremost objective was, or should have been, to draw the American fleet into a battle that it would have to come out and fight. To split off two small carriers for the Aleutian Islands operation was a mistake. The strategy to extend the Japanese defensive perimeter had stretched tactical capabilities too thin. It was time for tactics to counsel strategy, and tactics said that the Japanese navy had too many objectives.

Although we are not likely to see the Pacific war over island air bases reproduced, we can anticipate the recurring tactical problem that a commander with superior forces faces when pitted against enemies who know their own inferiority and decline battle. When mounting an attack on a land target is the decided-upon way of drawing out an inferior enemy, it is too easy for planners to permit the land attack to become the end itself and to forget that the attack is but the means to a greater end—in this instance that of destroying the enemy's seagoing forces.

Summary

In World War II aircraft became the chief naval weapon during daylight hours because of their effective range and their integral capacity for scouting, providing guidance to their target, and coordination. Not just any type of aircraft could do the job, and—considering the high combat-loss rates—not just any pilots.

The polarized overestimates and underestimates of air-strike effectiveness against warships that were made before the war led to unexpected tactical results during the war. Combat leaders, who by then had hard evidence that aircraft were effective against ships in daylight, had to learn the limits of the effectiveness—which was never more than sinking an average of one carrier for each air-wing attack—and change their tactics accordingly.

Meanwhile, as the war progressed, the balance that favored air offense at the outset shifted back in favor of ship defense—a development that also bore important tactical significance. It boiled down to a central tactical issue. If one carrier could sink two or three in an effective attack against any defense, there was no point in massing two or three carriers, which might be located together and sunk. If, however, it took two or more carriers—or repeated carrier strikes—to sink one carrier, then it was essential to *concentrate* sufficient striking force. (It was only necessary to *mass* forces if separate carrier task forces could not be coordinated by command-and-control).

As time went on, a third trend emerged in which the defensive firepower of two or more carriers operating in proximity could be massed to great effect. Concentration of force for offensive action became an automatic side-benefit and the problem of coordinating separated forces disappeared. It was *defensive* considerations that drove the decision to mass and in turn eliminated the need for stealth, deception, and divided forces.

The Japanese *had* to attack effectively first. A simultaneous exchange of attacks with similar losses on both sides would ruin them in the long run because they could not afford to exchange carriers on a one-for-one basis. They had to attempt stealth, deception, and divided forces as a calculated risk. They gambled, likely even believed, that one carrier could sink two. Even though they were wrong, it was still a good gamble at the beginning of 1942; by the end of 1942, it was a very bad gamble.

There were many reasons for the resurgence of defense. True, AAW guns alone could have been enough to cause it, but the final and decisive factors responsible for the success of American defense were two factors that the Japanese could not possibly fold into their early planning—radar and cryptanalysis. Except in the Battle of Britain, nowhere was radar more quickly put to decisive use than in the Pacific carrier battles. Cryptanalysis for its part almost eliminated the chance of the Japanese achieving surprise. Stealth and deception were foredoomed. Under the circumstances the Japanese might as well have massed their forces and taken their chances—especially in 1942, when they had numerical superiority and qualitative equality. By 1944 nothing they could do mattered. The Japanese would have less and less to show for their efforts, whether they were expended against a conservative enemy such as Spruance off the Marianas or a rash enemy like Halsey at Leyte Gulf. U.S. defensive strength ensured that the American fleet would survive long enough to counterattack, and U.S. offensive advantage ensured that the Japanese would lose the war at sea.

5

WORLD WAR II:
THE REVOLUTION
IN SENSORS

Scouting Measures and Countermeasures

Many of the postmortems of World War II have been more taken with the sensors that revolutionized naval combat than the weapons that were used in waging the war—including the airplane. Yet, focusing on sensors, weapons, or tactics in isolation is artificial; the battles were decided by all three together. The first step in analyzing how the new sensors affected tactics and weapon performance during the war is to establish a framework for discussion. Then look at radar as the most valuable of the new scouting devices. The nighttime surface combat of 1942 and 1943 in the Solomons campaign illustrates graphically the tactical potential of radar and the way the American cruisers and destroyers that fought those action-packed battles failed to take full advantage of it. Almost as important in World War II was the rise of communications intelligence. An examination of the way sensors were used in the submarine war in the Atlantic shows the great extent to which the information war was the decisive element in the defeat of the German U-boat. The recent declassification of the many closely held accounts of code-breaking in World War II enables us to grasp the full significance of cryptology as an element of scouting measures and countermeasures.

The sensor war was a duel. As the reach of weapons increased, electromagnetic science raced to stay abreast, inventing the means of detecting and communicating at long range. Concurrently, scientists were working on developing countermeasures to thwart the new electromagnetic technology. It is useful to think of the signals put out by these electromagnetic systems as measures that contributed to force effectiveness in one of two ways—scouting, or aiding in the detection, tracking, and targeting of the enemy; or controlling, to improve a commander's ability to execute battle plans. At the same time, the force was trying to use the new technology to diminish the effectiveness of the enemy's scouting and control systems.

One common way to categorize these countermeasures is to sort them according to the purpose for which they are used—as techniques for destroying, disrupting, deceiving, denying, or exploiting enemy signals. The possible actions, by no means exhaustive, have been laid out in table 5-1.

Table 5-1 is a static display. It gives no sense of pace or timing of signals exploitation, of buying time or of intruding in the timing and coordination of enemy action. Except subconsciously, warfighters do not deliberately think in the destroy, disrupt, deceive, deny, exploit framework, but rather leap at once to the possibilities of manipulating their own and the enemy's specific equipment and command structure. A more useful way to visualize signals exploitation is first to lay out the sequence of measures that must be taken for a fully effective attack, as table 5-2 does.

Evidently some scouting systems can perform more than one step. A surveillance-communications satellite could perform measures A, B1, B2, and B3. One of the advantages of aircraft has been that they can perform the tracking, targeting, attacking, and damage assessment functions in a single flight. By way of contrast, external scouting for surface-to-surface missiles must perform functions A, B1, and B2 before an attack. To ensure full effectiveness, thorough scouting may be necessary. To be sure of hitting the enemy's carrier or carriers, the attacker may need to know with precision both the enemy's position and formation. In addition, the attacker will need to know whether the enemy has cruise missiles of its own, located on ships other than carriers, that can be used in a punishing counterattack.

In principle, a single countermeasure anywhere can break the chain of measures necessary for an attack. A successful countermeasure can defeat, delay, or reduce the effectiveness of the attack by any break in the chain. This book will not discuss such measures and countermeasures in detail. Suffice it to say that each side strives to maintain the chain from A to C with some combination of redundancy, cover, covertness, cryptology, and sheer electromagnetic power while attempting to break the other's chain decisively at its weakest link. The sensor war aims to shorten the time it takes to complete one's own chain, and it aims to lengthen the enemy's time.

A modified table of measures, 5-3, emphasizes the relative consequences of a successful countermeasure.

Table 5-1. Countermeasures against Enemy Signal

| | Enemy Signal Function | |
	Scouting (e.g., radar)	*Controlling (e.g., radio)*
Destroy	Attack it	Attack it[a]
Disrupt	Jam it	Jam it[b]
Deceive	Provide false targets	Provide false targets[c]
Deny	Avoid the sensors[d]	Use covert transmission[e]
Exploit	Counterdetect enemy	Monitor enemy's traffic[f]

[a] In ships at sea, attacking the weapon system also usually meant attacking the signal system. From this derives the current interest in offboard command, satellites, land-based over-the-horizon radar, and other approaches, all of which complicate tactics.

[b] Jamming a scouting system usually buys range. Jamming a controlling system usually buys time. Either translates into a sought-after positional advantage.

[c] Deception also can be used against enemy weapons. Prominent examples include chaff used against missiles and noisemakers against homing torpedoes.

[d] Submarines challenge visual, radar, and infrared detection and sometimes, through quietness, passive sonar detection.

[e] There is asymmetry here, because covert signals like low-probability-of-intercept (LPI) radio transmissions are measures to confound major enemy countermeasures, namely, intercept and exploitation.

[f] Exploitation may be the most important component of this table, considering the strong possibility that the enemy will detect a scouting system before the scouting system detects the enemy. And radio transmissions may be heard and decrypted. In addition, the threat of counter-countermeasures enters in when the enemy suspects his traffic is being listened to. In that case, he can plant misinformation, taking due care to avoid self-deception. While there is a long history of strategic deception with assorted agents and double agents of espionage to do the communicating, this is not our concern. For an excellent and rigorous study of this subject, see Daniel and Herbig's *Strategic Military Deception*.

Table 5-2. Measures Required for Effective Attack

Strategic detection (A)	Observation of major enemy force presence or future presence in a region
Tactical detection (B1)	Location of the enemy for the purpose of attacking him
Tracking (B2)	Knowledge of enemy position sufficient to launch a successful attack
Targeting (B3)	Determination of enemy dispositions in detail sufficient to attack with maximum effectiveness
Attacking (B4)	Control of a coordinated, concentrated attack
Damage assessment (C)	Post-attack evaluation of the results

Observe that the countermeasure called exploitation has no place in table 5-3. That is because its effect is different from that of destruction, disruption, deception, or denial. Exploitation enhances one or more of the measures B1, B2, B3, and B4, which permits one's own attack. Exploitation has its own dynamics and fits into the tactical picture in a way best shown in the force-on-force model of modern warfare described in chapter 13.

To see the various roles played by the new sensors in World War II as well as the information war that they fostered, it is worth reviewing the dynamic processes that propelled signals warfare into prominence during those years.

Radar

Radar and radar countermeasures were the most important of the sensory tools that came of age in World War II. This category also includes the proximity fuze—a tiny, shock-resistant radar that significantly improved the effectiveness of weapons of many kinds. Used in shells fired against aircraft by a 5-inch, dual-purpose gun, the proximity fuze not only increased the allowable fire-control dispersion error by two or three times, it also simplified a three-dimensional fire-control problem by effectively turning the target area into a two-dimensional challenge.

The possibility of using pulsed radio waves to detect ships and aircraft occurred to scientists well before World War II. Several countries had secret research under way in the 1930s. Britain established the first five radar stations, on the east coast of England, in December 1935. Although radar was indispensable in the aerial Battle of Britain, it was not a secret weapon, unsuspected by the enemy, as cryptanalysis was then. Radar and radar countermeasures were part of a fast-paced technological race drawing on vast scientific resources, and all players quickly understood its significance. The radiation laboratory at the Massachusetts

Table 5-3. Effect of Successful Countermeasures

Strategic detection	(A)				Broad, general effect	Longest-lasting effect
		Time available to initiate countermeasures is shorter	Success of countermeasures is more quickly manifested	More precision of countermeasures timing is required		
Tactical detection	(B1)					
Tracking	(B2)				↓	↓
Targeting	(B3)				Specific immediate effect	Most transitory effect
Attacking	(B4)	↓	↓	↓		

Institute of Technology, for example, increased its hiring a hundredfold—from forty to four thousand—to accommodate research in the new field of technology.[1]

As a tool of war, radar was ubiquitous. By the end of 1939 shipboard prototypes were being tested for long-range aircraft detection, antiaircraft fire control, and surface tracking. British and American collaboration produced a series of remarkable breakthroughs beginning in 1940. Centimeter-wavelength radars were ready for production in 1942, offering sufficient definition to be used for detection of single aircraft, for fighter direction, day or night, and for accurate gun-laying for both surface and AAW targets. By 1943 radar had been fitted in enough reconnaissance aircraft to have a major influence on search-and-attack missions against surface ships, and in enough antisubmarine patrol aircraft to reverse the momentum of the U-boat campaign in the Atlantic. From 1940 on, radar was vital to fighter defenses over land, and it was the key to the effectiveness of the offensive fighter and bomber sweeps before the Normandy invasion. For antiaircraft defenses, radar was just as important over land as at sea.

Radar quickly became an indispensable navigating tool as well. It permitted high-speed surface operations in narrow seas, and it came to be relied upon so much that when a ship lost her radar at night she was literally and psychologically lost. As a direct instrument of war, in 1943 radar began helping guide bombers to their targets over Germany. Loran was used to aid ship and aircraft navigation everywhere that operations were intense. Radar was developed in the United States, Britain, Germany, France, and Japan. As aircraft operations, both offensive and defensive, became dependent upon the new technology, measures designed to counter radar acquired the highest tactical significance. The first great sensor war occurred in the air over Europe. World War II—specifically, from the Battle of Britain through 1945—offers the best case-study of the measures, countermeasures, and counter-countermeasures undertaken in scouting and weapon-delivery. The Battle of Britain is better for study than the Vietnam War because analysts have been denied access to documents that would accurately describe North Vietnam's tactical situation.

Radar gave the United States a big edge in the air over the Pacific. At the Battle of the Eastern Solomons in 1942, U.S. air search radar detected the approaching Japanese at eighty-eight miles—far enough out that American forces could scramble fifty-three fighters, the works, all with full fuel tanks. Radar gave U.S. admirals time to put interceptors in the air after the raid was detected; all fighters were vectored to the attack aircraft without fear of surprise from another quarter.

---

1   Brodie and Brodie, p. 209.

Because the Japanese were slow to develop radar, the U.S. Fleet had an unparalleled opportunity to exploit its surface-search advantage well into 1943. Indeed, U.S. naval forces were technologically well ahead of the Japanese fleet until the end of the war. In the Solomons, long-range patrol aircraft and coast-watchers gave the United States early warning of the approach of almost all Japanese aircraft and warships. (Cryptanalysis played no significant role in this strategic detection, since Japanese naval codes had just been changed.)

Because Japanese surface warships had to be well clear of U.S. air cover by daylight, the United States knew within a few hours when they would arrive. In eleven major engagements from August 1942 to November 1943, radar provided the United States with the means to detect, track, and target an approaching surface force and blast it out of the water with guns and torpedoes before it was aware of the American presence. Even so, the Navy still had not fully recognized that radar offered unparalleled opportunities and that the fleet would need to develop new tactics to take full advantage of them. There was a second problem that American tactical commanders had to solve. The Japanese also had a secret weapon—the Long Lance, a highly lethal long-range torpedo.

Night Surface Actions in the Solomons

The tactics used in night battles were a competition between these two new tools of war—American radar and the Japanese Long Lance. In five battles from August to November 1942 Japanese preparations paid off. The Imperial Navy had developed a coherent system of night tactics well before the war and had practiced it assiduously. Night action was part of Japan's pre-war recipe of equalizers designed to whittle down the U.S. Fleet before a conclusive battle-line engagement. U.S. Navy practice before the war had concentrated on daylight fleet engagements built on the column of capital ships. The American tactical concept was to seek a position that would facilitate—or at least not hinder—crossing the enemy's T. But American tactical training proved counterproductive in the Solomons.

Strategically the Solomons campaign was a contest over airfields on land and over flight decks at sea and for control of the air space around them. For the first six months, from August 1942 to January 1943, the campaign centered on Guadalcanal. In daylight the United States controlled the air around Henderson Field. The Japanese had the same advantage around Rabaul, New Britain, six hundred miles to the northwest. But when the sun set, airpower lost its grip, and surface combatants met and fought once more. Every night the Japanese threatened to rush warships south through the narrow waters of the Slot between the dual island chains that constituted the Solomons. To the Americans, the enemy warships were the fearsome "Tokyo Express," which was bent on delivering reinforcements to Guadalcanal or carrying a brutal gunnery bombardment to Henderson Field. Whenever American warships tried to stop the Japanese, the result was a lethal surface battle in the blackness of night.

In naval duels one side or the other almost always has the complicating problem of a beachhead or a convoy to protect. Every night battle in the Solomons was fought over some objective on land. In the first of these clashes, at Savo Island, the United States was defending the beachhead at Guadalcanal. In the next-to-last, at Empress Augusta Bay, it was defending Bougainville. In the battles between those two, the Japanese had the enduring problem of fighting an engagement while trying to reinforce or withdraw a garrison in the Solomons. Two carrier battles, those of the Eastern Solomons and the Santa Cruz Islands, were tied completely to events on Guadalcanal. The flawed strategy of piecemeal commitment of force in the Solomons gave Japanese tactical commanders the harder task. Keeping reinforcements flowing to sites where ships could not stay was difficult, because Japanese warships could only move for a few hours around midnight. It was a sharp disadvantage that American tacticians too long failed to exploit.

Despite their handicaps, the Japanese did well in the early battles, from August 1942 to July 1943. There were several reasons—the United States failed to grasp that the killing weapon was the torpedo; it had no tactics suitable for night battle at close quarters; it was slow to learn—and because of the rapid turnover of tactical leaders, the pace of the battles overwhelmed the Americans. Above all, the United States did not exploit its potentially decisive radar advantage, which combined both the edge in the first-detection and tracking capabilities that surface-search radar provided and in the targeting that fire-control radar provided. Although not all ships had both advantages from the start, the existing radar equipment should have been better utilized.

The U.S. Navy suffered from these shortcomings from August 1942 to July 1943. From August 1943 to the end of the surface fighting in the Solomons area in November 1943 it finally took advantage of the latent potential of radar, using new and compatible tactics.

Phase One, August 1942–July 1943

From the outset, Japanese tactics usually called for approaching in short, multiple columns, getting all ships into action at once, and maneuvering in defense against torpedoes. Sometimes destroyers would be positioned ahead as pickets to avoid ambush. When the pickets detected an enemy force, they would close, pivot, fire torpedoes, and turn away. Sometimes they would not fire their guns at all.

The U.S. tactic was to use a long, single, tightly spaced column. The Navy expected and achieved first detection and tried to position its columns so that all guns would bear across the enemy's axis of approach, crossing its T. A range of ten thousand yards would be safe from torpedoes and perfect for guns, it was thought, and if the enemy held to a steady column, the battle would be settled by guns before torpedoes entered the picture—a conjectured effective range of less than five thousand yards. The range closed too fast, however, the Japanese would not stand still, and their torpedoes were devastating.

At first, U.S. tactical commanders failed to appreciate the full danger of the threat from Japanese torpedoes. They operated from flagships that were not equipped with radar, commands were vague or tardy, and the battles were fought at point-blank range, sometimes in great disorder. The Americans eventually learned to respect the deadly effectiveness of a massive torpedo barrage against a long, tightly spaced column, but because the actions were closer than they wanted or expected they didn't grasp the fact that the Long Lance in barrage was effective at ranges equal to the effective range of cruiser and destroyer guns.[2]

The Battle of Cape Esperance, fought at the northern point of Guadalcanal on the night of 11–12 October 1942, marked the first time since the debacle of Savo Island five weeks earlier that the United States was able to put together a force to take on the Tokyo Express. It illustrates the phase-one tactics of both sides and the tempo of these actions. The United States had a nine-ship column capping the Japanese T, crossing ahead of an approaching force of three cruisers and two destroyers in "perfect" position. The four American cruisers were spaced at six hundred yards between ships, and the five destroyers were deployed at five hundred yards apart. The light cruisers USS *Helena* (CL 50) and USS *Boise* (CL 47)

---

2 A quick example of torpedo fire: Japanese spreads were thrown in the general direction of U.S. gun flashes (sometimes searchlights). A column of eight ships was about four thousand yards long. At a distance of four thousand to eight thousand yards, the torpedo spread was more than likely to be inside the end points of the target column. Ships were more than one hundred yards long and spaced at five hundred to six hundred yards, so about one weapon in six would hit. With as many as thirty torpedoes in the water, unseen and unsuspected, the results could be lethal, especially since one hit on a cruiser or destroyer almost always achieved a firepower kill. McKearney's study (1985) found that the average torpedo firing range over the entire campaign was 8,500 yards, which made the running range on the order of 7,000 to 7,500 yards (p. 154). He concluded that the average hit probability for all engagements was .06, but at the battles of Tassafaronga and Kula Gulf torpedo hit-probabilities approached .20 (compiled from appendix A, pp. 188–246). Not all U.S. columns were as long as eight ships, not all torpedoes would have been reliable, and toward the end of the campaign the Americans learned to comb the tracks, so his numbers corroborate the theoretical estimate.

had their SG surface-search radars on. In the USS *San Francisco* (CA 38), the flagship of ADM Norman Scott, USN, the radar had been turned off because it was an older model with a longer wavelength that was vulnerable to Japanese intercept. Figure 5-1 shows the speed of events as the battle unfolds.

2325   The *Helena* detects at fourteen nautical miles. Spotting planes are in the air, but are ineffective. The *Helena's* captain ponders, but reports nothing. Seven minutes elapse.

2332   Admiral Scott reverses course for tactical reasons that are sound only because he is unaware of the enemy closing at almost half a mile a minute. But his ambiguous signal results in a maneuver that puts the three lead destroyers directly on the engaged side of his cruisers, racing to regain their van position. Ten minutes elapse.

2342   The commanding officer of the *Helena* reports the enemy at six miles directly on the starboard beam, a position ideal for gunfire except that, without radar, Scott can't see his three destroyers. Scott, in a quandary, asks the destroyer division commander where his destroyers are. The commander, CAPT Robert G. Tobin, USN, says he is dead on the starboard beams of the cruisers, right in the middle. He is correct about only two of his destroyers, because the third, the USS *Duncan* (DD 485), is not astern. Having seen the enemy on radar at four miles, and believing that Tobin is charging them, the *Duncan's* crew is headed toward the enemy and is now in the middle of no-man's-land. Three minutes elapse.

2345   The five Japanese ships, still oblivious to their danger, are at two-and-a-half miles and visible in the *Helena*, whose crew, having detected the enemy on radar, knows where to look. The captain asks permission to open fire. The signal is ambiguous. Admiral Scott thinks the *Helena* is asking whether Scott is acknowledging another voice-radio transmission.[3] Scott says "affirmative," and is shocked to see the Helena open up with fifteen 6-inch and four 5-inch guns. One minute elapses.

2346   The Japanese are even more stunned than Scott. Until that instant they had been oblivious to the presence of U.S. ships, and they were now as vulnerable as U.S. ships had been at Savo. They corpen-18 away and for once fail to fire torpedoes.[4] The range is two miles, point-blank. One minute elapses.

---

3   Interrogatory Roger was the ambiguous signal book query.
4   A corpen is a follow-the-leader maneuver. Corpen-18 means to reverse course by turning in succession 180 degrees to starboard.

2347   Scott orders check-fire, even as all ships but his own flagship open up.
        The order is for good reason because the *Duncan* and the USS *Farenholt*
        (DD 491) are in line of fire and will show American 6- and 5-inch shell
        holes on their port sides after the battle. Four minutes elapse.

2351   Scott orders resume-fire, but most ships had never stopped. His ships
        have no fire-distribution plan and concentrate on what they can see—
        two already crippled destroyers ablaze. Gunfire distribution is a problem
        that will never be solved.

The Japanese fled, and no one seems to have suggested a hot pursuit. Four U.S.
cruisers and five destroyers had totally surprised three enemy cruisers and two
destroyers. The United States sank or damaged two destroyers and one cruiser
and saw two of its own destroyers and one cruiser sunk or crippled. Much of the
damage was self-inflicted. Before the *Duncan* sank, sailors on nearby ships could
see the hits made in her hull and superstructure by U.S. gunfire.

The U.S. Navy counted Cape Esperance a victory, but given the U.S. firepower potential and advantage of initiative, it should have been an annihilation.
In those early days of the sensory revolution, the Americans used radar, radios,
electronic countermeasures (ECM), and the signal book ineptly. At Cape Esperance they did not fire a torpedo. After that, the enemy was never caught so unprepared, so unready to counterattack, or so lightly loaded with its killer weapon, the
Long Lance torpedo.

The United States was using pickup forces in many of these engagements.
Naval historian Samuel Eliot Morison said the force had no battle plan, but in fact
the gun-column deployment *was* the plan. There was no sense of pace in the decisions made between first radar detection and the time for attack. What was worse,
because Cape Esperance was counted as an apparent victory, it seduced the United
States into using the same tactics at Tassafaronga and later battles.

Six weeks later, the Battle of Tassafaronga exposed all the U.S. shortcomings—the
scratch team, the inexperienced leadership, and the obsolete, tightly spaced single
column. The U.S. force once again enjoyed an overwhelming force of five cruisers
and six destroyers against eight Japanese destroyers, six of which were laden with
supplies, and they achieved total surprise, detecting the enemy by radar in ample
time. The Americans opened with radar fire control at the ideal eight thousand
to ten thousand yards, but because of an inadequate sense of timing, their torpedo fire was held too long, and the U.S. captains held course, thinking they
were out of enemy torpedo range. This time, however, they faced the redoubtable

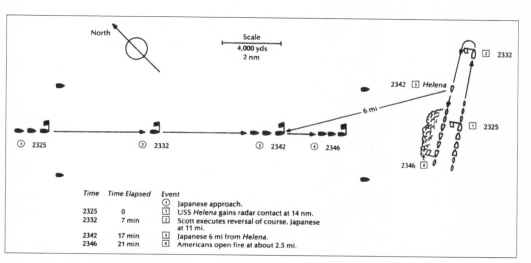

Figure 5-1. Tempo of the Battle of Cape Esperance

Rear Admiral Raizo Tanaka, who had been drilling destroyer teams since 1941. His destroyers were trained to wheel and fire their Long Lance torpedoes when surprised. They did, and as a result four of the five U.S. cruisers were sunk or damaged; Tanaka lost only a picket destroyer. The U.S. commander was RADM Carleton H. Wright, USN, but the plan was not his; he had relieved someone else two days before the battle. When it was over, Nimitz said the lesson of the battle was "training, training, and TRAINING," but the tactical lessons still slipped through American fingers.

Phase Two, July–November 1943

It was a full year after Savo Island and three battles later that the U.S. Navy got it right. The Japanese continued to operate as before, but they did so more proficiently and with better scouting. They used night air reconnaissance, radar electronic countermeasures (ECM), and rudimentary radar. U.S. forces would now be taking on a tougher enemy, but they also would be fighting more skillfully themselves. First, they now had properly trained units. Second, they had finally adopted sound tactics. Torpedoes would be fired by small, compact divisions of three or four destroyers. Two divisions would be sent in; one would fire and turn away; then the other would fire; then both would mop up with gunfire. When cruisers were present, they were to be kept at a distance of more than ten thousand yards, for fear of becoming targets for the deadly Japanese torpedoes. But it was best to let the destroyers do the damage: they had the most effective killing weapons.

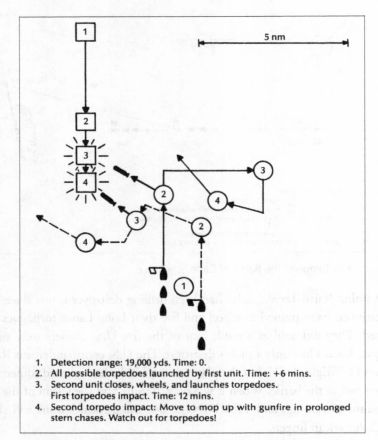

1. Detection range: 19,000 yds. Time: 0.
2. All possible torpedoes launched by first unit. Time: +6 mins.
3. Second unit closes, wheels, and launches torpedoes.
   First torpedoes impact. Time: 12 mins.
4. Second torpedo impact: Move to mop up with gunfire in prolonged
   stern chases. Watch out for torpedoes!

Figure 5-2. The Battle of Vella Gulf, 6–7 August 1942

It was at the Battle of Vella Gulf on 6 August–7 August 1943 that U.S. tactics came together. The Navy had its usual advance knowledge about a Japanese reinforcement mission. This time destroyers alone were sent hunting, and CDR Frederick Moosbrugger, USN, had the mission, the firepower, the scouting advantage, and the tactics to fuse all three. According to naval historian E. B. Potter, Commander Moosbrugger used the battle plan developed by then-commander Arleigh Burke.[5] The plan, illustrated by the scheme in figure 5-2, has Burke's flair. There were two units of three destroyers each, all well-drilled and tactically disposed to stay out of each other's way with the help of radar. They would maneuver with lightning precision. The first division, under Moosbrugger, carried forty-four torpedoes, and it would fire as many of them as possible. The second triplet of

5 Potter, p. 313.

destroyers, under CDR Rodger W. Simpson, which was heavier in AAW batteries, carried only twenty-four torpedoes. Both divisions would move in, their bows to the enemy torpedo threat, wheel around, and launch their fish. As with Japanese tactics, all this would be done stealthily, without gunfire. After the shock of the torpedo barrage was over, gunfire and aggressiveness could be used in proportion to the damage done, but at that stage the destroyers would have to watch out for the death-sting of the now alerted enemy.

On the night of 6 August tropical rain beclouded the SG radars of Moosbrugger's short twin columns. The islands around Kolombangara and Vella Lavella confused the radar returns and presented the usual complications of a military operation. Having been spotted earlier by an American night-search plane, the Japanese were on the alert for a U.S. force. Their mission was to reinforce the Kolombangara garrison. They had four destroyer transports, a two-to-three disadvantage. Yet, those were odds they had beaten before.[6]

Moosbrugger's force detected the Japanese at 19,000 yards. Every ship was notified at once. Moosbrugger shifted course right 30 degrees by twin corpens to hit the four enemy destroyers port-to-port. Gun and torpedo fire-control solutions were cranked in as the unseeing enemy cooperated with steady course and speed. Just seven minutes later the range was four miles. With lookouts estimating the visibility at two miles in the blackness of night, it was time to act. Moosbrugger gave the order to fire, simple and unambiguous, setting all the tactical flywheels of his semiautomatic plan churning in sync. The portside torpedoes twenty-four in all—hit the water from three ships. The firing range was just 6,300 yards for a running range of 4,000 yards—as good a setup as could be expected, and all one could ask for. A minute later, a "turn nine" order came from Moosbrugger. His division executed a simultaneous 90-degree turn to starboard to clear out, combing the wakes of the predictable enemy torpedo counterattack. At the same time, Simpson wheeled his three destroyers to port and bored in.

The men in three Japanese destroyers scarcely knew what hit them. On the U.S. side there was tension aplenty to grip the Americans, who could well remember the chagrin of earlier battles lost during what should have been the mop-up phase. But not that night. As in all good naval battles, the outcome was determined by the adoption of a feasible plan whose tactical cohesion came from training, good scouting, and the swift thrust of a killer weapon. Three of the four Japanese ships were sunk, while the cost to the American side was a gun-loader

---

6 However, neither side had very accurate estimates before that battle or any other.

suffering a crushed hand. Like Nelson, Moosbrugger made implementing sound tactics look easy. At last, the U.S. Navy had found the tactics to match its radar advantage and neutralize the enemy's edge in torpedoes.

They could now beat the Japanese with torpedoes—their adversary's superior weapon. Good sensors, tactics, and scouting could overcome better firepower. And the United States would win with small ships because the destroyers carried the big weapon. It was the destroyers' torpedoes—not the cruisers' guns—that ruled at night. Hit-and-move was the answer, not crossing the T; units had to be nimble rather than fixed in a sturdy, steady, cohesive—and suicidal—column.

There would be a setback at the Battle of Vella Lavella on 6 October–7 October 1943. It was another case of an unbloodied commander with a scratch force—three U.S. destroyers, instead of the optimal six, facing six Japanese destroyers, instead of the normal nine. Despite the disadvantage, the American commander, CAPT Frank R. Walker, USN, chose to go in with his three ships rather than wait for three more to join him from ten miles away. He had the usual radar advantage, fired fourteen torpedoes at seven thousand yards, and then gave the game away by opening up with guns while his torpedoes were still running. Staying broadside to the enemy, his three destroyers paid the penalty: two of them were torpedoed and the third collided with one of the victims. Three destroyers were put out of action in exchange for one Japanese destroyer sunk—the one that turned *into* the U.S. torpedoes instead of away from them.

But then came the masterful battles of Empress Augusta Bay and Cape St. George, fought by tacticians *par excellence*—RADM A. Stanton "Tip" Merrill, USN, and then-captain Burke. It is not necessary to recount all the details. The confrontation at Empress Augusta Bay (2 November 1943) looks less decisive in the box-score than it was in fact: U.S. forces sank a Japanese light cruiser and a destroyer, and a heavy cruiser was damaged in a collision; one U.S. destroyer was damaged. Merrill's mission was to defend the landing beach on Bougainville. His force of four light cruisers and eight destroyers was pitted against an enemy that consisted of two heavy cruisers and eight light cruisers and destroyers. On paper these were equal forces. The tactical plan was for Merrill to keep his cruisers at longer range, about 16,000 yards, executing 180-degree turns timed to upset Jap-anese torpedo-fire-control solutions, while staying between the enemy's heavy cruisers and the beachhead. To do all of this at once he had to sacrifice gunnery effectiveness, a small penalty because closer in his 6-inch guns could not fire for long enough to be effective before they were put out of action by the Long Lance. The destroyers, four under Burke at the head of the column and four astern under

CAPT Bernard L. Austin, USN, would be the untethered mad dogs, charging in and inflicting the torpedo damage.

The three separated formations lost control, so the results were mixed. Some of Burke's four ships scattered, and he had to mill around bringing them back into formation, at one point firing 5-inch guns at Austin. Merrill kept his four light cruisers under tight rein and away from the danger of torpedoes. His ships smothered the enemy with shells and occupied its attention while the destroyers made their charge, doing what moderate damage they could. The American attack so bewildered the Japanese that they turned and got out, abandoning their mission. In the battle the Japanese ships were almost completely ineffective. The U.S. force had learned to survive by lightness of foot. Its gunfire was not much—Morison estimated that it achieved only twenty 6-inch hits out of 4,600 rounds expended. Night-spotting of gunfire proved to be terribly difficult; the Japanese later said the Americans were consistently off in deflection. Merrill wisely declined to pursue the Japanese force because dawn was coming and this time, for a change, it was the Americans who would be subjected to land-based air attack, from Rabaul.

At the Battle of Cape St. George, on 25 November 1943, Burke had the chance to use his signature tactic of hitting with the left and following with the right. He had five destroyers split into units of three and two, supporting one another five thousand yards apart. His nominally equal enemy had two new destroyers escorting three destroyer transports, which were trailing 13,000 yards (a twenty-minute run) behind. The Japanese commander did not have his radar on, and his second force was effectively a protected group, not a mutually supporting one. Against Burke's force that was fatal. Burke detected the enemy on radar at eleven nautical miles and adjusted course. Fifteen minutes later, at three nautical miles, his three destroyers launched fifteen torpedoes—undetected—mortally wounding both lead destroyers. Burke then took after the three destroyer transports. With their bows to the enemy, his ships evaded a mess of torpedoes in a two-hour stern chase and ended up sinking one destroyer. It is fitting that the man who had conceived Moosbrugger's tactics could finish the Solomons night actions with his own little tactical masterpiece.

The Solomons: A Conclusion

How then to recapitulate a year and a half of night actions, eleven of which were designated battles? Radar was the new sensor; it had to be integrated tactically, and nighttime provided a magnificent opportunity for doing that; black night was radar's element, and it should have given the United States a decisive advantage.

In the conditions under which these battles were fought, crossing the T meant very little. The best tactic was to approach on a broad front, bows on (short columns abreast in practice), wheel anywhere within range and fire a barrage of two or three dozen torpedoes, then point all sterns toward the enemy's reply. One of the American errors was to forget that combat is two-sided competition. Line tactics were based on the strength of the broadside, which nominally had twice the firepower that could be unleashed end-on. Line tactics overlooked the fact that a beams-to column exposed ten times as much hull to torpedoes as a line abreast pointed toward or away from the enemy. In force-on-force computations, by using the line-ahead formation the U.S. Navy imposed a fivefold penalty on itself.

There was a no-man's-land of at least five miles in which no cruiser belonged. Experience had shown that with a torpedo barrage a handful of small ships could destroy a force that was larger and superior in killing power, at least by conventional reckoning. Somewhere in the Valhalla of warriors, Jellicoe must have looked down on those dark nights punctured with the violence of the torpedo and with a thin smile, shaking his head at the Americans who took so long to learn what he knew in 1916.

In the early battles the United States had been foredoomed by deploying pickup forces, thrown together and untrained, using the only tactics that surface officers had practiced—those of the fighting column. Perhaps at first they were the only tactics the Americans were capable of executing in the face of both the Japanese threat and the hazards of steaming at high speed in darkness and mostly uncharted shoal waters.

Still, the impression remains that the early tactical commanders did not know better—did not grasp the importance of their radars and the dangers of a long column. Particularly in the early battles, they seem not to have had the sense of pace to keep control while the opposing forces were closing at speeds of a mile a minute. Tactical commanders sometimes drove their van destroyers until they were in danger of colliding with the enemy before directing them to open fire. The Japanese never had that problem. As soon as they spotted an enemy, they pivoted and launched their spread of torpedoes. Their tactics were coherent. Before the war they built torpedoes into their cruisers, while the Americans took them out in the belief that all modern battles would be settled by guns outside of torpedo range.

From the outset, the Japanese tactical commander was up front, usually in the lead ship, in the fashion of the great Admiral Togo. The American commander, in his cruiser flagship, was far back in his single column—indeed, in two of these battles the flagship was sixth in line. When fast action was required, maneuvering from the middle of the column was ineffective. The mess at Cape Esperance illustrates the kind of problem that resulted. Placing the American flagship in the middle was a consequence of a loss of tactical good sense—an example of tradition reigning over an appreciation of new tactical circumstances. In the last five battles of 1943, including Empress Augusta Bay after Merrill turned his destroyers loose, the American tactical commanders were at the head of the formation, and the results were salutary. The Japanese had practiced their night tactics in peacetime and knew how to fight from the beginning. To the Americans, it became evident only through hindsight.

Reflecting on the details of these battles, it may seem as though each American commander improved by learning on the job and training his units accordingly. It is true that the intense operations in the Slot helped to school and steel leaders and their crews in 1943. And focusing solely on the major battles misses the fact that ships were out night after night, patrolling, stalking, engaging in shore bombardment. Yet, with one exception we cannot find an American tactical commander who fought *two* night battles and improved. This is a commentary on the rapid turnover of ships and staffs. Already noted were the cases of Wright and Moosbrugger, who took command within forty-eight hours of battle. ADM William F. Halsey, USN, as commander in the South Pacific, never let pass an opportunity to fight, and was always scratching for ships, especially destroyers. No officer ever led more than two battles or commanded exactly the same set of ships. The single officer who fought two battles and improved was Arleigh Burke, and even he was not in overall command at Empress Augusta Bay. We may wonder how it might have been if Burke or Merrill had fought as many battles as Nelson. Burke would have been the best prospect against a tactician whom he never had the chance to fight—the redoubtable Japanese wizard, the tenacious Admiral Tanaka.[7]

Old ideas of massing force came into question in the Solomons. A smaller force had the firepower at the prevalent short ranges to smash a larger force and survive. Americans had to hold in abeyance the commonplace principle of victory by superior concentration of offensive force. No doubt, naval leaders will again see circumstances in which the wisdom of the Solomons prevails—when small ships armed with many missiles have the firepower to take out more than their weight of opposing force.

---

7 In fairness it must be pointed out that the Japanese also fought with cruisers and destroyers that had *not* operated together. But doctrinal integrity and much practice in night operations kept them cohesive.

It is appropriate to conclude this section with an observation on strategy, specifically the strategic significance of the tactics in the Solomons. There appears to have been a tendency on the part of the Japanese to abandon winning positions—at Pearl Harbor, Coral Sea, Savo Island, Samar, for example—and stubbornly to pursue losing causes, such as the whole of the Guadalcanal campaign, Tanaka's dauntless reinforcement of Guadalcanal, and the Battle of the Philippine Sea. The successful Japanese night tactics in 1942 were hit-and-run.[8] The successful American tactics in 1943 were hit-and-duck and hit again. American forces were sometimes punished because it was ingrained in them to stay when they came. Yet, what was costly tactically may have paid off strategically in the end.

Radar and Air Defense

There is a coda to the Battle of Empress Augusta Bay that says much about the ability of the U.S. surface fleet in 1943 to defend against air attack with radar. After the battle, Merrill was well within striking range of the great Rabaul base, and knew he would see a full-scale Japanese air attack in the morning, mirroring the American air attacks on the withdrawing Tokyo Express that were launched from Henderson Field during the Guadalcanal campaign.

Merrill gathered up his four light cruisers and four of his destroyers in their tight AAW wagon-wheel. The attack came, one hundred strong, and if there was ever evidence that a modern surface fleet, concentrated and well-handled, could deal with aircraft, this battle was it. Merrill's ships bristled with guns, for AAW defense was their business. The cruisers alone fired 1,000 5-inch shells and more than 13,000 40-mm and 20-mm rounds. The Japanese achieved two bomb hits of minor impact and lost seventeen aircraft. The attack took seven minutes, which meant the cruisers fired about thirty-five rounds a second, a withering barrage.[9] Radar had given Merrill early warning, radar fighter direction steered his inadequate land-based CAP, and radar proximity fuzes made his 5-inch dual-purpose guns the most effective killers in the battle.

That was on 2 November 1943. Three days later, Halsey sent the carriers *Saratoga* and *Princeton*, under RADM Frederick C. "Ted" Sherman, to deliver air attacks on Rabaul. Up to this point Rabaul had been forbidden fruit. With at least seventy fighters on the ground, a harbor ringed with antiaircraft guns, and the firepower of seven or more heavy cruisers and a flock of lighter warships, the

---

8   This is not to deny Japanese courage in stopping to rescue survivors, which was done at great peril. Japanese tactics conformed to the prewar strategy of whittling the American fleet down to size.

9   S. E. Morison, vol. 4, p. 321. Note that the cruisers fired more than eight hundred shells for every enemy aircraft splashed.

defense should have been overwhelming. But the Japanese were gearing up for a massive sweep, and Halsey, with not one heavy cruiser to fight a night action, felt he had to risk an air attack. The carriers that he sent struck with forty-five attack aircraft and fifty-two fighters.[10] Japanese reconnaissance aircraft muffed their attempts to report the force, and Rabaul, which had no radar warning, was completely surprised. The American strike force attacked in the tightest of massed formations and came away with losses of only ten aircraft. It damaged four heavy cruisers, two light cruisers, and two destroyers, and the Japanese abandoned all thought of another night sortie to relieve Bougainville.

To appreciate the significance of radar, one merely needs to reverse the locations and missions of the two fleets. American aviators had asserted their ascendancy over Japanese aviators, but U.S. warships helped, accelerating the process, and radar proved effective in early warning and AAW gunnery.

Submarines and Sensors

This book says little about the submarine wars. That is because amphibious operations and air strikes required surface ships, and because fleet actions offered the best chance of controlling the seas. Submarines could deny control of the sea, but they could not exploit it. Submarines were spoilers, and still are—except in nuclear war, where they are intended to play a central role.

Submarines play two major roles—supporting the fleet and attacking shipping in a kind of guerrilla warfare at sea. To support the fleet, submarines scout where other warcraft cannot go; then they attack to weaken the enemy—major missions for the German, Italian, British, Japanese, and American navies.

The Battle of the Philippine Sea in June 1944 serves as well as any to demonstrate the effectiveness of submarines in supporting the fleet. Submarines first sighted the Japanese force and reported its general composition. Before the end of the battle they sank two big Japanese carriers—a decidedly better score than Mitscher's aircraft achieved. If one counts large, light, and escort carriers together, then during World War II the aircraft of all countries sank twenty carriers, totaling an aggregate 342,000 tons. By comparison, submarines sank fifteen carriers amounting to 306,000 aggregate tons. (At Midway the crippled *Yorktown* was actually sunk by the Japanese submarine *I-168*, but the credit for the destruction of the carrier beforehand should go to aircraft.) For their part, surface warships sank only two carriers, for a total of 30,000 tons.

---

10 Observe the fighter-heavy ratio. At Halsey's express orders, Sherman sent everything he had. His carriers were supposed to have been covered by land-based fighters.

There were three major efforts in the submarine guerrilla war—the German campaign in the Atlantic, the British campaign to interdict the German resupply of North Africa, and the American submarine campaign to isolate Japan from oil and other resources. All were formidable by any standard, and the U.S. campaign to isolate Japan actually can be called successful. Even the U-boat campaign in the Atlantic, which resulted in unparalleled destruction of some of the bravest men ever to put to sea, can be considered a strategic success because of the vast and disproportionate response imposed on the Allies, who, as Fleet Admiral Sergey Gorshkov of the Soviet navy later pointed out, were forced to expend many times more manpower and materiel to defeat the U-boat threat than Hitler's navy had to commit to pay for it. Then again, barring certain inefficiencies on their part, the Allies had no choice. Nazi Germany had tremendous leverage and exploited it ruthlessly; the Allies needed control of the ocean's surface.

The submarines were the latest in a long tradition of raiders at sea. In the most rewarding of all guerrilla eras, Francis Drake and John Hawkins and their Elizabethan compatriots reaped a double profit for their country: they deprived the enemy of the riches of the ships they captured and they took their booty to England. Raphael Semmes, captain of the Confederate ship *Alabama*, could destroy enemy vessels, but he rarely could keep his prizes. By World War II, surface raiders such as the *Graf Spee* and *Bismarck* were doomed by cryptanalysis, aerial surveillance, and radar. To escape a similar fate, twentieth-century raiders had to disappear under water. Throughout World War I and at the beginning of World War II submarines essentially were surface raiders that submerged to evade attack. The significance of this was that U-boats that were forced underwater by aircraft—usually far from the convoys—were ineffective. In the middle of 1943, it was aircraft that broke the back of the peak effort by U-boats, when on an average day 104 German submarines lurked in the seas. The Allies won the Battle of the Atlantic by a combination of offensive air patrols in the Bay of Biscay and defensive air patrols around convoys. At first, aircraft with radar slowed U-boats that were in transit; later, they drastically curtailed the submarines' maneuvers in the vicinity of the convoys. Radar was essential to the Allied effort.

The search radars also stimulated one of the first big measure-countermeasure duels in the scouting business. This book will not recount the details of how the British kept ahead of German detection devices by changing frequency, but it is an instructive story. British operational researchers learned how to gather data that told them whether the U-boats were monitoring Allied radar frequencies.[11]

---

11 Blackett, pp. 222–23. Among the several accounts of this electronic duel, one of the best and most concise is in Tidman, pp. 75–80.

In fact, such analysis was not necessary. The innermost circles of the Allied command already knew because the British had cracked the German code.[12]

Exploitation of the U-boat cipher—the Ultra secret—was the most important weapon of sensory warfare in the Battle of the Atlantic. Admiral Karl Doenitz directed his U-boats from ashore. By 1942 wolf packs were being used to scout and concentrate attacks on convoys. Since the U-boats could not communicate freely, Berlin played the role of tactical coordinator, opening up an opportunity for the greatest of all tactical signals exploitation. In May 1941 the British had pilfered a German cipher machine from the *U-110* and had begun to read the enemy's signals—though intermittently at first. In addition, the Allies triangulated U-boat positions, using radio direction-finders (RDF) to supplement cryptanalysts. German submariners thought that very short, technologically sophisticated burst-transmissions would be impossible to use for triangulation; they were wrong.

The deciphered information was of the highest strategic importance. Intelligence gave an exact count of the U-boat fleet, in both the Atlantic order of battle and the shakedown training in the Baltic Sea. The code-breakers provided invaluable information about the movements of U-boats and their plans of attack, which had been developed and ordered from thousands of miles away in Berlin. As Beesly wrote:

> Another incalculable benefit of having been able to read Hydra [the cipher initially used by all operational U-boats] for so long was the insight which it had given us into the way the U-Boat war was being conducted, and perhaps even into the way that Donitz's [sic] mind worked. We knew the U-Boat's methods, the average speed of advance when proceeding to and from patrol, the endurance of the various types of U-Boat and characteristics of their many commanding officers, the types of patrol lines favoured and the exact meaning of the short signals used for making sightings, weather or position reports.[13]

---

12 By 1943 American operations analysts had deduced this. As Tidman reports, Jay Steinhardt calculated that locations purportedly based on RDF (radio direction-finding) fixes were ten times more accurate than analysis showed they should have been. He took this puzzle to Philip Morse, head of the ASW operations analysis group, who confronted his naval boss with the data. The cat was out of the bag, and Morse and Steinhardt, at least, were told the truth. Yet there was never a whisper of the secret in the vast outpouring of operations analysis literature.

13 Beesly, p. 116.

Small wonder that superb American tactical study *ASW in World War II*, published in 1946 and classified at the time, is so rich in detail; it even includes the names of German aces.[14] The marvel is that the secret of Ultra was kept so well. In this official study virtually the only mention of code-breaking is in connection with the capture of the *U-505* in June 1944. The authors write that it gave the Allies important information about the German codes. The truth is that the USS *Guadalcanal* (CVE 60) and her escorts were able in quick succession to dispose of four U-boats, one of which was the *U-505*, because the Allies already possessed the code and knew where to send the hunter-killer group commanded by RADM Daniel V. Gallery, USN.

From what we know now about the influence of code-breaking in the Atlantic and the Pacific, it is reasonable to infer that

- A guerrilla campaign at sea—a modern *guerre de course*—that is not covered will fail because of the capabilities of modern surveillance.
- Due to overconfidence in high places, signals from shore to sea are especially vulnerable. Operational command from afar, which is tactical and reveals battle information, requires special signals discipline.

Tactical Interaction between Land and Sea Forces

We come to the last important factor regarding sensors, scouting, and countermeasures. As emphasized in chapter 1, the *strategic* interplay of events ashore and at sea has always been the major determinant of the scene and scale of most naval battles and of the aims of the respective combatants as well. The added importance of *tactical* interaction, owing primarily to the new role of aircraft, was a major development in World War II. The sensory revolution, which opened so many new possibilities, also had a major impact on the information war and on naval command. This new exploitation of information warfare is likely to expand rapidly and become a central element of twenty-first-century fleet tactics, affecting not only command-and-control, but also the structure of the fleet to fight in a more distributed, effective, and enduring way.

For the first time, tactical command was exercised from ashore to a significant degree. Yamamoto, Doenitz, Nimitz, and Halsey all participated to greater and lesser extents in the battle movements of their forces. In the record of Halsey's signals from ashore in Noumea are orders to begin South Pacific operations at

---

14 Sternhell and Thorndike, pp. 4, 10, 11, 20, and 81.

explicit latitudes and longitudes at specific times. Tactical command and campaign execution were exercised from ashore so that a striking force of ships and aircraft at sea could keep radio silence until its presence was discovered by the enemy. Even when cryptanalysis and RDF could not be used to full advantage, traffic analysis of the volume of signals revealed impending operations. Often when the text could not be decrypted the address headings could be decoded, revealing the commands and ships involved.

The Japanese and Americans both used land-based reconnaissance aircraft, partly to help conceal the location of ships and aircraft at sea, but also because land-based patrol aircraft had very long range and endurance. The Japanese, more than the Americans, used external reconnaissance to husband carrier assets for the attack. In the Mediterranean one of the most serious deficiencies, which sapped the Italian navy's confidence and morale, was the failure of land-based air reconnaissance.

While navies have expanded the reach of their sea-based air attacks against shore targets, what might be noted is the outcome of land-based attacks against targets at sea. Both the Italian and American air forces were supposed to attack warships at sea, and they largely failed. The Italian fleet, having been denied a naval air arm by dictator Benito Mussolini, had to depend on reconnaissance by the Italian air force and was grievously crippled by inept support. The Japanese, however, flew naval aircraft from fields ashore with success, most notably sinking HMS *Repulse* and HMS *Prince of Wales* with torpedoes. There is nothing inherently wrong launching air attacks from ashore against warships if the pilots are trained and aircraft are armed for the mission. Lack of mobility and the power to concentrate were the tactical constraints on the strike effectiveness of land-based aircraft in World War II. Weak command structure and neglect of the special training required to hit maneuvering warships were the main—and unjustifiable—reasons for the widespread failure of air strikes from land to sea.

Land-based maritime patrol aircraft proved highly effective against submarines because they could sortie on solo patrols safely and at long range. The nature of their tactics enabled navies to acquire patrol planes that were large and plodding. The British were slow to see their possibilities. After HMS *Courageous* was sunk by the *U-29* during the first week of World War II, the Royal Navy failed to exploit the fact that land-based aircraft were a safe way to fly against U-boats. For three and a half years the British demurred, until the exigencies of the war in the Atlantic drove them to it. The turning-point came in early 1943 with the transfer of bomber command squadrons to coastal command. At the same time, the British persuaded President Franklin D. Roosevelt to earmark new U.S. B-24 Liberators, which had just begun coming off the production lines in large numbers, for ASW patrol—a mission that suited the characteristics of those remarkable long-range aircraft.[15]

Nazi Germany missed a golden opportunity to exploit land-based aircraft at sea. After the fall of France, a few sorties by the Luftwaffe demonstrated that its medium-range bombers could attack Allied Atlantic convoys effectively. But Hermann Goering's penchant for attacks on land targets ruled out the development, production, and commitment of German aircraft to attack shipping in great numbers. The possibility that Germany might wake up to the opportunity haunted the harried Royal Navy through much of the war.

A separate book is needed to put amphibious operations in perspective. They usually—and properly—have been studied for their strategic content. Yet, the growing reach and range of weapons and the maneuverability of ships and aircraft unquestionably changed the nature of amphibious assault between the Napoleonic Wars and World War II in fundamental ways that are almost impossible to exaggerate. Since World War II, amphibious landings have demonstrated the growing land-sea interface and have spawned the development of new tactics. Among the fruits of this have been the stunning operation at Inchon; the landings at Wonson, which were confounded by minefields; the British destroyer *Glamorgan* being struck by land-based missiles from East Falklands Island; America's swift use of aircraft and warship mobility in the taking of Grenada; and the American amphibious demonstration and threat of an assault in Kuwait during Operation Desert Storm.

The multifaceted growth in the potential of land- and sea-based forces to operate against one another has received careful study. But the roles of scouting, communications, the control of forces, and the countermeasures against them have risen in importance relative to those forces and will continue to grow. The cause of all this was the sensory revolution. The growth of land-sea tactical interactions and of sensor technology are two of the great developments in tactics. And the trend continues, wrought by unmanned and autonomous vehicles, computer power, Google maps, ship-tracking systems, the extraordinary reach and invisibility of cyberoperations, and the potential of man-machine teaming leveraging artificial intelligence. These are all elements to make and execute better decisions faster.

---

15 Blackett, p. 227.

6

AFTER WORLD WAR II

New Kinds of Naval Operations

When World War II ended, the U.S. Navy shifted its focus from battle tactics to a wide array of fleet operations that included an unprecedented long-term presence in the European and East Asian theaters. With one exception—the Inchon Landing in South Korea in 1950—there have been no large amphibious assaults during this period. Although this book is not about wartime operations, it is worth pausing to point out the types of battles that the United States has *not* had to fight since World War II. This chapter will show the fuzzy boundary between the tactical and campaign levels of war. The "Battle of the Aegean" in chapter 15 discusses the conduct of a modern campaign through a series of imaginary interrelated twenty-first-century "battles" that we have conceived to illustrate our point.

U.S. naval operations in the post–World War II era have been continuous, widespread, and influential. The most obvious of these was the Navy's role in the United States' sustained support of the North Atlantic Treaty Organization (NATO) to help contain the Soviet Union. Yet, U.S. naval forces also have supported many campaigns ashore without fighting at sea and without losing a soldier whom they have delivered across the oceans. More recently, the suppression of piracy, interdiction of drug-running, and irregular warfare worldwide have been major elements of U.S. naval actions.

In this book the word "campaign" is being reserved for wartime operations. The term should be applied to a series of encounters by opposing forces over a wide geographical area. Past antisubmarine warfare (ASW) campaigns—along with

one against the Soviet fleet for which the Navy planned but never carried out—
looked nothing like fleet tactics. Each campaign comprised many different ASW
forces that operated in a series of engagements over the span of several years and
in areas as broad as the North Atlantic or Mediterranean Sea. The intensity of battle
waxed and waned in those campaigns. Small formations of escorts or individual
search vessels and aircraft participated in a slow-acting but arduous series of
engagements, often against jointly deployed U-boat "wolf packs" operating in
what today we would call swarm attacks. In the Mediterranean two submarine
campaigns were mounted simultaneously. The Axis forces attacked allied shipping traveling east and west, while the Allies targeted Axis shipping flowing north
to south to North Africa. At the same time, the two sides fought surface and air
campaigns on both land and sea. When ASW forces were absent or inadequate, as
sometimes was the case in the Pacific, submarines—in this case U.S. submarines—
were able to conduct a deadly campaign against almost defenseless Japanese shipping.

This "operational level" of war can be intricate. Essentially, there are two kinds
of naval campaigns.[1] One is an almost continuous interaction, as when antisubmarine forces seek to destroy submarines in order to protect shipping; the results
of such campaigns are *cumulative*. The second variety comprises a series of *sequential* battles in which each new engagement depends on the success of the previous
one. Examples of this are the campaign in the Solomon Islands in 1942 and 1943,
or the sweep across the central Pacific by the U.S. Third Fleet and Fifth Fleet,
from the Tarawa atoll in the Gilbert Islands in November 1943 through the landings at Leyte Gulf in October 1944 for the liberation of the Philippines. Naval
historians are most familiar with sequential campaigns conducted at sea, dating
from Greek and Roman times through the Napoleonic Wars. In World War I, the
Royal Navy began a distinctive cumulative campaign against German raiders that
extended around the world. Simultaneously the British and Germans fought skirmishes in the North Sea that included ships as large as battle cruisers, leading
to the climactic Battle of Jutland in May 1916. After Jutland the German navy
shifted to an unrestricted submarine campaign against shipping that ultimately
resulted in the United States' entry into the war for Europe.

The U.S. Navy did not acknowledge the existence of the operational level of
war until 1994. The change grew partly out of postwar pressure by the Marine

---

1   The two are described in depth by RADM J. C. Wylie, USN, in *Military Strategy*, first
    published in 1967. The book was republished by the Naval Institute Press in 1967 as part of its
    Classics of Sea Power series, with additional essays by Rear Admiral Wylie and an introduction
    by John Hattendorf.

Corps for developing a common terminology that would acknowledge the "operational level" between strategy and tactics in the list of officially recognized elements of war at sea. The two services formally instituted the "operational level" in *Naval Doctrine Publication 1, Naval Warfare.*[2] Meanwhile, the Navy continued its "presence" operations around the world much as it had before.

The new war-at-sea component might well have been called "operational logistics" because the huge geographical span typical of operations at sea entailed the movement of maritime forces over vast distances. A map of a maritime theater usually covers an area at least ten times as large as that of a typical ground campaign, and some 80 percent of the planning and effort in a modern naval campaign—or even a peacetime "presence" operation—involve supplying vessels and air fields with the supplies and ammunition that they need.

Purposes of Naval Operations

Over the centuries the foremost objective of sea power has been to influence events on land by delivering ground forces and supplies to the battlefield via the oceans and, more recently, by conducting air strikes against targets on land and destroying enemy resistance when necessary. Only secondarily have naval forces conducted operations exclusively for a narrowly maritime purpose, such as protecting fishing and offshore oil rigs. In the winter 1995 issue of the *Naval War College Review*, Frank Uhlig Jr. wrote a concise yet durable account of the many roles played by the U.S. Navy since its birth in 1775. Uhlig emphasizes three ways that the Navy has contributed to U.S. success: (1) to ensure "that friendly shipping [in the broadest sense] can flow"; (2) "to ensure hostile shipping cannot"; and (3) having accomplished these two things, "navies can risk landing an army on a hostile shore, supporting it with fire and logistics." Uhlig also reminds us of two times that the fledgling Navy failed in a fourth role—to protect the homeland from invasion. One pithy paragraph stands out as especially relevant today: "As the age of sail faded away, the U.S. Navy had already demonstrated all the reasons [that] a nation owns a navy. Even if the enemy lack a navy, there was no reason for the United States to deprive itself of one."[3]

The oceans are a vast two-dimensional highway, and historically the shipping that traverses them has required naval protection. Whichever country has controlled the seas has enjoyed a great advantage; invariably, losing that edge has led

2   Naval Doctrine Command, Norfolk, Virginia, 1994.
3   Uhlig, "How Navies Fight, and Why." The article was a precis of his book *How Navies Fight: The U.S. Navy and Its Allies.*

to dire consequences. There is uncontestable historical evidence that naval powers usually defeat land powers. That was the theme of Mahan's work, beginning with *The Influence of Sea Power upon History, 1660–1783*. Mahan's series of volumes showed the durable effect of command of the seas from Greek and Roman times through the end of the Napoleonic Wars. Professor John Arquilla of the Naval Postgraduate School has provided a recent, more quantitative book in his landmark treatise, *Dubious Battles*, in which he offers evidence of an even bolder assertion— that in conflicts since 1815, land powers not only have usually ended up being defeated by sea powers, but they almost always have started the wars they later lost.[4]

Both Mahan and Arquilla offer compelling *strategic* reasons for these phenomena. A fundamental factor is financial, they argue, because land powers usually must field substantial armies to accomplish their objectives; only the most prosperous of them can simultaneously build and maintain a formidable navy as well—a factor that France discovered to its disadvantage in the eighteenth century, when it was forced to confront the British Royal Navy at sea. However, neither explains the *operational* advantage that a sea power exploits over a land power. We will address the advantage below in a section entitled, "Two Great Constants: Operational Maneuver and Efficiency of Movement."

Functions Performed by Naval Operations

Historically, navies have performed one or more of four functions, and their structure and composition are designed to support those missions.

On the seas

- To protect the movement of shipping and the means of war on the oceans and ensure the safe transportation of goods and services. Navies also help safeguard stationary forces. By achieving control of the sea, a navy protects both the sea lines of communication (SLOCs) and on-station forces, such as ballistic missile submarines, blockading warships, and coastal patrols, from attacks at sea.
- To prevent the movement of enemy shipping and deny the other side the ability to wage war at sea.

From the seas

- Navies can deliver goods and services to their own countries' ground troops, put land forces ashore to seize and hold territory, and launch air and missile strikes for a variety of purposes.

---

4   Arquilla, *Dubious Battles: Aggression, Defeat, and the International System*. Arquilla had once proposed the title *Why Losers Start Wars*.

- They can prevent the enemy from delivering goods and services to its forces across an ocean, and they can protect their own homeland from every kind of threat.

Navies do not seize and occupy land, as armies do. A navy is a means to the end of controlling an enemy land force. Although there have been some exceptions, rarely has the center of a military conflict been on the oceans or in the air. Sea power's greatest payoff comes from the highly efficient movement of goods and services into either friendly or hostile territory. Today, however, many littoral waters have become dangerous, and are likely to erode the advantage that U.S. naval forces have held.

Since the 1970s the Navy has described its missions as control of the seas, power-projection, deterrence, and presence. Although these terms generally served the U.S. Navy well during the Cold War (although one Chief of Naval Operations denied that "presence" actually qualified as a mission), they do not always fit the missions typically assigned to the navies of smaller countries. By contrast, the functions described under the subtitles "On the Seas" and "From the Seas" above apply to navies and countries of all sizes and descriptions, not just to those that are major maritime powers. Most navies of the world emphasize the fourth function on the list—to prevent an enemy from delivering seaborne goods and services (i.e., soldiers, air and missile strikes, unmanned aircraft operations, and other means of war) against their homelands. And a coastal navy does not have to be a sea power to be competent and tough within its domain. A small navy may not be able to stop a foreign intrusion in coastal waters, but it can make delivery from the sea a serious burden for the invading power. Sea control is usually associated with winning fleet battles in blue water against a first-class navy or with suppressing a raider war conducted by a second-class navy.

Operations of Navies at Sea

The fleets that perform naval operations comprise four categories of forces. The first three are taken from Sir Julian Corbett, who has long been regarded as the best of the naval writers. More recent favorites include Geoffrey Till, Frank Uhlig, and John Hattendorf. (Indeed, author Hughes regards Hattendorf as a mentor who broadened his horizons.)

Here are the categories of ships that the fleet of a sea power is likely to contain:

A *battle fleet* of capital ships and accompanying forces meets and destroys the enemy's battle fleet. Mahan said, correctly, that the purpose of a battle fleet is to gain and maintain command of the sea wherever necessary. In the past, capital

ships—from oared galleys to ships of the line, battleships, and aircraft carriers—
were large and expensive. The beginning of the missile age in the early 1970s
sparked a change in thinking in most navies. It will be increasingly characterized
by swarms of smaller ships, armed with missiles and unmanned systems, that can
substitute for large, expensive capital ships in a more distributable, mobile, and
collaborative battle fleet.

Cruisers attack enemy commerce or help defend it from attack. Unlike Mahan,
Corbett saw that large capital ships were inefficient or incapable of defending
very large numbers of merchant vessels, even after the battle fleet had established
unchallenged command of the sea. Before World War I cruisers had dealt primarily with raiders, privateers, and pirates. Since then, however, surface raiders
have been supplanted by submarines, and since World War II, they sometimes have
been replaced by long-range, shore-based aircraft. A country that does not have
the means to challenge a big navy for command of the sea can challenge its unimpeded control by resorting to a *guerre de course,* a guerilla war at sea, to threaten
commerce. Hence, a necessary component of any naval force must be a sufficient
number of fast, medium-range cruisers capable of defeating smaller cruiser-raiders.
Corbett argued that when submarines superseded surface raiders, fleets needed
a large number of antisubmarine forces, which Corbett also labels as "cruisers."
Will a new battle fleet of easy to deploy but lethal combatants be able to disperse
and fill the role of the cruiser to protect other vessels from raiders, pirates, and drug-
runners? It appears so, because, unlike the current relatively small number of large
capital ships such as aircraft carriers and guided-missile cruisers, a battle fleet of more
numerous and distributable "capital ships" might be able to serve double-duty.

A third category for today's fleet is a *flotilla* that operates in littoral waters that
are too dangerous to expose a battle fleet of large capital ships. Since the beginning of the twentieth century maritime powers have used a distinctively different
fleet of small combatants, usually armed with torpedoes, to fight the enemy in
the coastal waters of the Baltic, North Sea, and Mediterranean Sea, and in the
Dardanelles. Sometimes destroyers were small enough to risk, as had been the case
in the Solomon Islands and in Norwegian waters during World War II. The characteristics of ships that made up these flotillas in the past sound quite similar to
those of a distributable battle fleet today, except the operating radius of individual
flotilla ships need not be as great.

Distinctive classes of easily deployable capital ships, cruisers, and flotilla craft
are probably desirable, albeit with some overlap. Indeed, we favor the use of combatant vessels that are designed to perform single functions—and trained to do
one, or a few, things well.

The emphasis of Mahan and Corbett is on control of the oceans and coastal waters, (functions 1 and 2 on our list, and to some extent function 4). To them we would add a fourth category—amphibious forces, designed to perform function 3, the efficient delivery of ground forces from the sea. Books by Philip H. Colomb and Frank Uhlig make clear that "delivery of goods and services" from the sea— that is to say, projection of power—is the operation with which larger navies have been most concerned.[5] Throughout history the delivery of forces for ground operations has been a function to which navies have committed as much effort as they have exerted to safeguard the sea lanes. But building amphibious forces designed exclusively to conduct opposed assaults is a relatively new phenomenon, developed during World War II by the U.S. Navy and Marine Corps. Mahan emphasized that the term sea power included merchant ships as well as combatants, partly because the merchant fleet had been the means of delivering armies to the battle-field in the seventeenth and eighteenth centuries.

Note that there is no evident congruence between functions and forces— between the means and ends of operations. It takes only a little thought to see that a navy's operational functions constitute the means of achieving the ends of a national maritime strategy. To describe the relationship in detail would require a new study by itself.

Operational Constants, Trends, and Variables

In future chapters we avoid setting down any principles of war as a way to enlighten naval tactics. By nature, principles are intended to apply to policy, strategy, operations, and tactics; they also are expected to be timeless. As a result, the principles must be so all-encompassing that they risk ending up as platitudes of limited utility. Instead, chapters 8 through 11 will describe *tactical* constants. *Constants* are practices that have not changed over centuries of naval operations and so are not likely to change in the future. *Trends* are developments that have changed in one direction and so are likely to continue in the same direction in future operations. We will pay particular attention to the expansion of information warfare as a trend affecting both operations and tactics whose importance is growing rapidly. *Variables* at the operational level of war stem not from technology but from social and political change. They do not signify a change in one direction, but will wax and wane as societies and nations change their goals.

---

5   Colomb; Uhlig (1994).

Two Great Constants: Operational Maneuver and Efficiency of Movement

"Operational maneuver from the sea" is a modern term coined by the Marine Corps, but the efficacy of overseas expeditionary operations in support of land war—which the new moniker describes—has long been an advantage of sea power. Thirty years ago Otto Bubke, a German army officer, wrote a short essay describing the operational reasons that control of the sea is advantageous.[6] First, sea power prevents the enemy from attacking from the sea. Second, it gives a maritime state the freedom to choose the scene of action anywhere on a land power's coast.[7] The reason, Bubke explained, was the operational movement advantage that ships have over almost any form of ground transportation. At sea an amphibious force will move around five hundred nautical miles a day. Fast containerships will move farther still, but in the twentieth century the norm for merchant ships was more like four hundred miles a day. By contrast, on land an army moving at operational speed against weak opposition will advance only about twenty-five miles a day. The famous German blitzkrieg in Poland and France in 1939 and 1940 moved no faster than that. In operation Iraqi Freedom in 2003 the American army took three weeks to reach Baghdad, which was hailed as a swift advance against moderate opposition of fifteen miles a day.[8]

Thus, in terms of speed, ships involved in an operational movement have at least an order-of-magnitude advantage over an army advancing against light resistance on land. In terms of the number of logistical personnel required to move a force to the scene of action and sustain it, the advantage of ships over land transport is one or two orders of magnitude. In the weight of combat potential carried to the scene of action per unit of energy expended, the ships' advantage can be two or three orders of magnitude.[9] Transport aircraft and aerial logistics complicate this simplified description, but aircraft have never sufficiently changed the

---

6 Bubke.

7 There is a third, but tactical, advantage of a superior navy. The geographical effects of terrain are muted or absent at sea. There are no defensive positions, as there are in land combat. Thus, in a fleet action, a small initial advantage in combat power is more likely to be decisive.

8 Rates of advance of land forces are more complicated and variable than those for fleets. In 1990, Robert L. Helmbold was a military analyst at the Army Concepts Analysis Agency when he conducted his comprehensive four-volume study. For our purposes the first volume, *Rates of Advance in Historical Land Combat Operations,* is most relevant. There is nothing comparable published on rates of movement of naval forces at sea.

9 In advanced economies with efficient railroads and paved highways already in service this may overstate somewhat the advantage to sea transport, but we have in mind regions such as those in the Middle East and Africa.

threefold advantage of ships compared to ground transportation so as to offset the advantage of sea power. Intercontinental ballistic missiles with nuclear warheads potentially attenuate a sea power's mobility advantage, but the change is not yet sufficient to alter the stark advantage of movement by sea as a constant of naval operations.[10]

Bubke did not say, nor do we, that sea power's advantage is the power to attack a strong land power's physical center of gravity, because the land power will defend it strongly. Nor does a sea power's advantage enable it to strike quickly, except with missiles. Britain found that it could not land on German soil in World War I, and even an expeditionary operation against Turkey at the Dardanelles proved to be too ambitious. In World War II, the Allies had to defer their carefully planned Normandy landings until 1944. Nevertheless, Bubke shows clearly that because a sea power cannot be invaded it does not have to maintain a large standing army in peacetime, and often it can find and fund allies for coalition operations against the dominant land power that threatens them.

A Great Constant: Land Battles Are Much More Frequent

Any encyclopedia of war will show that there have been far fewer sea battles than land battles throughout history. We shall return to the matter of frequency later to see why.

A Great Trend: Changes in Scouting Effectiveness

The scouting process is as important in naval campaigns as it is in battle tactics, and its progress illustrates a trend stemming from advances in technology. The improvements came first in an expansion of the range of coverage. Later, the volume increased and the information that flowed for intelligence operations became far more accurate. Soon very small robotic devices will be able to penetrate and look inside structures. Undersea search technology has not yet equaled these advances, but that may soon improve for littoral waters. Historically operational scouting has been a severe challenge to fleets. If a naval force blockading a port permitted an enemy to escape to sea it often was difficult for the blockaders to regain contact. When the French fleet and transports under Nelson's watchful eye escaped from Toulon in 1798, Nelson spent weeks sailing all over the Mediterranean trying to track them down before he finally found and destroyed them in the Battle of the

---

10 For a detailed appraisal of transportation considerations see O'Hanlon, pp. 141–67.

Nile. Until the twentieth century surface raiders and pirates routinely evaded searchers for months at a time. The onset of aviation enabled army (and later navy) scouts to cover wide swaths of ocean and report the raiders' positions by wireless radio. Within a decade, the raiders had all but disappeared. Later, commerce raiders began using submarines, which could dive below the surface to avoid detection by aircraft. To a much greater extent the location of an enemy fleet—and later even individual ships—had become less of a guessing game. Better scouting had changed naval operations fundamentally.

The trend continues, as satellites, unmanned aerial vehicles (UAVs), over-the-horizon radar equipment, and other technological advances enhance surveillance at sea. Some navies have adopted the low-cost expedient of using fishing boats and innocent-looking coastal traders to serve as scouts. The greater challenge now is how to *process* all the information that is being collected. As a result, the quest now is to find new ways to fuse and interpret the massive amount of intelligence data in a form that commanders can use to make decisions and act.

To a great extent, tactical and operational scouting overlap, so the information that is collected can be used for either purpose. UAVs, for example, can be launched to carry out strategic missions—that is, to provide surveillance and warn commanders of an approaching threat—but they also can be employed tactically, to guide weapons to specific targets. The initial, highly effective, land campaign against the Taliban in Afghanistan is a good illustration of operational and tactical scouting carried out by the same aircraft.

A Recent Trend That Will Become More Extant

Historically, naval strategists have sought to equip more and more ships, including commercial vessels, with weapons. In the Anglo-Dutch wars, for example, both sides employed armed merchant ships, which could be built quickly in large numbers and armed with the best weapons of the day. Today missiles of various ranges and homing characteristics can be placed in manned and unmanned ships and aircraft at a relatively low cost. With the onset of information-warfare concepts, this looks like the beginning of a lasting change in naval warfare.

The Greatest Variable: Social and Political Changes

The history of the U.S. Navy has been rife with changes in operational doctrine that have resulted from social and political changes. The development of steel warships with large guns created a split among government leaders. Some wanted to continue deploying U.S. warships around the world—in independent units or in very small squadrons—to provide a presence. Others argued that the Navy should assemble a fighting fleet whose ships would train together and develop tactics. Both sides justified their case on one function—the need to ensure the safety of commerce at sea. By 1885, when bigger warships were being built, the issue was resolved in favor of assembling and training a fighting fleet.

The next peacetime shift in U.S. operational planning came after World War I. Most analysts expected that the postwar Navy was going to be a major influence in world affairs, with a modern blend of capital ships and smaller vessels that could perform the "cruiser" function of dealing with raiders and submarines. There was no doubt among Navy leaders that battleships should fight as a fleet. The Naval War College war-gamed fleet actions assiduously, and annual exercises at sea also were organized as fleet-on-fleet actions. The so-called Rainbow Plans drawn up by the Army and Navy war colleges experimented with Japan, Germany, Italy, and even Great Britain as the enemy, but the main focus was on the Pacific and the Imperial Japanese Navy. Intense discussion about—and experimentation with— the roles of aircraft and aircraft carriers helped prepare the Navy for the World War II transition from battleships to flattops as the core of the Navy's battle fleets. The Marine Corps emphasized the need to project power to the Pacific islands, fashioning new tactics to exploit the increasing capabilities of landing craft and naval gunfire support. Navy–Marine Corps cooperation in the Pacific was crucial in preparing for Army-Navy amphibious operations on an even larger scale in the Atlantic and Mediterranean. The Navy itself concentrated on hammering out suitable tactics and campaign plans for a war in the Pacific.

For the forty years following World War II, U.S. defense planners were preoccupied with deterring a war with the Soviet Union. The Navy's focus was once again primarily on sea control—to keep the lines of communication across the Atlantic safe enough to defeat a large Soviet submarine force and to deter long-range Soviet bombers armed with antiship cruise missiles (ASCMs). The Navy maintained ballistic-missile-carrying submarines to deter nuclear war and deployed carrier task forces in the eastern Mediterranean, the Norwegian Sea, and the northwest Pacific, but the essential element of the Navy's contribution was to establish and maintain a secure link between the United States and Europe. The United States developed new technologies and tactics against submarines and practiced them assiduously. During the years that planning centered on deterring the Soviet Union, the Navy supported many small wars, some lasting for years. Because the job of confronting the Soviet Union came first, the U.S. Fleet often was less than optimal for these contingencies, but the payoff was a perfect record of safe delivery of men and material to many scenes of action.

When the Soviet Union collapsed in 1989, bringing the Cold War to a successful conclusion, the United States reduced the number of ships in its fleet by 40 percent. At the same time, however, the number and length of contingencies increased from their levels in the Cold War era. Sea control could be taken for granted initially, and the focus was entirely on forward presence and projection of power into distant lands.

After the terrorist attacks on the World Trade Center and the Pentagon in 2001, the Navy's focus shifted again. Its earlier concentration on power-projection waned, and in recent years the need to support large Army and Marine Corps operations overseas has diminished. Instead, the Navy has applied itself to carrying out irregular warfare, humanitarian relief, anti-piracy missions, Arctic operations, and other forms of presence and contingency missions.

Today, fighting fleets are undergoing a transition that is just as dramatic as the nineteenth-century shift from sail to steam, wood to steel, and small guns to larger ones, and the contemporary tensions are just as deep. The choice is between whether to maintain a forward presence in small units—with a shrinking fleet—or to assemble warships as fighting units for tactical development.

The list of challenges facing the Navy today is changing rapidly.

- Just as Navy planners had to prepare for the transition from battleships to aircraft carriers after World War I, similar preparations involving unmanned aerial vehicles are going on today, and these weapons almost certainly will take on expanding roles.
- As they did before the war in the Pacific in World War II, the Navy and Marine Corps must develop new tactics and capabilities for rapid deployment at likely hotspots (see nine locations indicated below).
- As the Cold War required until its end in the late 1980s, the Navy must rethink its plans for developing the tactics, training regimens, and technological advances that today's conditions demand. Navy leaders recognize that lesser contingencies will arise that will have to be met with less than ideal forces, but if the service gives equal weight to humanitarian relief and fighting irregular wars, its combat readiness will be diluted severely.

The Navy also must regain its focus and, insofar as tactical readiness is at issue, settle on where and how it will fight in the age of information warfare and robots. The littoral regions around the world have become both the centers of need and the centers of danger. The prospect of naval conflicts in the Baltic Sea,

Black Sea, Aegean Sea, and the eastern Mediterranean, especially, demand a new kind of tactical competency. Equally important are the Arabian Gulf, the South China Sea and East China Sea, the Yellow Sea, and the Sea of Japan. Each region demands new forms of operations in the information age. Chapter 13 closes by addressing the tactical implications inherent to these regions after we lay a foundation that describes the processes of naval combat over the centuries. Our intent is to emphasize that fleet combat readiness results from concentrating tactical efforts on a primary function. We have specified where the focus of American tactical readiness for today must be. The littoral regions of interest have become dangerous, and tactical effectiveness in them will be difficult to achieve.

Part Trend, Part Variable: Fewer Battles at Sea

Early Greek and Roman maritime campaigns against land forces or fleets were much more prevalent than they are today. The same was true in the Mediterranean Sea in the fifteenth and sixteenth centuries, when the Ottoman Turks, the Barbary States, and the leading powers of Europe—Spain, France, and the Holy Roman Empire—all contended with one another in prolonged and bitter operations. In the seventh century the Dutch and English fought repeated campaigns that were almost completely restricted to the seas. This phenomenon was tied to technology. At the time, an entire fighting fleet could be built in a few years. A country's whole navy could be lost in a crushing and decisive battle, yet it could be restored and ready for action within a few years. Hence a fleet was more often risked.

The eighteenth century marked a transition period in which ships became larger, more heavily armed, and more expensive. There were fewer battles, and naval commanders became more cautious, partly because it took much longer and cost more for a defeated state to replace its losses or build a new navy. During the battleship era of the early twentieth century the number of battles continued to decline. Between 1890 and 1910 the world's sea powers built seventy-four pre-dreadnought *classes* of battleships; yet, during the entire battleship era, from roughly 1885 to 1935, there were only seven fleet actions for command of the sea.[11] The statistics provided strong evidence to support the maxim that arms races do not lead to war, but rather that the prospect of war leads to arms races.

---

11 There were two decisive fleet actions in the Sino-Japanese War (1894), two in the Spanish-American War (1898), two in the Russo-Japanese War (1905) and only one—the Battle of Jutland (1915)—in World War I. We are dismissing battles such as the Coronel, Falklands, Dogger Bank, and Heligoland Bight as either cruiser warfare or skirmishes. If one includes dreadnoughts (all large-gun battleships) completed during the same period (between 1905 and 1910) it adds only another six classes to the seventy-four pre-dreadnought classes. Before any more sea battles were fought, the battleship era was over.

At the same time, the effectiveness of statecraft also has proven to be a factor in determining the number of major battles on the high seas. Part of the reason for the decline in the incidents of major sea actions was the dominance of Great Britain, with its policy of enlightened self-interest, during the nineteenth-century era of *Pax Britannica*. Under British policy, the Royal Navy protected the trade of all friendly nations. As a result, the number of naval battles fought on the high seas (and those fought near land) remained low from 1815 to 1894. That in turn explains to a large extent why there were so many different designs for capital ships during the battleship era—and why some of them were foolish.

The stability of the *Pax Britannica* period was destroyed by the rise of Germany and the German High Seas Fleet. As the German navy expanded, many other countries felt compelled to compete. The fact that these fleets existed itself generated more naval operations, and the pace continued through the end of World War II. After the war, the dominance of the U.S. Navy created a new era of stability, when once again only small-scale fleet actions ensued. Even so, there was no lack of naval *operations*, as the ascending U.S. Navy and other declining but still formidable navies projected their countries' power overseas.

The infrequency of major naval battles during this period has stemmed from other factors as well. First, the rapid pace of technological advances spawned larger and more expensive warships, aircraft, and command-and-control systems. Second, under the umbrellas of *Pax Britannica* and the more recent *Pax Americana*, countries around the world have been willing to cede protection of international sea lanes to a single dominant sea power. Today, with the geopolitical situation changing, there are signs that U.S. domination of the seas is now being challenged.

Command Processes Govern Campaigns

By definition, *strategists* devise long-range plans in theaters of operation, deciding specifically where to act and why and determining what forces to commit to an impending campaign. *Tactical* commanders work out how to confront and fight an enemy at the scene with the forces that have been made available—in other words, how to transform latent combat potential into visible combat power. The *operational* commander is in the middle. He or she delivers the combat forces to the scene of action and sustains them there for the duration of the campaign. To a great extent, however, the three must work together. Before the campaign is initiated it will take a combination of strategic and operational thought to estimate the size and makeup of the combat force that will be needed to achieve the strategist's objective; whether that potential can be achieved in the face of the expected opposition; and whether that force can be delivered to the scene of action and sustained for the time needed to accomplish the mission. It is not always that clear-cut, however. Strategists have their own staffs to make such estimates, but their team does not actually have to perform the acts of supply, and the operational commander's staff frequently has better local knowledge of the temper and capacity of the opposition. Tactical commanders, too, will make their own estimates about sufficiency and form their own opinions about the enemy as they construct battle plans to defeat the enemy.

The World War II campaign for Guadalcanal in the Solomon Islands illustrates these roles. After the Battle of Midway in early June 1942, the Joint Chiefs of Staff, at the urging of ADM Ernest J. King, USN, the Chief of Naval Operations, decided that the geographical area around the Solomon Islands in the southwest Pacific was of supreme importance as a potential staging area for U.S. forces to begin taking the offensive. To gain this ground, the Navy proposed blocking the Japanese advance by a swift assault on Guadalcanal Island before its airfield became operational and while the Japanese navy was still licking the wounds that it had suffered at Midway. Since time was critical, the attack was scheduled for early August 1942. As the operational commander in-theater, ADM Chester W. Nimitz, USN, the commander in chief of the Pacific fleet, had to decide whether the forces that the Joint Chiefs had envisioned would be adequate. There were ample ground forces in the Pacific, but there were only enough ships available to deliver and sustain one Marine Corps division in the far-off Solomon Islands. It would be the task of the tactical commanders, ADM Frank J. Fletcher, USN; ADM Richmond K. Turner, USN; and Gen Alexander A. Vandegrift, USMC, to land the 1st Marine Division, establish a perimeter on Guadalcanal, and quickly activate the airfield. Much of the United States' Pacific fighting fleet was assigned to support the landing and forestall a Japanese response, but there were very few aircraft carriers to spare for that mission, and they were worth their weight in gold. There were some serious operational constraints that U.S. military planners had to overcome—such as why only one Marine division was tapped for the initial assault. Nevertheless, the U.S. invasion force fought well and exhibited a high degree of interservice cooperation, and the attack, which succeeded after a shaky start, remains one of the cleanest examples of the interwoven roles of strategy, operational (or logistical) execution, and tactical skill needed to win or draw consecutive battles in an extended campaign.

The American success at Guadalcanal also owed much to the tepid Japanese reaction to the attack. Misled by faulty intelligence, the Japanese limited their response to a series of night attacks conducted by forces that were readily available, while at the same time attempting to reinforce their ground forces on the island. The result was a bitter, six-month-long campaign for the perimeter around Henderson Field on Guadalcanal that eventually was won by U.S. forces.

Japan's piecemeal response stemmed partly from logistical difficulties—the long distances involved in transporting available troops to help defend the island. And their efforts were confounded further by the fact that they had to come at night to evade American aircraft, which flew primarily during daylight hours.

Postwar speculation has suggested that the Japanese intelligence failure was, first, to underestimate the American buildup ashore and afloat, and second, not to appreciate the resolve of American land, air, and sea forces. Apparently, Japanese planners did not fully appreciate the strategic importance of Guadalcanal to their U.S. counterparts, and as a result did not provide their own tactical commanders what they needed to destroy the American beachhead.

Tension between Cohesive Action and Delegated Authority

The ideal in both peacetime operations and in wartime campaigns is to obtain the full collaboration of all commanders, vertically and laterally, to produce the sort of cohesive action that helps bring about success. Since the prosecution of war requires some degree of decentralized authority and responsibility, that goal in its purest sense is unattainable; the art of warfighting almost always involves some compromises.

Nevertheless, experience shows that prospects for approaching the ideal can be significantly improved if participants follow these guidelines:

- Develop sound combat *doctrine* that fosters cohesion.
- Conduct sound tactical *training* that prepares all echelons for coherent decisions and cooperative execution. (The exception is at high echelon levels where elected officials are likely unaware of the intricacies of a maritime plan.)
- Tap planners who have acquired sound fighting *experience* in the areas that will be used in the upcoming campaign so staff officers know what degree of cooperation to expect from counterparts in various positions of authority and responsibility. Having inexperienced planners can be a significant limitation.

There is little evidence that legislation intended to foster cooperation among the services has resolved these tensions. Indeed, the increasing emphasis on "jointness"—when not executed in the proper context—will come at the cost of downgrading Navy-unique tactical competencies and combat readiness. In the wake of fifty years of "unified" leadership and the inevitability of the problems described here, the best advice is to expect—and adapt to—imperfection; to be aware of the complexity of joint operations; and to include the roles of space and cyberoperations.

Improving Wartime Operations with Campaign Analysis

We conclude with a few words on the value of *operations analysis* in improving the outcome of wartime campaigns. Our own review suggests that using quantitative *operations analysis* techniques has yielded greater benefits in achieving wartime success than employing *tactical analysis*, which relies on highly variable hit probabilities, damage estimates, casualty ratios, Lanchester and Salvo equations, and other measurements to evaluate combat performance. The concept of *operations research* was developed in the late 1930s, when British scientists believed they needed to deploy into the field to show radar operators how the new radio-enhanced search technology worked. Dramatic proof of the value of the new interaction between scientists and radar users came in 1940 with England's victory in the Battle of Britain, which was based partly on the improved effectiveness of radar when it was combined with a swift-acting, effective command-and-control system. With it, Royal Air Force fighters successfully fought off German fighter escorts and shot down the attacking Luftwaffe bombers that the Nazi fighters had accompanied. The victory was crucial because Germany had needed to achieve air superiority in order to launch an invasion of the British Isles. In employing such operations research, British scientists had made a new and vital contribution to the life-and-death campaign going on in the skies over England. In the wake of the RAF's bold experiment, the Royal Navy and the U.S. Navy adopted the technique to win the Battle of the Atlantic, which involved submarines and ASW forces. It was another example of how to enhance the effectiveness of rapidly changing technology in both strategic and tactical planning. Similar partnerships would lead to breakthroughs in information warfare, through code-breaking and radar search and countermeasures.

To be sure, operations analysis had been used in previous campaigns. The cryptic bits of wisdom proffered by Chinese general Sun Tzu contained some quantitative estimates. And in the last chapter of this book, we will appraise war-gaming at the Naval War College in the 1920s and 1930s, which proved to be a valuable, if crude, operations analysis for helping Navy leaders prepare campaigns at sea in World War II. The familiar three-to-one rule of thumb that purports to describe the amount of force advantage that an attacker would need to win a land battle has a basis in fact, but it has to be supplemented with operations analysis to show the caveats in the resulting recommendations. Moreover, the need for a three-to-one advantage has never applied at sea because the open ocean offers no terrain, so historically a smaller warship advantage usually has been sufficient.

After World War II, operations analysis conducted by the fleet was generally superb, and for the next forty years fleet analysts played a key role in planning the campaign to contain the Soviet Union. Their techniques also were quite effective in enhancing the contribution of naval aviation to the air war over Vietnam. With the downsizing of the fleet after the collapse of the Soviet Union, the Navy shifted its focus on analysis involving ground-warfare operations. Quantitative analysts at the Pentagon turned their attention to procurement and budget decisions. Today it would be profitable to redeploy more analytical skills and resources to the crucial theaters of prospective operations, applying some of the atrophied skills of fleet analysis to restore efficient search-and-screening, command-and-control, delivery of fire, and *operational logistics*, updated to enable analysts to make twenty-first-century advances in surveillance, command, cyberwarfare, and precision strikes more effective.

7

THE EVOLUTION OF TACTICS IN THE AGE OF MISSILE WARFARE

Nuclear Warheads and Long-Range Missiles

Near the end of World War II, Germany paved the way for missile warfare with the development of the V-1, which was a prototype cruise missile, and the V-2, which was an unguided rocket. Germany fired more than 25,000 of these weapons at London and Antwerp between June 1944 and March 1945. To end the war, the United States dropped atomic bombs on Hiroshima and Nagasaki. The shocking destruction of the two Japanese cities, each with a single bomb, threatened to change the face of war, if not to make it unthinkable. It also gave impetus to the Navy's push to develop missiles—first Regulus and then Polaris—that could deliver warheads at very long ranges with reasonable accuracy. The new missiles were called "strategic" weapons because, much like strategic bombers, their purpose was to destroy an enemy's means of waging war.

Immediately after World War II, when the United States had a monopoly on nuclear weapons, the atomic bomb was delivered solely by aircraft, using B-29 strategic bombers, which had carried heavy bomb payloads against targets in Europe and Japan. This led to a bitter rivalry between the newly created U.S. Air Force, which claimed the mission as its own, and a recalcitrant Navy, which saw difficulties with intercontinental bombing at the time and balked at the hidden costs of maintaining bombers at fixed bases far forward in host countries. The Navy proposed delivering nuclear bombs from carrier-based aircraft, arguing that the mobility that ships offered would enable the bombers to fly shorter distances and would be less vulnerable than land-based airfields. The success of the Soviet Union in exploding a nuclear device in 1949 intensified the competition between the United States and the USSR and forced the development of more complex strategies and tactical analysis for a possible general war between the two countries. When the Soviet Union developed its own missiles for delivering nuclear warheads, the United States made the deterrence of general nuclear war a cornerstone of national strategy. That heightened the importance of trying to find ways to control—or at least influence—Soviet ambitions without resorting to general war. In the 1950s, with remarkable energy and technological acumen, the Navy developed and deployed Polaris missiles—and long-range submarines to carry and fire them—arguing that the undersea craft constituted a more stable and survivable deterrent than bombers and land bases because they could not be pinpointed for attack. It then began extensive tactical studies of submarine detectability, a command system to order an attack, and a "control" system to prevent an unintended or rogue attack. When the Soviet Union deployed its own sea-based systems in the 1960s, the tactics of survival and delivery became more symmetrical. As both sides developed land- and sea-based missiles, the tactics of general war became more and more complex. The analysis of such an intercontinental battlefield was rather stylized. Deterrence was the underlying aim because real war on such a battlefield had become so dreadful to contemplate. By the 1960s, both countries sought to maintain a stable situation through such strategic concepts as mutual assured destruction—the fear and certainty that both sides would be destroyed if the two became embroiled in an all-out war—and graduated response.

Effect of Nuclear Weapons on Fleet Tactics and Ships

The tactics designed for use in a general nuclear war did not directly involve fleets, but the need to maintain a secure nuclear deterrent shield affected all the Navy's tactical development and operational decisions. In Corbett's time, the first function of a navy of a maritime power was to safeguard the movement of trade on the sea lanes and the means of waging war at sea. When the United States began deploying nuclear weapons on board aircraft carriers and ballistic missile submarines (SSBNs), however, the function was broadened to include safeguarding the strategic forces at sea in both peace and war.

As such, the development of nuclear missiles had major effects on fleet tactics. Some of the early Soviet missiles were cruise missiles, fitted with nuclear warheads and designed to be fired by Russian warships—submarines, surface ships, and long-range land-based aircraft. Their targets were to be American surface ships, particularly aircraft carriers. Since detonating even one nuclear weapon in the vicinity of a ship was certain to destroy it, staying power derived from armor, compartmentation, damage-control techniques, and large displacement would have little value. Using antiaircraft guns in an effort to shoot down an attacker would be useless if a nuclear weapon were designed to detonate when the warhead was hit. The U.S. Navy developed surface-to-air missiles (SAMs) to destroy a bomber or missile far enough away for the ships to be able to survive. Indeed, Talos, Terrier, and Tartar SAMs—all *defensive* weapons—were the Navy's first substantial venture into guided-missile technology.

The tight defensive formations of World War II no longer were appropriate; adjacent ships would be incapacitated by the massive explosion and poisonous radiation. Designers initially intended that SAMs would cover several ships at the same time, employing the World War II tactic of defending your neighbor while defending yourself. SAMs were expensive, however, and any one ship could only carry so many. They had to be delivered accurately because commanders could not fill the sky with them by the hundreds the way 40-mm and 20-mm shells were expended in World War II. If anything, SAM distribution against incoming aircraft or missiles had to be coordinated so that commanders could rely on an efficient system of assigning targets to individual ships.

In time the formations were loosened even more and spread out in dispersed configurations. One such was a "haystack" disposition, developed so that enemy bombers could not easily locate the vital ship—the carrier—especially where commercial shipping resulted in the generation of many radar contacts. The fleet's prime targets were supposed to disappear like needles in a haystack. Survival by dispersion was a sharp departure from the fleet tactics that had been used at the end of World War II and through the Korean War, when effective air defense depended on a tight formation and mutual protection with a barrage of antiaircraft gunfire.

Tactical Legacies of Strategic Warfare Thinking

The modern U.S. Navy is a victim of outmoded nuclear war thinking. To this day, most warships have little staying power. One or two hits with modern missiles such as an Exocet or Harpoon will put most warships out of action. To survive an attack and continue to perform a task, a modern American warship depends heavily on reduced susceptibility—avoiding detection and carrying the kind of technology that will enable it to prevent incoming missiles from hitting at all.

Until very recently U.S. warships have depended on SAMs that can defend many ships within their coverage area. In the 1970s the United States and its allies made a meager start at developing a backup with point defenses, using the NATO

Sea Sparrow, a short-range missile, and CIWS, a rapid-fire gun close-in weapon system. Yet, until recently the U.S. Navy did not pursue point-defense systems—or soft-kill, with chaff and electronic countermeasures—as vigorously as most of the navies of the world.

The third legacy of nuclear weapons is a move away from tight formations for mutual defense. The Vietnam War contributed to loosening up American formations because warships were able to stand off at sea to deliver ordnance while they themselves were relatively safe from attacks. In fact, U.S. maritime supremacy was so certain that with the rarest of exceptions no enemy has dared to target American ships at sea. The result has permitted one-sided operations in which the U.S. Fleet delivered its combat power without any enemy response—a sharp departure from the longstanding tactical paradigm that fleet tactics are force against force. Doubtless the aviators and Marines who fought over or in enemy territory had a different viewpoint, but the Navy has enjoyed the almost unimpeded advantage of operational maneuver on and from the sea for the past fifty years. The paradox of that happy situation is that although fleet tactics were designed to survive Soviet attacks in the blue water, U.S. naval forces exercised striking power in conflicts, small and large, right into the confined waters of the Yellow Sea, the Sea of Japan, the Taiwan Strait, the Gulf of Tonkin, the eastern Mediterranean, and, most recently, the Persian Gulf. As a consequence, the American Navy has acquired the habit of operating ships singly or in small, loose formations that have emphasized effective offense.

At present the ocean sanctuary to which the Navy has become accustomed seems insecure. The longer reach of land-launched enemy missiles will be teamed with new targeting capabilities against U.S. ships. The commitment to joint littoral warfare entails operations near the shore, which subjects U.S. ships to a complex cruise- and theater ballistic-missile threat from many kinds of land launchers, aircraft, and small surface combatants. The implications will be discussed further in chapter 13.

Missiles in Maritime Warfare

It is easy to show that the world's navies are in a new age in which antiship missiles are the most influential weapons shaping tactics. Start with a quick survey of cruise missiles employed against shipping and how they relate to other weapons in what has become the first large-scale campaign in the sea lanes since the end of World War II. History's most profuse application of cruise missiles has been against tankers and other commercial ships in the Persian Gulf. The attacks started in May of 1981 and continued for seven years, until mid-1988, ending a year after U.S. intervention that provided protective escorts for ship traffic.

Data compiled by Navias and Hooton in their book, *Tanker Wars*, shows the dominance of missile and rocket attacks in the conflict.[1] French arms sales equipped Iraq well to carry out air-launched Exocet missile attacks. Seemingly, missiles had been used between 257 and 261 times, or in about 80 percent of all Iraqi attacks on commercial ships. Iran was less well-armed with operable missiles, but being positioned athwart the sea lines through the Strait of Hormuz and up the Gulf, it was able to attack 207 neutral ships in a wide variety of ways, with mines, gunfire from warships and flotilla craft, and rocket-propelled grenades. Opponents launched nine Silkworm cruise missiles against at least two neutral targets. Iraq and Iran used antiship missiles in more than half of all attacks on shipping. In terms of damage inflicted, cruise missiles were even more important, since they were the foremost cause of ships actually lost.

Iraq and Iran conducted two major, simultaneous, and intermingled campaigns. More than 400 ships were hit in some fashion—411 according to Navias and Hooton. Some 60 percent of the victims were tankers, attacked by one state or the other. The other 40 percent comprised containerships, bulk carriers, general cargo ships, and smaller vessels. Only a quarter of the ships hit were destroyed; large tankers proved to be the sturdiest and most resilient.

The so-called Tanker War constitutes by far the biggest campaign against shipping since World War II. Far more ships were sunk in the 1941–46 era; U-boats sank 2,828 Allied merchant ships in the Battle of the Atlantic alone. Several hundred more were torpedoed but not sunk.[2] But an average World War II ship sunk by a U-boat had a gross registered tonnage of five thousand tons, about one-fifth the size of a modern cargo ship, and the difference is even more pronounced for tankers. So in terms of quantities carried, the Gulf maritime campaign was very serious indeed. Estimates show that by 1986 the tonnage damaged beyond economic repair already had reached some 20 percent of all Allied merchant ships sunk during World War II.[3] Navias and Hooton estimate that less than 1 percent of the 800 to 1,000 ships that entered the Gulf each month were hit—about the same overall total as the fraction of sailings lost in the Battle of the Atlantic, although not as bad as the worst of that period, when up to 20 percent of merchant

---

1   Navias and Hooton.
2   Roskill, *The War at Sea*, p. 447, and Valle.
3   Navias and Hooton, p. 129.

traffic was lost.[4] Also reminiscent of the Battle of the Atlantic, there was a remorseless buildup of shipping losses in the Gulf until the United States responded to pressure from the neutral states there and started to convoy reflagged Kuwaiti tankers.

A Campaign Perspective of the Tanker Wars

There is a direct and immediate comparison with the use of torpedoes against merchant shipping. Like torpedoes, tactical missiles were conceived and developed to attack warships. Destruction of commercial targets is not force-on-force combat, but a one-sided, predator-prey form of warfare. Just as submarines stalked and destroyed merchant shipping with torpedoes, so the unprotected tankers were stalked and destroyed by Iraqi and Iranian attackers with missiles and other weapons. In both cases, the commencement of escorted convoys made a substantial, if not crucial, difference. Escort of convoys against air and surface attack in the Persian Gulf is a reminder that the direct protection of vital shipping has an honorable history that goes back long before submarines became the high-seas raiders and buccaneers of the twentieth century.

The campaigns against shipping in the Persian Gulf illustrate the overlap of tactics and operations and the need to treat them together in littoral conflict. As a campaign, the American objective in Southwest Asia exemplified the first function of a navy—to "safeguard the movement of goods at sea." Broadly, the carrier battle groups of the U.S. fighting fleet could not offer direct protection for tankers sailing up the Persian Gulf; only individual convoy escorts could fend off attacks by the Iranian threat, which in this instance comprised land-based aircraft and a flotilla of assorted small coastal combatants. But the security of the escorts depended upon air cover, present or prospective, from the American carriers standing outside the Strait of Hormuz.

Safe transit through the Gulf waters also depended on mine-clearance operations, carried out largely by European countries, which had joined the effort by the mid-1980s. In NATO, mine clearance is a national responsibility; at the time, Europeans were better equipped for that than the U.S. Navy was.

The Persian Gulf example shows how missile warfare in the littoral environment is clouding the distinction between a navy as a set of warships and aircraft and a "fleet" whose purpose is to control a coastal region that delivers firepower from both land and sea. The distinction is of paramount importance. The axiom that "a ship's a fool to fight a fort" is tempered by the caveat that in order to influence

---

4   Ibid, p. 130.

events on land, navies must either circumvent or destroy the enemy's ability to send land-based aircraft and missiles over the coastal seas. To affect events on land, a maritime state must deliver the resources of war across the narrow seas and onto the shore. The littorals are not only where the clutter is, but they also are where the forts are.

Missile Combat between Fleets: The Record

Although the Navy has not employed fleet tactics involving force-on-force since World War II, there has been plenty of fighting, all of it in littoral waters. A 1994 master's thesis by then-lieutenant John Schulte, USN, at the Naval Postgraduate School details the prominent role that missiles have played in these engagements.[5] In the first cruise-missile attack on a ship, during the Arab-Israeli War of 1967, an Egyptian salvo of four Soviet-made Styx missiles sank the Israeli picket-destroyer *Eilat*. In 1970 the Egyptians conducted what was in effect a live-target test of the ability of the Styx to home on targets smaller than a destroyer; they fired four missiles and sank an Israeli fishing boat, the *Orit*. In the Indo-Pakistan War of 1971, India successfully employed nine Styx missiles against Pakistani warships and merchant vessels, some of which were in port.

Next came the best wartime laboratory for study of missile combat—the Arab-Israeli War of 1973. The two sides exchanged 101 Styx and Gabriel missiles in five separate battles with devastating effects on the Syrian and Egyptian flotillas and no harm whatsoever to the Israelis. After that came the South Atlantic War of 1982, in which Argentina achieved well-publicized results with air-launched Exocets and, for the first time in combat, with land-launched missiles as well. In the same war, but less well-known, Royal Navy helicopters launched Sea Skua air-to-surface missiles at two Argentine patrol boats, sinking one and severely damaging the other.[6] In February 1991, during the Persian Gulf War, two Silkworm anti-ship cruise missiles (ASCMs) were launched from a land site in Kuwait, aimed at the USS *Missouri* (BB 63), which was bombarding Iraqi positions with 16-inch shells. Although the Silkworms malfunctioned and did not inflict any damage, the incident is noteworthy as the first and only time in a war that a ship-fired surface-to-air missile has shot down an ASCM, the honor going to a Sea Dart fired by

---

5   Schulte, pp. 3–14. Unlike Navias and Hooton, who compiled the number of targets attacked, Schulte's objective was to record ASCM attacks and determine their effectiveness from the attacker's viewpoint. His data for attacks in the Tanker War are truncated and limited to missile attacks in the period from 1981 through 1984.

6   Argentina's cruiser *General Belgrano* and submarine *Santa Fe* were defeated with underwater ordnance.

HMS *Gloucester.* Other incidents were the Gulf of Sidra (1986; six Harpoons); the attack on the USS *Stark* (FFG 31) (1987; two Exocets); and Operation Praying Mantis near the end of the Tanker War (1988; eleven Harpoons and five Standard missiles in surface-to-surface mode, plus one Harpoon fired by Iran). Altogether, Schulte records a total of 155 missiles launched against warships. Whether in terms of incidents, damage achieved, weapons fired at a target,[7] or cost of ordnance expended, missiles and missile warfare dominate modern combat at sea.

Chapter 13 looks closely at the hit-probabilities of ASCMs. Briefly, large, defenseless commercial ships showed very high hit-probabilities, but the damage by no means has been uniformly fatal. Hit-probabilities against warships that defended themselves were far lower, yet substantial and usually with devastating effect. Perhaps the most interesting and alarming statistic is the number of successful attacks on defendable ships, such as HMS *Sheffield,* that failed to protect themselves.

Disconcerting in its tactical implications is the case of the *Atlantic Conveyer,* hit and destroyed in the South Atlantic War. Two Exocets, launched by a pair of Argentine Super Étendard jet fighters, homed on HMS *Ambuscade,* one of the screen ships in the Royal Navy formation stationed east of the Falklands. The *Ambuscade* launched chaff, which distracted the ASCMs and saved her from harm. But once the Exocets had flown through the chaff cloud they searched for another target and found the SS *Atlantic Conveyor,* destroying the ship and the important cargo on board. By saving herself, *Ambuscade* failed in her mission to protect the other ships in the formation. A further irony is that the Argentine pilots actually had hoped to hit the aircraft carrier HMS *Hermes,* which was also in the formation and had a flight-deck full of Harrier jets. Despite modern sensors and precision-guided munitions—or perhaps because of them—naval warfare in the twenty-first century will continue to be full of confusion and surprise.[8]

---

7 One ought to be careful that something was shot at. More than two hundred antisubmarine attacks, often with expensive torpedoes, were made by the United Kingdom against an effective order of battle of one Argentine submarine. In 1969 the USS *Morton* (DD 948) fired more than 15,000 shells in the Vietnam War, and this was by no means close to the record for a deployment. But most of it was a blanket of harassment and interdiction fire. A typical target was a suspected bunker.

8 See Woodward, pp. 293–96 and elsewhere. His *Memoirs of the Falklands Battle Group Commander* is head and shoulders the best book about the realities of modern naval tactics by an operational commander and vividly portrays the additional burdens placed on such leaders by the missile threat.

Lessons of the South Atlantic War

Although navies have entered a new era of missile warfare, other weapons clearly have not lost their potency.[9] The short, furious war between Argentina and the United Kingdom over the Falkland Islands not only spotlighted the emergence of the missile threat but also underscored the need for navies to relearn some old tactical lessons.[10]

Some of the conclusions proffered at the time were inaccurate; others were right on the mark.

The inaccurate pronouncements included:

- The sinking of the Argentine cruiser *General Belgrano* demonstrated a startlingly new deadliness in nuclear submarines.
- The sinking of the HMS *Sheffield* followed a few days later by the damage or loss of other British surface warships showed their surprising vulnerability to air attack.
- Therefore surface warships are obsolete—especially large and costly ones.
- Fatal attacks will come without warning.
- Had nuclear weapons been used, warships would have been even easier targets.
- Naval combat is becoming more lethal for the participants.

Wiser conclusions, grounded in the history of war at sea, are:

- The sinking of the *General Belgrano*, which was built before World War II, showed again that it takes modern weapons to fight a modern war. The British navy outclassed the Argentine navy, notably in nuclear submarines. In the open ocean, a fighting fleet that is even slightly inferior will usually be defeated decisively by a superior enemy and inflict little damage on him. The Argentine navy, having appreciated its inferiority, was quite right to retreat into its territorial waters, effectively taking itself out of the war. Submarines are capable warships, able to attack anything on the surface, but this is nothing new. In World War II, U.S. submarines sank 1,300 Japanese ships, including a battleship, eight aircraft carriers, and eleven cruisers. Nuclear power only amplifies submarine potency.

---

9   As an aside, fourteen of the eighteen times that U.S. Navy ships have been sunk or damaged by enemy ordnance since World War II have been due to mines. See Horne, p. 82.

10 Called the Malvinas in Argentina.

- The *Sheffield* and the three other British escorts were lost in the course of successfully doing their job, which was to protect the aircraft carriers and troop ships. Because Americans have not seen a fleet action since 1945, the United States has forgotten that it is the nature of naval combat to be fast-paced, deadly, and decisive.

  If there is a new lesson from the South Atlantic War, it is not that warships are vulnerable to missiles, but that aircraft armed with bombs cannot compete against warships that are equipped with modern defenses. In the course of sinking half a dozen British ships, the large Argentine air force was almost destroyed after conducting three days of courageous, intensive attacks. Four of the six warships were sunk close to the Falkland Islands. In an amphibious operation such as the one that the Royal Navy was conducting, a fleet temporarily surrenders the tactical advantage of mobility while it guards the beachhead. Since the enemy's scouting problem is solved, the fleet is more vulnerable at that time and must depend on its active defenses to fend off attacks.

- The United States cannot permit its surface warships to become obsolete. It depends on the safe passage of merchant ships at sea and the use of the seas—with amphibious landings if necessary—to protect its interests overseas. It cannot do this without surface warships. Large, protected ships such as battleships are valuable partly because they can take hits and continue fighting.

  Before the British amphibious landing in San Carlos Sound, the mobility of the British fleet enabled it to operate safely east of the Falklands. Unsupported by sea, the Argentine ground forces on the islands were essentially cut off from the continent, and the Argentine air force was too far away from the scene to contribute in a decisive way.

- In modern naval combat, effective scouting is the key to effective weapon delivery. Both the Argentine and British forces were hampered by inadequate scouting. The Argentine air force and Argentina's lone submarine needed better reconnaissance to track and, more important, to target the key British ships. The British needed reliable tactical warning of impending attacks. Although their submarines were useful for early warning, at least two surface ships were attacked while they were on radar picket (scouting) duty far away from the main force. Ships must have warning in order to deal successfully with missile attacks. In modern sea warfare the outcome between two forces armed with missiles will often be decided by scouting and screening effectiveness before any missiles actually are launched.

- The South Atlantic War taught nothing about the tactics that navies should employ during a nuclear war. Yet, when weapons of mass destruction are employed, fixed targets ashore are likely to be more vulnerable than ships at sea, which are able to maneuver to evade attack.

- Naval combat at sea has always been highly lethal to the participants, but the Falklands actions confirm the trend toward fewer casualties per vessel for each ship put out of action. Modern war on land and at sea has become more destructive of machines, not people.

Casualties at Sea
Data compiled by Blood and his fellow researchers enables us to be more specific about the decline in personnel casualty rates.[11]

Killed and Wounded in Action
In the South Atlantic War there were 23 incidents of damage to British warships and auxiliaries. The casualty average was 5.8 seamen killed and 8.3 wounded per attack. By comparison, in World War II the U.S. Navy average for 513 incidents among warships destroyer-sized and larger was 38 killed and 35 wounded. Among amphibious ships and auxiliaries, the average for 355 incidents was 11 killed and 16 wounded. In other words, personnel casualties in the South Atlantic War were only about 20 to 25 percent of what they were in World War II. If the severe Argentine losses in the *General Belgrano* are included, the loss rate is much higher; on the other hand, in World War II the Royal Navy suffered 1,421 lost when HMS *Hood* blew up—a victim of the *Bismarck*—and 1,204 died when the HMS *Glorious* was sunk by gunfire from the *Scharnhorst* and *Gneisenau*. Catastrophes happen.

Ship Casualty Rates
For the Royal Navy the Falklands operation was intensive and dangerous to the 36 warships and 23 auxiliaries present. During the period 30 April–16 June 1982, Blood and his coauthors count 1,723 ship-days and 23 damaging attacks, for a hit-rate of 1.34 ships per 100 ship-days of operations. The comparable World

---

11 Blood, Jolly, and Odowick, pp. 124–34.

War II hit-rate for the American Navy during Pacific operations is much smaller, only .32 hits per hundred ship-days. During the intense and stressing Solomons campaign in 1942–43, however, American ships suffered hits at a much greater rate. For example, for the Guadalcanal-Tulagi landing operations in August 1942 the record shows 6.36 ships hit per hundred ship-days. Interestingly, during the Okinawa campaign, when the U.S. Navy suffered an unprecedented 290 hits on it warships in two months due to kamikaze attacks, the hit-rate itself was only .44 ships hit per hundred ship-days because the U.S. force on scene was so massive. Casualty rates can vary all over the map, but when the fighting is intense many ships will be sunk or damaged. One also can conclude that a fleet action is not necessary for intense fighting—unless the term fleet action is defined to include the fighting between ships and forces based ashore.

Damage per Quantity of Ordnance

Additional data also have been gathered since the first edition on the relationship between the number of hits and the damage done.[12] Understandably, the bulk of the data for damage and sinkings of warships, destroyer-sized and larger, comes from World War II. In two different studies, Richard Humphrey and Thomas Beall drew from the same data source, which assembled forty-nine cases of damage from bombs, thirty sinkings from bombs, forty-nine incidents of damage from torpedoes, and forty-eight sinkings from torpedoes, of German, Japanese, French, British, Italian, and American warships.[13] Unlike Humphrey, Beall included data on damage from shells, but he only looked at ships put out of action. Humphrey and Beall used different approaches in analyzing the data, so their results tend to reinforce each other's. Table 7-1 shows the average amount of ordnance required to put ships of different sizes out of action.

Beall plotted the mean number of bombs or torpedoes, while Humphrey expressed his results as the probability of a firepower kill for a given number of notional hits. The best comparison is Humphrey's 50 percent probability of a firepower kill. Beall concluded that a salvo of shells was two and a half times as destructive as a bomb with the same amount of explosive because of the greater kinetic energy and penetrability of a shell. Nevertheless, it took many shells to accumulate the same effect as a 1,000-pound bomb, which carried 660 pounds

---

12 Prominent sources are Beall, Humphrey, and Schulte.
13 Brzozosky and Memmesheimer. They refer in turn to Souchard, a CONFIDENTIAL study.

Table 7-1. Ordnance to Achieve a Firepower Kill on a World War II Warship

Warship Displacement	Beall	Humphrey
In average number of 1,000-pound-bomb equivalents (TPBEs)		
3,000 tons full load	1.00 TPBE	0.71 TPBE
15,000	1.7	1.6
45,000	2.5	2.7
90,000 (an extrapolation)	3.1	3.9
In average number of 21″ torpedo equivalents		
3,000 tons	0.8 torpedoes	0.6 torpedoes[a]
15,000	1.4	1.3
45,000	2.0	2.2
90,000 (an extrapolation)	2.5	3.2

[a] A fractional torpedo means that the explosive warhead in a U.S. 21-inch submarine torpedo was more than enough, on average, to put a 3,000-ton ship out of action.

Table 7-2. Ordnance to Sink a Warship in World War II with 0.8 Probability

Warship Displacement	1,000-Pound Bombs	21-Inch Torpedoes
3,000 tons full load	4.0	1.6
15,000	9.0	3.5
45,000	15.5	6.1
90,000 (by extrapolation)	23.0	8.6

of explosive. Humphrey also computed the amount of ordnance to achieve a sinking.[14] Table 7-2 displays the number of bombs or torpedoes for an 80 percent probability of sinking.

In World War II it took a lot more punishment to sink a warship than to incapacitate it. Comparing tables 7-1 and 7-2, the average was five times as many 1,000-pound bombs and two or three times as many torpedoes. World War II ended decades ago. What can we say about modern warships and weapons? For any given weight of attack, today's warship is unlikely to be more survivable than then, because staying power has not been built into modern ships as assiduously. Although the postwar sample size is small in comparison with World War II, Humphrey compiled and analyzed the results of hits from thirty-eight attacks of

---

14 Beall was interested only in firepower kills because his purpose was to validate the firepower equations illustrated in chapters 1 and 4.

all descriptions. He concluded that the results since World War II correlate with results during that war. One difficulty he faced was that the modern ships that were hit were relatively small ones. The old cruiser *General Belgrano* of 13,000 tons was the largest fighting ship sunk, and the USS *Tripoli* (LPH 10) of more than 18,000 tons was the largest one put out of action. Most of the combatants were of 5,000 tons or less.

In passing, Humphrey noted that small ships were difficult to hit. But wartime hit-probabilities of all kinds of ordnance against both large and small warships have disappointed the attackers for a long time, and there is no reason to believe that this constant of naval tactics has changed. The exceptions come when torpedoes and missiles are fired at defenseless merchant ships. These had a hit-probability more like that of peacetime training performance. Large modern merchant ships and tankers are easier to hit but harder to sink than small modern combatants or merchant ships of the sizes that were attacked in the two world wars.

Separately, Schulte analyzed the damage from thirty successful ASCM attacks. He recognized that kinetic energy and residual fuel in a cruise missile could be as important as the warhead size. He experimented with three measures: warhead explosive content (250 pounds for an Exocet), total missile weight (1,439 pounds), and total missile kinetic energy (at a speed of Mach 0.93). He arrived at a best fit with a function of missile kinetic energy.

It took extreme dispersion in the amount of ordnance to achieve a ship kill. Schulte's summary plot, figure 7-1, takes care of that. It shows that even the best fit tells very little in forecasting any particular outcome. Analysis in engineering detail can calculate how the damage will change depending on where the missile strikes, but there is no way to know in advance what the location of hits will actually look like. The lower curve in figure 7-1 shows the mean number of Exocet missile equivalents (ECMEs) required to put a ship out of action, as a function of displacement. The upper curve shows the Exocet equivalents to sink the same-sized ship. The dots and squares indicate the amount of dispersion. Schulte truncated his plot at 6,000 tons full-load displacement because data are so sparse for larger ships.

Figure 7-1 shows that for small, modern combatants it only took about twice the number of missile hits to sink a ship as to put it out of action. That is probably because much less lethal energy than was delivered by an Exocet would have been sufficient to incapacitate most of its victims. When the Egyptians experimented by firing four large Styx missiles against the tiny *Orit*, none hit, but one near miss was enough not only to immobilize the vessel but to sink it. The Styx is designed

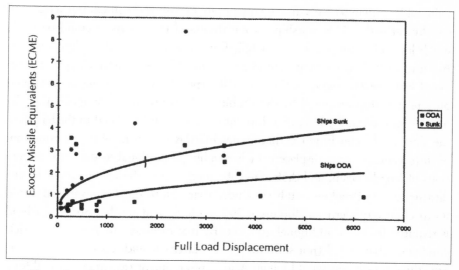

Figure 7-1. Exocet Missile Equivalents versus Full Load Displacement for Ships Out of Action and Ships Sunk

for use against large warships. It has a 700-pound warhead, nearly three times that of an Exocet. Just as pertinent, a Styx weighs 5,000 pounds. Traveling at Mach 0.7, it produces a lot of kinetic energy.

Every effort to ascertain the relationship between hits and damage from historical data must struggle with the problem of "overkill." The incidents above the two lines in figure 7-1 record actual hits, which could well be more than were necessary for a sinking. A lesser problem could be called "underkill." For the squares below the ship OOA line, were all the ships really put totally out of action and, if so, for how long?

The wide spread above and below Schulte's best-fit regression line is found in the Beall and Humphrey plots as well. One may conclude that there is little purpose in trying to cut the cloth too fine when trying to forecast outcomes. On the other hand, the rough estimate represented by Schulte's mean will permit very useful calculations similar to those done for the era of carrier warfare in chapter 4. Similar calculations for the missile era appear in chapter 13.

Damage versus Warship Size and Armor
None of these analyses reflects design considerations other than warship displacement. Is there another, more design-specific source that takes armor, magazines, and other properties into account? The Naval Surface Warfare Center (NSWC), Carderock Division, at the David Taylor Model Basin has been doing excellent

vulnerability analyses for years. Its quantitative work is classified, but its general conclusion is that U.S. warships of ten thousand tons or more could be made much less vulnerable to firepower kills from cruise missiles than they are now. An unclassified assessment, entitled "Cruise Missile Warfare," appeared in Naval Institute *Proceedings* in October 1985 (pp. 97–101). The results are based on a relationship proposed by the Brookings Institution, which asserts that the number of hits required to put a ship out of action can be related to the length of the ship. Beall's conclusion is that vulnerability is proportional to the cube root of displacement. Since displacement is roughly proportional to the three dimensions of length, beam, and draft, the cube root reduces the measurement to one dimension. The Brookings study concluded that a hit by one large warhead would incapacitate a modern warship up to 300 feet long, and another similar warhead is required for every additional 100 feet. By that measure, the *Proceedings* article concluded that to kill (not sink) an aircraft carrier would require seven missile hits, three missile hits would kill an Aegis cruiser, one or two were required for a frigate, and one would be enough for a patrol craft. The NSWC and Brookings studies depend on models, and most damage models have not reflected the progressive effects of fire and flooding very well.

One detailed study completed by the chief of the Bureau of Ships in May 1944 in response to a request from ADM Ernest J. King, the Chief of Naval Operations, estimated the vulnerability of warships to attacks by airborne weapons—bombs and torpedoes—including the effects of near-misses. Thinking in strategic rather than tactical terms, the CNO asked only for the number of hits (or near-misses) needed to sink a ship. The data available to the Navy's Bureau of Ships (BuShips) were more sparse than Humphrey's were, so the report was in the form of a set of theoretical calculations and judgments, corroborated by actual wartime data.[15] BuShips' discussion of the calculations was extensive. Magazine vulnerability and protection are given great weight, as well as the tactical choice of armor-piercing (AP), semi-armor-piercing (SAP), and general-purpose (GP) bombs. Although air-dropped torpedoes were in question, BuShips increased its sample size by including torpedo attacks from surface ships and submarines as well. Thus, the devastating Japanese Long Lance was treated the same as a smaller U.S. Mark XIII air-dropped torpedo. BuShips' conclusions are tabulated for eight ship types, from destroyers to battleships. The tables show the probability that a given number

---

15 Only U.S. ships were included. For battleships, there were four torpedo incidents. Two ships survived and two sank. There were seven bombing incidents, in which five battleships survived and two sank. The sinking incidents were probably from the Pearl Harbor attack. Humphrey worked with twenty-two incidents of battleships in high conditions of damage-control readiness.

of hits (or near misses) will sink a ship. Table 7-3 displays BuShips' results side by side with Humphrey's at the 80 percent level. It also includes Schulte's data, to indicate that an Exocet has about the same effectiveness as a 1,000-pound bomb.

The results are disconcerting to the tactician because all of them show the flatness of the kill curve. In fact, the BuShips data indicate that only a few more hits were required to sink a battleship or carrier than to sink a heavy cruiser. Can modern designs be effective against cruise or theater ballistic missiles to keep a modern combatant in action? The classified 1990 study by NSWC Carderock asserted that a great deal can be done; moreover, the toughening will come at only a modest increase in cost.[16] Whether this is so, the Navy's current inventory is mainly in large warships that are potent offensively but depend almost entirely for survival on reducing susceptibility by a layered defense of combat air patrols, SAMs, and hard-kill and soft-kill point defenses. Even more important, American warships depend for survival on out-scouting the enemy and attacking him not only effectively, but decisively first. These are tactics suitable for a fleet in the open ocean. The tactics will lose their efficacy in littoral waters.

Tactical Considerations of Staying Power

The results of these studies are not definitive. Certainly the data were gathered responsibly and the statistical analysis carried out in scientific fashion. The data are an accurate representation of history, but the damage assessment is too open-ended to say that such-and-such a number is conclusive for tactical planning or future designs. Tacticians should follow the philosophy of author Damon Runyon's horse-race gambler: "The race is not always to the swift, nor the battle to the strong. But that's the way to bet." Here are inferences that are warranted in placing bets on the future staying power of American warships.

Only one or two missile hits are needed to put a warship out of action if its armor, compartmentation, and other protective measures are meager. It takes more ordnance to sink a large ship than to achieve a firepower kill, but readers should be suspicious of the suggestion that it took five times as much ordnance to sink a ship as it took to put one out of action. Most likely the ratio for small ships is about two to one, and for large, protected ships it is about four to one. Part of the reason is overkill. As chapter 5 pointed out, there is a propensity for the attacker to pour shots into a visibly crippled ship until it sinks—even at the cost of letting other enemy ships continue to fight. The torpedo and large missile that will usually sink patrol craft and frigates outright carries lethal potential well in excess of what is needed for a firepower kill.

---

16 Hansen and Gray.

Table 7-3. Rough Comparison of Ordnance to Sink a Warship, Then and Now (in number of bombs, torpedoes, or Exocet missiles)

Displacement/Type[a]	BUSHIPS		Humphrey		Schulte ASCMs
	Bombs	Torpedoes	Bombs	Torpedoes	
1,800 tons/prewar DD	1.3 GP	1.2	3.0	1.5	2.2 Exocets
2,400 tons/*Fletcher* DD	2.0 GP	2.0			
3,000 tons/current frigate			4.0	1.6	2.8
15,000 tons/*Baltimore* CA	4 SAP, 6 GP	3.0	9.0	3.5	
33,000 tons/*Essex* CV	6 GP	3.5			
41,000 tons/*Washington* BB	6 AP; many GP	5.5			
45,000 tons/current amphib			15.0	6.0	

[a] BUSHIPS data are given in standard displacement, common then, so we have inflated them by 15 percent to approximate full load displacement.

Small ships armed with missiles will draw disproportionate attention to themselves in littoral operations. Just as destroyers, submarines, and PT boats armed with torpedoes once were used to threaten battleships and cruisers, today's small and numerous missile-armed combatants will draw a lot of fire from large ones in modern combat.[17] Small ships with a big punch *ought* to draw fire because they can inflict disproportionate damage to big, expensive ships. The tactical rule is to put every threatening enemy ship out of action first. A firepower kill is the proper *tactical* measure of effectiveness; a sinking may be a broader campaign goal.

The study by BuShips is the least valuable, primarily because it has the smallest data sample. That is good news for the Navy, because the BuShips data show that a ship three or four times larger than a heavy cruiser is only slightly more resistant to sinking. But to achieve the staying power that Humphrey derived for capital ships, the vessels must be built with the protective armor and supporting components of capital ships such as the *Bismarck, Scharnhorst, Yamato,* and *Musashi,* all of which suffered enormous punishment before sinking.

Littoral Warfare: Measuring Performance
In evaluating the designs of warships, American systems analysts almost invariably use deliverable combat potential as the principal criterion for making decisions about its characteristics. Since a large ship enjoys economies of scale, it will carry

---

17 The Navy usually treated the commanders of PT boats as dangerous cowboys who put Americans more at risk than the enemy. The point is, their stealthy approach with torpedoes was seen as a highly lethal threat to larger ships.

more fuel, ordnance, aircraft, or Marines than several smaller ships of the same total cost. The analytical conclusion is, therefore, "bigger is better." The important disadvantage of a large, supposedly efficient ship is the hazard of putting many eggs in one basket. Indeed, the Beall, Humphrey, Schulte, and BuShips studies all reflect a diseconomy of scale. If a 60,000-ton ship carries twenty times the payload of a three-thousand-ton ship but can only take three or four times as many missile or torpedo hits as a small one before it is out of action, then that is a substantial disadvantage offsetting its greater payload.

For ship procurement decisions a better analytical criterion than combat potential is: *Maximize the net delivered combat power over the combat life of the ship*. This takes into account the possibility that the ship will be incapacitated in the midst of fulfilling its mission.

Several ships with complementary capabilities can be gathered into a task force tailored for a mission. Several ships of a single class can be operated together or with others in complementary combinations. For operational planning, the best criterion for evaluation is: *Maximize the net delivered combat power over the effective life of the task force*.

As a tactical factor, large ships with big payloads should be protected by small screening ships, the loss of which can be accepted. Susceptibility to hits can and should be attenuated by defensive firepower and soft-kill, but these may not be enough in littoral waters, where sudden attacks at relatively close range will be more frequent. Littoral waters will be a critical arena of modern fleet actions.

Littoral Campaigns

Littoral operations are of two kinds, with innumerable variations. The navies of small states and continental powers will treat their inshore waters as their ocean of interest, where they protect their coastal activities and deny them to an enemy. Usually the foremost consideration in their naval strategies is to deny delivery by an enemy of the means of war, either by invasion or by strikes with missiles or aircraft. Coastal navies use land installations to scout and attack from as safer, cheaper, and more resilient than large warships. Their fighting ships are small and heavily armed. They depend for success on stealthy attack and surprise by out-scouting the enemy. Their ships are short-legged with austere habitability, because they can sortie to perform brief, stressful tasks. A neighbor is usually seen as the principal foe, at least for fleet design and planning. For examples, take the navies of China and Taiwan, North and South Korea, the Baltic states, Peru and Ecuador, and Colombia and Venezuela.

Two articles describe the strategies and tactics of coastal navies in detail. One is "The Seapower of the Coastal State," by Jacob Borrensen, a Norwegian, in the March 1994 issue of the *Journal of Strategic Studies*. Borrensen puts the operational aim of a competent coastal defense in full strategic context: a coastal state will not attempt to defeat the navy of a maritime state, but instead will endeavor to inflict sufficient pain on that navy in an extended campaign so that the enemy will not think the game worth the candle. More recent, and rich in tactical detail, is an article by Commander Tim Sloth Joergensen, Royal Danish Navy, appearing in the Spring 1998 issue of the *Naval War College Review:* "United States Navy Operations in Littoral Waters, 2000 and Beyond." Joergensen offers a pointed warning that the U.S. Navy is not sufficiently configured or practiced to defeat a coastal power without severe losses. The implication of both articles is that it will not take a high-technology coastal defense to inflict pain and suffering on a high-technology, blue-water navy.

A maritime power conducts the second kind of operations. The U.S. Navy's principal responsibility is to safeguard the oceans almost anywhere, though not everywhere at once. The other side of the coin is to deny movement of enemy shipping and the means of war—an easier mission that usually comes with the territory when the first mission is achieved. Weakness that comes from disregarding these two missions invites another country to build up a blue-water fleet to move into the power vacuum. Provided that the U.S. Navy keeps a quantitative and qualitative edge, it probably will remain unchallenged on the high seas well into the twenty-first century, or at worst face a guerrilla campaign conducted by submarines and long-range aircraft. When the oceans are secure, the U.S. Navy will operate along the world's littorals to ensure delivery of the means of war and prosperous peace.

National interests introduce hybrid forms of this simple dichotomy. The navies of South America; the Indonesian navy, which must patrol 13,000 islands; and the navies of India and Pakistan all have variations tailored to their strategies. The South Atlantic War produced unexpected and difficult combat circumstances for the forces of both Argentina and the United Kingdom. To contribute, the Argentine navy would have had to operate 400 miles and more offshore. The British navy, designed for ocean escort, had to be reconfigured as a full-fledged fighting fleet for the first time since 1945.

In the littorals the primary mission of a maritime power such as the United States is to deliver or show the capacity to deliver its combat potential across the coastal waters and into enemy territory. Strikes with missiles and aircraft by the blue-water fleet can often be delivered from outside the coastal clutter, safeguarded by defense in depth. There its susceptibility to attack is reduced by SAMs, point-defense, soft-kill measures, decoys, and a new capability that has not been tested in battle—low-observable characteristics, or *stealth*.

At the same time, the American Navy will operate inside of the littoral waters to bring the means of war safely into a host nation's ports or to force an entry with an amphibious operation. It will wish to destroy enemy coastal shipping and fishing fleets. It is in these coastal waters where a maritime fleet and a coastal fleet confront each other with their own distinctive operations and tactics. Indeed, the coastal navy's home playing field. A wealth of experience in past littoral campaigns illustrates the challenge—campaigns for Santiago, Port Arthur, Gallipoli, Norway, Guadalcanal, New Guinea, North Africa, Okinawa, and Inchon are examples of the risks and rewards when a maritime navy clashes with a coastal state's navy and fortifications.

Summary
Navies are in a new tactical era characterized by missile warfare. Cruise, theater ballistic, defensive, and air-to-air missiles compose an assortment that is large and growing larger.

Coastal regions will be where operations will take place. In fact, littoral waters may be usefully defined as where the clutter of friendly, enemy, and neutral coastal trade, fishing boats, oil rigs, small islands, dense air traffic, large commercial ships, and an intricate tangle of electronic emissions all create a confusing environment in which stealthy attack can come suddenly and almost without warning.

Fleet actions in the missile age have been fought in coastal waters, but not by the U.S. Navy. These battles have been fast, furious, and decisive. Tactics were dominated by the use of missiles. Combat actions tended to be either at night or to involve aircraft.

Recalling that "the second-best weapon frequently does the most damage," the fact that mines were the cause of fourteen out of eighteen incidents hurting U.S. Navy warships during the years after World War II, while important, hardly affects the dominating influence of missiles in littoral operations. There has been one very extensive antishipping campaign in which air-launched antiship cruise missiles were the most effective weapon. The campaign led to a revival of escorted convoys, covered by a battle fleet.

For littoral operations, it is no longer possible to define a fleet merely as a set of warships, because land-based systems play a prominent part. Off-board, land-based sensors contribute to detection, tracking, and targeting. The reach of missiles between land and sea will result in naval "battles" that are an almost continuous string of operations in which lethal little engagements take place within a campaign that looks more like the stretched out Battle of the Atlantic than the short, intense Battle of Midway.

The kamikaze attacks off Okinawa marked a turning point in operations at sea and metaphorically represent the start of the missile era. In that campaign, the U.S. Fleet, with nominal command of the sea, was severely stressed by land-launched suicide attacks.

The tactical purpose of a fighting fleet has been to take control of the local seas by destroying the enemy's fleet. The fighting fleet does so to allow free movement of goods and services on and from the sea and to deny these advantages to the enemy. When there is no fleet action in prospect, then the fleet with maritime preponderance supports the campaign on land directly with air and missile strikes. The usual measure of a fighting fleet's performance, enemy warships and aircraft destroyed, cannot be used then. A better measure is combat power delivered by the forces afloat.[18] But ships that are sunk or out of action cannot deliver anything, so the offense, defense, and staying power of a ship or force all need to be evaluated together. This can be done by estimating the net delivered combat power of a ship or force over its combat life.

---

18 Since the battle fleet does not itself transport many elements of power, a comprehensive view would include shipping protected as well as organic materials delivered. However, for practical purposes, it is difficult enough to measure just the fleet's own effectiveness.

8

THE GREAT TRENDS

On the Principles of War

In one of his most widely quoted maxims, Alfred Thayer Mahan wrote that "from time to time the structure of tactics has to be wholly torn down, but the foundations of strategy so far remain, as though laid upon a rock." What Mahan meant was that the principles of strategy are more lasting than tactics because they deal with broader, longer-term concepts, where the principles of tactics involve "using as [their] instruments the weapons made by man," which he said "shares in the change and progress of the race."[1]

Even so, there is a distinction between military principles—Mahan's or anyone else's—and the actions that derive from them. Just as the existence of strategic principles does not mean that strategies cannot change, tactics also change, but that does not preclude the search for tactical principles; both tactics and strategies are influenced by "weapons made by man." We can forgive Mahan for not foreseeing how weapons of the future would influence strategy, but there was evidence of change even as he wrote. During the transition from sail to steam propulsion, naval leaders had to revamp all the strategic practices of blockading. Sailing ships that stayed on station for months were being replaced by ships that lacked endurance and depended on coaling stations, the competition for which itself had a profound influence on strategy.

Philosophers sketch out a hierarchy of enlightenment that begins with truth, which they say exists, but never is known with certainty. From truth come principles, which express our contemporary vision of truth. From those principles come programs for concerted action—policy and doctrine. From those come strategic

---

1   Mahan, pp. 8, 88–89.

or tactical decisions, which are individual actions guided by policy and doctrine. Finally, throughout this construct error creeps in. Mahan's skewed prognostications of World War I strategy, based on his own principles, illustrate as well as anything the margin for error.

The armies of the world are much more given to studying principles than navies have ever been—a condition that Mahan deplored and which has not changed much. Most students of military history have avoided the problem of differentiating between strategic and tactical principles (and underlying logistics) by simply classifying both as principles of *war*. The search for enduring truth has ended in the compilation of many transitory lists. In an unpublished paper, CAPT S. D. Landersman, USN, assembled twenty-three lists of principles of warfare, including some written by naval officers.[2]

Principles on any subject have exceptions, and the exceptions to the principles of war tend to be crucial. "In war every problem, and every principle, is a duality," wrote Liddell Hart. "Like a coin, it has two faces. This is the inevitable consequence of the fact that war is a two-party affair, so imposing the need that while hitting, one must guard."[3] Clausewitz, who made no lists of principles himself but who was the father of lists, confounded his readers with propositions and variations, some of which were counterpropositions. He is the practitioner's delight and the theorist's frustration. On the subject of strategic concentration of forces, he wrote a very short chapter that can be quoted in its entirety:

> The best strategy is always to be very strong; first in general, and then at the decisive point. Apart from the effort needed to create military strength, which does not always emanate from the general, there is no higher and simpler law of strategy than that of keeping one's forces concentrated. No force should ever be detached from the main body unless the need is definite and urgent. We hold fast to this principle, and regard it as a reliable guide. In the course of our analysis, we shall learn in what circumstances dividing one's forces may be justified. We shall also learn that the principle of concentration will not have the same results in every war, but that those will change in accordance with means and ends.
>
> Incredible though it sounds, it is a fact that armies have been divided and separated countless times, without the commander having any clear reason for it, simply because he vaguely felt that this was the way things ought to be done.

---

2 His lists are included in appendix B.
3 Liddell Hart, p. 329.

This folly can be avoided completely, and a great many unsound reasons for dividing one's forces never be proposed, as soon as concentration of forces is recognized as the norm, and every separation and split as an exception that has to be justified.[4]

The principles of war must have important exceptions because most of the lists collectively conflict and few lists present their principles in order of priority. This is as it should be. Principles that conflict—such as concentration and economy and security and surprise—create a dynamic tension that is a small safeguard against heedless conformity, and the absence of priority forces the list-memorizer to pick and choose. Lists of principles help us deal with the entropy of war. The danger lies in the reader's memorizing lists as a substitute for study. A senior officer can hardly do more mischief to young officers than to lecture on a list of principles. He or she should lecture on their content instead.

The second weakness of principles of war is that they are usually reduced to key words, such as *concentration*. A word is not a principle. A principle is a statement of general truth. "Concentrate force" is a minimal statement of minimum value. "Mass superior force on a portion of the enemy's" is more specific and therefore more valuable. "Concentrate combat power at the decisive place and time to destroy the enemy, but do not mass your force so that it is vulnerable to enemy firepower" is still more specific, but it does not hold historically, even though it may be suitable today. Then there is the compelling way that the same principle was expressed in Soviet theory: "Concentrate the main effort and create superiority in forces and means over the enemy at the decisive place and time." Is that what we mean as well? At the very least, to be useful a principle of war must be current and prescriptive, clearly implying what actions must be taken to put it into practice.

A third weakness of the principles of war is that, uninterpreted, they do not distinguish strategy from tactics (or, if one insists, from "operational art"). Useful interpretations can be made, but in the transition from the general to the specific there is room for error. The Soviet military laws of war and "law-governed patterns" were cogent but also very abstract. The system of military science in the Soviet Union was one of the tightest ever constructed: confidence in theory and faith in determinism were between them the key to interpreting Soviet military plans and forecasting Soviet military actions.

---

4 Clausewitz, p. 204.

Another problem with the principles of war is that they fail to distinguish between land and sea combat. Regardless of the trend toward greater tactical interaction between land and sea forces and the fact that the *strategic* influence of sea and land forces has always existed and has not changed much, in combat there are salient differences between military and naval principles of action. The following list compares statements by T. N. Dupuy on army battle next to Hughes' statements on navy battle. The left-hand column is taken from chapter 1, "Timeless Verities of Combat," of Dupuy's book, *Understanding War.* The right-hand column is the naval counterpart to Dupuy's statements.

Land battle	Sea battle
1. Offensive action is essential to positive combat results.	True of sea battle.
2. Defensive strength is greater than offensive strength.	Defense is usually weaker.
3. Defensive posture is necessary when successful offense is impossible.	Defensive posture is inherently risk-prone and subject to incommensurate losses.
4. Flank or rear attack is more likely to succeed than frontal attack.	Attack from an unexpected quarter is advantageous, but the concept of envelopment has no parallel with land tactics.
5. Initiative permits application of preponderant combat power.	Initiative is especially valuable at sea.
6. A defender's chances of success are directly proportional to fortification strength.	Defensive power is solely to gain tactical time for an effective attack or counterattack.
7. An attacker willing to pay the price can always penetrate the strongest defense.	This is true of sea battle, given the wherewithal.
8. Successful defense requires depth and reserves.	At sea, setting aside reserves is a mistake.
9. Superior combat power always wins, if one takes into account the value of surprise, relative combat effectiveness, and the advantages of defensive posture as elements of strength.	When the appropriate qualifications are considered, it is possible to say that superior force will always win at sea. However, it is better to say that when two competitive forces meet in naval combat, the one that attacks effectively first will win.
10. Surprise substantially enhances combat power.	True of sea battle.
11. Firepower kills, disrupts, suppresses, and causes dispersion.	True of sea battle.
12. Combat activities are slower, less productive, and less efficient than anticipated [from peacetime tests, plans, and exercises].	Although this is often true, there are many examples of naval engagements in which the results come more swiftly than expected. Perhaps there is less friction at sea than on land.
13. Combat is too complex to be described in a single simple aphorism.	True of sea battle.

Although Dupuy's military verities do not consistently apply to sea combat, there is no reason to quarrel with them. Principles of war are useful. Like all good theory, they help explain the whys and wherefores—in contrast with practice, which deals with whens and wheres and hows. And yet, ultimately there is dissatisfaction with principles because they lead nowhere. After diligently distilling the statements of the wisest authorities into a flawless list—if it could be done—one would be positioned at an intellectual cul de sac. Without much loss, one might as well say that the contribution of principles to warfare boils down to out-thinking the enemy. Understanding the processes of combat is a better approach to tactics. Processes are the navigator's science and art; principles are the stars that mariners use to find their way.

The Processes of Combat

The key to fruitful study of tactics is an appreciation of how battles transpire in time and space. The activities—the dynamics—of combat are the wellspring of understanding. *Dynamics* suggest time-dependent models—descriptions of combat processes. Generally, models are images of processes; specifically, they are mathematical models, simulations, and war games that probe and add detail until the battlefield itself becomes the ultimate laboratory of understanding. That the study of battlefield dynamics constitutes the proper approach to study is reinforced by the universal terminology of warfare; the terms *power, potential, energy, pressure, mass, momentum, movement,* and *force* refer to the dynamics of physical bodies that warriors apply to the processes of combat.

Looking at fundamental processes enables tacticians to reexamine history and frame some conclusions about trends, constants, technology, and battlefield contexts—how technology wrought a change in the way each process was executed. As was noted in chapter 7, the delivery of firepower changed significantly when the age of sail gave way to the era of the big gun; big guns later gave way to the age of airpower. Technology changed the delivery process, and with it the tactical manner of concentrating firepower. Trends that are evolving now provide clues to combat in the missile age and the emerging new era of robotics and cyberwarfare.

The abstractions below do not follow from history the way that a falling apple inspired Sir Isaac Newton to develop the law of gravity. Evidence for social phenomena seldom is as conclusive as it is for physical phenomena, but it will serve well nevertheless.

Naval tactics are built on five propositions, each of which involves a process:

- Naval warfare centers on the process of attrition. Attrition comes from the successful delivery of firepower.
- Scouting—locating the enemy sufficiently to deliver effective firepower—is a crucial and integral process of tactics.
- Command-and-control, or C^2, is the process that transforms scouting and firepower potential into the reality of delivered force.
- Naval combat is a force-on-force process that often is accompanied by simultaneous attrition on both sides. To achieve victory one must attack effectively first. Therefore, actions taken to interfere with the enemy's firepower, scouting, and C^2 processes also are fundamentally important.
- Maneuver also is a tactical process. In fact, maneuver in battle was once the classic definition of tactics. Maneuver is the activity by which command-and-control positions forces to scout and shoot. Battle maneuver deserves—and receives—attention, but in the discussion that follows it is an orphan, no longer warranting its earlier status because maneuver is understood as more seamless now.
- The essence of information warfare is to interfere with the enemy's three fundamental processes—firepower delivery, scouting, and C^2—and defend our own.

Firepower delivery, scouting, and C^2 can be viewed not only as processes but as functioning elements of naval forces—firepower, scouts, and C^2 systems. Confronting these elements of force are three opposing elements: counterforce, antiscouts, and command-and-control countermeasures (C^2CM) systems.

Firepower and Counterforce

Firepower is the capacity to destroy the enemy's ability to apply force. Counterforce is the capacity to reduce the effect of delivered firepower. We could refer to offensive and defensive power, but it is useful to retain the asymmetry of counterforce as the defender's response to firepower. Although the practice is less common today, navies historically have answered enemy firepower by building survivability—known as "staying power" in the days of 16-inch guns and 18-inch turret faces—into the hulls of warships. Today, deception devices, chaff, and decoys substantially substitute for armor and physical staying power.

Scouts and Antiscouts

Scouts gather tactical information about the enemy's position, movements, vulnerabilities, strengths, and, in the best of worlds, intentions. To do this, they use several means—reconnaissance, surveillance, cryptanalysis, electronic signal detection, and other forms of information operations. But scouting is not completed until the information is delivered to the tactical commander. Antiscouts destroy, disrupt, or slow enemy scouts. This might be called interference screening, but screening has come to mean both antiscouting and counterforce—that is, ASW and AAW screens put as much or more emphasis on countering an enemy attack as on reducing the quality of its information.

C^2 and C^2CM Systems

There are two basic processes in command-and-control, or C^2. *Command* decides what is needed from forces and *control* transforms that need into action. C^2 systems are defined, perhaps a bit artificially, as the equipment and organizations by which the processes are performed. Command is embodied in commanders, their staffs, and material resources—for example, tactical decision aids and displays of processed scouting information. Control is embodied in communications equipment, the operation order, fleet doctrine, and a signal book. Command-and-control countermeasures (C^2CM) are steps to limit the enemy's ability to decide (command) and disseminate decisions (control). C^2CM devices include missiles that destroy command centers and flagships. More commonly they are communications-jamming equipment. At its most subtle, C^2CM is carried out by espionage agents planting misinformation and by false contacts, when they are used to confuse the tacticians' decision rather than divert their weapons. However, spies can perform acts of scouting, and signals exploitation—by RDF, for example—can be a form of scouting, too.

A tactical commander uses C^2 to allocate forces for four activities: firepower delivery, counterforce delivery, scouting, and antiscouting. Meanwhile, the enemy commander is doing the same thing. Many weapon systems have some capacity to conduct all four activities. From the fleet commanders' point of view, one of their major tactical responsibilities is to assign functions to their forces. They also must integrate the expected contributions of systems that are not under their direct command, such as national surveillance satellites, army surface-to-air weapons (when their own vessels are in port or unavailable), and air force interceptors that stand between their fleet and the enemy airfields—to include all tactically relevant contributions from allies and partners.

We shall now examine the historical trends that have altered the character of each process and the tactics that are associated with them. This chapter concentrates on the causes and effects of tactical change. In the next chapter we will examine the historical constants—what tactics have not changed—such as surprise, which continues to play an unwavering and important role. Knowledge of trends and knowledge of constants are equally important.

However, analyzing the processes separately can be deluding. Concerted action wins battles. The processes must be coordinated by a tactical commander in the way that a conductor manages and blends the instruments of an orchestra. The challenge for tactical commanders, however, is that at the same time their enemy counterpart is making decisions about their own forces and the timing of their attack. Both sides take steps building toward the climax and outcome of the battle. Except in battles where the result is a foregone conclusion, the winner will be the fleet most united in seeking the opportunity to attack effectively first.

Maneuver

Maneuver has a unique place in the list of processes. Through maneuver the elements of a force attain positions over time. The best hope of victory comes when all elements are in good positions to execute their assigned functions. At sea, positions are not fixed geographically (although some fleet components may be at fixed sites ashore).[5] Positions of opposing fleets exist in relation to one another, and, as elements maneuver their relative positions, are always in flux. In naval combat, the relationship between the range and bearing of one force to the other is a paramount tactical consideration that changes continually as vessels maneuver. Tracking the relative positions of one's own forces also is crucial—and sometimes frustratingly difficult to achieve.

During the age of fighting sail, ships used to stay in a tight column for cohesion and sought to be to windward or leeward of the enemy. Battleships maneuvered to cross the enemy's T. Picket submarines are pre-positioned to scout and attack in waters through which the enemy may pass. Aircraft are put on a CAP station so they can be vectored to a target or can maneuver on their own to attack. Deck-launched interceptors are in a state of readiness that is predetermined to give them time to move into a position for attack. In each case the emphasis is on the *timely positioning* of forces, which enables one to scout and shoot better than the enemy. *Maneuver* is the means to the intermediate end of establishing relative positions toward the ultimate tactical end of delivering firepower.[6] Particularly in modern naval combat, when weapon and sensor ranges so dominate the ability of

---

5 Ground combat seems different. Defendable positions achieved first have absolute value.
6 Again, we would not take the same stance regarding ground battle or tactics.

ships and aircraft to shift position, maneuver should enter into tacticians' calculations as the vital feasibility check against their plans for positioning and timing.

Moreover, the physical speed of ships, aircraft, and weapons can easily be confused with the speed of decision and the speed with which the decision is executed. To eliminate ambiguity would be to forgo any understanding of the interrelationships. Sun Tzu is often quoted as saying, "Speed is the essence of war." But it is apparent from his next sentence—"Take advantage of the enemy's unpreparedness"—that he was speaking of command. He also was speaking of mobility, for he then says that in order to capitalize on this unpreparedness one must move swiftly to the enemy's area of vulnerability. Mahan's aphorism "The true speed of war is . . . the unremitting energy that wastes no time" is deliciously ambiguous, although he referred specifically to battle-line speed. Mahan grasped as well as anyone that timely delivery of concentrated firepower involved the conjoining of everything—decisions and their dissemination, strategic aggregation, tactical positioning, and fast, accurate gunfire.

Maneuver and *mobility* are terms sometimes used interchangeably. Mobility is an element of strategy, operational art, or grand tactics. When Mahan described mobility as "the prime characteristic of naval strength," he was expressing a truth of strategy. Mobility consists of the ability to accomplish these actions:

- To move long distances in a self-sustaining manner. Mobile logistic support forces have made this possible.
- To move apace, that is, quickly in relation to the movement of ground forces or the establishment of new airfields or missile bases ashore.
- To operate at length, up to several months on or near station. Both naval bases and mobile logistic forces have made this practical.

For mobility, ships without mobile logistic support forces must have their own built-in range and endurance. Nuclear propulsion in surface ships is an attribute of strategy. In contrast, nuclear propulsion in submarines is an attribute of both mobility and effective tactical maneuver and stealth.

Maneuver is *tactical* speed and agility. Fleet maneuver must be collective, coordinated motion, so it is impossible to divorce C^2 and speed of decision from this discussion. Trade-offs can be made between the amounts of time it takes to scout, to assimilate information, to decide, to order, to maneuver, and to deliver effective firepower. Speed and agility of platform—a warship or a warplane—are two elements of speedy action. Enjoying an advantage in maneuverability helps compensate for shortcomings in other areas.

Two trends have become evident in maneuver today. The first is a shift of emphasis from speed of platform to speed of weapon. Until World War II, maneuvering the fleet was the very heart of tactics. During the war, aircraft speed took precedence over ship speed. Since the war, missile speed and range have created a tactical environment in which weapons are delivered without much change in ship position. Missile speed and agility are nullifying even aircraft agility, and farsighted combat aviators concede that missile maneuvers now dominate air warfare, as aircraft dominate ships' tactical maneuvers.

The second trend of maneuver is a corollary of the first. Ship maneuverability has diminished in importance and given way to scouting. "The fundamental tactical position," wrote Guiseppe Fioravanzo, "is no longer defined by the *geometric* relationship of the opposing formations, but by an *operational* element: the early detection of the enemy."[7] The significance of this development is that firepower might be more easily concentrated at long range, when naval forces are physically divided. This is a possibility emphasized by ADM Elmo Zumwalt, ADM Worth Bagley, and ADM Stansfield Turner.[8]

We have alluded to the larger no-man's-land brought about by longer weapon range. It is more difficult now to distinguish between movement to the scene of battle (known as strategic mobility) and movement to attack and win (called tactical maneuver). Since battles can occur at very long ranges, the value of mobility has been diminished or modified, and, in theory, the existence of very long, powerful missiles has neutralized the strategic capacity of mobile forces to shift the scene of action. On the other hand, long-range delivery systems in effect endow speed with a new *tactical* attribute by enabling a ship to move out from under an enemy's own targeting solution for long-range missiles.

Historically, maneuver has been used for three purposes:

- Advantageously concentrating offensive or defensive force—except that strategically the importance of fleet motion has diminished.
- Striking more quickly. Important as this element of tactics is and always will be, the relative importance of speed in ships and aircraft themselves is diminishing.

---

7 Fioravanzo, p. 209.
8 These officers were prominent leaders of the U.S. Navy in the early 1970s. Zumwalt was CNO from 1970 to 1974, and Bagley was his vice chief during much of the same period. Turner's influence on the Navy was probably at its peak when he was president of the Naval War College, from 1972 to 1974. They were creative, imaginative and—in the collective mind of the conservative Navy—unconventional.

- Protecting a force by evading the enemy's weapons. The value of speed in self-defense is increasing. Agility is still important, but hardly more so than in the past.

Firepower

The most conspicuous trend in the history of warfare is the increase in weapon range, from two miles or so in the days of fighting sail to fifteen miles or more in the era of the big gun, three hundred miles during World War II, and six hundred miles or more today. Since intercontinental missiles with nuclear warheads reach halfway around the world, we have arrived at a plateau: in nuclear warfare the potential tactical battlefield is the globe.

Regardless of this trend, *maximum* weapon range has never been very interesting to the tactician. What matters is the *effective* range. The long guns of sailing ships were effective at only about three hundred yards, and carronades were limited to an even shorter distance. Around 1900, before continuous-aim fire, it was estimated that a battleship would take fifty minutes to reduce an enemy to impotence at a range of 2,500 yards. By 1914 it would take only ten minutes, in good visibility, to put an enemy out of action at ten thousand yards. The effectiveness of the major-caliber battleship guns at the time of World War I is shown in figure 8-1, which assumes good visibility, acceptable sea states, and the use of visual range-finding equipment. Fire control was the key in that war. The performances in figure 8-1 are nominal and take little account of the smoke of gunfire or of destroyer smoke screens. At the Battle of Coronel, the Battle of the Falklands (1914), or the battle cruiser action at Jutland, when visibility was pretty good, the outcome would be decided outside ten thousand yards. Nevertheless, when visibility was an issue—in the action between the battle lines at Jutland, for example—a fleet could save itself by opening out expeditiously, as the German High Seas Fleet did.

In World War II, radar ranging changed that. Gun ballistics became so accurate, with refined fire-control systems, that even medium-caliber 5-, 6-, and 8-inch guns could be fired accurately almost to their maximum range.[9] In the half-century from 1898 to 1948, the effective range of naval weapons increased about tenfold.

The increasing effectiveness of shipboard gunfire was obscured by the growing use of aircraft for bombing early in World War II. But aircraft themselves

---

9   We should never forget, however, that situations can arise such as those described in chapter 5 regarding gunnery effectiveness in the Solomons.

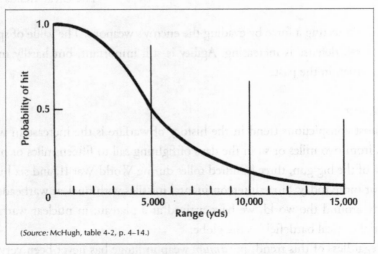

Figure 8-1. Probability of Hitting with Battleship Guns as a Function of Range, ca. 1916

(*Source:* McHugh, table 4-2, p. 4–14.)

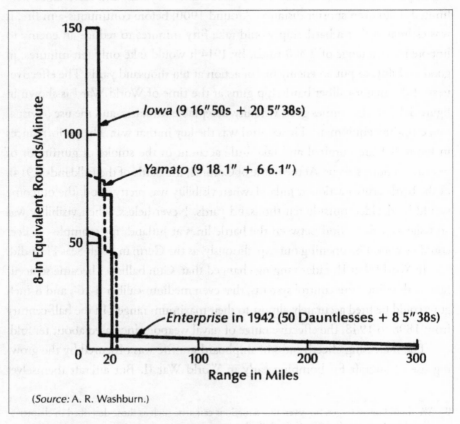

Figure 8-2. Rate of Fire versus Range in 8-inch Rounds/Minute Equivalents

(*Source:* A. R. Washburn.)

exhibited a visible distinction between gross weapon-delivery range and effective range. In the 1930s engineers designed land-based B-17 bombers specifically to carry out attacks on warships at great range. Yet, horizontal bombers turned out to be almost totally ineffective; they had difficulty finding naval targets at long range and experienced even more difficulty hitting them at any range. Naval aircraft of much shorter ranges proved to be the best ship-killers.

In a short unpublished paper, A. R. Washburn of the Naval Postgraduate School makes a comparison between naval aircraft and naval guns. For representative battleships and aircraft carriers, he plots firepower versus range, as shown in figure 8-2, which displays the weight-rate of firepower delivered in 8-inch-gun equivalent rounds. The firing-rate for the main battery of the USS *Iowa* (BB 61) was two rounds per minute; for the Japanese battleship *Yamato*, it was one round per minute; for the aircraft the turnaround time was estimated as one hour. By comparison, the entire "main battery" of the carrier USS *Enterprise* (CV 6) was paltry; instead, the range of the ship's aircraft was decisive against enemy carriers because the weight of attack, in 1942 and 1943 at least, was *sufficient* for decisiveness. Before the war, the tactician's mental model looked a lot like Washburn's curves. The pro-battleship community doubted that the weight of an air strike would be sufficient for decisiveness, especially when defensive considerations were factored in. But the pro-carrier community tended to think of the weight of attack in terms of the attacking wave of bombers sixty times as great as what the

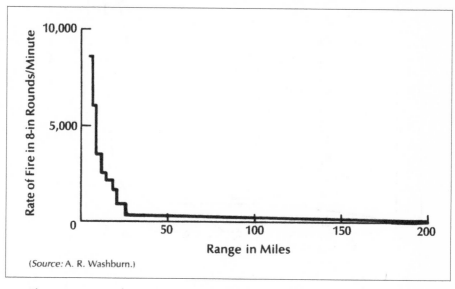

(*Source:* A. R. Washburn.)

Figure 8-3. Rate of Fire of the Entire U.S. Fleet in 1939

figure shows. An air-wing attack was to be a decisive pulse of power. Washburn also aggregated the firepower of the U.S. Fleet in 1939, the result of which is shown in figure 8-3. The result shows why the question of the potential that carrier aviation might have for decisive action was controversial before World War II.

Today, the trend continues—toward greater nominal range, through more compact ballistic- and cruise-missile propulsion systems, and toward greater effective range by means of sophisticated fire-control and homing systems. There also is a trend toward increased raw destructive power. The growth in weapon lethality has been as important as the increase in range. This has been systematically

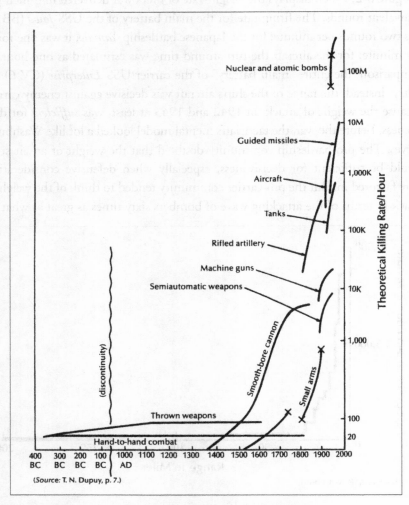

(Source: T. N. Dupuy, p. 7.)

Figure 8-4. The Increase of Weapon Lethality over History

studied for land-combat weapons by T. N. Dupuy, whose work on the increase of theoretical lethality is displayed in figure 8-4.[10] Notice that the vertical scale is logarithmic. After concluding that, even omitting nuclear weapons, the lethality of weapons has increased by five orders of magnitude—that is, 100,000 times—between the middle of the sixteenth century and the present time, Dupuy uncovers a paradox. While weapon lethality on the battlefield grew, the rate of personnel casualties per unit time shrank. Why? One prominent reason was the increased dispersion of troops on the battlefield.

Hanging over the head of civilization is the Damocles sword of nuclear weaponry. To an extent an intercontinental exchange of weapons between North America and Asia has been replaced by the threat of a terrorist attack by nuclear, chemical, or biological weapons. In the closing days of the Soviet Union it was small comfort to observe that the U.S. and Russian arsenals had reached a plateau in the increase in the range and lethality of individual nuclear weapons. Speaking tactically, there is some uncertainty as to whether the *effective* range of these weapons is truly intercontinental, since they have never been employed. Both civilization, which must suffer the consequences of badly aimed weapons, and tacticians, who must deal with the uncertainties of ineffective delivery, can hope *for* missiles, ballistic or cruise, that will travel thousands of miles and land as predicted, within a few score meters.

As we saw in chapter 7, the threat of nuclear weapons created enormous practical difficulties. Yet, even apart from nuclear warheads, the increased effective weapon range by itself points to these developments:

- A change in the form of defense. This will be taken up in the next section of this chapter.
- A further erosion of the distinction between land and sea battle, to be discussed in chapter 11. The emphasis here is on the greater potential for combat between land and sea forces; this is an important *tactical* trend that heightens the struggle between land forces, which have greater recuperative power, and sea forces, which are more difficult to target because of their maneuverability.
- The fusion of strategy and tactics for unlimited war.

The last of these is worth considering first. Because of the unpleasantness of the prospect of unlimited war—and a general trust in the ability of the nuclear

---

10 Dupuy (1979). See especially p. 7 and chapters 1 and 2.

umbrella to deter it—too little thought has been given to the combat execution of intercontinental war. The term *strategic weapons* itself is beguiling: if a general nuclear war breaks out, the entire world is effectively a tactical battlefield, directed by commanders and staffs operating in the highest-level command posts. It is crucial that tacticians direct attention to this area.

In the 1960s and 1970s, the paradigm of nuclear war was this: the president pushes the red button, which dispatches thousands of Minuteman and Polaris missiles in one huge spasm. One does not have to take that flawed and now obsolete model literally to see the need for a more effective—and rational—method of command-and-control in the twenty-first century. In such a war of supreme destructiveness, the centers of C^2 themselves would be attacked with unprecedented ferocity. Commanders and their staffs in positions up through unified and specified commanders would be the officers in tactical command, selecting targets, gathering intelligence, issuing orders to fire, and conducting the battle on a worldwide scale. All of the usual tactical responsibilities would devolve on these commanders and staffs—for operational plans, for communications with forces bearing arms, for timeliness of commands to move and shoot, for access to survivable scouting information, and for tactical training in the heat of simulated battle. Even the combatant commanders, four-star flag and general officers, cannot think of themselves any longer as dealing solely with strategy and logistics. When they control the targeting and release of all manner of weapons, they will serve as tactical commanders on the vast field of battle.

Counterforce

The prominent trend in defense is away from survivability through armor, compartmentation, bulk, and damage control, and toward cover, deception, and dispersion. To discuss defense a distinction must be made between "dumb" weapons such as shot, shells, and bombs and "smart" weapons such as manned and unmanned aircraft and guided missiles. For purposes of analysis, aircraft are guided missiles, except that they can be used more than once.

When shells, torpedoes, and bombs dominated warfighting, there was every possibility of building substantial staying power into warships. Since battles were fought within visual range, there were limited means of achieving cover and deception. The smoke screen was the most common cover device. Bombs from horizontal bombers could usually be evaded, and salvo chasing had some temporary effect.

Torpedo countermeasures were the prototypes of today's defenses against missiles. A torpedo was highly lethal, and the best defense was to avoid it. To compensate, attackers fired spreads. Submarines tried to fire them at point-blank range, and surface ships tried to coordinate simultaneous attacks in the greatest numbers possible. In every case, brave attackers closed as much as they dared, because torpedoes, once fired, were irretrievable. There are many parallels between the torpedo and the modern missile scenarios.

Even in their heyday, armor and hull strength were rarely thought of as offering as much security against shells as deep bunkers in the ground. Armor was a dilatory device, used to forestall enemy firepower until one's own offensive power took effect. In those days, there was much discussion of the division of a ship's displacement between firepower, staying power (protective armor), and propulsion power. Before and after World War I, each country had its own style: Americans sacrificed speed for guns, armor, and radius of action; the Germans opted for staying power; the Italians emphasized speed; and the British (like the Americans today) incorporated habitability for extended worldwide deployments in big ships.

In the war games of the battleship era, the typical first-line dreadnought had a life of about twenty major-caliber hits; the pre-dreadnought had a life of twelve hits.[11] The loss of firepower and maneuverability was treated as a nonlinear function of the number of hits—that is, a dreadnought suffering ten hits in U.S. war games would lose more than half its firepower and speed.

In the 1920s game experts at the Naval War College saw that it was possible to aggregate the effectiveness of the battle line, taking both firepower and staying power into account. Figure 8-5 displays a comparison between opposing battle lines on parallel courses, with all ships' broadsides able to bear, and with *unimpeded* visibility. The U.S. Pacific Fleet (shown as blue force) comprises ten battleships. All are more heavily armed and armored than the six battleships and four battle cruisers of the Japanese (shown as orange force). At 15,000 yards, in *three* minutes the Japanese line will lose 20 percent of its original life, the American line only 15 percent. The relative Japanese strength will deteriorate very rapidly. If the Japanese are to have hope of winning, they must count on their speed to cross the T before the range is closed, or they must try to maintain an interval between battle lines of about 25,000 yards, where they have an advantage.

As suggested in chapter 4, both the Americans and the Japanese knew these relationships in the 1920s. American fears centered on the Japanese advantage in line speed (twenty-three knots for the Japanese versus eighteen knots for U.S.

11 Around the time of World War I, one or two torpedo hits were considered fatal.

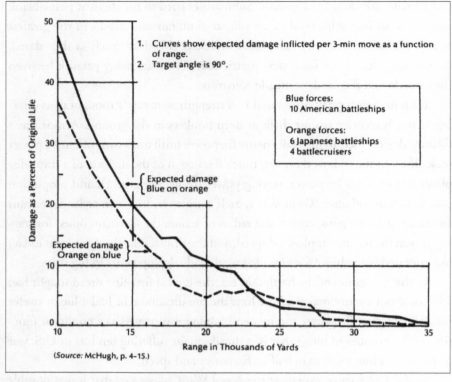

Figure 8-5. A Naval War College Comparison of Opposing Battle Lines, 1926

forces), the possibility of surprise, and the lurking danger that the U.S. Fleet would be too crippled after eliminating the Japanese to fulfill its mission. (In war games, this was the relief of the Philippines.) The Japanese hoped that their submarines would inflict initial damage, their aircraft and Long Lance torpedoes would effect further damage, and that their *Mogami*-class light cruisers, retooled secretly with 8-inch guns, would significantly augment the battle line. There were, as we know now, catastrophic surprises to both sides after the war in the Pacific commenced. It is useful, nevertheless, to recall once more the coherence of planning on both sides, the legitimate American concern for the unexpected, and the lightning pace of decision. The kinds of force comparisons shown in war games were familiar, and the games were played through to add dynamics to static plots such as that presented in figure 8-5. Although the pace of destruction rarely unfolded as rapidly as that figure foretold, it still was furious, and we can believe that the friction of war was not wholly discounted when these pre-war planning aids were used.

In World War II defensive *weapons* assumed unprecedented prominence. By 1942 a flood of AAW weapons was being installed, with radar sensors, deadly proximity fuzes, and new, capable fire-control systems to lead and hit fast-moving targets. By 1944 attacking aircraft faced a veritable curtain of fire. In the last year of the war, modern surface combatants had redressed the balance of power they had lost to naval aircraft.

The ascendancy of the ship lasted a mere moment, for at the end of World War II it was eclipsed by the atomic bomb, and armor was not effective as a protection from nuclear blasts. Cover and deception and the urgency of a first strike took on overwhelming significance. Air interceptors, AAW missiles, and ASW weapons were more than ever temporizing weapons. The American posture was all the trickier because the U.S. Navy could never attack first, certainly not with nuclear weapons. How to buy enough time to deliver a massive strike ashore was the tactical question. Judging from the enormous Soviet naval effort to counter U.S. carrier task forces, the Americans were eminently successful. But they paid a price: with nuclear war in mind, they built ships without much survivability against conventional munitions. They concentrated on long-range defensive weapons—air interceptors and missiles—and neglected the guns and the modern close-in "point" defenses that were analogous to the 20- and 40-mm guns of World War II. They also neglected the development of new soft-kill devices— short-range systems that could not reach out far enough against nuclear weapons. The Royal Navy followed a similar bent and neglected damage control and point defense. It suffered the consequences when its ships fought to retake the Falklands with conventional weapons. By contrast, Israeli warships prepared for the 1973 war by developing soft-kill defenses against Syrian and Egyptian weapons so successfully that they all survived unscathed.

The preceding section on firepower mentioned T. N. Dupuy's paradox— that although weapon lethality has increased one-hundred-thousand-fold since the sixteenth century, the casualty rate in ground combat has diminished. The data in chapter 7 show a corresponding reduction in casualties at sea. The trend is toward greater destruction in materiel, not lives. Why is this?

First, the number of highly capable weapons per soldier on the battlefield has decreased; weapons such as tanks, fighter-bombers, and heavy artillery account for much of the rise in the theoretical killing-rate. In actual battle, however, a greater percentage of today's casualties sometimes has been inflicted by other weapons. For example, infantry small arms exceeded artillery in producing casualties *after* the range and lethality of artillery rose dramatically. Often the second-best weapon performs better because the enemy, at great cost in offensive effectiveness, takes extraordinary measures to survive the best weapon.[12]

Second, in the past, ground combat weapons often could not be aimed at their targets when those enemy forces took cover, and therefore they were less than nominally effective. As weapon range increased, the effects of inaccuracy in weapon delivery increased greatly. Area fire breaks up concentration of force and suppresses enemy fire, but it is inefficient for killing.

Third, increasingly troops have been dispersed for survival. Dupuy estimates that between the Napoleonic Wars and the 1973 Arab-Israeli War the average density of troops on the battlefield was diluted by a factor of two hundred.[13]

Of special relevance to naval warfare is that the rate of destruction of hardware, tanks in particular, has far exceeded that of troops. A highly dangerous enemy machine draws fire because it is dangerous, but it is not correspondingly manpower-dense and so not many casualties result from its being put out of action.

Ground forces disperse over the battlefield in clusters, not evenly. A platoon of men is a small cluster of force, a tank is a big one. Ships at sea are still bigger clusters of force, whether measured in firepower, manpower, or dollar-value. The smallest unit that can be dispersed is a ship. When dispersion is an important means of defense, small ships and distributed firepower are an important advantage. Much of the modern debate over the size of warships concerns the comparative merits of dispersal in small ships, used to complicate enemy targeting, and of concentration of force in large ships to fight off the enemy. The Pacific carrier wars provided some insight that illuminated the problem. It was *defensive* fighting power that decided whether a force should mass or disperse. Today if fleets comprise large ships with strong defenses, commanders mass them and fight the enemy off. If they have small ships or weak defenses they must disperse. In either case they are buying time to carry out their mission, which is not to steam around waiting to be sunk. If the defense cannot buy time for the offense to perform, then the fleet ought to be somewhere else.

---

12 We saw this phenomenon in the Falklands War. The Argentine air force lost only eight, or about 10 percent, of its aircraft to the British ships' most expensive AAW defense, their SAM missile batteries (Sea Darts). The Argentine pilots knew that if they hugged the water the SAMs would be ineffective, and the British ships shot down most of the attackers with short-range weapons. Nevertheless, the "ineffective" SAMs were vital to the defense because they constricted the Argentine pilots' maneuvering room, helped make the British close-in defenses more effective, and forced the pilots to drop their bombs at so short a range that sometimes the ones that hit had had no time to arm.

13 Dupuy (1979), figure 2-4, p. 28.

The American experience since World War II has been in conventional warfare, with U.S. warships for all practical purposes operating in a sanctuary, either out of range of enemy weapons or fighting an enemy such as North Korea, North Vietnam, or Iraq that lacked the force to attack effectively. As the U.S. Navy's bread-and-butter missions for thirty years, these "projection" operations have probably bred complacency about the nature of combat, which is not always so one-sided an affair; until recently, they have clearly affected American attitudes toward defense, damage control, ship construction, and survivability.

There also is a paradox in contemporary American naval doctrine for operational maneuver from the sea. Much emphasis is placed on small, agile forces ashore because of the hazard from enemy precision munitions. Equal attention should be given to the threat of precision missiles incapacitating U.S. Navy ships off the enemy coast in support of ground operations.

Tacticians should always remember that the reason for building survivability into a vessel is to gain time for the offense. Critics who talk about surface ship vulnerability ignore this. The less knowledgeable assume that expensive ships should stand up in combat forever; the wiser contend that big ships are not worth the money, and that if someday there is an alternative that delivers superior net force—that is to say, delivers firepower over a ship's combat lifetime—they will be correct.

Important to understanding these discussions is the way the fleet tactician looks at defensive force. Defensive systems collectively act like a filter (not a wall or a Maginot line) that extracts a certain number of incoming aircraft or missiles. As it is able, a hull absorbs hits and enables the warship to conduct curtailed offensive operations.

World War II AAW weapons destroyed some air attackers and distracted others with a curtain of fire. Modern hard- and soft-kill defenses do the same. Up to a point, the defense takes out a high percentage of the attackers. When the attack is dense and well coordinated, an active AAW defense will become saturated at a certain point, beyond which most missiles or aircraft will get through. The modern concentrated air or missile attack aims to reach past the saturation point of the defense.

Two other trends bear mentioning. One is the growth of a tactical no-man's-land, a region where neither side can operate its main force and where pickets (aircraft, submarines, and small-surface missile craft) will fight fierce subordinate engagements to create weakness or gather information. The no-man's-land exists because defense needs room. In conventional war, battle space translates into time to react against attack. In missile warfare it may be that no defense is adequate and that space is needed simply to stay out of reach or to make it too difficult for the enemy to target moving ships. A smaller no-man's-land has long existed. In the past, daylight surface actions that used guns did not occur at less than two thousand yards: action was fatal before the range closed to that point. Battle lines did not expect to fight at ten thousand yards, the zone where destroyers lurked. Carriers did not want to approach other warships closer than one hundred miles. A miscalculation or an adverse wind would put guns within range, and it would all be over in fifteen minutes. HMS *Glorious* discovered this, and many more of the U.S. jeep carriers off Samar might have been sunk at the Battle for Leyte Gulf had Vice Admiral Takeo Kurita not lost his nerve and retreated with his overwhelmingly superior Japanese surface fleet.

The second is the growing vulnerability of ships in port. Ports have traditionally been havens for navies superior and inferior. Although few harbors have ever been absolutely safe from attack, the strategy of the nation that has the weaker navy has been heavily influenced by the consideration that a fleet-in-being could be reasonably safeguarded in port. But this has changed; the security of ports has diminished. Pearl Harbor, of course, marked the transition, as did several other striking if less well-known events. On the night of 11 November 1940, for example, a handful of torpedo planes from HMS *Illustrious* surprised the heavily protected Italian fleet at the port of Taranto. They put three of six Italian battleships out of action for six months and one for the rest of the war, and the Italian fleet fled to Naples.[14] After Sherman's carriers struck Rabaul in November 1943, the Japanese navy was so stunned that it soon withdrew to Truk. Not much later, in 1944, carrier strikes penetrated Truk, and the Japanese, unable to challenge the United States at sea and completely frustrated by the U.S. Navy's ability to concentrate overwhelming air power against any island bastion, withdrew into the western Pacific. Today, almost half a century later, ships are often safer outside of home port than in.

Scouting

The goal of scouting is to help get weapons within range and aim them effectively. Scouting gathers information and reports it. The dominant trend in scouting has been the increasing rate of search and the increasing range of reconnaissance, surveillance, and intelligence-gathering systems. The reason is obvious: longer-range

---

14 Roskill (1960), pp. 110–14.

weapons demand such improvements. Less obvious is the reason that scouting has had to struggle to keep up. Weapons fire in any direction. In figures 8-1 through 8-5 we saw firepower represented in one dimension. Figure 8-6 considers an aircraft reconnaissance mission in World War II whose search-area looks like a pie-shape. Double the range of the enemy's attack aircraft and you quadruple the area to be searched. A barrier search—a scouting line—can sometimes cover the perimeter of this expanded area. The bent-line screen invented late in World War II to detect submarines in front of a carrier is an example. Still, tactical commanders cannot often be satisfied with a scouting *line*. For one thing, it is usually pervious: submarines that can approach submerged and launch missiles are a threat that seemingly springs from anywhere at or inside a missile range. For another, searches cannot always be continuous. In World War II, when scouts or patrol planes in tactical support were launched by the Japanese and Americans at dawn after a night without reconnaissance, they were never sure how far out the enemy might be found.

Most commanders today would like to track every ship and aircraft that might be a threat. As weapon range has increased, the area involved, expanding as the square of weapon range, stretches the surveillance capacity of most nations to its limit. Even American surface surveillance is challenged, not so much by the ability to see contacts as by the ability to classify them either enemy or harmless. This is especially true of contacts in cluttered coastal waters.

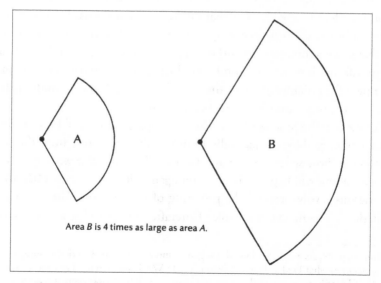

Area *B* is 4 times as large as area *A*.

Figure 8-6. Illustration of Search Capacity as an Area Concept

There is a second development that has affected scouting. Recall the scouting line thrown out in advance of the World War I Grand Fleet. Its placement was not governed by gunnery range, but by calculating the time it would take to relay a signal to Jellicoe by wireless, plus twenty minutes to allow for the shift from cruising formation to battle line before the enemy closed to weapon range. As we have noted, in warfare space is equivalent to reaction time. Now that missiles can approach at twice the speed of sound or greater, reaction time is so compressed that the scouting line must account for both missile range and the time it takes to act against air, surface, or submarine launch platforms. Some authorities illustrate this with three circles or pie slices. The smallest is the region of *control:* any enemy inside it must be destroyed. The next is the region of *influence* or competition, something like a no-man's-land. The largest is the region of *interest:* friendly ships must be prepared to deal with an enemy inside it. Scouting seeks targeting data in the first region; tracking in the second; and detection in the third. So the effect of the increase in weapon system range and speed has not been simply to increase the area in which weapons may be delivered, but also to expand the size of the battle-field so that it includes the entire region of scouting and preliminary maneuver.

The vertical dimension of the battlefield also has been extended—deeper beneath the surface to the seabed and higher above it to space. This complicates the tactician's thinking enormously. One must deal simultaneously with operations on multiple levels or domains, each with its own set of weapon ranges and con-straints and scouting capabilities—and each also continually evolving. Ballistic missiles have trajectories, torpedoes have drag, and air-to-air missiles have g-limits. The commander's bedevilment is that tactical decisions must be woven into all domains. Submarines torpedo enemy surface ships, of course, but the complica-tion is that when submarines or surface ships fire missiles, a subsurface or surface threat transforms into an "air" problem. Tactical commanders are not playing three games of simultaneous chess; they are playing one game on multiple boards with pieces that may jump from one board to another.

Warfare is in the process of extending into space. Space will be an additional plane of action, as different tactically from the air as the air is from the surface. No one knows how space combat and tactics will evolve, but we may be certain that space warfare will happen. James Dunnigan writes in *How to Make War* that "air operations revolve around the gathering of information. They always have; they still do."[15] The first wartime role of aircraft, on land and at sea, was scouting.

---

15 Dunnigan, p. 98. As a creator of good war games and a critic of bad tactics, Dunnigan is to this generation what Fred T. Jane was before World War I and Fletcher Pratt was before World War II. If Dunnigan does as well as Jane and Pratt, he will be almost right about 75 percent of the time, which is not so bad.

Aircraft were so successful in this that the antiscout—the pursuit plane—was invented. In World War I all other aircraft roles were inconsequential by comparison. The same sequence of events is certain to hold in space. Space satellites already are enormously important for surface surveillance. In some particulars they are peerless for scouting. Like antiaircraft fire in World War I, earth-launched anti-satellite systems are not the best countermeasure. Neither are the current means of cover and deception. As a direct result of the fundamental importance of scouting, "pursuit" systems in space will be invented to destroy surveillance satellites. Space bombers will follow some day soon. If the past offers insight, a descendant of Giulio Douhet will prophesy the end of ground combat with the arrival of strategic space bombers, and a twenty-first-century Billy Mitchell will prematurely predict the victimization of all warships from space.

Antiscouting

Before the age of the big gun, the only cover at sea was incidental gunsmoke or accidental fog. With the advent of the big gun, weapon evasion was recognized as an important tool of war. Surface warships could avoid or delay being hit chiefly by putting up smoke screens, chasing salvoes, and combing torpedo wakes.[16] These were antitargeting devices—ways to confound the enemy's weapon delivery. As the destructiveness and range of weapons grew, the means of surviving weapon attacks diminished and the emphasis shifted to reducing the enemy's scouting effectiveness. Antiscouting became possible when tacticians began to conduct scouting at long range to account for the phenomenal growth in weapon range. Antiscouting by cover, deception, and evasion would now aim at limiting detection, tracking, or targeting.[17]

Submarines stayed submerged to avoid detection as well as to attack. Carrier task force commanders tried to stand aside, avoid detection, and attack enemy carriers first. Spruance decided to guard the beaches at Saipan and Guam because he thought the enemy might move in around him. The Japanese especially exploited the cover of weather, and the cover of night allowed high-speed carriers to run in

---

16 The idea behind salvo chasing was this: If the enemy observed shell splashes that fell short, he would correct by adding range to the next salvo. If you steered in to close the range, you would do so in the hope that his next salvo would be too long.

17 Other terms include *stealth* for cover; *distortion* and *disinformation* for deception; *obfuscation* for evasion with jamming or decoys. Cover prevents the enemy from knowing your presence. Deception makes him think you are elsewhere and draws his fire away. Evasion ruins or delays his attack. Ervin Kapos likes to speak of "C and D" as confusion and dilution. Another complication: in the U.S. Army, *cover* means protection. Soldiers take cover by digging foxholes or getting behind rocks.

and attack airfields ashore. Land-based aircraft usually outranged the carriers, but their airfields were fixed and known.

Radar was a terrific scouting system, but passive radar-detectors could pick up the enemy at longer, tactically significant ranges. Radar countermeasures gave early warning, but it did not provide counter-targeting information. For German U-boats trying to evade—not fight—the aircraft of the British Coastal Command, passive detection was enough. For the Japanese in the Solomons, early detection was important, but they did not provide the targeting information that they needed to deliver firepower.

By World War II, communications countermeasures were as important as search and targeting countermeasures. RDF and code-breaking positioned the enemy sufficiently to concentrate an attack. In an important example of this, German surface raiders, merchant raiders, and an extensive network of resupply ships and tankers were located and swept from the seas in 1941 not by aircraft scouting, as was commonly believed, but by Allied code-breakers reading the coded traffic that was being transmitted to German vessels.[18]

A natural result of search and communications countermeasures was counter-countermeasures. At Cape Esperance, Scott turned off his flagship's radar at great tactical cost; he thought the enemy would otherwise be alerted. The whole structure of communications since World War I has been based on the reasonable proposition that whenever you talk, the enemy listens. During the war, the assumption was usually that plain talk would be understood while encoded talk would alert the enemy, sometimes giving away one's location but without revealing anything about intentions. As we now know, using code was riskier than this. Also, simple factors such as the time it took to encrypt and decrypt messages and the chance of adding error or misunderstanding during transmission tremendously frustrated commanders when speed and accuracy were vital. For at least the first six months of the war, American tacticians manifestly underestimated the friction and confusion caused by communications security.

People who think that automated encryption and decryption have solved the problem would do well to reconsider. Beyond the threat of pilfered information, the equipment costs money, there never is enough of it, and incompatible interfaces turn up at just the wrong moment, especially in joint operations such as the invasion of Grenada. On the face of it, these and the other possibilities inherent in very-long-range warfare portend antiscouting opportunities and scouting inhibitions in combinations that almost are beyond our grasp. The trends of warfare say this will be so.

18 Beesly, pp. 91–97; Hughes and Costello, pp. 153–55.

C² and C²CM

In the first edition, the text concluded that C² trends are less important than constants. This is probably still true, but there is a widespread belief that information warfare is new and revolutionary. This section has been reworded with particular care because some experts in technology expect that future tactical commanders will have a clear and immediate picture of the battlefield. A contradictory—and more accurate—assessment is emerging concerning the tactical *uncertainties* about the impending battle. Chapter 13 discusses the unstable conditions that aggravate the uncertainty in missile warfare. Modern tactical commanders work mostly with electronic clues about their enemy (and often even about their own forces). A commander of fighting sail saw much more of the battle than today's commanders can see through their electronic eyes, but still he could not see everything. Jellicoe and Scheer, Spruance and Nagumo, and Tanaka and Burke all lacked crucial information and had to make pivotal tactical decisions while operating literally or figuratively in the dark. If this lack of information were simply a tactical constant and no more of a burden than before, it would be sobering enough. But a reasonable conclusion from naval history is that the next battlefield will spring more surprises. Now, without good scouting, the enemy's missiles can come anytime, and with speed that was never possible under sail and only sometimes possible in World War II. A commander at sea faces a twenty-four-hour war. The nighttime Battle of the Nile was an anomaly in 1798. In modern war, night action is commonplace.

The increasing value of surprise is directly supported by the research of Barton Whaley. In his book *Stratagem: Deception and Surprise in War,* he analyzed eighty-six land battles that took place from 1914 to 1953. Later he extended his study, covering twenty-five more cases that carried him up to 1973.[19] Whaley concludes that during these years the use of deception increased in order to achieve surprise, and that surprise became more difficult to achieve without deception. For similar reasons, deception probably grew more important on the oceans. Today new and remarkable surveillance and reconnaissance systems make it more difficult for a fleet to mount a coordinated attack without giving the enemy any inkling that it is coming. But the range, complexity, and redundancy of scouting systems and

---

19 His extensive research work was completed in 1969. It was supplemented by Whaley and Ronald Sherman in Daniel and Herbig, pp. 177–94. Although strategic deception was Whaley's emphasis, research by CPT William Van Vleet, USA, led to similar conclusions on the value of tactical surprise and deception in land warfare. Van Vleet also records the most common methods of success on the battlefield.

the complicated process of fusing their products opens new doors to the ingenuity of a tactician who is disposed to deception.

The continuing pressure on tacticians will be unparalleled. What sort of combat leader is suited to this new environment? People of youth, vigor, and moral and physical stamina, as important as they have always been, will assume even greater prominence.

Another consequence of the twenty-four-hour battlefield is that ships will fight important engagements at "condition" watches. In World War II it took a while to adapt to condition II and III watches[20] and dawn-and-dusk general-quarters alerts. Husbanding the crew's energy became an around-the-clock concern of every captain in the war zone, especially during the Battle of Okinawa. That battle, with the kamikaze threat and the continuing pressure for days on end, is the best laboratory we have had to observe the psychology of the modern battlefield. The pressure on ships' crews was just as remorseless and enervating as it was on captains. War's prolonged tension is a new phenomenon. Crews will suffer fewer hours of boredom and more hours of fear. True, there will be regions of the open seas in which American ships will be safe, but inshore off a hostile coast, the need for alertness and flawless decisions hovers over warships like an albatross. Tension resulting from the near-constant threat of a surprise attack will be continuous and remorseless. The inadequacies of C^2 in the *Stark* and the *Vincennes* illustrate the dangers, even when the enemy does not have a well-calculated attack under way. For coastal navies the pressure will be evident every time their warships put to sea. In today's Navy, ship design and manning increasingly incorporate the requirements for battle under conditions II and III. In such combat, tactical commanders and their captains will have to imbue a sense of presence-in-absentia, because the action may be over before the captain is on station, won or lost by an officer who asked self-reflectively, "What would the captain do?"

The great deadliness of modern surprise attack can be illustrated numerically. When guns answered guns, a two-to-three disadvantage could not easily be offset by surprise. For example, according to Bradley Fiske's model of exchanged broadsides, to gain equality the inferior force (call it B) would have to fire for ten minutes unanswered by *A*. That is about 60 percent of the time it would take *A* to eliminate *B* if both sides exchanged fire. For *B* to obtain a two-to-one advantage over *A* before *A* started to return fire, *B* would have to fire unanswered for twenty

---

20 Readiness conditions less than general quarters—the former kept roughly one-half of the crew at battle stations, the latter one-third.

minutes, the military equivalent of the *Chesapeake* being caught unprepared by the *Leopard* in 1807. Compare this with the model of carrier warfare in World War II. If *B*, with two carrier air wings, could surprise *A*, with three, *B* would sink two carriers at a blow and have instant superiority. Coordinated modern missiles have the potential of inflicting similar shock on a fleet. A surprise attack of the scale from which a fleet might recover in the age of big guns will be decisive in a modern naval war. The range of weapons has increased the demand for scouting range, and the speed of weapons has increased it still more.

As the potential for sudden, coordinated shock attack grows, and that is the obvious trend, the roles of C^2 and of countermeasures against the enemy's C^2 take on new and compelling significance.

Tacticians will need every promise fulfilled of swift, accurate information processing and display just to stay abreast of the trend. Think of it this way: the increase in weapon range demanded an increase in sensor coverage roughly in proportion to the square of the weapon range. Greater weapon velocity—for instance, the difference between a Mach 1 cruise missile and a Mach 3 or 4 ballistic missile— will demand a shorter C^2 response to keep up with the threat. Large missile warhead size and kinetic energy leave no margin for error. Will technological advances reverse the trend toward greater tactical uncertainty and command confusion, and give commanders the potential to clarify their situations before and during a battle? We will not know until the next fleet action, but astute commanders will be suspicious of promises that their understanding will be enhanced by the vast knowledge that is accessible to them. This much seems certain: the preferred solution to attack effectively first has become even more compelling, and that will require dominance over the enemy by well-synthesized battlefield knowledge.

Modern tactical commanders will expend relatively less energy on planning for and delivering firepower, and relatively more on planning and executing a scouting effort and forestalling that of the enemy with antiscouting and C^2 countermeasures. Why this is so becomes clear when we consider that the modern equivalent of obtaining a gunnery fire-control solution involves what are loosely thought of today as reconnaissance and surveillance systems. The direction of tactical developments now evident will heap more and more hot coals on the heads of fleet commanders and staffs as they try to compensate for deadly surprise with C^2.

9

THE GREAT CONSTANTS

Maneuver

One problem of combat theory is how to define the beginning and end of a battle. Does the exchange of lethal force—firepower—open the battle? Consider the story of the cobra and the mongoose, told by Norbert Wiener in his book *Cybernetics*. The mongoose has the peculiar ability by some combination of mental and physical agility to stay ahead of the cobra's capacity to strike. At the right moment the mongoose attacks behind the cobra's head and the fight is settled. Did the battle consist of one leap by the mongoose? No. Nor does combat begin when the first shot is fired. Sun Tzu, Liddell Hart, and John Boyd would insist, correctly, that combat is more than the application of firepower. In a proper battle, firepower is preceded by maneuver, which bears on the outcome. In Mahan's words, tactics is "the art of making good combinations preliminary to the battle as well as during its progress."[1]

Throughout history the purpose of maneuver has been to establish a superior fighting posture. Fioravanzo gives us a clue to the constant that connects maneuver old and new. He refers to the fundamental tactical position as the relative location that affords earlier or greater concentration of firepower.[2] Speed and time, which are dynamic, translate into position, which is static. In the age of fighting sail, admirals knew the importance of maneuver before ships came within fighting range and lost speed from damage. In the age of the big gun, the greater speed of battleships was more than offset by the speed with which the battle might end from gunfire. Maneuver played its part principally before ships opened fire. We

---

1   Mahan, p. 10.
2   Fioravanzo, p. 209.

know the situation today: with a potentially huge battlefield and fast-acting weapons, maneuvers of even the most agile ships appear to be carried out at a snail's pace. Still, tacticians seek some superior position. Obtaining that requires speed and time; the tactical commander contributes foresight as well. In sum, the modern commander must not be deceived by distances; what may seem like strategic movement may be a battlefield maneuver. Nor must commanders forget that although their aim is position, they must use speed and time in order to achieve it.

In peacetime tacticians usually have overrated the wartime advantage of more speed in combatant ships. High speed is expensive in money, weight, and space. Peacetime planners too often overlook the tactical reality that a formation is tied to the slowest ship in the force, whether due to its design or incurred through malfunction or damage. As a squadron commander, Arleigh Burke told his captains that he would never leave a damaged ship, but he admitted later that he was speaking with his heart and not his head. The usually astute Fiske was so taken with speed that he placed it first in importance in his 1905 Naval Institute Prize Essay, ahead of both "manageability" (command-and-control) and firepower. Mahan, however, was not deceived; he spoke of "homogeneous speed" and influenced the decision to build pre–World War I battleships with arms and armor at the expense of speed. Baudry scornfully referred to armored cruisers not as the analogue of cavalry—which, compared with infantry, was "an arm *deluxe*"—but rather as an engine of war "on the cheap." "Whoever heard of squadrons of zebras ridden by children armed with sticks?" he wrote.[3] Jackie Fisher, father of the battle cruiser, a ship whose fatal tendency it was to blow up under the briefest of fire, would have done well to heed Baudry's contempt for speed. Winston Churchill wisely preferred fast but well-armored battleships that could operate ahead of the battle fleet in support of the scouting line.

Modern naval analysts have been notably unsuccessful in making a case for the cost-effectiveness of speed; their few successes have been mostly in relation to *defensive* tactical maneuver, not *offensive*. Neither the hydrofoil nor the surface-effects ship has proven its case; the speed of these vessels brings too many penalties in its wake. Even the new faster attack submarines were rationalized on sandy ground.[4]

---

3   Baudry, p. 47.
4   Speed in solo-performers such as submarines and single aircraft conducting low-altitude penetrations is subject to its own analysis. Questions of the homogeneous speed of a force and what to do with damaged ships become moot. The thing to bear in mind is that by definition solo performances are unconcentrated, and without concentration a unit depends for long-term survival on remaining undiscovered. And unfortunately speed usually is the enemy of stealth.

Uhlig points out that carriers *must* be swift to operate aircraft. It is fascinating to speculate what their speed ought to be if this were not so. The question is not idle: we may see the widespread use of very short takeoff and landing (VSTOL) aircraft in the future. The cost penalty of vertical lift—which is the VSTOL's greatest liability—could be offset substantially by reducing the propulsive power of the *entire formation.* We should remember that with half the propulsive power a ship can travel about 80 percent as fast. In addition, speed creates noise in the water, and noise draws submarine missiles. There are times when the ability of a carrier to operate its aircraft at low speed—or even at anchor—is a valuable attribute. Even so, strategic speed—when a force moves into the Indian Ocean, for example—remains a precious capability. And speed for tactical evasion and counter-targeting is at least of some importance.

In World War II the *North Carolina, Alabama,* and *Iowa* classes were the only battleships that could keep pace with the carriers, and it seems pointless to ask if another class of AAW ship might have played the role of the fast battleships better. When new technology offers more speed without much compensatory cost, we should embrace it. But when technology offers speed only if this or that is given up, we should not be beguiled. History tells us that that extra bit of speed in ships and speed and maneuverability in aircraft is dearly purchased and has not increased in fifty years.

Firepower

At sea the essence of *tactical* success has been the first application of effective offensive force. If the tactician's weighty weapons substantially out-range the enemy's, then the objective is to stand outside effective enemy range and carry out the attack with sufficient concentration of force to destroy the enemy. If the enemy out-ranges the attacker, then the tactician's aim is to survive any blows with sufficient residual firepower to carry out the mission.

It is all the more important now for a tactical commander to have the means to concentrate effective firepower and deliver enough of it to accomplish the mission before the enemy can bring decisive firepower to bear. Without such means, one should not wish to engage the enemy, for the attacker is likely to lose with very little to show in damage to the enemy. The second great constant of offensive force applies here: Other things being equal, a small advantage in *net* combat power will be decisive and the effect will be cumulative. The necessary margin of superiority, however, widens when the enemy seems likely to deliver a first, but inconclusive, attack. An inferior force cannot assume a defensive position and exact a substantial toll, as can be done in ground combat. An inferior fleet must be disposed to risk and must find a way to attack effectively first. Otherwise, it should be ordered to avoid battle and to adopt a strategy of evasion, survival, and erosion, which it must hope to achieve with skill and good fortune.

In the previous chapters we have seen some of the theoretical and empirical bases for this conclusion. It was also buttressed by some of the strategic gaming at the Naval War College before World War II. There the results of engagements between "detached squadrons" were decided by the following sort of set-piece evaluations: In cases where there were two forces with relative strengths (not simply numbers of ships) of two to one, the inferior force was removed from the game. When the odds were three to two, the lesser force lost half its strength. With odds of four to three, the superior force defeated its adversary but was incapable of carrying out any large operations during the remainder of the game.[5]

Our own numerical estimate is that superiority in net combat power of four to three has been conclusive at sea, except in the case of an effective enemy first attack. An advantage of three to two will crush the enemy. At times countries have sought a numerical advantage of five to three or two to one, but those numbers are based on strategic rather than tactical considerations.[6]

Another recurring tendency, perhaps common enough to be called a constant, is to overestimate the effectiveness of weapons before a war. The abysmal ineffectiveness of naval gunfire in the Spanish-American War came as a shock. By 1915, after ships' fire-control problems had been largely straightened out, ten or twenty minutes of accurate gunfire was conclusive. Nevertheless, at Jutland the High Seas Fleet escaped destruction because the British battle line was unwieldy, the German fleet maneuvered skillfully, and smoke obscured the scene of action. Before the Pacific carrier battles commanders were too sanguine about the effectiveness of air power. And the chaotic night surface actions did not at all reproduce the clean, decisive battles that had been played out in prewar board games because firepower was not as effective as expected. This rule abides: Watch for the fog of war, and do not underestimate the propensity of the enemy to survive your weapons. In the next war at sea we will see ships with empty missile magazines and little to show for the expenditure of what should have been the decisive weapon.

---

5 McHugh, pp. 4–28 and 4–29.
6 In negotiating the Washington Treaty, the United States, on the basis of strategic responsibilities in both the Pacific and the Atlantic, held out for a five-to-three advantage over Japan in capital ships. At the beginning of the twentieth century, Great Britain, fearful of a two-power alliance against it, adopted a two-power standard, which meant that its navy was to be as large as the next two strongest navies combined.

When Admiral Burke, the last of our World War II tacticians, was asked what he would change in the new class of guided-missile destroyers—his namesake, the *Arleigh Burke* class—he said he would add a brace of cutlasses.

Still, the possibility of a decisive outcome has almost always been latent. There have been times when offensive effectiveness was confounded by bad tactics—under the Permanent Fighting Instructions, and by a combination of good armor and poor shooting and maneuvering after the Battle of Lissa. In general, however, offensive firepower always reasserts its domination over the defense, and we should be no more surprised by the destruction of the *General Belgrano* and the *Sheffield* in the Falklands campaign than Beatty was when two of his battle cruisers blew up in five minutes. Nor should we be surprised that HMS *Hood* proved to be too delicate a greyhound; that the back of the Imperial Japanese Navy was broken in one morning at Midway; or that the U.S. Navy, with overwhelming naval superiority, was nevertheless losing more than one ship a day to kamikazes in the bloody Okinawa campaign. In modern battle, ships and aircraft will be lost at an agonizing rate. But we observe no trend toward *greater* destructiveness; we see a continuation of the decisive and destructive nature of naval combat.

Is there inconsistency between one paragraph that says offensive weapon performance will be overestimated and another that says naval combat will be bloody and decisive? The reconciliation lies in this: even though tacticians probably will need more offense than they foresee, the offensive capacity for great destructiveness and potential decisiveness will still exist. Dewey and Sampson won decisive battles with horrible gunnery. Jutland may have been tactically inconclusive, but the battles of Coronel and the Falkland Islands certainly were not. Even the inconclusive naval battles in World War I hung on a knife's edge, minutes away from decisiveness. After four big battles in 1942, carrier air power was decisive enough to sweep the Pacific Ocean almost clean of carriers. The fact that airplanes were less effective than predicted was important, since it influenced their tactical employment; to the Pacific Theater strategists, this hardly mattered.

Counterforce

While the success of defense against firepower has waxed and waned—and at present is on the wane—the importance of diluting or destroying enemy offensive firepower continues. These characteristic constants of counterforce include:

- Except for brief periods and in unusual circumstances, defense at sea never dominated offense in the sense that Clausewitz and other observers intended to convey about land combat. The potential for decisive attack at sea has almost always been latent.[7]

- Defensive force has demonstrated unanticipated resiliency. Its contribution is seldom greater than to give time to attack effectively. But if too much is not demanded of defense, new means can be found to impede new threats.

- Defense will sometimes look more effective in practice than it did during planning because offense will not be as effective as it is calculated to be in peacetime.

- Offense and defense will both fumble at the onset of a war. However, offense will show better early in the war.

Another constant of maritime warfare is that navies are difficult to replace. For this reason ships of the line did not engage forts with the same number of guns, battleships did not venture into mineable waters, and aircraft carriers did not attack airfields that based similar numbers of aircraft. Ships *did* attempt such actions if they had preponderant force in the sea-shore battle and if they had established sea control. The Gallipoli operations in the spring of 1915 illustrate both the prerequisite preponderance of force and the hazards of engaging shore batteries in mineable waters. Three French and British battleships and a British battle cruiser were sunk or damaged, and the fleet's attempt to penetrate the Dardanelles was called off on the very brink of success.

Carrier operations against airfields bear similar risks. Compared with damaged aircraft carriers, damaged airfields can be reconstituted quickly. In conventional war, there is less possibility of concealment, survivability, and recuperation at sea than on land. The compensatory virtues of warships have been their greater mobility and potential for concentration.

Should nuclear war come, it will alter these generalities. Surface warships will be more durable than land-based forces because of the capacity for both strategic movement away from the threat and for tactical movement out from under a missile attack. The capacity for survival of submarine-based submarine-launched ballistic missiles (SLBMs) through concealment exceeds that of land-based intercontinental ballistic missiles (ICBMs). Nuclear war also changes the replacement

---

7   Clausewitz wrote, "We maintain unequivocally that the form of warfare we call defense not only offers greater probability of victory than attack, but that its victories can attain the same proportions and results" (p. 392). He was speaking of the defensive *battle*, and this in a tactical sense, so he is being taken in a fair context. It is well to add, however, that elsewhere, and in a broader strategic context, Clausewitz wrote, "If the defense is the stronger form of war, yet has a negative object, it follows that it should be used only so long as weakness compels, and be abandoned as soon as we are strong enough to pursue a positive object" (p. 358).

equation: conventional naval forces are more difficult to replace than conventional land-based systems, but in nuclear war, when no warheads are replaceable, this liability disappears altogether.

Scouting

Sun Tzu wrote:

> Now the reason the enlightened prince and the wise general conquer the enemy whenever they move and their achievements surpass those of ordinary men is foreknowledge. What is called "foreknowledge" cannot be elicited from spirits, nor from the gods, nor by analogy with past events, nor from calculations. It must be obtained from men who know the enemy situation.[8]

This is found in the chapter entitled "Employment of Secret Agents." We can imagine Sun Tzu fairly rubbing his hands together with glee on his first encounter with modern cryptanalysis and surveillance satellites.

Naval commanders have always sought effective scouting at a range consistent with their weapon range. That is, they have sought data about enemy forces far enough away—or *soon* enough away, remembering the time-movement relationship—to deploy for effective offensive and defensive action. And the data have included a plot of the commanders' own forces. An amateur who imagines a chessboard war cannot conceive of the frustrations of keeping this plot. It is not rare in peacetime exercises for a commander to target his own forces. Every professional should reacquaint himself or herself with the hazard and reread Morison's detailed accounts of the Solomons night actions, including the Battle of Cape Esperance, in full and sobering detail. The choice of tactics must be compatible with force proficiency. Unpracticed, widely dispersed forces on a modern battlefield that is dense with long-range missiles run great risk of self-destruction. Some planners assert that the widespread use of the global positioning system (GPS) will end fratricide. If so, then GPS will have changed all previous experience in war at sea.

The great constant of scouting seems to be that there is never enough of it. In the days of sail commanders deployed a line of frigates ahead to conduct strategic search (in those days the great naval problem was to *find* an enemy at sea). There were few other means of knowing the enemy's strategic objective or where its forces

---

8 Sun Tzu, pp. 144–45.

were operating. Like modern satellites or over-the-horizon radar, sailing frigates doubled as tactical scouts, and there was no conscious distinction between that role and the strategic role. When the frigate made contact, she scurried back within flag-signaling range. The ships of the line then had ample time to form in column. Without enough frigates, fleets under sail could be caught in disarray. For the French and Spanish in the Napoleonic wars, the Battle of Cape St. Vincent was one such embarrassing instance among several. Naval commanders cried out in frustration for more frigates.

In chapter 3 we saw the tremendous amount of force involved in scouting. Jellicoe committed 25 percent of his heavy firepower, and Scheer allocated almost as much. By World War I scouting resources involved more than ships and aircraft. Both sides also tried to exploit signals intelligence. (Scouting includes the delivery of information, but not the analysis.) It is hard to see how fleets would have managed their scouting problem without the wireless; radio communications were handy for fleet maneuvers, they were vital to successful scouting.

Between the world wars aircraft became the principal scouts—for detection, tracking, and, as gunfire spotters, for targeting as well. The French Admiral Raymond de Belot, writing about the World War II battles for the Mediterranean, said the Italian navy was continually pleading with the air force for scouting aircraft and was demoralized without them.[9] The Americans and Japanese employed submarines and land- and sea-based patrol planes for early warning or strategic scouting. The U.S. carrier force added large numbers of dual-purpose scout bombers for tactical reconnaissance, with great effect. The Japanese, slower to use carrier aircraft for search, sought to rely more heavily on cruiser-based floatplanes and, whenever they could, on land-based search. Yet, their skimping on reconnaissance aircraft cost them dearly. The best commanders never hesitated to augment single-purpose scouts with dual-purpose ships and aircraft, sacrificing fighting mass in order to find and target the enemy. The contribution to U.S. tactical effectiveness of air-search radar engaged in detection and targeting is probably undervalued in the history books. Despite the misuse of radar in the early night actions in the Solomons, the benefits of superior air-search and radar-search on the Pacific battlefields can hardly be overstated.

Tactical commanders today also can believe they will never have enough for search efforts. The distribution of all search equipment according to range, center bearing, and spread-angle will be one of their most important tactical decisions. As Spruance, Mitscher, and Halsey did with their scout bombers and Jellicoe

---

9   Belot, pp. 41–44, 67–68, 71–72, and 86.

did with his fast battleships, commanders today sometimes will have to sacrifice massed firepower to augment scouting. If there is global nuclear war involving ICBMs and SLBMs, tactical scouting will play its role, as it has in other wars. Resources in space and on the ground will be necessary for targeting, assessing damage, and estimating residual fighting capacity. What will technology produce as the next "radar" device for that war, and will we use it well or squander it, as we did in the Solomons with outmoded tactical plans? A good guess is that the next "radar" will be small, unmanned vehicles, especially aerial devices. Yet, the difficulties of integrating these into a scouting network should not be underestimated. Scouting always has been an important constant of war: winners have out-scouted the enemy in detection, in tracking, and in targeting. At sea, better scouting, more than maneuver, as much as weapon range, and often as much as anything else, has determined who would attack—not merely who would attack effectively, but who would attack decisively first.

C² and C²CM

Dr. J. S. Lawson, who was the chief scientist of the old Naval Electronics Systems Command until he retired, uses the term *command-control* to mean the process by which commanders exercise authority over and direct their forces to accomplish the mission. Around 1977 Lawson and Professor Paul Moose of the Naval Postgraduate School devised the decision cycle depicted in figure 9-1.[10] Their system entails *decision* (part of commanding), *sensing* (part of scouting), and *acting* (largely a part of control through communications), as well as all tactical processes. By incorporating *sensing* and *acting* into the C² *process* and building them into a feedback loop, Lawson and Moose and their compatriots permit C² to look outside of itself. They also make possible the study of its effect on the activities of firepower delivery and scouting—for example, on the rate or quantity of firepower delivered or on the rate or quality (i.e., tactical significance) of reconnaissance and surveillance information. With the command-control cycle it is possible to examine the tactical context and "productivity" of C², observing the steps involved in the delivery of firepower, in scouting, in C², or in all three. A tactical analyst can hold two processes constant while exploring the third in detail. For example, one might

---

10 Independently, Dr. Geoffrey Coyle of Shape Technical Center established a similar paradigm. There is also unclassified evidence in Soviet scientific research in cybernetics that the Russians produced the equivalent C² model as early as the 1960s. See Abchuk et al., and Ivanov, Savel'yev, and Shemanskiy, which are revisions of earlier works published in 1964 and 1971. James Taylor, pp. 36–41, has a useful commentary on this aspect of Soviet research on C².

assume some tactical scouting and weapon-delivery plans on both sides, and then devote attention to the movement of necessary information into and within the flag center—that is, to the command process. Alternatively, one might study the flow of orders to units on communications circuits—to localize and attack a submarine, for example—with emphasis on traffic routing and the time involved in consummating an attack (the control process).

At first, one of the conspicuous deficiencies of Lawson's 1977 model was that it treated control as a one-sided process. Lawson now believes his model should accommodate an enemy control cycle, which would operate on both the battle environment and on one's own forces.[11] The resulting force-on-force activity is shown in figure 9-2. The picture seems obvious, but there is nothing obvious about the complex analytical problems that result from the simple step of including the enemy's control cycle. To begin with, we might like to know the effect of operating, say, 20 percent faster inside our control loop than the enemy is able to do. Does this give us a negligible tactical advantage in controlling the battlefield environment, a 20 percent advantage, or virtually total control? We presume that there is no general answer, but the details of the specific tactical problem at hand

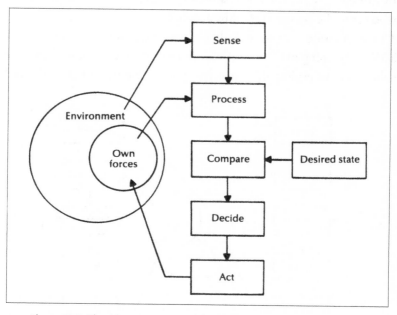

Figure 9-1. The Lawson Command-Control Cycle

---

11 From conversations with Lawson in Monterey, California, winter 1985.

still must be addressed. Not everyone who has played with the cycle has grasped the fundamental distinction between an engineering loop with feedback, which controls "nature," and a pair of military control loops, which operate with contrary objectives.

Lawson emphasizes the fact that command-control is a process, that is, it shows how to do something. His control model is an abstraction, operating in time without specific tactical content. The emphasis advocated in this book is on command—that is, what is to be done. Command is concerned with the distribution of force—the allocation of combat power. Power distribution is the business of C^2. The distribution of force by command is spatial and temporal, and it is also functional (force is distributed between scouting and striking, or between offensive and defensive firepower, for instance) as well as organizational (force is distributed laterally between the subordinate commanders and hierarchically among the electronic warfare staff officers).

Tactical content is closely akin to Lawson's *desired state*—the result that command wants to achieve. Early in a battle the desired state has much to do with the assignment of tasks and force positions and with influencing the activities of the enemy through C^2CM. Later in a battle, the desired state of C^2 is the first delivery of firepower to the enemy in effective batches.

Unless doctrine is fairly well-drawn and the nature of naval operations is predictable, planning in C^2 must deal with tactical content—the *desired state*—in generalities. Let us explore this important point. One style of ground attack is to

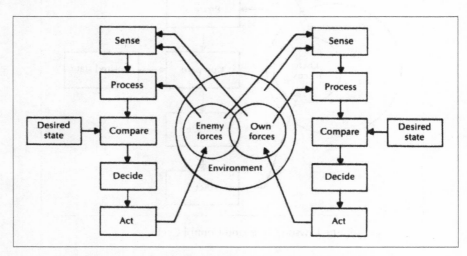

Figure 9-2. Enemy and Friendly Command-Control Cycles Operating Simultaneously in the Same Environment

direct operations along a front by specifying for each force element a geographi-cal objective—its *desired state*. Reinforcements are then sent to the places where operations are experiencing the greatest difficulty. Success is viewed as the simul-taneous attainment of all objectives. In this case, victory depends on the absence of exposed flanks. A second, contrary style is to strengthen places along the front where operations are succeeding, reinforcing success with the object of snowball-ing it. In this case, victory depends on a breakthrough followed by exploitation. In naval operations, the successful defense of a battle group depends on the timely augmentation to handle air, surface, or sub-surface attacks. The best screen for-mation to use for shooting down incoming missiles is seldom also the best one to detect, deter, and destroy attacking submarines or small fast-attack surface craft. In strike operations two virtues of naval mobility are the widespread threat of attack and the exploitation of enemy vulnerability when it is found.

Generally, when he or she is defending, a good commander reinforces weak-ness; when attacking he or she reinforces success. How does this constant of tac-tics apply today? It means that on offense, modern networking permits a highly coordinated strike in time and space at a critical point from widely dispersed forces. After damage assessment, initial success can be followed with other deliberate, measured attacks. That is the essence of the American operations called *dominant battlefield awareness* and *precision strike*. It also means—and this is what needs the greater attention—that on defense, when the initiative is the enemy's, the forma-tion and C^2 doctrine should be designed for rapid, independent response by any ship at the instant it is threatened. Under such a weapons-free defensive doctrine, the tactical decisions of formation choice and relative emphasis on the threat from air, surface, subsurface, space, and land must all have been made in advance. That entails assignment of free-fire and keep-out zones. When the attack comes, the com-bat decisions of a commander in defense are mostly reduced to plugging the gaps opened by the enemy and to aiding helpless, damaged ships. After one of his first engagements then-commander Arleigh Burke wrote in his after-action report, "There is no time in battle to give orders. People must know what they do before they go into battle."[12]

A commander and his staff synthesize information, using decision-support sys-tems when they will help do the job better. Modern displays, geographic and alpha-numeric, assist in this process. So does artificial intelligence, which emulates the

---

12 Quoted in Callo, p. 64.

thinking process and automatically makes decisions on its own when it surpasses that process. There is no conspicuous example of a military command decision-aid that unequivocally decides better than the human mind, but there are many systems that do *part* of the job better. Some weapon fire-control systems assign priorities to address threats, lay guns, and fire missiles without human modification, and they have existed since World War II. The Aegis missile system, while still subject to human intervention and to override, is designed to operate on preprogrammed tactical doctrine adjusted and activated by humans in advance.

Control is the act of executing decisions that have been made. Verbal, visual, and electronic communications are the great instruments of control. Effective planning and training lay the groundwork for control. One measure of the effectiveness of C^2 is the length of time that a plan endures before it must be changed. Another is the amount of communication required to change the plan.

Time and timing are the crucial elements. Time is duration and timing is the point in time when the commander takes a proverbial deep breath and issues tactical commands. Time is a quantity to save; timing is a moment of choice.

Time is saved when compact signals and communications nets are used to process and disseminate orders more quickly. Time is also saved by decision aids. The other great timesaver is teamwork, achieved through training and doctrine. The time *killers* are lethargy, befuddlement, physical exhaustion, and disintegrating morale. Most likely many more disastrous tactical decisions than the history books tell us have been made by leaders whose spirit was used up and by fighters who were exhausted. Without doubt the debacle at Savo Island—the worst battle in U.S. naval history—can be attributed to exhaustion. It explains the hasty, maladroit American force distribution and the failure of the American picket destroyers to detect the passage of Vice Admiral Gunichi Mikawa's cruiser force.

Timing is the kernel of successful fighting. The ancient Greeks had an expression for that fateful moment of opportunity—or the favorable time to seize an opportunity. Tacticians constantly wrestle with the question of whether they have enough structured information to launch a successful attack, knowing that the enemy is gathering information for the same purpose. Even if the tactician has complete information, that alone cannot ensure success between evenly matched forces. Consider chess. Both players know everything and are in perfect control of their forces. The winner is not determined by tactical information. Good timing is not only the product of information but also of native ability and experience.

In other respects chess is a poor simile for war. Its problems are wholly intellectual. There is no need to factor in the fog of war, the threat, the struggle to reduce mental chaos, and the pressure of timing the attack. Burke has been quoted many times as saying that the difference between a good leader and a bad one is about ten seconds. A commander should always have both time and timing in mind. Another difference between good and bad leaders lies in what they see when they look, what they hear when they are told, and what they communicate when they speak.

The first aim of command is to maintain order—to keep control or, as Bainbridge-Hoff wrote, "to keep confusion away as long as possible."[13] If doing so is only a beginning, nevertheless it is the place to start tactical planning. Recall that Blake and the other generals at sea first set out to stamp order on their heterogeneous forces by forming columns. After order came the concentration of force. Most likely, Americans fought in column during the early night actions in the Solomons partly because they could not expect much more of their ships without losing control. Even later, when Burke conceived his tactic of hitting successively in small teams, two teams were the most he could coordinate. At Empress Augusta Bay, Merrill's cruisers formed a point of reference while two teams of destroyers sprang from each end of the column. The use of three formations resulted in a grand melee and only modest damage to the enemy. Burke's forces separated, and for more than an hour he milled around, gathering them up. *Everyone* "lost control."

With characteristic pith, MG Jasper A. Welch, USAF (Ret.), once indicated his criteria for a "perfect C^{3}I system." They are listed in order of importance:

- Preserving the order and cohesiveness of one's own forces.
- Controlling the pace of battle and avoiding fatal blunders. (These first two criteria are Welch's "prerequisites to avoid defeat.")
- Ensuring "non-zero effectiveness." (This is Welch's first prerequisite for winning.)
- Optimizing allocations, strategies, or force compositions—C^2 of ensured efficiency. (Welch says this would rank close to seventeenth in its relative order of importance.)[14]

LTG John Cushman, USA (Ret.), says something along the same lines with regard to communications.

---

13 Bainbridge-Hoff (1894), p. 86.
14 Hwang et al., pp. 4–6.

Imagine a meter for measuring the commander's satisfaction with his communications, reading from zero to 100, zero being that he had none, and 100 being perfect. If a commander had only very rudimentary communications, barely adequate but at least something, he might be up to 50 or so on the meter. He gets only double that with a perfect system.[15]

Tactical complexity is a peacetime disease. After the transition from peace to war, a marked simplification of battle tactics occurs. The tactical theorist underestimates the difficulty of executing complex operations in the heat of battle, and military historians are too quick to point out opportunities that could never have been exploited. Even peacetime naval leaders fall victim to this tendency. Cleverness, ingenuity, and complex maneuvers work best for solo performers such as submarines and small units that can be highly trained. Extraordinary evolutions, such as the High Seas Fleet's proficiency at executing a 180-degree turn in the midst of battle, must be doctrinal, heavily practiced, and few in number. Since the enemy can be expected to know about anything that has been practiced very much, complex fleet tactics must work even when the enemy is aware of them. Because of the tactical trend toward more capable communications and decision aids, the temptation to equate complex tools with complex tactics will be almost irresistible. Complexity, however, should only be added after great deliberation and much training.

Since the art of concentrating offensive and defensive power is complicated, it is easy to exaggerate the potential of the enemy to master it. While it may be fatal to underestimate the enemy, it is not sufficient simply to plan for the worst and act accordingly. Sometimes we are taught to base actions on demonstrated enemy capabilities. That is wrong. Actions should reflect full consideration of all enemy capabilities—a vastly different notion. Readers who understand game theory know that it is like the commander's formal "estimate of the situation," in which values are attached to each choice-pair. One arrives at the game-theory solution upon discovering the best action to take against the enemy's best action, considering all choices by both sides. But as with most formal schemes for optimization, the estimate of the situation (with or without numbers) becomes distorted in practice. For one thing, the estimate is static and battle is dynamic: time and timing will add and subtract alternatives. (In the Shenandoah Valley campaign of May–June 1862, Stonewall Jackson *created* alternatives simply by starting earlier

---

15 Cushman, pp. 6–111.

than the enemy and marching faster.) For another, new knowledge unfolds unforeseen contingencies. A battle plan must make provisions for ways that the balance of power may shift before the main strike—something that an estimate cannot predict. Consider the Battle of the Philippine Sea, in which the Japanese long-range carrier air strike was doomed before it was launched, because Spruance had already destroyed the land-based Japanese air component and his fighters dominated the airfields on Saipan and Guam, where the carrier aircraft would have to land.

The limits of the estimate are seen most fully if we consider the inferior force commander. For him, worst-case planning is not a winning option. One way to use the estimate is to find the enemy option most adverse to you and try to eliminate it, by such means as scouting, deception, or a quick thrust. For the superior commander, a riskless battle means the loss of great opportunities. If he accumulates force to cover every eventuality, he has cheated his neighbor of force or else has cheated himself out of time, and time is the strategic equivalent of tactical force. Halsey, who fought with more heart than head, was forgiven his blunders because his command was always moving forward in either strategy (when he was commander, Southwest Pacific) or tactics (when he was commander, Third Fleet). Nevertheless, when we rank the big-league tactical commanders of history, Halsey trails Spruance, who fought with both heart and head.

The role of the estimate of the situation is a constant. The estimate is as important as ever in its influence on a tactical decision, but it never governs a decision. For the inferior force commander, the estimate is important because it offers clues about how to take risks, which during battle are inevitable for the inferior force.

Much has transpired to accelerate financial, transportation, and commercial information transfer and integrated decision-making. One reads that new opportunities and competitive advantages come from the resulting knowledge. Every day this is proclaimed as a great trend, and progress. The U.S. armed forces embrace the fruits of commercial cybertechnology, too. The goal is to adapt business successes for rapid, accurate decisions reaching widely dispersed forces to achieve accuracy in time, space, and cyberspace (i.e., electronic information channels and nodes). But business *competition* depends on information-exchange *cooperation*. Information warfare seeks to destroy enemy information. The technology is indeed affecting American strategy: the so-called CNN effect—immediate reporting and a continuous news cycle that can influence opinion—is only one consequence. But on balance, in force-on-force circumstances the benefits of C^2 countermeasures will keep pace with C^2, so that in the tactical domain there will be no improvement in command decisions over those in the past.

A fleet commander in battle would be wiser to think of the speed of decision and the reliability of executing decision as constants. In his valuable book *Command in War,* Martin van Creveld traces the history of ground combat command from ancient times to the present. Naturally enough, he points to uncertainty as the central problem with which all command systems have to deal. But, he writes, "the most important conclusion of this study may be that there does not exist, nor has there ever existed, a technological determinism that governs the method to be selected for coping with uncertainty." From smoke signal to telegraph, from radio to communications satellite, technology is a snare that will trap an unwary military organization. Instead of patterning actions after what available technology can do, we should, as van Creveld eloquently concludes, "understand what it [technology] cannot do and then proceed to find a way to do it [accomplish the mission] nevertheless."[16]

The time it took to read and act on tactical signals by flag hoist or signal light was about equal to the time it takes to do the same today between widely dispersed ships and aircraft. During the age of sail, the smoke of battle interfered with the ability to read signals. Recall the abominable frustration of VHF radios that failed because of a bad patch between the radio shack and the bridge, or of an ASW aircraft that burned holes in the air for lack of a UHF crystal or the right communications plan. We had better remember today's data-link outages, communication bridge failures, and the daily difficulties of email, chat, and other electronic transmissions, as well as the enemy's ability to jam conversations or hack into and infect computer networks with viruses. It is still awkward to talk with submarine crews. Weapon range and lethality open out formations, and open formations must depend on satellite communications, which are not always reliable. It comes down to this: despite advances in the speed and volume of communications, the capacity to command and control a force in battle probably has not changed.

Why does this matter? Because it affects the timing of the decision and the distribution of orders. Good plans have faltered when commanders underestimated the time it took to communicate and overestimated the clarity of their communications. Among the universe of examples are Callaghan's struggles to manage his unwieldy thirteen-ship column at the Battle for Guadalcanal and Scott's confused maneuvers and orders to begin firing at the Battle of Cape Esperance. Technology is hard pressed to keep up with the need for systems to control forces. Modern commanders can pick up inestimable insights from history regarding the drumbeat of battle and their own difficulty in marching to its cadence. There is no peacetime counterpart.

---

16 Creveld, pp. 268 and 274–75.

To stay with the cadence, commanders and their staffs lay their plans. Planning is a function that unites disparate forces into a task force. To achieve the full cooperation of all components, one staff only—that of the task force commander—should do all operational planning. The distribution of forces for air, surface, subsurface, amphibious, and strike operations is a function that the commander must lead rather than arbitrate. The planning and execution of a united scouting effort, including the management of all electronic emissions in his forces, rest on the commander's shoulders throughout the operation and should not be delegated. This does not obviate the decentralized application of force by his subordinate commanders, but the commander and the command staff must be completely competent in *all* aspects of fleet operations if the fleet is going to execute its mission well. Since the days of battleships, cruisers, and destroyers, tactical commanders have directed all components for united action. Only the tactical commander can act as the centripetal force.

The development of doctrine is also part of C^2. Tacticians preparing for battles in the littorals must have companionable combat doctrine and fighting instructions that are practical, prevalent, and practiced throughout the fleet. Good tactics in wartime derive from good tactical study in peacetime. Sound practice comes from sound doctrine, sound doctrine from sound tactical thought, and sound thought from a foundation of tactical theory. That there were few tactical surprises at sea in World War I can be attributed partly to the outpouring of naval tactical writing in the early twentieth century. Surprisingly, tactical and doctrinal readiness at war's outbreak seems to have little relationship to the pace of technological change or the number of wartime opportunities to observe warships in action. In World War II the U.S. Navy did better adapting naval aircraft for battle than at adapting the more familiar gunship for night action. Tactical effectiveness correlates best with the quality of tactical thought in various publications. U.S. naval warfare publications should compare in tightness, focus, and readership with the old fleet tactical publications that preceded them. Articles on tactics should dominate Naval Institute *Proceedings*, as they did in the period from 1900 to 1910. The hard core of the Naval War College curriculum should be naval operations, as it was in the 1930s. War games should stress not merely training and experience but the lessons learned from each game's outcome, as in the 1920s and 1930s. In intellectual vigor our modern tactical writing should compare with the best in the world. Yet the renaissance in tactical thought started by Admiral Hayward when he was Chief of Naval Operations is faltering. The tactical proficiency achieved for blue-water operations has not been matched by proficiency and fighting instructions for littoral warfare. The quality of our writings is the best clue—even

better than the conduct of a peacetime exercise at sea against an "Orange enemy"—
to our probable tactical competence at the outset of a two-sided coastal campaign.
To date the writings are deficient—long on expressions of alarm but short on
tactical solutions. In fact, four of the best articles in professional journals dealing
with littoral combat operations and the tactics of inshore warfare are by foreign-
ers. *The Seapower of the Coastal State,* by Jacob Borreson (Norwegian) and "U.S.
Navy Operations in Littoral Waters, 2000 and Beyond" by Commander Tim Sloth
Joergensen (Danish) already have been cited; the third is "Non-intervention:
Limited Operations in the Littoral Environment," by Lieutenant Commander
Jeremy Stocker, RN,[17] and the fourth is "A Word of Caution," by Rear Admiral
Yedidia "Didi" Ya'ari (Israel).[18]

What is the greatest of all constants of peacetime command, nothing barred?
Army general Cushman believes that since accomplishing the mission comes first
in wartime, preparation to do so should come first in peacetime.[19] Perhaps he is
right. Should we quote Clausewitz's "Habit breeds that priceless quality, calm"
and say that habit that bred before combat must derive from training, which takes
first priority? Good habit is a worthy candidate. Or should we say, "Know your
forces, know your enemy, and know yourself," as Sun Tzu implied? This is all
splendid advice, but nothing takes precedence over the peacetime commander's
job of finding and developing combat leaders. Let him do his best to find them,
send them to sea, and keep them at sea. The first aim of every seagoing captain
and commander should be to find two officers better than himself or herself and
help in every way to prepare them for war. That done, everything else will follow.

Summary of Tactical Trends and Constants
Trends in the History of Naval Battles

- Speed in the weapon (torpedo, aircraft, missile) has increased faster than
  in the platform (ship or element ashore) delivering it.
- Speed of delivery is governed by scouting and C^2 processes as well as the
  sheer velocity of weapons.
- Maneuverability of a formation of warships has become less important
  for concentrating force and striking first in battle but still is important
  for securing concealment and evading enemy weapons.

---

17 Stocker.
18 Ya'ari has now retired as Vice Admiral Ya'ari.
19 Cushman, pp. 4–13.

- The absolute and effective ranges of weapons have increased. Effective weapon range has come to be more advantageous than weight of deliverable firepower since the aircraft carriers replaced battleships in achieving command at sea.

- The lethality of individual weapons (a torpedo, aircraft bomb, or missile) has increased, especially against the naval machines of war.

- Weapon range and lethality have expanded the size of the no-man's-land between fighting fleets. Small combatants, some unmanned, must occupy the intervening surface, and the importance of aerial and undersea vehicles has been promoted.

- Growth in weapon range and lethality has led to an increase in land-sea interactions. Naval battles increasingly include forces based ashore.

- Scouting systems have had to race to keep up with longer-range weapons. Scouting must be carried out in two dimensions and so the scouting effort increases as the square of weapon range.

- The trend in defense has been away from staying power (the ability to keep fighting after absorbing hits) and toward defensive force (firepower and soft-kill measures).

- There is a trend toward spreading forces out, while using C^2 to concentrate firepower from dispersed formations and dispositions.

- Ships in port and aircraft on the ground have become more vulnerable to attack. Harbors are not the safe havens of the past.

- The region requiring scouting has expanded vertically. The effects of space, air, surface, and subsurface operations are increasingly interrelated because more weapons now cross the domain boundaries.

- Combat has become a twenty-four-hour hazard. With early positioning for long-range attack now so important, it will be difficult to define the beginning of a modern battle.

- Tactical commanders have had to devote more of their attention to scouting relative to that for delivery of fire.

- The breadth and intricacy of sensor and communications networks and meshing technologies are growing at a very rapid pace, especially in the past two decades.

- Tactical commanders have had to increase the proportion of forces devoted to scouting and screening at the sacrifice of fleet firepower.

- The historical trends in naval warfare are usually related to machines and the technologies that created them.

Constants in the History of Naval Battles

- First application of effective firepower is the foremost tactical aim.
- The purpose of defensive measures is to delay the effect of enemy fire until one's own fire has taken effect.
- Maneuver in anticipation of combat is, as always, an important part of battle, but today most maneuvering is carried out before the shooting and on a grand scale.
- Navy forces take longer to replace than army forces. That fact and the predominance of the offense at sea have led to greater reluctance to risk forces afloat than on the ground, including airfields.
- The advantage of ship speed is overrated in peacetime. Its tactical value must be weighed against what is sacrificed to attain it.
- Under continuous-fire conditions, a small advantage in net effective force is not only decisive but will succeed without compensatory damage inflicted by the weaker enemy. The same is true of pulsed fire with salvoes, except that a weaker enemy that succeeds in a surprise first attack will be greatly rewarded, and sometimes he will win a battle he would otherwise have lost.
- Firepower is less effective than anticipated from peacetime tests and firing exercises. Nevertheless, there is usually the potential for decisive fire and victory embedded in fighting fleets.
- Thus far in history naval battles have been fought best without retaining a tactical reserve, the way ground forces do.
- Antiscouting and its likely exploitation have become major constraints on enemy scouting effectiveness.
- The possibility of tactical surprise is a great constant. Remarkably, surprise may come from enemy action, from one's own force mistakes, or by chance.
- Command-and-control technologies—from early signal flags, to voice-radio commands, to the most modern electronic transmissions—have always been hard-pressed to stay abreast of the demands that it enable a tactical commander to execute his plans.
- Though seemingly new, modern decision aids and the growth of artificial intelligence should be seen as serving a tactical commander within a constant framework of compressing the *time* he has to gather information and *timing* of his attack to achieve victory, which is almost always with less than complete information.

- The first aim of command has usually been to keep control. But sometimes a melee and loss of control has been an advantage, usually to the inferior force.
- Surprisingly the pace at which control of a fighting fleet can be exercised has not changed much throughout history. The fact of very sudden unexpected missile attack may have suggested a speed of timely decision that does not often happen.
- The advantage of faster movement of ships at sea over horses, railroads, or trucks on the ground has been an abiding advantage, as has the economic efficiency of movement by ships.
- Planning, doctrine, and training as well as combat experience help reduce the possibility of a commander and his fleet being overwhelmed by the tempo of battle.
- The development of complex tactics in peacetime has been a longstanding predisposition. After the first battle, tactics are usually simplified.
- The historical constants in warfare are usually related to human personality and skills.

10

THE TRENDS AND CONSTANTS OF TECHNOLOGY

Technological Pace and Tactical Change

This chapter is a postscript to the great trends and constants of tactics. Technology is renowned for the way in which it prompts changes in tactics: tactical trends develop *because* of technology, and tactical constants abide *in spite* of new technology. As a result, technological advancement and its periodic overthrow of tactics are themselves a central constant of warfare. The key question is whether the increased *rate* of scientific discovery today translates into a military trend. Do we see more than just the continuing influence of technology on tactics? Do we see acceleration of that influence as well?

We need to know whether the faster rate of technological change gives way to more rapid introduction of potentially revolutionary weapons and sensors in order to answer two tactical questions:

- How often will the effect of new technology be great enough that if it is exploited in a series of battles it will affect the outcome of a war? That is, what is likely to be the frequency and magnitude of technological opportunity?
- How well will these technological opportunities be seen and acted upon when they arise, so that naval leaders can actually exploit them in battle?

Dupuy, in unpublished papers, accumulated evidence that in ground combat the impact of a new weapon upon the outcome of a war usually has been local and almost always has been transitory. He believed that a technological surprise by itself never has won a war on land, but that technology accompanied by a tactical revolution has. Napoleon's tactical use of mobile artillery was revolutionary; the field artillery itself was not new. It is ironic that the Germans exploited tanks so effectively with their Blitzkrieg, for one of their victims, the French, possessed more and better tanks, and another, the British, had invented them. In these instances the new tools, artillery and armor, were no secret at all. In contrast, when tanks were a surprise, first used in substantial numbers by the British at Cambrai in World War I, the British forces achieved local successes but could not exploit their new weapons. Some argue that the British prematurely squandered tank technology before the accompanying tactics had matured. That illustrates the first question: is it possible in wartime to develop a weapon—along with the tactics and training—in secret and in such numbers that it will serve as a war-breaker? Or will the technological impact of the weapon almost inevitably be local and transitory?

Secret Weapons and Wartime Surprise

Because there are fewer big battles at sea, the potential for decision by technological surprise is greater. At least one weapon is comparable in decisiveness to cryptanalysis, which wrought the great increase in Allied scouting effectiveness: it is the *kwi-suns*, or turtle boats, of Korean Admiral Yi Sun-Sin, which in 1592 helped win two decisive battles against the Japanese at Pusan and in the Yellow Sea.

Another secret weapon sprung long after its prewar invention was the Japanese Long Lance torpedo. As late as the summer of 1943, the U.S. Navy did not know exactly what the Japanese weapon was or why it had been so effective. The Long Lance had been developed in the early 1930s, and Japanese cruiser and destroyer men had trained extensively with it. American scorn for Japanese technology takes much of the blame for the U.S. Navy's overconfidence at the start of the Pacific war, which was almost as foolhardy as German and Japanese overconfidence in the immunity of their own ciphers.

Then there is the atomic bomb. Although it was not specifically a naval weapon and not numerous enough to be regarded as tactical, the bomb was the shocking weapon that administered the coup de grace to Japan in 1945. The science and technology took four years to develop, and only two bombs were built. Is it possible to keep the development of an "ultimate weapon" a secret in peacetime? Evidence suggests that it is not possible, at least not in the United States. Many people in this country believe secret weapons are proper public news. With his book *On Strategy,* the late COL Harry C. Summers Jr., USA, helped revive an awareness that a country cannot fight effectively for very long without accounting for the temper of its people. The message would not have seemed so new or fresh if more journalists had read Mahan, the Soviet Russian laws of war, Clausewitz, or even Sun Tzu. Now, the nature of a free population, its society, and its government will also decide the extent and kind of secret weapon developments that are possible. The reader should pick up Vannevar Bush's *Modern Arms and Free Men,* published in 1949. Bush concludes that the open society, with its greater exchange of knowledge, outperformed the closed fascist societies of Germany and Italy in the exploitation of science and engineering during World War II.[1] Surely, however, to win the technology war one must have either better science or greater secrecy. One cannot concede both to a foe.

In most instances the hoped-for surprise of new weapons in wartime has been muted in some way. Here are some examples of weapons, mostly naval, that brought disappointment in World War II:

- Magnetic influence mines. Germany introduced them against shipping in the estuaries of the British Isles. They were effective, but they were used prematurely. As a result, they turned out to be vulnerable to countermeasures.
- Magnetic exploders in American torpedoes. Developed before the war, they worked badly and were a great setback to U.S. operations. In a short war, American torpedoes would have been an unmitigated disaster. The British and Germans also experienced early problems with their sophisticated torpedoes.
- Proximity fuzes. For much of the war they were restricted to use over water out of fear that the Germans would recover one and adopt the technology against U.S. strategic bombers.
- Night fighters. These were highly effective, but there were too few of them to be decisive.
- Submarines. They had a powerful impact, but their role against warships was well recognized before World War I.
- Sonar. This was a crucial response to the submarine, developed in secrecy. It was not enough to neutralize the threat.
- "Window," the strips of aluminum foil used to jam enemy fighter-direction radars. The Germans had window early in World War II, but they delayed

---

1   Bush, pp. 193–232.

its application until the Allies used it in the bombing of Hamburg in July 1943. Both sides appreciated the fact that window was a doubled-edged tool of war—of value to both sides.

- Jet aircraft, V-1 and V-2 missiles, and snorkeling submarines. All arrived too late in the war to have much effect.

Here are some reasons that new weapons, whether secret or known, do not always deliver what they promise:

- Production limitations, as with magnetic mines
- Testing limitations, as with torpedo exploders
- Great complexity, requiring skilled operators and integration into fleet tactics, as with radar and night fighters
- Great simplicity, threatening adoption and exploitation by the enemy, as with window
- The risk of failure after introduction, as with the U.S. magnetic torpedo
- Exaggerated expectations, as with sonar
- The penalty for maintaining secrecy during a lengthy period of development, as with Nazi Germany's secret weapons

We can conclude that decisive technological surprise at sea is difficult to achieve in wartime. As a result, there is little reason for authorities to hold back a new weapon in wartime until the numbers, tactics, and training exist to guarantee that it will be decisive. Certainly, the instinct of wartime leaders is to rush a tool of war into the fray, and their professional instincts are correct. The enemy—the side responding to a new technology—can only adopt an attitude of wartime wariness, but not paranoia.

Peacetime Evolutions and Revolutions

The situation in peacetime is a sharp contrast. New weapons technology usually is discovered in plenty of time for the enemy to react to it before war arrives. (For secret sensors the evidence is shakier.) But will the tactical significance of a new weapon, developed in peacetime, be grasped in wartime? Too often, warfighters underestimate a new enemy weapon or fail to invest money in developing countermeasures or do not expend enough tactical thought and training on an adequate response. The tacticians' province is to do what is possible with existing tools. Should these tools be used for dispersion? Evasion? Preemptive attack? Or should tacticians downgrade the role of the newly obsolescent weapons systems and focus on the use of what is left in new or better ways? If the tacticians do not see the threat and prepare for it, then perfectly visible peacetime technological advances will turn out to be decisive wartime weapons that may as well have been secret. There lies the real danger. What are these weapons? New technologies are on the horizon in chemistry, materials, space, lasers, stealth, cyber, unmanned vehicles, autonomy, and mine warfare. Do we see them?

We have a recent example in Operation Desert Storm, fought in 1991, where one side failed to anticipate the technology and tactics being used by the other. Since the war there have been many interpretations of the results and differing emphases on American weapons, sensors, and C^2 systems. The brilliant tactical application of them all together was even criticized as imperfect! In any case, the results illustrate the theme. As was the case in the Blitzkrieg attacks in World War II, the success of the U.S. attacking forces in Desert Storm came primarily because the Iraqis were not prepared for what would happen on the battlefield, even though they knew about almost all the innovations they would face, from stealthy aircraft and cruise missiles to satellite surveillance. Iraqi generals simply could not conceive how crushing these elements could be when they were applied in a tactically integrated way. It was not only the Iraqis who were surprised, however. Soviet military leaders also seemed to have been awed by the tactical superiority of the U.S. forces, which appeared to be far beyond anything they had imagined was possible.

Now we come to the more subtle issue: the quickening pace of scientific research. Doubtless the current acceleration can be called a trend, but there is little evidence to show that it has led to faster improvement in weapons design than has occurred before. The United States now exhibits slower gestation periods for warships, warplanes, weapons, and sensors. In the Anglo-Dutch wars, entire fleets were built in a year or two. If the English or Dutch had invented a new naval weapon during those wars, they could have put it to sea within that timeframe. In the United States today, it takes fifteen years to conceive a new warship design, marshal support for it, push through the appropriations, and build the first prototype. Another question: if modern war is decided by the pace of modern technological advances, then why do we ascribe a useful combat life of thirty years to our warships and half that time to our fighters and attack aircraft? Why do the Russians, who seem to be able to deploy new designs faster than the Americans, nevertheless keep obsolete ships and aircraft in inventory for so long? Decisive tactical surprise is not likely to derive from the acceleration of scientific research—at least not in this country. Here, high technology is the *enemy* of speedy exploitation.

Even so, let us postulate a new weapon of war that has the potential to change the face of battle—that is, to break open the war. Just four of the impending possibilities are cyberoperations, robotic vehicles, long-range land-launched missiles, and the use of more compact launch systems to permit the broader employment of missiles in other-than-traditional cruiser-destroyer warships. The Navy first experimented with submarine-launched cruise missiles in the 1950s and deep-sea homing mines in the late 1960s. The question is how to transform the technology into combat reality at sea. The answer is that technology should be introduced by *evolution* instead of *revolution.* The evolutionary approach can work in a free society. Yet, Americans persist in haggling over and redesigning every ship and aircraft and sensor to the point of exhaustion before it is produced. In the case of the cruise missile, the Navy decided to hold up production for thirty years because it could not demonstrate an efficient method for targeting the weapon. The maxim should be: develop the weapon and the targeting system will follow. It would have been sad indeed if development of the major-caliber gun had been deferred until the details of its fire control had been worked out.

U.S. treaty cruisers are the perfect example of a successful evolutionary approach. The limits on heavy cruisers prescribed by the naval armaments treaties negotiated between the world wars were 8-inch guns in a ten-thousand-ton standard-displacement hull. The design aim under the treaties became "tonnage-effectiveness" instead of "cost-effectiveness."[2] Two cruisers of the *Pensacola* class were "designed to weight." They were called dogs, top-heavy and poorly armored. Even while the *Pensacola*s were under construction, design lessons were being incorporated into the second class, and every couple of years a better class was authorized. The culmination of the series of four cruiser classes, each an improvement, was the magnificent *Astoria* class of seven superb and much-admired ships. In World War II the *Pensacola*s fought side by side with the *Astoria*s, and it would be difficult to say which class performed better in combat. The *Pensacola*s may have been prototypes, but they were not *merely* prototypes. They were imperfect but effective warships, and they showed the way to something better. The real breakthrough came with the heavy-cruiser designs produced in wartime—the *Baltimore, Oregon City,* and *Newport News* classes, fully outfitted with AAW weapons, search- and fire-control radars, and ultimately semiautomatic 8-inch guns.

There are many examples in which important improvements in combat capability have been hidden. One is the rifling of gun barrels. Another is the improved

---

2 Rear Admiral Stalbo, in the Red Navy's *Morskoy Sbornik,* writes that even now this is the most important criterion of warship construction. See Stalbo, p. 25.

fire-control systems in dreadnoughts. New engines barely can be detected from an aircraft's appearance, but they can vastly change the plane's performance. Changes in computer reliability or cryptology or in scouting systems in outer space are invisible, at least to an amateur observer. Karl Lautenschlaeger asserts that the most important characteristic of the Soviet *Oscar*-class submarine was not its great size, but the likelihood that its missiles were guided by space-based sensors.[3] Submarines that depend on acoustic stealth are in a continuing competition to operate more quietly than the enemy; the quieter they become, the more "invisible" they are. All of these important alterations are possible because there was a combat ancestor upon which to improve.

On Great Transitions

When a technology is potentially revolutionary—as the sail was during the age of oars, as steam was during the age of sail, and as the aircraft carrier was during the age of the battleship—the practical matter of exploiting the new opportunity is exceedingly complicated, even after you know where you want to go. The objective of an orderly phase-in is not to evade the attention of those guarding the status quo. The Old Guard sees real threats while the technological changes are still wisps of smoke on the horizon and warns of many potential dangers that do not even exist. Rather, phasing in the new technology provides time to solve a monstrous transition problem. If it is hard to develop new tactics for new systems, then it is even more difficult to design tactics that blend the old and the new. Consider the false starts that occurred when Navy leaders had to work out new roles for carriers and battleships in mutual tactical support. Building a new navy from scratch, as the United States did with the New Navy of 1881–1914, is simplicity itself compared with the job of transforming a navy that already exists and plays a vital defense role, as the U.S. Navy does today.

Even if the technical development of an astounding new weapon system can take place in an orderly fashion, there still is much more that follows—retraining, integrating old tactics with new, handling logistical support, and attending to a host of mundane details. These are just the substantive problems. Arranging such transitions is not the technologists' responsibility, but it is *the* problem with revolutionary technology. Moreover, it is not likely that a less expensive new weapon with greater capability can produce significant savings in the defense budget. First,

---

3   Lautenschlaeger, p. 57. A former naval air intelligence officer, Dr. Lautenschlaeger was on the research staff of the Los Alamos National Laboratory.

during the introduction of the new weapon, the cost of new production and of temporarily duplicated training and logistic support will add substantially to the budget. Second, the advantage of a new weapon system to the developer will eventually become an advantage to the adversary, who can leverage the same cheaper technology to buy more of the weapons than the United States.

But the main technology issue remains how to make the transition from an old navy to a new one. As the situation in America today shows, it is a huge problem. On one side are the American aircraft carrier proponents, who remind us that other navies are starting to build their own carriers; on the other is almost everyone else in Washington. Critics say the Navy should restructure itself in some new, imaginative way, but it is not that easy. Former undersecretary of the navy R. James Woolsey once complained that the Navy has more views on the correct composition of its forces than it has warships. During his term as chief of the office of naval material, ADM Isaac Kidd Jr., USN, is supposed to have said, "Our Navy is being nibbled to exhaustion by a flock of ducks. The bites aren't fatal, but you spend all your time fending them off." Often it seems that too many people in Washington can say no to an innovation and no one can say yes. Vannevar Bush once said that the unity of decision under a totalitarian regime was a recipe for making colossal technological mistakes, whereas the prevalent confusion of decision-making in a democracy was more efficient. He could not have anticipated the tortuous system of procrastination that characterizes modern American defense procurement.[4] Even so, frustrated tacticians should understand that even in better times there were great burdens on those who had to choose where defense dollars would go. The noise of modern Washington's quarrels is "duck quacks" compared with the roars of the old-time lions. In his writings, Bernard Brodie reminds us of the difficulties that confront men in the best of worlds:

Men who have been condemned out of hand as unimaginative or unprogressive may simply have been much more acutely aware of technical difficulties to overcome before a certain invention could be useful than were their more optimistic contemporaries. The mere circumstance that one man was proved wrong in his predictions and another right does not prove that the latter was the more discerning observer. . . .

This question is closely related to the whole issue of conservatism in high military or naval circles, upon which there has been a good deal

---

4   Bush, p. 193.

of dogmatic writing. It is natural that inventors or cranks should inveigh against the persons or political bodies whom they believe to be capaciously placing obstacles in the way of their own recognition. In the aggregate such condemnation mounts up to such a hue and cry that even the disinterested observer is likely to take it up. Writers vie to surpass each other in hurling invectives at the "big-wigs" or the "brass-hats."

In 1842, Sir Robert Peel, defending the Board of the Admiralty against charges of having ignored Captain Warner's torpedo invention [the whole Warner scheme was commonly referred to in later years as the "Warner hoax"], pointed out some of the problems facing a public body in respect to the adoption of a new invention. "I think," he said, "that on the one hand a public man is culpable if he wholly disregards suggestions of this nature, and on the other, equally culpable if upon slender grounds he lends himself too unreservedly to their support. . . . Every man in office has been in the habit of receiving applications of this nature—not a day passes without something of the sort."[5]

The Story of the *Wampanoag*

Elting E. Morison has been at once a sympathetic interpreter of naval conservatism and a critic. In one of his essays, he tells the story of the *Wampanoag*, an astonishing product of the technological genius of Benjamin Isherwood that the "Old Navy" laid up to rot.[6] On her sea trials in February 1869 the *Wampanoag* made seventeen knots in heavy seas, and later, returning to New York in calm water, she made twenty-three.[7] The fastest ship outside of the United States at that time was the British *Adriatic*, which once ran a measured mile in calm water at a speed of fifteen knots. No other ship would match the *Wampanoag*'s speed for twenty years.

The *Wampanoag* was fast because she was designed by Isherwood as a whole ship—with a mission. The mission was to hunt down Confederate raiders or else (as an afterthought) to act as a raider herself, preying on British commerce. She was a sprinter—and therein lay the problem. To the westward-looking, insular, Indian-fighting, railroad-building American nation of 1870–90, the *Wampanoag* (and, in a sense, the entire Navy) seemed to be superfluous. Elting Morison speaks out against a reactionary Navy that wanted to follow the old ways and was blind

---

5 Brodie (1943), pp. 438–39.
6 E. E. Morison (1966), pp. 98–122.
7 Pratt (1941), pp. 343–46.

to the future even when it lay tied up in New York Harbor. He is right about the blindness. He is wrong to assign blame to the Navy alone; the entire nation was responsible. The grizzled old sea dogs of the Secretary of the Navy's board, who rejected the *Wampanoag* on absurd grounds, were guilty of nothing more than being inarticulate—an old problem among naval officers. They were practical men, working with a budget that had been all but eaten up by government apathy. And worse, they were trying to run a Navy that was maintaining a distant and poverty-stricken presence around the world. The *Wampanoag* could go like a flash for five hundred miles or cruise for a few days on coal, but what good was that on the African station? With a shallow draft, slender lines, and the ability to move nimbly as a greyhound under steam, she was as awkward under sail as a seaman recruit. In the 1870s Navy, ships had to have endurance to execute their pathetic little mission. It is true that Navy leaders might have been more indignant. Instead, VADM David Dixon Porter, USN, hero of the Civil War, champion of sail, and an enemy of engineers, would order cruises under sail for economy and to "instruct the young officers of the Navy in the most important duties of their profession." While the West was being won nobody cared about a navy. For most of two decades, an unarticulated national policy decreed that there was no place for the *Wampanoag*. The decision to lay her up seems sad, but inevitable.[8]

We are not quite finished with the story of this remarkable ship, so pregnant with technical and military implications. The effectiveness of raiders was on the wane. From the days of Sir Francis Drake to Raphael Semmes and James Waddell, the payoff of *guerre de course* waned. In 1875 the smoke of twenty knots could be seen a long way off, and one ship under steam did not evade squadrons of two or three for long. Imagine how a navy of commerce raiders would have affected the New Navy a decade later, around 1889. You can hear the Old Guard complaining: *Fine thing this fancy new doctrine of Mahan's about command of the sea, cultivated by that academic, Stephen B. Luce, up there in Newport, Rhode Island! We have the fastest cruisers in the world, we have, all descendants of the master-engineer Ben Isherwood's first greyhound! We know our mission—it's commerce-raiding. Let's have speed, battle cruisers will be next, then the* Indefatigable, *the* Hood, *the* Repulse. The children of the *Wampanoag* could have been a navy like Mussolini's—the fastest in the world—but with never enough fuel to train, hardly enough fuel to go to battle, and not even enough speed to run away.

---

8   For more on the nadir of the U.S. Navy, also see Albion, pp. 199–204. I am less pro-*Wampanoag* than the historians, who seem enchanted by technology for its own sake. Until 1902 the British, who also had many remote stations to patrol, built one-thousand-ton sloops of war to cruise under sail.

Effecting a Transition

Everyone should read Elting Morison. He is almost always right about the U.S. Navy. His examples of its technological myopia are withering. He explains with magnificent understanding why this is:

> And the Naval service of that time [mid-nineteenth century] was more than a set of regulated routines, ordered procedures, and prescribed tables of organization. If not quite a whole society, it was, at least, almost a complete culture. . . . It can seem at times arbitrary, discriminatory, elitist, insensitive. . . . And, like any closed system, it was limiting on the higher flights of imagination and longer reaches of intelligence.
>
> But there were great and redeeming features, some of which, perhaps, it would be nice to have today. . . . The whole structure of the Navy was shrewdly designed to enable men to deal effectively with that unforgiving, incalculable element, the sea. Furthermore, it was imaginatively designed to enable men to live and work together in confined spaces, in uninsulated intimacy, for long periods of time in isolation from the rest of the world. . . . The meaning of this relationship of the man to the service, to the authority of culture, had in it something of that governing power that moves the churchman.[9]

In all his writings Morison expresses well why the modern Navy needs a research and development base, the vision to see what that base offers, and the power to act on insights. And yet there is the *Wampanoag,* the ship without a mission, to remind us that technological anticipation is not enough. It must be accompanied by a naval policy compatible with technology, a strategy, a competitive price, and, last but not least, an appreciation of the tactical context into which more speed, or more armor, or more endurance, or more firepower, or a better sensor is going to fit.

Usually more than one piece of technology is required to create a revolution. Sail and cannon together replaced the oared galley. Steam power alone was not enough to replace the ship of the line; it took the steam engine, the screw propeller, and the metal hull all together, which in turn made possible the big gun and the marriage of rifling, breech-loading, and an effective fire-control system. Big aircraft carriers were nothing without powerful aircraft engines to lift bomb-loads worthy of the name, and big aircraft required powered elevators, catapults, arresting

---

9   E. E. Morison (1977), p. 14.

gear, and the science of long-range navigation over water. The big naval revolutions depended on both a polyglot of technologies and a synthesis of leadership. Even the *Polaris* submarine, the embodiment of a naval revolution as neat and swift as we are apt to see, would not have arrived without the inspired marriage of two technologies, nuclear propulsion and solid-fuel rocketry; and the work of two great technical leaders, ADM Hyman Rickover, USN, and VADM William F. "Red" Raborn, along with Arleigh Burke, a Chief of Naval Operations who understood warfare, politics, and the value of swift action.

When the big-deck aircraft carrier that has been the mainstay of American sea power passes from the scene, the change will be grand and intricate—technologically, strategically, fiscally, and tactically. You cannot say that Elting Morison's truism about Navy conservatism does not apply, for indeed even among businesses such as the steel and automotive industries, which *do* know the direction they should be taking, there is powerful inertia—a tendency always to defer things for just one more year or two. But in the Navy's case, there is no clear direction. Besides short takeoff, vertical landing (STOVL) and VSTOL aircraft and UAVs, there are at least three other major technologies that might serve as the basis of a new force structure. Let us call that new force structure System X—actually a web of systems. When the nature of System X becomes clear, the Navy must work out its transition problem, for carriers will remain useful instruments of sea power long after System X becomes the sword-point of battle. During transitions, old technologies linger, and for good reason. This was the case with the battleship; it abided, although it was prematurely maligned after having been almost undone by neglect during the Washington Treaty years. The same was the case with small guns, which were still used after the advent of the big gun, whose propitiousness was overrated at first. It also was the case with wood and sail, when steel and steam were in the offing but not geared to the American mission. Even today, it is the case with antiship missiles—as replacements for manned aircraft in the world's navies.

Strategically, System X must guard the surface and allow the continued movement of commerce and military force to transit across it. In turn, guarding the surface means dominating the air space above it. These are special American national interests, which represent both vulnerability and opportunity at once.

Technology, strategy, and budget all are contributions that friendly outsiders can make to the great transition. The Navy's own unique contribution will be fleet tactics for System X. However the system works, naval officers will need to shape it imaginatively, not simply by updating old operational requirements for missile cruisers, fighter aircraft, or communications satellites. The transition from oar to sail was more than a change from line abreast to line ahead; the change was essentially from old tactics such as those used on land to unprecedented new tactics to be used at sea. Although a column under sail looked much like a column under steam, the tactical rationale for one column was vastly different from that for the other. If this book helps lay the groundwork for the new tactics that accompany System X by unfurling some professional sails in the imagination of officers who will someday work them out, it will have served a better purpose than the one intended, which is to spawn a debate over the tactical employment of *current* weapons and the development of tighter doctrine for them.

In any event, System X will not be imposed on the Navy from outside. Technologists may offer a menu of alternatives, strategists may propound the policy context, comptrollers and congressional committees may cajole or threaten, foreign navies may offer new threats to render the old means of sea power obsolete, but in the end the Navy must find its own way. The aim of this section has been to make clear to the civilian that a major transition is a deep maze. While there is no guarantee that the navy will find its way through the maze, evidence suggests that the amateur zealot will only lead the Navy into blind alleys.

Summary

Tactical and strategic change wrought by technology is a great constant. Today, there does not seem to be a speedup in the advent of new and revolutionary weapons that matches the accelerating pace of technology itself.

Occasionally the introduction of a remarkable new weapon developed in the midst of war has had a decided effect on the outcome of a campaign. Usually the effect is limited because of the need for secrecy, testing, complexity, production, and training, and because of the threat of enemy discovery. When a new weapon system is developed during war, it should be put into action quickly.

New weapons and scouting systems developed overtly in peacetime can win wars when they are accompanied by sound tactics and suitable doctrine and are used by well-trained forces. Weapons and scouting systems that have been developed carefully but secretly in peacetime can be expected to have important consequences, but these are limited to the extent that production, doctrine, and training are curtailed by secrecy. To respond to clandestine and not so clandestine enemy instruments of war, doctrine must be adaptable at war's outset. Someone outside of the Navy's regular training and operating establishment must be thinking about the tactical ramifications of surprises, so that new tactics may be swiftly introduced, practiced, and put into action.

New weapons often require the development of new tactics by persons of great vision. Both weapons and tactics will be perfected more quickly if a series of similar fighting machines are built, each model following rapidly on the heels of its predecessor. It is impossible to design the perfect weapon for large-scale production and employment without practicing with it; even then, it takes three or four generations of hardware before a weapon realizes its full potential.

Tactical hopes and technological opportunity are separated by an invisible wall. In the past, naval tacticians have been guilty of trying to fit new capabilities into the tactical framework with hidebound lack of imagination. Inventors have been guilty of advocating new capabilities, such as the *Wampanoag*'s speed, that are too fragile, too narrow in their purpose, or too expensive for tactical adaptation.

As for the great transitions in naval warfare, these take longer than expected, not only because of the time required to perfect a new instrument of war and to build it in numbers, but also because a shakeout of tactics takes time. While the new manner of warfare shapes up, plans must be formulated for a transition, during which the old and the new both have combat roles to play. These roles are decided by evolutionary tactics, doctrine, and training—that is to say, by the warfighting customers. But the ultimate *impact* of a great transition in the hands of a master tactician may be felt like a bolt from the blue, even when technology has introduced the new weapons in front of our eyes.

Great transitions require the engineering insight to fuse several scientific potentialities into a dramatically different weapon or sensor; the tactical insight to see how the weapon will change the face of battle; and the executive leadership to pluck the flower of opportunity from the thorns of government. The inspiration for these transitions often comes from outside a navy. The perspiration always comes from within it.

11

THE GREAT VARIABLES

Theory, Planning, and the Battle's Proximity

In his book *Discussion of Questions in Naval Tactics*, Russian Vice Admiral Makarov related a remark that Napoleon made to the Russian ambassador to France in 1812: "All of you think that you know war because you have read Jomini. But if war could be learned from his book, would I have allowed it to be published?"

True, if theory won battles, theory would be a state secret. But it does *not* win battles. Even Communist regimes publish military theory openly in the interest of fostering a unified purpose. Theory falls short because it cannot predict the variables that decide battle tactics and outcomes. Theory sees trends and constants, but not the contexts of time, place, and policy—that is, those determinants of tactics that are unknown in advance of war and those variables in each commander's equation that change from battle to battle, region to region, season to season. Theorists are limited in their power to assist commanders who are operating in the context of actual warfare. Tactical possibilities can never all be abstracted from a study of theory or history.

If that were all, we could omit this chapter. But consider the influences on battle. Theory is the most general and remote of these. The next-most-remote is the burden of responsibility on the peacetime commander. In wartime, the mission is every commander's paramount consideration, according to the axiom. In peacetime, however, the commander's whole purpose is to prepare to execute the wartime mission. But what *is* the mission? Modern U.S. naval forces have a wide array of potential objectives, in terms of both the scale of war and the location of operations.

Peacetime commanders are the professional ancestors of men who fight. In the Navy's inner circles we honor leaders such as William Moffett, Joseph Reeves, and William Pratt who helped prepare for our battles, but who were never privileged to lead them. Charitably, we forget others—officers who were devoted to inspections, paperwork, freshly painted hulls, and elegant wardroom appointments. Peacetime leaders forget that their first responsibility is to keep doctrine current and train to it. Working machinery, full supply bins, and reenlistments matter, too, but since they are more tangible than combat readiness they tend to divert attention from it. Smartness and impressive correspondence are indices of energy and intelligence, but in peacetime they too often come to be mistaken for substance. Peace should be a time for renewing tactics and doctrine.

Some variables are quickly known in wartime. There is a national aim and a military strategy. There are theaters of action and choices of forces. The war a navy foresees governs the structure of that navy and constrains and shapes its doctrine. If we have built and trained a force against the wrong enemy in the wrong scene of action, there is little that can be done at the onset of war to change either the equipment or the doctrine. Having been so heavily committed over the years to widely dispersed operations in small detachments around the world with the aim of preventing or containing war, the U.S. Navy of today will be ill-prepared to fight as a coordinated fleet of many ships. Fleets fight as they have trained. If the Navy has no experience with battle fleets, it will only fight competently in units that comprise a small number of ships.

More variables are resolved for the tactician as the battle approaches. The commander knows the mission and the orders of battle, but also must work with what he or she is given. Commanders may conduct additional training, tune doctrine to the current circumstances, and infuse the crew with a certain spirit and style—but only if time permits. Every commander should be troubled by every change of commanding officer and by every transfer of a line or staff unit. Commanders should be haunted by the memory of the brave but inept pickup forces in the Solomons battles. A fleet fights on the momentum of two flywheels. One is fleet doctrine; the other is stability in the fighting force. Woe is the fleet that is sent into battle with neither. Not even Nelson could have triumphed over both handicaps.

The final influence is the proximity of the previous battle. The first battle of a war is like a football game in which both sides have practiced plays without body contact, or like a chess player who has practiced only against a computer. No one can know the final context of a battle until the fighting is under way and the abilities of leaders, people, and weapons have been revealed. As for a tactical commander's choices of tactics, whether they are solid or deceptive, simple or complex, tightly or loosely controlled, only the battle itself tears away the last veil and reveals its final variables. And yet, beware commanders who believe that they can establish their tactics as they wait for battle. Those officers will never know enough to make a sound tactical decision. Sound theory, peacetime preparation, wartime experience, and the commander's tactical plans together build the possibility of victory.

Missions and Forces

As battle looms, two things come into focus. The first is the mission. The second is the size and makeup of the forces involved. Mission and forces should match hand and glove. The U.S. Navy invented task forces years ago to coordinate the two. The task force is a marvelous concept—an assembly of just the right forces in the right numbers to carry out a specific task. The ability to assign forces in proper kind and quantity is a subject to which we will return at the end of this chapter. Everything governing the tactical commander's plan of operations derives from the mission. We will take this up first.

Mission: The Link to Strategy

Having a knowledge of the mission implies knowledge of geography and oceanography and of any other physical factors that will affect tactics. None of these is known precisely. But the mission itself is handed down by a more senior command and has definite parameters. It also is the commander's tyrant. With the description of the mission come the forces assigned to carry it out. Sometimes the mission comes because of the existence of previously constituted forces.

Strategy determines the forces and objectives of a battle, but that is not the same as saying that strategy dominates tactics. Rather than viewing strategy as something that looks down upon and governs tactics, it's best to see it as Clausewitz does: "[E]verything turned on tactical results. . . . That is why we think it useful to emphasize that all strategic planning rests on tactical battle . . . this is in all cases the fundamental basis of the decision. Only when one has no need to fear the outcome . . . can one expect results from strategic combinations alone."[1] Sound strategy depends on enough knowledge of all forces and their tactics to estimate the probabilities of winning. At the Naval War College it will not do to

---

1   Clausewitz, p. 386.

study strategy and offer strategic plans without first studying in detail the forces and tactics on which those plans depend. Strategy and tactics are related like the huntsman and his dog. The hunter is master, but he will not catch foxes if he has bought and trained a bird dog.

Still, higher authority always determines a tactical objective in a strategic context. Sea battles support some larger purpose ashore. In theory, we know that a fleet's foremost objective is the destruction of the enemy's fleet in a decisive battle. The basic premise of naval strategy is that the destruction of the enemy's fleet opens all doors. In practice, a great battle for command of the sea seldom occurs unless both sides choose to fight. What Clausewitz said of war applies here to decisive naval battles—that the decision for war originates with the defense, not with the aggressor; the ultimate object of the aggressor is possession, not fighting.[2] Naval history is replete with examples of one side deciding to avoid decisive battle, which helps explain why there have been so few battles at sea.

There was a time when a group of ships was kept in port as a "fleet-in-being." The idea was to prevent the defending force from being defeated without having inflicted enough damage on the attacking force to deny them the opportunities they could otherwise enjoy after winning. A survey of modern naval weapons suggests that keeping a fleet-in-being is more difficult than it once was, but that it is not yet an outmoded strategy in conventional war.

As outlined in the chapters on World War II, the inferior force will wish to fight only when the other fleet is at a disadvantage in the pursuit of its operational objective. The goal of naval operations is usefully thought of as either sea control or power-projection. Sea control aims at protecting the sea lines of communication, but it usually focuses on the destruction of enemy forces that threaten these lines. Power-projection aims at employing sea control, primarily by strikes ashore or amphibious landings. Power-projection would be clearer if its definition included the safe movement of shipping and the timely military reinforcement and resupply of ground operations, but usually it does not. We saw how in World War II a commander either defending a beachhead or attempting to reinforce one was caught between divided objectives, which no statement of primary mission could entirely clear up. Spruance clung tenaciously to his mission and defended the beachheads in the Marianas and was criticized for doing so. Halsey carried out his mission to destroy the enemy fleet so single-mindedly that MacArthur barely escaped a debacle at the Leyte beaches. In the Solomons one side or the other was

2 Ibid., p. 377.

always hampered by a mission associated with the fighting on the ground. An enemy can exploit the problems of a superior force whose plate is too full. It is axiomatic that strategy never should allow the tactician's plate to overflow.

The point is that strategy cannot always fulfill its obligation. It is an observable—and understandable—phenomenon that to draw the enemy into decisive battle a "projection" operation must threaten it. The extended reach of modern weapons means that a major projection operation adds to the tactical commander's burden. The tactical commander must have in mind that which is paramount—that is, either the destruction of the enemy at sea or the safeguarding of an operation connected with events ashore. We observed that paradox in the Pacific war. The Japanese navy usually tried to destroy warships first: sea control was its first priority. Although the American Navy was schooled in the philosophy that the enemy's fleet is the primary objective, it stubbornly protected its beachheads, sometimes at great cost. Nevertheless, the obvious conclusion—that ensuring the success of the projection operations is the wiser course—is not fully endorsed by the facts. If the U.S. Navy had not had the advantage in radar, cryptanalysis, and shipbuilding, the more classical efforts of Japanese strategy might have been less futile.

There were other examples of projection operations in World War II—more single-minded than these—that flew in the face of the dictum that made sea-control the primary objective. The Allies staged the North African landings in November 1942, well before May 1943, when the back of the U-boat threat was broken. The German campaign for control of the Suez Canal, which Field Marshal Erwin Rommel conducted in 1942 without having eased the threat from Malta or the British submarine threat in the Mediterranean, almost succeeded. British naval operations in support of Greece and Egypt were carried out with the most tenuous of sea control. When the Germans seized Norway without having gained command of the sea approaches, the British Admiralty was stunned, and Prime Minister Churchill was enraged. The capture of Crete from the air cost the German army so much that no such operation was ever repeated. Even so, it still succeeded, and the Royal Navy paid dearly in the number of warships lost during the assault.

Yet, these operations are unique to World War II. From the centuries spanning Hannibal's campaign and Tsushima, one searches in vain for an example of an overseas operation succeeding on the ground without the attackers having gained control of the intervening sea. A successful overseas operation depends on the ability to operate on the ocean's surface. The initiation of both air strikes or amphibious operations and the support of forces on the ground require use of the sea, and the dual objectives of these operations will continue to plague tactical commanders. The modern American Navy emphasizes precision strikes from the safety of the sea. But this approach is twice in error. First, to believe in the sufficiency of air and missile strikes against the land is to believe in "victory through air power." The strikes may be necessary in all instances, but they will not always be enough to achieve a national military purpose. The partial success of the NATO navy and air force strategic bombing campaign in the spring of 1999 confirms the limitations of air supremacy. The attacks from the air punished Serbia for intransigence, but they did not achieve their purpose of preventing atrocious behavior on the ground by Serbian forces in Kosovo Province. Second, a fleet is incomplete without elements that can enable it to operate in waters next to the enemy coast. A fleet is not worthy of the name unless it can move troops and trade safely through coastal waters and keep the enemy out of its own waters.

The Intensity of War

Another mission-related variable that cannot be resolved in advance is the scale, or intensity, of the war. At one end of the spectrum is a crisis somewhere in the world that some countries want contained to satisfy their national interests. At the other extreme was—perhaps still is—unconstrained nuclear war. In between there are many gradations of theater war.

Containing crises has been the bread-and-butter mission of the American Navy for seventy years. Some have been deterred—and therefore have been undervalued; others have involved brief combat. Since World War II none has seen successful attacks on U.S. warships on the high seas. Dealing with these crises has been one of the continuing successes of U.S. naval operations.

Up the scale of intensity lies active war with conventional weapons. The war in Vietnam is an imperfect example: it might also be categorized as the upper extreme of a war of crisis-containment. Except for the incidents in the Tonkin Gulf, all the naval operations—from air strikes and naval gunfire-support to blockade-like, "market time" operations and the riverine wars in South Vietnam—were conducted in support of ground operations. Since the enemy posed no maritime threat, the United States could take the movement of shipping and sea control for granted. These days it is dangerous to believe that the U.S. Navy will continue to operate from an ocean sanctuary without significant challenge or losses.

General nuclear war has been so awful a prospect that Americans have preferred not to speculate beyond the concept of deterrence. Even many military planners who speak of absolute deterrence as unrealistic shrink from thinking through the tactics, command-and-control, and weaponry to be used against weapons of mass destruction. America's firsthand experience with vast destruction is limited to the Civil War. A better example of total war is the Punic Wars, which ended with the utter destruction of Carthage. Russians, who have seen more of war's devastation, had more realistic plans to fight and survive nuclear war than we Americans.

When nuclear war is not in the offing, what can be said about preventing other bloodshed? Throughout history deterrence has been a function of military force at all levels of war. The correct way to think of the array of naval functions—again with the U.S. Marine Corps a prominent naval element—is in relation to the deterrence as well as the conduct of war, from local crisis to total engagement. Sometimes we hear that deterrence is not a mission. That is to remind us that deterrence that is not backed by the capability and the will to fight is hollow. The deployments of Marine Corps forces in Lebanon in 1983 and Army forces in Somalia in 1993 were a bluff, both of which were called and collapsed. Every deterrent force, from Clemenceau's famous "one American soldier" on the Western Front to the elaborate NATO naval exercises in the Norwegian Sea, is a thrust. Those who would thrust naval forces into an exposed position should ponder what lies beyond these tokens of resolve. On occasion there will be a test of will and blood spilled. In 1787 Thomas Jefferson said, "The tree of liberty must be refreshed from time to time with the blood of patriots and tyrants. It is its natural manure."

To see that deterrence is a weighty responsibility that distracts attention from tactical development, one merely has to look at the Navy's rigorous peacetime operating schedules and the mischief they create when fleet schedulers try to maintain stable task forces to train together. Since the 1990s, the Navy has committed itself to respond to crises at a rate that has been unparalleled. Seagoing American sailors know this, but for those who believe the end of the Cold War reduced the pace of their involvement, the following statistics will set them straight. Take 1990 as the year that the United States realigned its strategy after the collapse of the Soviet Union. In the European and Central command regions, from 1970 until 1990 the average of new crisis responses involving naval forces was 2.9 a year. From 1990 to 1996 the average was 5.0 crisis responses a year. (In all, there were 91 crisis actions over 27 years, or an average of 3.4 a year.) At the same time, the active fleet shrank by 40 percent. Perhaps even worse, the duration of each crisis increased by more than an order of magnitude, from a median length of less than a month through 1989 to more than a year from 1990 on.[3]

A fire department is effective when it puts out house fires before they spread. It does not have to put out a Chicago fire to be regarded as a success. Most of the fleet's deployments have been to fight the house fires of the world. There lies the dilemma of the Navy and Marine Corps regarding missions, tactics, training, and deployment. Naval forces must aim to deter at all levels, and when that fails they must aim to fight the blaze at the lowest level while continuing to deter at the next level. No naval force or any military establishment ever before faced such a plethora of responsibilities and mission ambiguities.

An implication of multiple responsibility and mission ambiguities relates to C^2. To conduct sound C^2 planning, it is necessary to distinguish the characteristics of the different levels of warfare. Most American C^2 planning seems to emphasize the first level, crisis or confrontation, in which the purpose is containment with a satisfactory political or strategic resolution. At this level, naval forces operate under strict rules of engagement. A major tactical problem is to apply pressure with visible presence while facing the continuing threat of an enemy surprise attack. In crisis containment visible presence is an asset; in active combat it is a liability.

U.S. crisis situations have been handled under the tight control of the National Command Authority (NCA). In effect, tactical command has been exercised from Washington, with much of the formal chain of command bypassed. To strengthen this sort of prompt regulation of events, the NCA has made a great effort to build a C^2 system for direct communication worldwide, even reaching fairly low-level units.

A truism of international conflict is that a nation must succeed both militarily and politically. During a major war the political elements are subordinated. World opinion and international law are slighted at best, flouted at worst. At the crisis level both military and political considerations weigh heavily; circumscribed force is the order of the day. The military tactician thinks in terms of executing a combat mission with minimum losses. The statesman, on the other hand, thinks in terms of the political objective that precipitated fighting or the threat of such action. These military and political objectives often come into conflict. Tactical commanders in a crisis or confrontation cannot escape the friction between military and political aims; the goals of statecraft confine their military plans.

---

3   Taken from an analysis in *Crisis Response: Analysis of Historic Data*, December 1997, by C. B. Barfoot, the Center for Naval Analyses representative on the London staff of the Commander in Chief, U.S. Naval Forces Europe (CINCUSNAVEUR).

Although military leaders at the scene of action and in the chain of command may bridle at the amount of control exercised from Washington in a crisis, the record of fifty years of crises suggests that such control will continue. Detailed oversight of localized transitory military operations, even those involving shooting, has flowed—and probably will keep flowing directly from the seat of government to the tactical commander at the scene of action—because of its enormous political content. It would be wise to construct C^2 doctrine accordingly. The doctrine should (1) lay down a *modus vivendi* that unites the NCA so that when it approves operations it speaks with a single voice;[4] (2) specify that the chain of command always be included in orders going to the scene of action; (3) provide for suitable explanations to accompany the assignment of forces, reinforcements, and logistical support from intermediate commanders; and (4) hedge against the possibility that containment will fail and that a conflict will escalate—by preparing for a delegation of authorities and an expedited means of C^2 when it becomes necessary.

There is nothing inherently illogical about providing detailed direct orders from the NCA if this four-point doctrine is faithfully followed. Command can be efficiently exercised at the highest level that meets two criteria. First, the command's span of control must not be exceeded. Combat activity must be localized so that the commander deals with a manageable set of subordinates. Second, pertinent and timely tactical information must be accessible. With the modern means of scouting and communications, a commander sited in a command post remote from the battlefield may have as much or more information than the on-scene commander in a ship. Although experience shows how easily the officer in a command post can overestimate the quality and timeliness of the picture of the battlefield, it also shows that the on-scene commander can underestimate the strategic and political implications of his or her tactical decisions.

If a crisis escalates to theater war, there is a danger, perhaps the preeminent danger, that communications to subordinate commanders at the scene will deteriorate, that the span of control will overwhelm the NCA, and that the tempo of war will demand local initiative and authority. This is one reason to provide doctrine for a short-circuited command. The NCA may not appreciate the need to relax the reins, as in the Vietnam War, when there were too many off-the-scene orders. But the greater danger is the inculcation in our tactical commanders of an

---

4   The NCA can be a Hydra whose heads speak with inconsistent political motivations. When the United Nations is in charge the direction from the top is even more convoluted.

attitude that will cause them to freeze and wait for orders when initiative is called for. In theater war, pace and timing will be everything, even as communications deteriorate and the fog of war descends.

When long-range missiles are employed, the conditions will be even more chaotic—with or without nuclear, chemical, or biological warheads. Sound defense requires plans, facilities, and doctrine that will provide for recovery when C^2 nodes and links are destroyed. Operational commanders fixed ashore can be pinpointed, attacked, and disrupted or destroyed. It would be absurd for defense plans to depend on the unequivocal supposition that the president and Joint Chiefs of Staff will survive an intercontinental attack. To cover such cases there should be preplanned actions that forces would take automatically. Another unsound defense measure is to base all surveillance-processing activities ashore. Many tacticians believe that surveillance information should be collated at sites such as Pearl Harbor, then transmitted in near-real time to the tactical commander afloat. The shore facility is more survivable in theater war, but in general war it will be pre-targeted, so a mobile afloat facility is preferable. Airborne command posts are survivable, but ingenious provision must be made for their logistic support after a matter of only a few hours. A seaplane command post—a craft that can sit on the water but also move quickly to avoid attack—is a better way to combine survivability and greater logistic endurance.

Missions and Strategies of Inferior Navies

Theorists are prone to think in terms of two great sea powers in conflict. The policies of continental powers are also worth examination, because those policies eventually affect the tactics of both land powers and sea powers. We saw what happened when Britain's eighteenth-century navy, accustomed to the aggressive Dutch, attempted to use the same tactics against the reluctant French. British tactics, ill-suited to the new enemy, failed. The French spoke of the ultimate objective, the higher purpose of navies, and French governments would not send their fleets into decisive battle. The British, who understood their own navy's role, scorned this policy, regarding it as the rationalization of inferiority. But the French were right, and often their strategy was sound. The ultimate objective of navies is to influence the lives of populations on the land.

When policy results in an inferior navy, the first thing to observe is that a defense by fleet action will fail. What have been the options of the inferior navy? One is to maintain a fleet-in-being, as the Germans did with their High Seas Fleet after Jutland and the French often did with their sailing navy. But the competence of an inactive navy withers away and over time the superior navy will be able to take successively greater risks to exploit its command of the sea. A second possibility is to try to whittle the enemy down to fair odds in decisive battle. That was the wartime objective of the High Seas Fleet before Jutland and the training objective of the Imperial Japanese Navy before World War II. The High Seas Fleet developed tactics that emphasized deception and trickery to gain an advantage in battles between small detachments. The peacetime Japanese developed tactics appropriate to inferiority—and later exercised them from habit during the war, when Japan actually enjoyed superiority.

A third approach, when the ratio of forces gives the smaller fleet a chance, is to catch the enemy with a temporary vulnerability and exploit it to gain command of the sea. The inferior navy cannot base its actions on enemy capabilities, but must be prone to accepting risk and willing to act on an estimate of enemy intentions. Doubtless that was what Nimitz had in mind before the Battle of Midway, when the American fleet was outnumbered. His orders to Fletcher and Spruance were to fight on the basis of calculated risk.[5] An inferior navy should put unstinting emphasis on superior scouting. Nimitz and his two combat commanders based their battle plans on good intelligence from code work. To attack effectively first, an inferior force must overcome its limitations by some combination of initiative and surprise.

A fourth approach is to establish local superiority, as the Germans did in the Baltic during much of World War II and the Italian navy and air force did at times in the Mediterranean.

The fifth possibility for an inferior navy is simple sea-denial. The goal of sea-denial is to create a vast no-man's-land. Why should command of the sea be necessary for a continental power to achieve its purpose on land? Denying the coast to the enemy may suffice. The U-boat campaign against British shipping in two world wars was an unambiguous attempt at sea-denial in the service of continental aggrandizement. The British submarine, surface, and air campaign against Rommel's sea line of communication is another, less pure, example. Sea-denial, extended long distances at sea by air and submarine attacks, was the core Soviet naval strategy against NATO and the U.S. Navy.

---

5 In a special letter of instruction supplementing the operation order, Nimitz wrote: "In carrying out the task assigned . . . you will be governed by the principle of calculated risk, which you shall interpret to mean the avoidance of exposure of your forces to attack by superior enemy forces without good prospect of inflicting, as a result of such exposure, greater damage on the enemy" (S. E. Morison, vol. 4, p. 84).

When sea-denial fails as a war-winning strategy, it can still contribute to the war effort if it can be used to provide leverage. The U-boat campaign was a success, at least in terms of the cost of the response that it required from the Allies. The kamikaze pilots could do nothing about restoring Japanese command of the sea, but they could hope to cripple and delay the U.S. Navy and so help to defend the Japanese homeland. Today the coastal defenses of many states that are no threat whatsoever on the high seas could deliver punishing attacks, even to the American fleet, if their national survival were at stake.

There is another possibility that Mahan's disciples tend to slight. The continental power may achieve a maritime objective by action on land. Before World War I, one school of opinion held that Britain must avoid committing a large army to Europe—that Britain's military role should be to protect its colonies and trade in the rest of the world and carry out its policy to maintain a balance of power on the continent. The other school, which included British army General Douglas Haig, maintained that standing aloof from the war on land could lose the continent to Germany. Enemy dominance on the continent might not be fatal to Britain in the short run, but it was undesirable, to say the least, this school contended. In World War I, army opinion won the day and the British Expeditionary Force was rushed to Belgium, where it suffered grievously.

The advocates of a maritime strategy felt vindicated, and there was a great public outcry against sending British boys into the trenches. Nevertheless, in World War II a larger expeditionary force was delivered to the continent. During the Blitzkrieg of spring 1940, Nazi troops quickly overran Belgium, the Netherlands, and France, spawning the miracle at Dunkirk. Whether the British should have been committed to the ground under the circumstances will not be addressed here. More important was the difference in the effect on Britain's maritime strategy of its experience in the two world wars. In World War I, when France survived with Britain's help, Germany had to base its fleet and U-boats in the North Sea. In World War II, after France was overrun, the U-boats were unleashed from the Bay of Biscay, and if Hitler had chosen he could have devastated Allied shipping with aerial attacks from French airfields. The fall of France had made the operations of the British navy tenuous in the extreme. Events on the ground had drastically altered—and almost crushed—Britain's maritime strategy. Sir Francis Bacon's hoary dictum, "He who commands the sea . . . may take as much or little of the war as he will," has to be considered next to Clausewitz's observation that when one takes little of a war, one is in peril of giving the enemy what he seeks. Not only is the influence of sea power slower and less direct than that of ground action, but it is more affected by events ashore than naval officers are wont to admit.

In sum, we have made three points concerning tactical missions. First, while it is true that the object of a mission is clarified as the time of action approaches, the commander's choice of tactics is constrained by the chain of preparations for battle. Second, the nature of these preparations is influenced by the tremendous span of missions that must be contemplated and anticipated in peacetime. Last, naval tactical commanders need to pay attention to the interaction of sea forces with events on the ground. There are three good reasons for this. The first is purely tactical: there will be more interaction between land and sea in the future. The second relates to the nature of any probable enemy: its fleet, its organizational structure, and its military philosophy will be land-oriented and foreign to us. The third is that we have inherited from Mahan a tendency to focus attention too readily on the big battle. Maintaining the security of the seas is a big task, with or without combat. Contributing to a land campaign directly with combat power is another big task, so in performing it we should be mindful of the need to control and use the adjacent littoral seas. This book about tactics treats an area much neglected, but it does not espouse the big battle as the be-all and end-all of a fleet. Fleets superior and inferior have other, less glorious missions and purposes.

Forces

To carry out a mission a commander is assigned forces. To build a cat's cage, a carpenter is given lumber and nails. The carpenter can measure the materials he needs for his task, but the tactician cannot be sure whether the enemy will be a pussycat or a tiger. During the Grenada operation, the size of the beast was underestimated. Fortunately the forces of VADM Joseph Metcalf, USN, the tactical commander, were augmented and he was able to get his job done.

One purpose of strategic scouting is to determine what the opposition comprises. The higher commander decides on the basis of the intelligence estimate what forces to allot the assigned tactical commander, allowing a margin for error proportionate to possible inaccuracies. That is the concept.

If the strategic commander has an abundance of forces available, as was the case at Grenada, time and timing come to dominate the calculations. The assembly and deployment of more force always takes more time, and time is as precious to strategists as it is to tacticians. At Grenada time was critical, for Metcalf found newly arrived Cubans in the act of building up their defenses as his paratroopers and marines landed. When the tactical commander makes his own estimate of the situation, the forces he has been assigned imply how thoroughly he can hedge against every enemy capability—or contrarily, they suggest the risks that the strategic commander compels him to take.

There is another way to look at forces vis-à-vis mission: for the *strategic* commander to tailor the task to an existing force. The advantage of this is coherence of operations. There are many examples. The Third/Fifth Fleet in World War II was a trained, tactically united entity. The old ASW hunter-killer groups of aircraft and destroyer escorts maintained their integrity as they moved from one submarine target to the next. Every Marine Corps ground-air-ship team depends heavily on continuity for effective amphibious assault. In these cases time, not force size, is the free parameter in operational planning. The measure of the *tactical* commander's effectiveness is the pace at which he or she carries out successive missions.

The Correlation of Naval Force
The root of effective tactical action is an appreciation that force estimation is a two-sided business and that not all elements of force are found in the orders of battle. The term "correlation of forces" is so concise and expressive that it is a wonder how military officers have been able to communicate without it. It took the laconic Sun Tzu forty-eight words to express its meaning:

> Now the elements of the art of war are first, measurements of space; second, estimates of quantities; third, calculations; fourth, comparisons; and fifth, chances of victory. Measurements of space are derived from the ground. Quantities derive from measurement, figures from quantities, comparisons from figures, and victory from comparisons.

It is intriguing to consider what Sun Tzu, intellectual master of the intangibles of warfare, meant by quantities. The intention of Soviet doctrine for conflict in peace and war was to incorporate all quantities in the correlation of forces and means, including geographical and temporal advantages and disadvantages.

What follows is only one of many ways to parse the elements that a commander must correlate.

Leadership
Theory has little to say to potential combat commanders about leadership. Most tacticians accept Thomas Carlyle's philosophy that "the history of the world is but the biography of great men," and they reject George Orwell's notion that leadership is only doing what is expected of a nominal leader—merely "shooting an elephant" to please the crowd.

The correlation of forces involves a comparison of leadership. History offers many examples of the value of knowing the enemy commander's habits. Knowing those of Villeneuve and de Ruyter resulted in the use of different tactics. The Japanese could depend on Spruance's conservatism to tie him to the beachheads. Usually, however, naval operations offer fewer opportunities than ground operations for evaluation in action. The personalities of army generals such as Montgomery, Eisenhower, Rommel, Guderian, and Patton were well known, and their styles were carefully drawn in the enemy's mind. Through the years naval officers have had fewer occasions to telegraph their temperaments, notwithstanding such exceptions as Nelson, Jervis, Yamamoto, Halsey, Hughes, and Suffern. (Hughes and Suffern, of the British and French navies respectively, must be the foremost example of a pair of naval antagonists. They fought each other five times in the Indian Ocean in 1782 and 1783.)

A combat leader's appraisal of leadership is objective. The Duke of Wellington surely knew that Napoleon's presence on the battlefield was worth "another forty thousand men," but Wellington would have been more interested in his own defensive positions at the Battle of Waterloo given the objective knowledge that Napoleon, because of his style, was sure to attack before Marshal Blücher arrived with his Prussian reinforcements.

Apart from strong numbers and successful scouting, the greatest determinants of victory are the very things that commanders will judge most badly: their own attributes and reputation. All good combat leaders are highly competitive; unfortunately, so are most bad ones. Under the circumstances, the best counsel is this: The untried commander should assume that he or she has average skill and not presume that he can overcome disadvantage with talents he may not possess. If a commander has talent, it will grow. A good reputation may be worth more on the battlefield than good attributes, and a bad reputation will mute even the best attributes. That is why Napoleon sought "lucky" generals. Explicitly, a tactical philosophy that *depends for success* on its leaders out-planning, outwitting, and outmaneuvering a first-class enemy is a philosophy of fatal over-optimism.

Training and Morale

"We learn how to do things by doing the things we are learning how to do," Aristotle observed in his *Ethics*. The mechanics of training should be seen not as an end but as the beginning of effective combat. In football, open-field blocking and tackling are creative skills, but they come from rote practice that is supplemented by competition on the field. Combat training is two-sided. Morale, too, is a relative property, both on the football field and at sea.

Theory leaves the final estimate of the states of training for the day of battle. If commanders are prone to exaggerate their personal virtues, that is counterbalanced by their propensity to undervalue the state of readiness of their own forces in relation to the enemy's. ADM George Dewey and ADM William Sampson won battles with gunnery that was execrable. In the circumstances, the U.S. admirals who served during the Spanish-American War knew that the Spanish fleet was even less ready and appreciated the need for quick, decisive action.

American ships in the Solomons were thrown together helter-skelter. Yet, it does not follow that the troubles there all stemmed from this deficiency, for at the same time on the Japanese side the redoubtable Rear Admiral Tanaka suffered as grievously and complained as bitterly about the heterogeneous forces that were thrust upon him. The point is not that incoherence is tolerable, but that training and morale must be compared with those of the enemy.

Hardware

The true orders of battle on both sides include a qualitative estimate of the state of equipment. Ships must drag inoperative equipment into battle along with the good. Most of the wartime life of the gallant USS *Houston* (CA 30) was spent fighting with one of three turrets out of commission. Propulsion plants are an interesting case. When navies depended on massing for concentration of force, a crippled engineering plant in one ship slowed the entire fleet; the alternative was to leave the speed-limited ship behind. The speed advantage that Togo had over Russian Admiral Zinovi Rozhestvensky was probably doubled by the pathetic state that the Russians' propulsion plants were in after their exhausting 18,000-nautical-mile cruise from the Baltic to the Straits of Tsushima. Today, with the dispersal of modern fleets in combat, it is more difficult to predict the effect of one or two ships with poor engineering plants on the composite maneuverability of a fleet.

All in all, the numbers, quality, and mix of a commander's own forces on the eve of battle are probably the easiest quantitative estimate to make, and that of the enemy's forces is one of the most difficult. A thorny problem of great significance is the estimate of scouting resources. The difficulty comes partly because of the wide array of potential sources of information, some of which will not be under the command of either battle commander, and partly because the active use of some sensors will depend on how the battle itself unfolds and on decisions regarding electronic emissions.

Endurance

Combat endurance is governed by the ammunition stocks and fuel capacity of the forces at the scene of action. It affects both tactics and strategy. Dewey suspended action at Manila Bay when an erroneous report told him his ships were almost out of ammunition. A Navy study in the 1960s concluded that ASW ships escorting military convoys across the Atlantic could easily run out of torpedoes by firing at false contacts—a prognostication that was corroborated during the Falklands War, when the British navy fired hundreds of ASW weapons against an effective Argentine order of battle that contained only one submarine. After the U.S. Navy's study, torpedo magazine capacity was tripled in the ship class involved. *Tactics* are affected when there is a real danger of running out of weapons—missiles, for example.

In the October War of 1973 the Israeli navy's fast patrol boats were able to close and sink Egyptian craft that carried missiles with nearly double the range of the Israelis' own by inducing the Egyptians to empty their missile magazines without effect. The U.S. Navy appears to be reexamining the number of offensive and defensive weapons that its ships carry. But there is an *upper* limit to desirable capacity. For one thing, magazines are hard to armor against enemy missiles. One does not choose to send ammunition ships in harm's way. For another, missiles, which are expensive, cannot be permitted to go down with the ship in large numbers. The research of a student at the U.S. Naval Postgraduate School, working on a thesis on the "correct" balance between area AAW missile systems and point-defense systems, produced an unanticipated side-benefit: he was able to examine U.S. and adversary warships to determine the relationship between the expected combat life of a ship—in terms of the number of incoming air-to-surface missiles—and the number of AAW missiles still in the magazines when the ship was put out of action. The results are classified, but the study demonstrates that a staff estimate of fleet endurance should be made with due consideration of the *net* missile firepower in relation to the expected combat lifetime of a force, which naturally will suffer losses.

It is important to assess fuel capacities in battle planning. The Battle of the Eastern Solomons in August 1942 gave us a memorable example of what happens when this area is neglected. Instead of three carriers, Fletcher had only two in the battle, because he had sent the USS *Wasp* south to fuel. She missed all the fighting and was sunk by a submarine soon after. Tactical endurance hardly ever enters into amateur force correlations, and, being a distraction, an aggravation, and a great source of friction, it is rarely given the place it deserves. Knowledge of the enemy's endurance deficiencies can lead to a decisive tactical advantage, as Togo demonstrated at Tsushima.

Resilience

The relative accessibility of mobile support ships, fleet repair facilities, and naval shipyards weigh in the commander's plans. A tactical concern is the job of reconstituting an effective fighting capability after an attack. Post-attack scouting for damage assessment and a simple, preplanned roll-call ought to be included in doctrine and implemented. Plans for post-attack rendezvous to refuel and rearm should be automatic. How to exploit the enemy's own post-battle confusion also is a consideration. The foe of resiliency is swift pursuit.

Since it is reasonable in war to expect damage and temporary suspension of air operations in a carrier, it often also is reasonable to expect quick flight-deck repairs and a return to offensive readiness. Any American operation order should include a plan to survive during the interim—not just for carriers, but for any key ship, such as an Aegis combatant, the commander's flagship, or an accompanying fast support ship that has been damaged. These crucial tactical variables must be thought through and communicated to the force some time in advance, because there will not be time to do so when the operation commences.

Tactical Environment

Meteorology, oceanography, the proximity of land, and the fact that mines, missiles, and submarines subject operations in coastal waters to a higher order of surprise also greatly influence the choice of tactics that are employed to carry out a mission. Littoral operations are now prominent and affect much tactical planning. Next to a coastline, the islands, inlets, shallows, coastal air and surface traffic, dense commercial electronic emissions, fishing boats, fog banks—all these things and more create their own local influence and tactical variability. A theme of this book is that sea battles differ from land battles because there is less influence of geography at sea. The closer the battle is to land, the more the shape of the land and the continental shelf change this general truth. This last variable may have, currently, the greatest influence to alter each operational setting. Theory that successfully identifies the great trends and constants can offer only limited practical advice about it. As Admiral Hayward said, "Every body of water requires a different set of tactics."

Payoff: The Synthesis of Force Attributes

Together, *leadership* and *training* describe force *competence*. *Endurance* and *resilience* describe combat support, but they connote something more as well. The term *hardware* is more comprehensive than *order of battle*, even after all scouting and communications assets are included, because the hardware evaluation is an attempt to balance force and mission and to assess the state of equipment readiness.

Leadership, training, hardware, endurance, and resilience are pieced together by the commander in a mosaic of offensive and defensive force potential. They also can be arrayed objectively by the staff to indicate readiness by individual unit, or by antisubmarine, antiair, antisurface, and strike capacity. These indicators of force competence are calculated for both sides and explicitly or implicitly weighed against each other to produce a net assessment for the mission.

The character of the *tactical environment* is shared by friend and foe. But it does not affect both sides equally or in the same way. There are day fighters and all-weather fighters, there are searchers, and there are evaders. (A dramatic example of contrasting influences is the different ways that the sonar environment affects the antisubmarine predator and prey.) The best procedure in practice is to develop values—numerical or symbolic—for leadership, training, hardware, endurance, and resilience; next, reduce or expand the values according to environmental influences; and finally to correlate the two forces.

Particularly with regard to the enemy, qualitative assessment may guide tactics as much as quantitative knowledge. Nelson did not much care how many French and Spanish warships his fleet would face. His tactical plan was based on the knowledge that his force had a great qualitative advantage in the type of ship-on-ship engagement that characterized the age of fighting sail. In the Solomons campaign Americans usually had a better estimate of where and when a night battle would be fought than what they would be fighting. It seems that Japanese tactics in the Solomons were robust—that is, ideally suited for a variety of conditions of surprise and uncertainty—where American tactics were not, at least in the beginning.

The correlation of forces is always mission-specific and is undertaken in the context of the tactical plan. Friendly and enemy force-relationships influence the estimate of the situation and the plan of action. But the plan of action must be unified and must allow variations for contingencies. As the experiences of Nelson, Togo, Jellicoe, and Burke suggest, a good plan is deceptively simple—a remarkable reduction of comprehensive considerations into a cohesive, feasible essence.

It accommodates timely modifications, but there must be few variations because it has a momentum to which every change adds drag and the risk of confusion.

Decision aids help battle planning and execution. Some are merely displays of the location and status of forces. Others help to position forces and structure scouting plans. Still others facilitate timely actions. Desktop microcomputers are a boon to decision-making. As surely as the world is undergoing a revolution in information processing, so its navies are in the midst of a computing revolution that requires them to run just to stay in place.

12

A TWENTY-FIRST-CENTURY REVOLUTION

The Influence of Information Warfare

The fastest-changing trend in naval tactics today is the effect of information warfare (IW). But information warfare and its subsets affect far more than naval tactics. A comprehensive study of IW requires a book to cover the subject, and several good ones have been written. At the most fundamental level, IW is about how to employ and protect the ability to sense, assimilate, decide, communicate, and act—while confounding those same processes that support the adversary. In this book devoted to tactics and campaigns, we emphasize sensing (scouting), commanding by links, and acting (shooting). In the information warfare domain, the methods of cyberattack and defense are executed differently in peace or war and in commercial or military operations. This chapter highlights some of the differences before focusing on how IW is changing tactics in combat. The most recent wide-ranging domains of IW include scouting with unmanned aerial and undersea vehicles, network-hardening and intrusions, and computer viruses.[1] There also are longstanding IW methods such as the employment of human spies, deception in many forms, surveillance of many kinds, psychological operations and perception management, and physical destruction of command-and-control capabilities.

Information warfare broadly conceived is orthogonal to naval tactics. As a consequence, IW is having major effects on all six processes of naval tactics used in fleet combat—scouting and antiscouting, command-and-control, C^2 countermeasures, delivery of fire, and confounding enemy fire. Chapter 13 will discuss

---

1   In the U.S. Navy system, IW embraces electro-magnetic warfare (EMW), computer network defense (CND), computer network attack (CNA), and other subsets.

the effects of IW on tactical planning. For example, electronic and acoustic emissions can be detected by an enemy who is well beyond the maximum range that these devices can function in locating the enemy forces for the ship or aircraft that is using them. This has always been true, but today tactical commands should be executed with barely detectable radiations because of the heightened risk that enemy missiles will be fired at a detected communication signal. The value of decoys imitating real targets has been increased because they create doubt in the enemy's mind or, in the best of situations, cause him to waste aircraft and missile attacks on false targets.

Naval tactics aided by IW govern the processes only in battle, but information warfare occurs in both war and peace and affects both military and nonmilitary activities. Information warfare is a competition that has its own distinctive tactical skills, laws, and ethical considerations. In 2016 Peter Denning, chair of the computer science department at the Naval Postgraduate School, recalled the vast change that has occurred in IW during the fifty years that he had worked in this field. "For the first 40 years, computing research—including mine—focused on developing hardware and software technology," he said. "For the last ten years it has been in employing the developments in many and widespread applications."

Another way to grasp the magnitude of the trend is to look at the pervasiveness of compact navigation systems, apps, and social networks such as Google, Facebook, Twitter, LinkedIn, YouTube, Instagram, Flickr, Snapchat, Vine, and Skype as new and popular modes of information transmission. People routinely walk down the street engrossed in smartphones, work out with personalized playlists and increasingly sophisticated wrist-worn fitness monitors, summon taxis or rent rooms in the new sharing economy, and play one of the many interactive commercial war games against distantly linked anonymous opponents. Ten years from now in this fast-developing field, these identifiers of today's commercial networks may well be replaced and forgotten.

Indeed, there is a mounting wave of concern about how far automation will expand and what its impact will be on the continuum of cognition from data to information to knowledge. In the past decade we have begun to learn how to automate "knowledge work," which for decades was thought to be immune from the kind of automation that replaces manual work. This new form of automation—and the application of artificial intelligence—is creating social stress. We cannot foresee whether knowledge automation will destroy more jobs than it creates or whether new professions organized around design and distribution will add to employment. Navies are facing similar uncertainties. They are drawn toward more automation because they fear that without it adversaries can seize the upper hand. At the same time they observe that automated systems can be too fragile to depend upon under fire. In addition, automated weapon systems could make mistakes too swiftly for human operators to be able to prevent a deadly disaster. In geopolitics, terrorists have exploited impressionable people around the world with new forms of propaganda, some of it ugly in the extreme. Authoritarian states employ the web for propaganda, censorship, and control that is unprecedented in its reach; at the same time, they risk losing the information war to new, creative forms of independent communication that resist restrictions or shaping.

Cryptography and Cyberwarfare

The information warfare revolution started early in the twentieth century with wireless radio accompanied by aerial scouting. Throughout World War I early aircraft with rudimentary radios affected the way battles were fought on land. At sea ships were subject to easier detection, and aerial scouting led to successful campaigns to eliminate surface raiders. The new scouting power was accompanied by an opportunity to intercept and exploit enemy communications. That led to encryption, which in turn led to code-breaking. Until now the effects of that first breakthrough in information warfare have never been exceeded. Today, the same radical effects on warfare have occurred with computer technology. Transmissions in cyberspace have led to intrusions affecting security that must be countered by defensive measures. Together they create a constant, pervasive "cyberwar" going on continuously, whether in peacetime, crisis, or full-fledged conflict.

Deception and Surprise

In chapter 8 we highlighted Harvard professor Barton Whaley's study of strategic deception—how to achieve it, its probability of success, and its value measured in enhanced casualty exchange rates.[2] Most deception in the twentieth century was supported by communications and other electronic media. Only 23 of the 115 deceptions that Whaley investigated from 1914 to 1968 involved naval operations, such as Pearl Harbor and Midway, and most of those dealt with amphibious assaults, such as the Normandy invasion. Nevertheless, many of Whaley's general conclusions regarding successful deception are robust for fleet tactics and campaigns as well. His prescriptions include

---

2 Whaley. A later and in some ways superior book is Rothstein and Whaley.

- Reinforcing preconceptions or expectations of the enemy commander; then do something different.
- Using deception, which he says is a low-risk endeavor, whether it works or not.
- Using multiple false clues—say up to six—because some clues will not reach the enemy decision-maker, and using more than one clue adds credibility to the ploy.
- Employing *strategic* deception does not cost much in forces or dollars, but it involves some devoted thinking by the deceiver and his staff. It is not certain that *tactical* deception will be similarly inexpensive in terms of the number of forces that are needed to achieve it.

How does Whaley's study of historical deception help plan for the twenty-first century? One example is the tension between invisibility and operational decentralization. Today American cyberwar in peacetime is closely controlled at a high level. There ought to be plans in place so that when the shooting starts commanders can shift control to allow decision-making involving deception within the theater of operations. An insightful historical cautionary tale is the very tight security that protected the Navy's code-breaking achievements before the Japanese surprise attack on Pearl Harbor. Authorities in Washington did not realize that they needed to reinforce the war warning that had been gleaned from having broken the Japanese diplomatic code. Only seven months later, cryptanalysis conducted locally by the Pacific Fleet command—which involved breaking the code used by the Japanese fleet—resulted in a happier outcome. Nimitz's shrewd conclusion that the Japanese were going to attack Midway Island had not been at all certain from the early clues reported by his cryptographers, and his willingness to bring his few carriers back to Pearl Harbor from the Southwest Pacific involved a degree of risk, as did his willingness to confront those in Washington, including Admiral King, as CNO, who wanted more evidence to support Nimitz' conclusion. Nimitz' exploitation of cryptanalysis at CINCPACFLT headquarters played an important role in the American victory.

In 2017 the Defense Department directed the elevation of the U.S. Cyber Command to a unified combatant command, giving it greater powers of decision and direction. Cyber Command now has charge of conducting all military and naval cyberoperations around the clock. Hopefully, it is empowered to coordinate with commerce and industry, which also suffer cyberattacks and must develop their own defensive measures. In addition, the new Cyber Command must coordinate closely with theater commanders, who must take the offensive when the shooting starts. Just as U.S. leaders worried about giving away code-breaking secrets before Pearl Harbor, we also risk revealing specific methods today if we act prematurely. The value of each application must be balanced carefully against its cost, weighing centralized direction against the perspectives and needs on scene. The new unified commander and staff will have a responsibility to plan for and train other unified commands in this rapidly evolving field. Agility will be essential in applying it across the spectrum of conflict.

The need to understand contemporary deception and surprise must not only be part of planning for major wars; it also must play a role in preparing for irregular warfare and for terrorist attacks and defense against such attacks. Here the intent is to indicate protective actions, but be aware a preemptive counterattack is sometimes the best defense. In a more recent book, *Intelligence and Surprise Attack: Failure and Success from Pearl Harbor to 9/11 and Beyond,* Erik Dahl cites two factors that are necessary for authorities to exploit intelligence collection without repeating past mistakes.[3] First, there must be a *tactical-level warning* that is sufficiently precise to warrant attention. Second, decision-makers must be receptive to the warning when it is timely and in sufficient detail. Dahl tempers Roberta Wohlstetter's well-known analysis, which concluded that when an intelligence failure occurs, it is likely to be because the clues are lost in a background noise of irrelevant information.[4] The recurring WikiLeaks phenomenon in peacetime by states or rogue individuals is a clue that military intrusions will be increasing in peacetime or war.

Today with the huge increase in data volume, gathering information is easier, sorting it is harder, and the chance of overlooking clues that might prevent surprise is greater than ever. Even though new analytical tools are being applied to aid in sorting, it is likely that deception, as an IW method, will endure and the level of sophistication will mount. Intelligence experts will be more challenged to stay alert to exploit or prevent surprise attacks. As information proliferates, surprises may be more likely, so it is prudent to plan how to recover from them. The normal assumption is that communications security will be effective. As a backup, there should be a continuing effort to evaluate contingency plans that assume that the enemy has broken our code and is "reading our mail." Does success *depend on* secure communications, or can operations be modified to compensate for possible enemy knowledge of it?

---

3 Dahl.
4 Wohlstetter.

The intelligence community carries the heavy burden of Dahl's insight that in order to be acted on a "strategic warning" must be specific. For example, an accurate forecast that, say, the Japanese were going to war in early December 1941 was not specific enough to forestall a major failure of American defenses. Dahl believes that it is insufficient merely to know that a terrorist attack is being planned somewhere in the United States. The intelligence community cannot assume that its job is done when it reports that an attack has become more likely somewhere. Bold, useful intelligence is not risk free and carries the burden that it sometimes may be wrong in the details. It is a cruel responsibility, because the intelligence community cannot risk getting the reputation of the boy who cried wolf, or no one will believe what it says when it has full, accurate information.

Exploitation of Unmanned Vehicles and Countermeasures

We are well into the robotic age of warfare. Unmanned vehicles that are either remotely controlled or programmed for independent action proliferate, with a variety of capabilities and purposes. Automation has been employed in defensive systems for several decades, including automatically controlled close-in weapon systems and the highly integrated Aegis combat system. Technology is now enabling higher degrees of automation with broader military application. A frequently seen metaphor imagines aerial robots cooperating like a flock of birds. Developments now under way include flexible and reliable automation for hands-off operations and improved energy densities for greater endurance in unmanned air, surface, and undersea vehicles. Technological advancements also are making it possible to blend offensive and defensive tactics. Autonomous systems hosting a variety of sensors may not need communications links for reconnaissance, but it would be valuable indeed if the enemy were not able to detect the reports they made back to the command. Researchers also are experimenting with technology and new combat doctrine to enable unmanned aerial vehicles to work in tandem with manned aircraft and warships.

A major tactical consequence of this activity will be to hasten the shift to smaller systems that are more numerous, less costly, and more difficult to detect. As the number of such robots increases, their inherent resilience will improve every country's ability to sense, understand, and act. Robotic craft serve to broaden the available options to operate independently, in small cooperating numbers, in groups large enough for swarm attacks, or in concert with manned systems.

Meanwhile, as commercial applications of unmanned vehicles proliferate, navies will borrow from civilian industry, and military applications will expand as public trust of unmanned systems grows.

Information Operations for Rescue Missions and Diplomacy

"Hastily formed networks" (HFNs) is a descriptive term for the way the Naval Postgraduate School has deployed information capabilities to scenes of natural disasters, such as a tsunami in Southeast Asia and Hurricane Katrina on the Gulf Coast. Other American and international agencies have supported disaster relief in places such as Haiti and in the mountains of South Asia. Rapidly deployed command-and-control connections are the foundation for useful rescue and humanitarian support in the future. The Cebrowski Institute's HFN program, coupled with tactical mesh network development at the Naval Postgraduate School, is in the forefront, not only for advances in technology and computer system advances but also in improving field operations—in other words, the tactics and procedures for disaster relief.

The means for responding to natural disasters such as earthquakes, hurricanes, and forest fires are steadily being improved by better information operations. Humanitarian field experience will better prepare armed forces for responding to successful enemy attacks such as those on the New York City World Trade Center and the Pentagon in 2001. Terrorist attacks with widespread consequences or their attempts will occur again, potentially in a U.S. container port, or to an electrical grid or a water supply. Peacetime experience with rapid emergency emplacement will help prepare authorities to exploit modern technology for diplomatic purposes or unforeseeable small-scale military operations around the world. An example of inefficient practice in peacetime—corrected since the event occurred—was a time-consuming decision to release closely held satellite surveillance information that was badly needed to execute humanitarian operations in Sumatra after an earthquake and tsunami.

Exploitation of Computing Machines and Information Flows

A longstanding debate is under way about when or if machines with self-improving artificial intelligence (AI) will supplant human thinking. Motion pictures have offered fictional examples of what might happen. In the 1968 film *2001: A Space Odyssey*, a thinking computer named HAL, installed to help human astronauts on a voyage to Jupiter, decides to eliminate the humans and take over the spaceship. The *Terminator* movie series, which began in 1984, features a post-apocalypse earth run by human-hunting robots that were created after a man-made information system had become "self-aware." Ever since these films reached local theaters, research on artificial intelligence has been haunted by the possibility that computer scientists will create a thinking machine that will become a Frankenstein monster.

The debate over AI is healthy, wide-ranging, and rich with possibilities. By and large it focuses on highly specialized *thinking* robots. There are also specialized *acting* robots that do things that are too dangerous or too tiny for a human and can perform important tasks that humans either cannot do as well or do at all. Two Naval Postgraduate School professors with technology and operational credentials espouse an approach with a more certain payoff. Peter Denning and John Arquilla argue that for the foreseeable future humans teamed with increasingly remarkable computer assessors, calculators, data-processers, and tactical exploiters will be the most effective.[5] An example they cite is experience with winning strategies for chess and the game of go. People and machines working together have been shown to be better than either a person or a machine working alone.[6] For further affirmation of the power of people and machines in combination, see the CNO Strategic Studies Group 35 Final Report, "The Network of Humans and Machines as the Next Capital Ship."[7]

The advantages of teaming humans and machines through technological advances should come as no surprise. Beginning with World War I, illustrations depicting great advances in warfare frequently showed a soldier being "assisted" by the protection of a tank. Today, tanks and other vehicles programmed to control themselves autonomously are being deployed experimentally, but their capabilities are less comprehensive than when a soldier is present to deal with decisions for which autonomous vehicles are not yet prepared. Autonomous vehicles can work well in specific situations, but they still suffer handicaps in flexibility and adaptability.

---

5   Peter Denning chairs the NPS Computer Science Department and Cebrowski Institute. John Arquilla, mentioned elsewhere in the book for his research into who wins wars and why, chairs the Defense Analysis Department and sponsors the NPS Littoral Operations Center.

6   Also see two papers with the remarkable conclusion that effective decision-makers themselves play a role as unique human *sensors* in a modern networked environment. Bordetsky and Dolk, and Bordetsky and Mullins.

7   Wisecup.

Denning points out that a new generation of AI-assisted technologies has arrived that may accelerate this pace. Developments include deep-learning algorithms that tap large quantities of data from a large network to produce ever-smarter AI assistance. We do not need to focus primary attention on advancing AI's self-learning capabilities; we can gain more by finding and capitalizing on synergies between humans and machines. This is the essence of human-and-machine combat-teaming and the ability to make better decisions faster and act on them swiftly to obtain maximum advantage in enhancing human performance. Just as giving a soldier a long-bow to replace a spear and putting a steam engine in a warship to replace the wind were major advances in man-and-machine cooperation, giving human decision-makers combat-oriented computer programs will enhance combat performance. We can take cues from the civilian world of iPads, Apps, Google Maps, ever-improving spreadsheet tools to expand and exploit computing power, cars that drive themselves, instant worldwide communications, and the future of artificial intelligence to make better decisions. Many commercial advances are being adapted for military operations, reliable logistics, and precision delivery of firepower.

The success and proliferation of unmanned *aerial* vehicles evolved quickly because of operational demand on scene, but that has not been the case for unmanned surface vehicles at sea. UAVs became popular because soldiers could observe their value in combat. By contrast, unmanned surface vehicles that operate in dangerous coastal waters will evolve quickly only after they are programmed with instructions how to carry out the specific tasks they are expected to execute. Judging from the many applications of UAVs, it is clearly time to develop unmanned technologies for surface vessels that can collaborate with manned systems in dangerous littoral waters.

Exploitation of Space Satellites

There now is worldwide recognition of the importance of satellites for communications, control, surveillance, and navigation. One of the biggest risks to the *military* is the growing possibility—indeed the likelihood—that an enemy will destroy our satellites or otherwise neutralize their effectiveness.

A telling example involves the satellites now being used for accurate navigation. The U.S.-developed Global Positioning System (GPS) has vastly improved commercial, personal, and military navigation. A major advance in weaponry was to use GPS to guide land attack missiles accurately onto stationary targets ashore.

No enemy will be content to accept the destructiveness of cruise missiles that are assisted by GPS navigation. It will do its utmost to destroy the satellite or the link that guides such missiles. With that in mind, it is prudent to design and acquire equipment and software and train personnel to carry out appropriate responses and alternatives.

Tactical Information Warfare in Combat

New technology to improve data collection, analysis, display, and connectivity is accelerating the breadth of information warfare.[8] In chapters 8 and 9 we addressed the combat role of information warfare and how it has evolved. The trends and constants of fleet tactics are catalogued under six combat processes, each of which is enhanced by information operations. These interacting six processes have feedback loops that are shown in the discussion of command-and-control. These diagrams are an attempt to reduce a highly subjective mental process to a formula that is too pedantic for practical application. Our emphasis here is more on good and bad tactical leaders who made, or failed to make, crucial decisions at critical points in time. Tactical instinct cannot be reduced to a formula or script. A new wrinkle introduced by information warfare is the need for education and training devoted to personal development in this new and separate domain of expertise.

There are several excellent books on the topic. One is *Information Warfare and Security*, by Dorothy Denning, which provides extensive coverage of offensive and defensive operations for both military and commercial purposes.[9] Denning's definitions and categories are comprehensive, and her illustrations cover every form of information operations. She includes the difficult subject of quantifying the *value* of information operations. Her bibliography is an excellent source for further reading, and seventy pages of endnotes have many more references to important publications such as "Cyberwar Is Coming!" by John Arquilla and David Ronfeldt.[10] Remarkably, the bibliography illustrates the accelerating pace of information-warfare activities. Her earliest citation is David Kahn's *The Codebreakers*, published in 1967. Of the approximately sixty publications in the bibliography, only five were published before 1990.

---

8. The U.S. Navy says every aspect of the way we task, collect, process, evaluate and disseminate—the TCPED continuum—is affected.
9   Denning.
10 "Cyberwar Is Coming!" may be found in another excellent source on the growing impact of information warfare, *In Athena's Camp: Preparing for Conflict in the Information Age*, by John Arquilla and David Ronfeldt.

Information Warfare in Education and Training

Navy leadership has recognized the need to expand the knowledge and skills of information warfare in every aspect of fleet operations. The challenge is to fill the need. The Naval Postgraduate School has set a high bar for graduate education and research in information warfare, whether tactical, operational, technological, or sociological. NPS has a rich program of curricula and research, including a Department of Information Science, a Department of Defense Analysis, the Cebrowski Institute devoted to fostering cyberoperations, and the CRUSER program to hasten the testing and introduction of technologies and tactics of unmanned vehicles. The faculty knows that staying current entails maintaining a running dialog with curriculum sponsors and industry.

Success also depends on filling quotas of the right students in each of the curricula. By the "right" students, we mean a mix of information professionals and seagoing officers in the surface, submarine, and aviation communities. VADM Patricia Tracey, USN (Ret.), former chief of naval education and training, once pointed out that her graduate education was a time to expand her horizons—a time for her to think as well as learn. She espoused graduate education as one of the most valuable opportunities that the Navy can give its future leaders. The book's first cornerstone is "sailors matter most." Military men and women must not only perform with skill and courage in battle or under stress, but also perform when they are not in combat or conducting difficult operations. The best officers and crew members must be prepared to *think* as well as act under pressure. Graduate-level education for information operations prepares these service members to contribute to technology-swift enhancements, and—just as important—to embark on a career of service as specialists or as IW-aware warfighters in the fleet.

Another valuable way that the Naval Postgraduate School and Naval War College advance the Navy's use of information warfare is by sponsoring workshops and monitoring conferences that help officers stay abreast of advancements in commercial technologies. NPS also conducts field experiments to achieve new, better, and usually smaller and cheaper means of detection, communication, and control for unmanned vehicles. The commercial world of Silicon Valley and its many savvy offspring often are more aware of the value of information operations than the Navy is.

For training, the emphasis must be on skill-sets. The art of working with intelligent machines will be a new and different skill. Perhaps we will even begin to train self-learning machines to work with their human companions.[11] There

---

11 The need to teach machines is suggested in CNO Strategic Studies Group 35 Final Report, "The Network of Humans and Machines as the Next Capital Ship," 31 July 2016.

is a no more complicated blend of technical knowledge and operational skills—information that leads to action—than in unmanned systems, cyberoperations, and information warfare. In chapter 8 we show that success in combat requires well-timed action based on a just-sufficient amount of information. Decision-focused sorting of the flood of information that flows into a command by a staff-commander partnership is an important part of time-critical decision-making. Tactical success comes from choosing the right moment to act, neither too soon nor too late; as a result, attacking effectively cannot be without risk. Sudden cyber-attack is not dependent upon geography, and a defender must be ever-ready to block an attack "from every direction." Cyberattacks can take place instantaneously anywhere in cyberspace. Training to *operate* in such a domain will be different and will require experienced, high-caliber teachers.

Not new, but likely to become more important is information warfare enhanced by virtual environments. Mock-ups used in Combat Information Centers and their successors beginning in World War II vastly improved combat readiness. Anti-submarine warfare trainers for hunter-killer task groups and convoys were used extensively in the 1950s. These were ways to provide vicarious experience for naval personnel in the increasingly fast pace of combat. Team-training within a ship or in a task group composed of ships and aircraft was especially beneficial. One modern equivalent is the use of virtual environments for the development of unmanned systems and for testing to augment field experiments. Flight simulators with realistic visual and motion properties were introduced in large numbers more than fifty years ago; it was only after the military installed aircraft simulators servicewide that tensions between the pilot training community and the simulator developers and education specialists came to the fore. The pilots saw the simulators as *supplements* to training in the air (albeit with a small increase in cost); the developers saw them as *substitutes*, with potentially large cost-savings. The debate continues, and it probably will become more important as trainers become more sophisticated.

There is one caution about vicarious training. One of our most realistic ways to teach ground tactics is on instrumented ranges that substitute lasers for deadly bullets and shells. English tactical analyst David Rowland, however, discovered the troubling fact that in infantry battles the difference between casualty rates inflicted in actual combat and those estimated on an instrumented range was less by *a factor of seven*. Soldiers are more cautious when excessive boldness results in death rather than embarrassment.

The Naval War College curriculum (and presumably all military education for senior officers) should be reexamined constantly to ensure an up-to-date understanding of potential influence of IW operations wrought by technological advances in the Department of Defense and in significant adversaries. Unlike the case with other combat tactics, there is plenty of opportunity to observe cyberattacks around the world in peacetime. The Naval War College itself was a victim of one such attack. The admonition of military operations research professionals also applies to IW and especially to cyberoperations: "When there is a war on, study the war; don't game it, or simulate it, or write sage papers about it."

Youth and Creativity

We conclude with a radical thought—an unproven hypothesis. Innovation in IW development and operations is probably a skill for which younger service members—both officers and enlisted personnel—are best attuned. Preparing future Navy leaders for information warfare should start early. The U.S. Naval Academy has established a new Center for Cyber Security Studies to imbue its students with an early introduction to IW.[12] Enthusiastic support for the center signals the importance that seasoned professionals place on starting young. Here are wise words regarding cyberwar by a Navy lieutenant: "The most talented graduate students at the best U.S. computer science and engineering schools are said to be those who leave their respective programs before graduation in order to pursue venture capital or other commercial opportunities to transition an academic project or hobby to commercial viability . . . resources championed in support of bringing an idea from concept to fruition is the essence of accomplishment in cyberspace. A service interested in pursuing excellence within its cyber forces must understand that it is the role of the service to administratively and organizationally reduce the various forms of friction that would inhibit those individuals and teams within their cyber forces from innovating, developing, and deploying capabilities faster than an adversary force."[13]

To add weight to the case for youth and the need for seniors to help them stay ahead in creativity we remind the reader of some combat leaders and the age

---

12 Its mission is "to enhance the education of midshipmen in all areas of cyber warfare [and share] expertise and perspectives . . . across the Yard . . . and harmonize efforts and shape a common framework for cyber warfare related efforts at USNA." The Army also recognizes the need to attract youth. West Point has established a new Army Cyber Institute with similar aims.

13 Meadors, prepared for and disseminated by VADM Jan Tighe, USN, deputy CNO for information warfare and director of naval intelligence.

when they achieved greatness: Napoleon was a general at age twenty-three, J. E. B. Stuart at age twenty-eight, and George Custer at age twenty-three; and LT W. B. Cushing was only twenty-two when he sank the CSS *Albemarle*. The list of past heroic military achievements by creative young men is a long one. Perhaps skill in information warfare among young men and women today is analogous to the talent exhibited early on by mathematicians and classical music composers. In both of these sharply contrasting professions the truly great ones made lasting contributions while still in their teens.

MODERN TACTICS
AND OPERATIONS

Missiles and Maxims

The goal of concentrating, or massing, offensive forces to attack has become widely accepted as the overriding maxim for tactical success. "Prescribing an approach which enables an action to be opened with full firepower enforces the soundest of all tactical maxims," the Robisons wrote in 1942.[1] It was a solid deduction from historical research of that era. Yet, an examination of the air and surface battles since then shows that the maxim occasionally must be tempered.

To understand what has changed in the intervening years calls for the development of a new model of the dynamics of modern combat. This chapter will not attempt to repudiate the concept of marshaling firepower—far from it. Rather, it seeks to examine each of the processes of tactics and freshen the doctrine of tactics to incorporate technological changes.

To begin we recall the description of an aircraft carrier attack as a phenomenal pulse of striking power with which an air wing theoretically could sink several carriers, although none did that during the Pacific war. Then recall the nighttime surface engagements in the Solomons and the shocking multiship destructiveness unleashed by a spread of torpedoes, analogous in power to a missile attack. It is apparent that a modern warship armed with ballistic or cruise missiles and supported with adequate scouting has the capacity to sink several of the enemy's warships.

If Trident submarines could be targeted, they would go down with many warheads—more than the number of nuclear weapons that would be expended to sink them. These huge submarines seem to have been designed on a cost-effective

---

1   Robison and Robison, p. 896.

basis—that is, economies of scale drove the concentration of twenty-four missiles in each vessel, each missile armed with eight multiple independently targeted reentry vehicle warheads (MIRVs), without regard for the possibility that the submarines might be detectable someday. Had the designers factored even the remote possibility that these boats might be tracked at sea or else attacked in port or at dispersed harbors they would have distributed Trident missiles on more submarines, even though that would have been less expedient.[2]

The most striking illustration of the concentration of warheads in the modern nuclear arsenal was the MX missile, which carried about ten. A natural but unforeseen consequence of the first strategic arms limitation treaty, or SALT I, which counted missile launchers rather than warheads, is that the land-based MX system was considered destabilizing because it offered the enemy an opportunity to destroy many warheads with one in a first strike.

Now, since each of these weapon systems constitutes an indivisible massing of firepower that is potentially vulnerable to successful enemy targeting and first strike, it creates a tactical problem. Set aside the particulars of each case and analyze the situation in more general terms, abandoning all preconceptions and leaving open all questions of massing, concentration, and the possibility of a reserve component. Now question one maxim in particular—the one that calls on tacticians "always" to use superior force to attack a part of the enemy, while forestalling him from doing the same.

A Salvo Model of Modern Missile Combat

Let us define the core characteristics of the kind of small missile ships that are typical of the warships for which we have combat data. We shall apply them in a "salvo model" that takes the same form found in a naval research journal and a publication of the Military Operations Research Society.[3] Assume two combatants, A and B, each having deployed several ships and having the following characteristics:

- *Staying power* of a defender, denoted a_1 and b_1, is the number of nominal ASCM hits by an Exocet or similar missile needed to put the ship out of action.
- *Salvo size* of each attacker, denoted a_2 and b_2, is the number of missiles that will be launched successfully. These numbers do not appear in the two salvo equations because only a fraction of the missiles will hit, denoted H_a and H_b.

---

2   Besides the cost premium of wider distribution, there also is the issue of control: more submarines create more control problems and hazards.
3   See Hughes (1995). The article includes thirty-eight references for further study.

- *Striking power* of each attacker, denoted α and β, is the number of accurate ("good") ASCMs launched. This is the number of missiles launched that will hit if there is no defense.
- *Defensive power*, denoted a_3 and b_3, is the number of good shots that each defender will destroy or deflect when alert and ready to do so. (*Survivability* is the combined resistance of a ship due to both defensive power and staying power.)
- The equations yield the number of enemy ships, ΔA or ΔB, put out of action by a salvo.

The two equations are:

$$\Delta B = \frac{\alpha A - b_3 B}{b_1}$$

is the effect of A's salvo in putting B's ships out of action.

$$\Delta A = \frac{\beta B - a_3 A}{a_1}$$

is the effect of B's salvo in putting A's ships out of action.[4]

Implicitly the missiles in the salvo are spread uniformly over the defender's ships. A uniform distribution is not necessarily best, because if each defender extracts an equal number of good shots, the whole strike may be defeated; by comparison, an uneven distribution concentrated against only some targets would put at least those targets out of action. It is easy to calculate what the distribution ought to be to achieve the most damage. In the past, the knowledge and control were never sufficient to distribute fire optimally when targets were in plain view, and it is even less likely that commanders will be able to distribute a salvo optimally in the future. Even so, assuming a uniform distribution, as this example does, makes for as good a proxy as any for these explanatory computations.

Also implicit in the equations is that staying power is linear—that is, if two hits put a ship out of action, one hit reduces its striking power and defensive power by half.

In the formula, defensive effectiveness ignores the existence of what are called leakers—the small numbers of missiles that sometimes penetrate a strong defense

---

4 The equations could be used to model the results of the air strikes in the Battle of the Philippine Sea. When the units are in aircraft carriers, and a carrier's salvo is its air wing, the values for α, β, a_1, and b_1 all equal one, and a_3 and b_3 are 1/2 and 1/7 for the United States and Japan respectively.

even after the targeted vessel has done its best to take them out. The aggregate defense is perfect until it is saturated with more attacking missiles than it can deal with. It is not hard to introduce the effect of leakers mathematically. That will come later in the section "Massing for Defense."

For simplicity, we are using the same procedures here—to help explain the nature of salvo warfare in the missile age—employed in the simple models of battle-line gunfire and carrier striking power that have been developed and applied over the years. First, we will insert some purely hypothetical numbers in the model to show the basic character of salvo warfare when a ship has the firepower to take out more than its weight of the enemy. To illustrate the effects of great striking power in a small warship, let us say that one of B's ships can launch eight missiles, of which six are well aimed, in other words $\beta = 6$ good shots. Also assume that one hit will put an enemy ship out of action (OOA), so $a_1 = 1$, and that each defender can shoot down one, but only one, incoming missile with point defenses, so that $a_3 = 1$. Then B, the single attacking missile ship, has the potential to put three of A's ships out of action:

$$\Delta A = \frac{[6 \times 1] - [1 \times 3]}{1} = 3$$

But all three enemy targets will only be destroyed if the circumstances are right, including first detection and tracking by B, perfect distribution of fire, and simultaneous attack with all targets within range. After allowing for imperfection, it still is evident that a massed force can be vulnerable to effective attack by a smaller force, because when one ship in a formation is tracked and subject to attack, then all the rest are as well. In this example, the defending ships have meager defensive power and staying power. The tactical effect when their defense is stronger is a consideration that shall be examined later.

If we construct a table like the one we did involving aircraft carrier pulsed power (table 4-1)—but with the dramatic increase in striking power conjectured above—it would show that B, even though outnumbered one to three, could win against odds that look impossible in a static comparison. Table 13-1 shows some basic possibilities.

Implicitly we have described the tactics depicted in figure 13-1, in which both sides have massed forces. In the example, ships on both sides carry great firepower that is overexposed to enemy surprise attack. So a better tactic would be to spread the missile ships in the hope that not all of them would be detected and attacked simultaneously (figure 13-2), or else to commit missile ships one at a time in the hope that at least one out of three would get off a first attack (figure

Table 13-1. First Strike Survivors (A/B)

	Initial Number of Missile Ships (A/B)				
	2/2	3/2	2/1	3/1	4/1
A attacks first	2/0	3/0	2/0	3/0	4/0
B attacks first	0/2	0/2	0/1	0/1	1/1
A and B strike together	0/0	0/0	0/0	0/0	1/0

13-3). We presumed earlier that something like the tactics in figures 13-2 or 13-3 was embodied in the Japanese carrier battle plans in World War II, where Japanese commanders sought to deliver a highly destructive surprise attack with one (undetected) force while using a second force—intentionally made known to the U.S. side—as bait to divert part of the American attack.

In the circumstances that have been outlined above, the battle will be decided by scouting effectiveness and weapon range—and these factors will also govern the choice of *tactics* to employ. For the sake of discussion, assume that scouting is accomplished entirely by on-board sensors, and that each missile ship has its own independent chance to detect the enemy. If *B* now tries tactic 3, a sequential attack, and if its sensors are as good as any of *A*'s—giving *B* an equal chance of detecting any one ship first—then *B*'s chance of detecting *A*'s force before his leading ship is detected by one of the enemy sensors is only one in eight. He will lose the advantage of surprise to *A*'s superior aggregation of scouting rather than to superior firepower. (We have omitted the complicating possibility of passive targeting, which will be taken up later.)

In the same circumstances, let *B* try tactic 2. In a formal sense, tactic 2 has no advantage over tactic 1. It is more reasonable to assume, however, that if *B*'s units have an equal chance of detecting *A* first, then *A* is confronted with the more difficult scouting problem of having to detect all of *B*'s ships *individually* first in order not to suffer the loss of three ships. Although it is likely that some of *B*'s ships will be detected first and lost, if only one of *B*'s ships detects *A* first it will devastate all of *A*.

Next, suppose that *A* has longer-range missiles, but that *B* has longer-range sensors. As in tactic 2, *B* should be disposed to try to maneuver so that at least one of *A*'s ships is within effective range. If *B* has good communications, only one ship need be radiating its sensors. Depending on the passive targeting potential of *A*, the radiating ship may be destroyed, but one of the others may be able to close and attack decisively. If one of *B*'s ships can track *A* while staying outside of

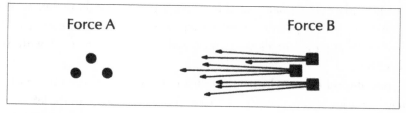

Figure 13-1. Massed Attack

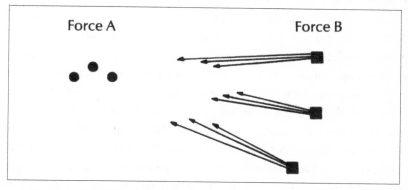

Figure 13-2. Dispersed Attack

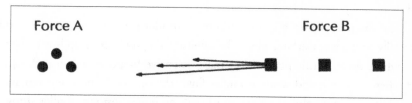

Figure 13-3. Sequential Attack

A's missile range, *B*'s tracking ship may be able to guide another ship quietly into range with a fire-control solution for a silent attack.

If one or both sides have off-board sensors—such as satellites—the analysis is quite different. If *A*'s missiles out-range *B*'s, then in the circumstances the battle is reduced to a contest where *A* alone is stalking. If the out-ranged force *B* must be committed to fight at all, it would try tactic 2 in hopes that *A* would make a mistake in the coordination and distribution of fire.

Perhaps *A* is predominantly land based. Then sea-based side *B* has a simpler scouting problem against his immobile enemy (precise targeting may be something else). *B* should try to close covertly and attack undetected. But recall the Battle of Midway and the effect that American air power based on the island had on Japanese plans. If A's land-based force also can tap a small, mobile sea-based force that can deliver potent offensive firepower, then his land base may draw enough of B's attention to allow A's sea-based component to attack with devastating effect.

These illustrations can be made explicit in the salvo equations by attaching a term for scouting effectiveness (in this case σ) as a component of the left member (e.g., $\sigma\beta B$). The scouting term takes value from zero to one. *Zero* means that there is no information about the enemy and that the attacker has no ability to hit any targets. *Zero* also means that the targets, although they have been detected and tracked, are beyond effective range. A value of *One* means all targets are within range and each is being tracked, so that every enemy ship can be targeted, provided there are enough missiles. To put a numerical estimate on σ it is necessary to run through a thought process as we have just done so that σ is a compact way to summarize a great deal of tactical thought. Another useful term is defender alertness (δ) to modify the right-hand expression (e.g., $\delta b_3 B$). Like σ, the symbol δ takes values from zero to one. Scouting effectiveness also affects δ, because full defensive potential is hard to achieve without an awareness of the enemy's presence and location. Both σ and δ also can represent human factors, such as states of training and readiness—always as a degradation from the full salvo potential (αA or βB) and defensive potential ($a_3 A$ or $b_3 B$).

The discussion above is a paradigm of modern missile warfare. It pertains especially to nuclear warfare, where the offensive firepower per ship is very destructive, where there is little potential to mass defensive firepower in mutual support, and where scouting and weapon ranges favor the offense in new and remarkable ways that encourage the distribution of striking power among smaller ships. Do these circumstances justify the commitment of one unit after another because of the greater potential destructive power of small units of force against larger units? The answer hinges upon the correlation of scouting potentialities.

Deployments of ballistic- and cruise-missile submarines mimic many of the attributes of single-file weapon systems—awkward C^2, virtually no defensive firepower, no capacity for mutual defense, and almost total dependence on first detection and targeting for success.[5] The force-on-force tactical relationships of nuclear war have not been discussed in unclassified literature, but perhaps open discussion is not yet necessary and may never be particularly desirable. Indeed, SSBNs

---

5 Many imagine nuclear war to be a matter of the pre-targeting of fixed sites and the early release of weapons in a general exchange. This is a flawed image on many counts, and, in any case, our intention is to keep the discussion more general.

are always subject to search and attack in some restricted way. The ramifications are explored in D. C. Daniel's *Antisubmarine Warfare and Superpower Strategic Stability*. Yet, his book and other less-well-developed open studies are primarily concerned with technology, strategy, and policy issues. The tactical side—how the battle would be fought, in detail—is at least as significant.

In his detailed technical analysis, Daniel shows that SSBNs at sea are very difficult to detect, track, and target, but that the submarines can be easily destroyed when they are found. This is the essence of the tactical situation under discussion. However, it is not only the presence of nuclear weapons that alters the classical tactics of massing. It is also the suddenness and destructive potential of the modern missile strike, even if it involves conventional weapons. "Use superior force" is a maxim that by itself is misleading; a markedly smaller force may have sufficient net striking power to win. The dual notions that govern modern tactics are, first, aggregating *enough* force and, second, using scouting and C^2 to strike effectively first. As for "forestalling the enemy," doing so by maneuver or greater weapon range—the traditional technique—has to be augmented with modern concepts of antiscouting.

Variations and Historical Numbers

As always, the numbers that go into the equations make all the difference. For example, if each B had twice as much staying power ($b_1 = 2$), then A's potential against him would be cut in half:

$$\Delta B = \frac{[6 \times 1] - [1 \times 3]}{2} = 1\frac{1}{2} \text{ (not 3) out of action}$$

But if B had twice as much defensive power ($b_3 = 2$), then

$$\Delta B = \frac{[6 \times 1] - [2 \times 3]}{1} = \text{none (not 3) out of action}$$

Many of the relationships among the various attributes of the warships in the equations have been worked out, and some are quite interesting. To discuss all the mathematical relationships would imply an excessive faith in a model. Nevertheless, four conclusions from the salvo model research paper mentioned above are solid, important, general properties that do not depend on particular inputs:

- *Unstable circumstances* arise in salvo warfare. The term *stable* means the persistence of victory by one side over the other in a variety of different combat situations. The instability is evident because small changes in the left- and right-hand terms of the numerator (striking power and defensive power) result in big swings in the number of ships lost.

- *Weak staying power* exacerbates the instability. Staying power is weak when the denominator is small relative to the numerator. This often occurs because only one or two missiles will put most contemporary warships out of action (the same is true for torpedoes and mines).

- *Staying power* is the element of ship design that is least affected by the particulars of a battle, including poor tactics. Good or bad readiness, scouting, equipment performance, and tactical coordination affect the outcome greatly and more or less unpredictably. A well-built ship with strong staying power (which makes a bigger denominator) acts as a hedge against tactical mistakes (which change the numerator).

- *Numerical superiority* is the force attribute that is consistently the most advantageous in an exchange of salvoes. For example, if *A*'s unit striking power, staying power, and defensive power are all twice that of *B*, there nevertheless will be a parity of outcome—that is, the same fraction of each force will be put out of action—if *B* has twice as many ships. This is a mathematical consequence of the equations.

If one wanted to play around with the salvo equations to reach one's own conclusions about missile combat, are there any real numbers to replace the ones that have been used up to now? The answer is yes, with the important proviso that the equations apply to engagements between small combatants. Only one incident has occurred in which ASCMs fired at warships were defended by surface combatants with long-range surface-to-air missiles. That was the Iraqi Silkworm missile attack on the USS *Missouri* described in chapter 7. The other battles were between corvette-sized ships or fast-attack craft. Schulte analyzed attacks totaling 222 ASCMs from 1967 to 1992—every one that his research could uncover in the unclassified literature.[6] Here are the results:

- Against defenseless targets, mostly large commercial ships, the 63 ASCMs that were fired scored 57½ hits.[7] As a result, 12 ships were sunk and 42 put out of action. The probability of hits per shot against defenseless ships was .913.

6 Schulte.
7 The half is a near miss by an Egyptian Styx missile that sank the Israeli *Orit* in 1970.

- Against defendable targets—in other words, warships that were capable of defending themselves but failed to do so, such as USS *Stark* and HMS *Sheffield*—38 ASCMs fired scored 26 hits. As a result, 6 ships were sunk and 13 put out of action. The probability of hits per shot against defendable warships was .684.[8]
- Against defended targets—in other words, warships that attempted to defend themselves—the 121 ASCMs scored 32 hits resulting in 13 ships sunk and 16 put out of action. The probability of hits per ship against ships that defended themselves was .264.

An important number to be inferred from these data is the *defender's* performance in defeating ASCMs. Clearly, some of the ASCMs that failed to hit a defended target would have missed if there had been no defense. If we assume the same fraction of ASCM misses that occurred in attacks against defenseless and defendable targets, then the fraction of ASCMs leaking through the defense was .320, not .264. Thus, defender effectiveness in defeating well-aimed ASCMs is a probability of .68, or about two out of three. Schulte could find no instance in which active point defense was the certain cause of success, because passive defenses in the form of jamming or chaff were used in every successful defense. Soft-kill systems were the more important defensive measure.

All of Schulte's data on ASCM attacks were gathered before 1994. An interesting fact is that the greatest number of attacks occurred between 1967 and 1987. Three more recent missile attacks on ships have been reported since Schulte compiled and analyzed the record, but all of them have been launched from ashore.

One was the attack on the Israeli ship *Hanit* off the Lebanese coast in 2006. One missile hit and damaged the vessel. During the attack a nearby merchant ship was hit and sunk by a second missile that missed the *Hanit.* In the second attack, on 1 October 2016, Yemeni rebels near the Bab Al Mandeb hit and severely damaged HSV-2 *Swift,* a UAE-operated support ship that had no defensive weapons. In the third, also in October 2016, just a week after the attack on the *Swift,* Yemeni rebels fired one or more missiles at USS *Mason* (DDG 87), which successfully defended herself. The missiles were believed to be Chinese-designed C-802s or derivatives, although this is not certain.

---

8   It is reasonable to ask why the hit probability declined when a defendable warship was the target. One certain reason is that defenseless targets were larger and easier to hit than the warships. A second possibility is that the attacker was free to take his time and attack the defenseless merchant vessels more boldly.

The most recent ASCM attacks from warships or aircraft were in the Falklands War in 1982 and in the extended Iran-Iraq War in the 1980s. This should be no reason for complacency. First, new missiles have become hotter and harder to defend against. Second, although there have been no recent sea-launched missile attacks on ships, there have been a great many attacks from the sea, using land-attack missiles. On land it is much harder to assess the number of hits achieved, the effects on the different conflicts, or the recovery time needed to restore an airfield, replace a missile launch site, or reopen a factory. Partly as a result of land-attack missiles from the sea, both states and insurgents have increased the numbers and ranges of missiles to counter them. Third, attacking ships by missiles is less costly than defending against them with hard-kill systems, especially with surface-to-air defensive missiles. Fourth, saturation attacks, in which many missiles arrive on a target simultaneously, have not yet occurred, but such tactics seem likely to be used in the future.

Planning with Salvo Equations

So far we have been using simple combat models to describe the nature of fleet actions with ships of the line, battleships, aircraft carriers, and now missile ships. The idea has been to get beyond firepower scores and other indices, such as tonnage, number of guns, and weight of broadside, and into the dynamics of the battle. Some naval officers have used similar simple methods to explore new equipment designs and better tactical doctrine. We do so now with the salvo equations.

Understandably, training commands have taken to using simulations and war games to teach and illustrate these tactics. Yet too often these exercises attempt to incorporate more detail than can ever be known about past or future battles. The alternative is to seek artful simplicity that is not pretentious but describes the circumstances clearly and understandably. We shall try to do this in the examples that follow. Readers who are put off by numbers and equations can skip to the section of this chapter, entitled "A Recapitulation," that summarizes what the calculations imply.

So far, we have made this fundamental point: that modern missiles have brought into question and sometimes overturned the principle of massing forces. In some tactical circumstances, a small naval vessel that is heavily armed with missiles can take down enemy ships out of all proportion to its size. Naval officers will want some other examples where the circumstances are less clear-cut and the situation is more competitive. Navy tacticians should be comfortable with quantitative thinking, because tactics and logistics have always required computations. Knowing how much, how far, how fast, and by whom is fundamental to the conduct of all actual military operations.

1. The Basic Case

Fleets of equal size: $A = B = 10$ small combatants (of say, 500 to 1,500 tons)
Same striking power: $\alpha = \beta = 3$ hits/salvo (from $a_2 = b_2 = 6$, and $H = .5$)
Same staying power: $a_1 = b_1 = 2$ hits/ship OOA
Same defensive power: $a_3 = b_3 = 2$ shots destroyed or defeated in self-defense
The two mirror-image equations give identical results, thus:

$$\Delta B = \frac{\alpha A - b_3 B}{b_1} = \frac{30 - 20}{2} = 5 \text{ enemy ships OOA}$$

In one exchange each side loses half its force.

2. Victory by Attacking First

If, however, B out-scouts A and delivers a first effective attack, then A's response with only five surviving ships will be inadequate and ineffective:

$$\Delta B = \frac{15 - 20}{2} = -2\frac{1}{2} < 0$$

None of B's ships are hit, with a five-shot defensive cushion as margin for error.

3. Victory with More Numbers

Change the size of B's force to $B = 15$, with all other inputs as in the basic case. Now if as before A tries and succeeds in distributing his missiles uniformly, the effectiveness of A's ten ships against B is:

$$\Delta B = \frac{30 - 30}{2} = 0$$

B's fifteen-ship fleet has this effect:

$$\Delta A = \frac{45 - 20}{2} = 12\frac{1}{2}$$

All ten of A are OOA, and B's salvo has $2\frac{1}{2}$ ships' worth of offensive overkill as a margin for error.

Notice how sensitive the results are to the inputs and the instability represented by these equations. For example, a moderate increase in the size of B's fleet creates a big change in his favor. Although this phenomenon probably is no more important than other factors—such as strike coordination and defense alertness achieved by using a tight command-and-control network—it is real enough. To illustrate this, work the equation using a degradation due to scouting deficiency on one side or the other ($\sigma = .7$) or a reduction in the defensive readiness of one side ($\delta = .7$).

4. Victory When Lesser Force Quality Is Offset by Greater Force Quantity

B's advantage in example 3 depends on having a larger force than A or deploying it more wisely. Now we give B a different fleet, which would cost about as much as the basic fleet. Change B's characteristics to these:

New fleet size: $B = 20$ (instead of 10)

New striking power: $\beta = 2$ (instead of 3)

New staying power: $b_1 = 1$ (instead of 2)

New defensive power: $b_3 = 1½$ (instead of 2)

Again, under the assumption that a commander succeeds in distributing his fire uniformly, the result for each side in an exchange of fire is:

$$\Delta B = \frac{30 - 30}{1} = 0 \text{ (none lost in the more numerous, more distributed force)}$$

$$\Delta A = \frac{40 - 20}{2} = 10 \text{ (all lost in the higher quality, less numerous force)}$$

This is a specific instance of the general truth about the salvo equations mentioned above. As far as the equations are concerned, a numerical advantage in ships always is the most valuable attribute a fleet can have. Specifically, if B is twice as numerous as A, then for parity in percentage losses each A must have twice the striking power, twice the defensive power, *and* twice the staying power of each B.

Salvo Equations for Impending Battle

Up to now we have restricted the use of models to illustrate combat dynamics of two sides in tactical action against each other. What about applying the salvo equations in real situations? Doing so depends on whether the contexts (the great variables) described in chapter 11 are sufficiently known. Uncertainties about coming combat events make it unlikely that a detailed simulation will offer much extra insight. In addition, a simulation usually takes time to prepare, make repeated runs, and analyze the results. Simulations sometimes can be useful for campaign planning when the pressure of time is less extreme. In 1991 and early 1992 the U.S. Army, Air Force, and Joint Staff used a variety of simulations and war games to anticipate the operations against Iraq and to compare various force distributions.

For battle planning and execution at the tactical level, something like the salvo equations, but which is easy to use and understand, will serve better. The simplicity helps underscore the fact that the results are not predictions. At the same time, the equations serve as a check-list of essential information. To apply the salvo equations, the tactical commander and the staff must know the characteristics of the two fleets well enough to write the inputs. The inputs must square with both the tactical commander's plan and the staff judgment concerning enemy capabilities and plans. The tactical plan includes the way scouts are deployed, the ships' formation or disposition, the expected coordination achieved by a communications network, and the tactical decisions that are needed to achieve deconfliction (freedom to fire without incurring severe fratricide). The plan affects σ and δ especially. Since a commander must consider such inputs in order to make tactical decisions, the staff must consider them thoroughly.

Unlike the four previous examples, the composition of each force is usually a mixture of different classes of ship in a heterogeneous fleet. The model is exercised with aggregated task elements, and the results are expressed as aggregate losses to the whole fleet. Let us see how the aggregation works when we use the equations to enlighten tactical circumstances and sharpen a commander's battle plan.

Competent planning requires dependable numbers. Ship characteristics and their effectiveness numbers can be provided by historical battle data—ship salvo sizes and hit probabilities, defense effectiveness, and ship staying power, observed in battles involving missile ships.

For the example, suppose that we are going to oppose two fleets of very different sizes. One fleet, called *Small* (or *S*), comprises seven 800-ton guided-missile corvettes. They are armed with a total of 56 missiles with Harpoon characteristics. The other fleet, called *Towering*, far exceeds *S* in size and combat potential and is labeled *T*. It comprises 25 warships ranging in displacement from 400 tons to 3,000 tons. Fleet *T* is armed with 180 missiles that have Penguin or Harpoon characteristics. Defenses consist of a variety of point-defense weapons, chaff, electronic jamming, and decoys. We will combine the characteristics of each side into a composite, using the following inputs:

Inputs for Small	Inputs for Towering	Observations
$S = 7$ with 56 PGMs	$T = 25$ with 180 PGMs	PGM means precision guided missile
[Missile launch reliability for all PGMs = .9]		[Approximating peacetime data]
$s_2 = .9 \times 56 = 50$ PGMs	$t_2 = .9 \times 180 = 162$ PGMs	PGMs launched in a complete salvo
[PGM hit probability $H = .6$]		[From the historical battle data]
$\alpha S = .6 \times 50 = 30$	$\tau T = .6 \times 162 = 97$	Well-aimed PGMs or good shots in an aggregate salvo
$s_1 = 1.0$	$t_1 = 1.5$	From combat data. T's large ships have more staying power
$s_3 = 1.0$	$t_3 = 1\frac{1}{2}$	Unit defensive power
$s_3 S = 7$	$t_3 T = 37\frac{1}{2}$	Aggregate fleet defensive power

The Case of an Inferior, Heavily Outnumbered Force

If a grand melee ensues in which all ships participate, the size of the disaster for S is computed to be:

$$\Delta S = \frac{97 - 7}{1.0} = 90$$

T has the striking potential to put all of S out of action more than twelve times!

$$\Delta T = \frac{30 - 37\frac{1}{2}}{1.5} = -7\frac{1}{2} < 0$$

T has a generous defensive margin for error.

The defeat of S is no surprise: when all ships are able to shoot at the entire enemy fleet, all of S's vessels are put out of action and none of T's is hit. Moreover, even if S surprises T and fires first, S fires ineffectively and does no damage. Perhaps the extent to which S is outclassed comes as a bit of a surprise? After all, S is inferior in firepower by only a little worse than three to one. If S does the calculation, S would not wish to fight; the commander will lose all his ships with nothing to show for their sacrifice, and he will lose the battle as well.

So far we have not given S a mission. Let us stipulate that the circumstances are so grave that S *must* engage T. Although S is certain to lose, he should try to sell his fleet dearly and damage the enemy as much as possible. If S's tactical commander sees the situation as we have exhibited it, then the staff can compute how much damage his fleet will do if it concentrates all fifty of its PGMs on part of the enemy. Since that may be difficult to do—tactics are notoriously hard to execute—we will keep the tactical commands simple and easy to execute. The intellectual part of the problem is to decide what fraction of the enemy to attack. Sometimes it is a tactical possibility to shoot just at the attractive targets. These would include the big ships, because they do not have much more defense or staying power than the small ones.

The attractive targets would also include transports or amphibious ships, if any were present. Recall the air attacks by Argentine fighter-bombers during the British landings in San Carlos Water in May 1982. The Argentine aircraft did not try to strike the amphibious ships. They behaved as if they thought they might gain ascendancy by wiping out the escorts, but that was too tough a task. The pilots said later that they merely followed their instincts to attack the ships that were shooting at them. If they had done some calculations in advance they would have realized their most effective action at the beachhead would have been to have hit some of the ships that were carrying troops.

For our exercises we are interested in allocating S's salvo against part of T, just to do some harm in an exchange. The S commander sees that each of his seven corvettes can launch eight missiles, of which about four will be good shots. Each enemy ship's survivability value is three shots (1.5 PGMs shot down and 1.5 hits to put a ship OOA). To keep the tactics simple, S's commander orders each ship to fire all eight of its missiles at a single enemy and in a compact pulse. The hoped-for effect would be that all S vessels firing together would take out seven of the enemy. Since by assumption all twenty-five enemy vessels are expected to be in a single formation so they can concentrate fire, the chance of two S ships choosing the same target is small.

Here is an alternative tactic and computation. If S were to attack only half of the enemy force—say the left or right half—then the attack would be mounted against about twelve ships. Applying the salvo model with the prior assumption that the PGMs would be spread uniformly over the twelve, the calculation is:

$$\Delta T = \frac{30 - (1.5 \times 12)}{1.5} = 8 \text{ OOA (out of 12 attacked)}$$

Either tactic by S would be far better for S than a general melee—seven or eight of T OOA as opposed to none—but S's commander should choose one tactic or the other.

What is mathematically the best average result that S could achieve? Maximum performance is achieved by firing at exactly ten targets, in which case $\Delta T = 10$. This is the sort of optimization calculation that operations analysts love, but it is impractical. It is important for S to see that his chances of winning are zero and that if his orders compel him to fight he must work out special tactics such as the two above in order to do any damage whatsoever. It is unimportant for him to obtain the mathematically optimum solution, because there are too many unknowables that will adversely affect the distribution of fire, damage effects, and the danger that neutral shipping in the area will end up as false targets. These and other uncertainties are assumed away in mean-value computations—or in any other analysis, for that matter.

To conclude this exhibit of how salvo equations could be used in real battle planning with real data and facts about the combat environment, it would be wise to remind commanders that the enemy also has tactical choices. Let us assume that T's tactical commander recognizes that S should try to attack only part of his force by using the same equations. He wants to attenuate the effect of S's tactical choices. He knows that he will win handily if he can concentrate the salvoes of enough ships and that firing salvoes from all twenty-five of his ships at once is excessive and wasteful and will expose too many of them to enemy attack. He is aware that he probably can win without a loss if he out-scouts S and attacks first, but his appraisal is that he will only achieve first detection some of the time. Moreover, in the time it will take for tracking, attack coordination, and missile flight, the enemy may detect him and launch missiles at him before his own missiles hit the enemy. He also acknowledges the possibility that S will out-scout him and that T could be the one to suffer a surprise attack.

Therefore, the proper response for T is to partition its fleet into separate elements and attack in waves of one element at a time. Its commander wants each wave to be strong enough to take out all seven corvettes in the enemy fleet. The average striking power of each of his own ships is:

$$\tau = \frac{97 \text{ good shots in an aggregated salvo}}{25 \text{ ships in the } T \text{ fleet}} = 3.5 \text{ good shots/ship}$$

He uses the equation for τ salvo effectiveness against S to solve for the number of T required to make $\Delta S = 7$:

$$\frac{3.5T - 7}{1.0} = 7$$

The solution is $T = 4$ ships in a wave. In practice the commander would worry about which ships to put in each wave—for instance, whether the smaller fast-attack craft with Penguins, the larger ones with Harpoons, or a mixture of both should be put in a wave. He would already have doctrine for formation spacing, but he would have to make many other battle-specific tactical decisions.

How much better will T do in reducing his own losses in an exchange? If he sends a wave of four, then S (which now outnumbers T's wave) will have an excess of firepower:

$$\Delta T = \frac{30 - (1.5 \times 4)}{1.5} = 16$$

Sixteen is fourfold overkill, so all four ships in T's first wave must expect to be put out of action and win many posthumous medals. Nevertheless, loss of four ships is better than the alternative, which is loss of seven or eight ships *on the average*. T has cut the cloth very fine, because four ships are mathematically just enough to destroy S with no margin for error. T should expect a few enemy corvettes to survive undamaged. On the other hand, unless the S fleet is remarkably skillful, it will have expended all its missiles at T's first wave and must confront twenty-one remaining, fully armed ships.

We have illustrated a way to carry out some of the tactical planning when a battle is imminent and when its context is known in part. When aircraft are available nearby for scouting or attack, many factors may change, but the salvo equation format still can be used. Some battle outcomes will be determined by out-scouting or out-ranging the enemy. The Navy's sorties against Libyan warships in the Gulf of Sidra in March 1986 are an example in which the United States succeeded in mounting effective attacks because of superior scouting and striking range and because Libyan defenses and staying power were completely overwhelmed. Superior training, deception, and C^2 also can be decisive. The sea battles between Israeli and Syrian or Egyptian combatants in October 1973 illustrate this, as well as underscoring the unstable tactical circumstances of missile warfare. Although the Israeli ships were nominally out-ranged, they suffered no hits; yet they achieved a very high hit-performance against their Syrian or Egyptian foes.

To develop scouting, deception, weapon range, and the role of aircraft more thoroughly demands more information and a more complicated analytical form than salvo equations require.

Tactical Networks

The U.S. Navy has devoted much thought and energy to tactical networks. Network-centric warfare (NCW) is an attempt to integrate operations, but it risks counter-detection.[9] It is part of information warfare. NCW is a comprehensive approach

---

9 The term was coined by Vice Admiral Cebrowski. The description of it is our interpretation of his still evolving concept.

that specifies three laterally connected grids. The first is a sensor grid to correlate acquired information; the second is a C^2 grid in which all units exchange operation plans, tactical tasks, orders, and changes to plans, tasks, and orders as events unfold; the third is a shooter grid, which assigns targets and coordinates fire. The grids are linked vertically so that a stream of actions flows from sensors through decision-makers to shooters. Although counteractions are not specified in the concept, it is implicit in NCW that antiscouting, C^2 countermeasures, and counterforce activities must degrade the enemy's tactical performance and interfere with his own grids. This approach also strengthens the resilience of the force. The NCW structure can employ multiple paths, compounding the enemy's challenges.

The salvo equations assume the existence of the three linked networks. The equations apply whether A is linking two ships, twenty, or two hundred. The linkages may be rudimentary—relying on sound doctrine to serve as the primary means of coordination—or they may be highly integrated and automated, which is the the design underlying intention and expectation of the American system.

The equations reserve no separate term for command-and-control because C^2 is embedded in the existing terminology. For instance, αA represents the best that each warship can do to achieve hits, multiplied by the number of warships. There is no allowance for situations in which two ships shoot at the same target, or for other waste and inefficiency in the fog of battle. The same is true of $a_3 A$. The coordination of defensive fire and soft-kill measures is implicit. In effect, the equations represent a networked force. One cannot expect a network-centric warfare *bonus* that provides better results than the equations yield. There can only be a penalty when the network is deficient. That is why the mathematical range of σ and δ is from *zero* (representing terrible networking) to *one* (representing ideal networking).

Massing for Defense

Networking permits widely separated shooters to deliver a pulse of striking power—the dispersed fleet's salvo—that is concentrated in location and time. But widely separated ships cannot provide a mutual defense; indeed, they can be vulnerable to defeat one at a time. By contrast, massing for mutual defense is advantageous if ships in a fleet can protect one another by protecting themselves. A fleet's carrier aircraft used as CAP is such an "area defense" capability. Surface-to-air missiles, with increasingly effective engagement ranges, will protect several ships in a formation, especially if they can deal with crossing targets, such as ASCMs homing on a nearby ship.

As the previous sections show, the most important factor in assessing a fleet's prospects is the number of ships. Many small ships offer more tactical flexibility. The smallest unit of disaggregation is a single ship. The Navy comprises significant numbers of large, highly capable ships, many of which have an area defense capability. It was more for *defense* than for *offense* that the American Navy sacrificed numbers for quality.[10] For the past several decades, American battle fleets have had to defeat any surprise attack that the enemy might hurl, using sea room and a layered defense in depth—nowadays, first with F-18s and F-35s, then SAMs, and finally point defenses. At one time strong staying power was another important component, but it is only rarely so now.

The principle of massing for defense holds that when major formations that are operating apart from one another are in danger of being defeated individually, they should be massed in one or more formations that are strong enough to ward off an attack. This is so whether or not they can muster an offensive strike by networking when they are apart. The advantage of mutual defensive support is evident even if one expects deficiencies in coordinating these formations and combined defenses are not as effective as hoped.

There is nothing new or surprising in this. It is a reminder that the decision to mass or disperse depends on defensive considerations, not offensive ones, and it has done so since World War II, when aircraft carrier battle tactics were developed. In cases when defenses are likely to be stronger when the ships are concentrated, the fleet should be massed the way the U.S. carrier fleets were concentrated in 1944. If defenses are weak, however, as they were against attack from the air in 1942, then a dispersed force is more effective and the need to out-scout the enemy and attack effectively first will be more urgent. If counterforce is weak and the C^2 network is capable of achieving offensive concentration of firepower over great distances, then a broad-front attack (tactic 2 in figure 13-2) is desirable.

The tactician should also remember the new possibility that a sequential attack (tactic 3) may be superior. That possibility is more likely to arise in littoral waters, where there is a constant danger of surprise and swift destruction. Such circumstances—a radar scouting advantage and the potency of a torpedo salvo—led to Burke's sequential one-two punch during the Solomons campaign in 1943.

---

10 Another reason is economies of scale. A large ship with three times the displacement of a small one will have three or more times the payload and probably cost only twice as much. Sometimes the ship must be big to carry and operate its payload; modern carrier aircraft illustrate. A large ship is also more comfortable for long cruises in many kinds of weather.

To consider the principle of massing for defense in quantitative terms, think of an American Aegis cruiser as a self-contained, one-ship fleet.[11] No other warship comes as close to that description; the Aegis has the ability to scout with radar, helicopters, and satellite information; it can strike with missiles; and it can control its battlespace against attacks from aircraft, submarines, and surface vessels. The mission for our one-ship fleet will be the classical fleet role—to control its sea space by defeating any nearby enemy fleet. The principle of massing for mutual defense holds that if one warship is not enough then commanders must provide for a two- or three-ship fleet, not necessarily all Aegis cruisers.

Force A in figures 13-1, 13-2, and 13-3 is a one-ship fleet, except that the three dots are compacted into one. The Aegis cruiser was designed to be large and powerful in order to mass a strong defense in a cost-effective way. The Navy did not wish to invest in its track-while-scan radar and luxurious C^2 facilities (which accounted for about half of the ship's total cost) without equipping the vessel with massive defensive firepower. Later, the ship's combat potential was broadened by providing it with additional offensive firepower as well.

When we explore the logic of fewer, larger ships for defense, we must face the absence of combat data. This is not a reason for gloom. Gunnery analysis in preparation for World War I was very helpful. Although data on peacetime performance were not very accurate—as always happens for peacetime periods, they were too optimistic—they successfully identified the improvements that were needed for gunfire effectiveness: range-finding, range-keeping (target position prediction), tight spacing, and optimal formations. (Note: The statistics in the following paragraphs will be helpful for understanding the situation, but they are not as precise as those used in the salvo equations earlier in this chapter.)

Our Aegis-like cruiser will carry 32 SAMs for defense against air, surface, or land-launched ASCMs. If doctrine specifies that two SAMs will be fired at each enemy ASCM, then its defensive power is $a_3 = 16$. To use the equations without modification, we shall assume that point defenses back up the SAMs perfectly so that there are no leakers—that is, no inbound missiles getting through the ship's defenses. In addition, there is enough sea room and warning so that the cruiser is fully alert, leading to the component $\delta = 1.0$. Each of the ship's additional 32 missiles for offense has a hit-probability of $H = .75$, so its offensive power is close to $\alpha = 24$. Its staying power, a_1, is uncertain, but it takes between two and four ASCM hits to put it out of action. In this example we provide the enemy ships the

---

11 The smallest tactical unit of warships should be a pair of mutually reinforcing types, but that need not detract from this thought experiment.

same characteristics as in the one used to illustrate figure 13-1—namely, striking power β = 6, defensive power b_3 = 1, and staying power b_1 = 1. The enemy vessels could be missile-carrying fast-attack craft or maritime patrol aircraft similar to a P-3C Orion carrying eight Harpoons, of which six would hit their targets.

How large a fleet with these characteristics can our cruiser put out of action? Solving for $\Delta B/B$ = 1, we find that it will destroy or disable 12 enemy ships or aircraft.

On the other hand, how big must the B fleet be to put A out of action if our cruiser is caught by an enemy surprise attack? Solving for $\Delta A/A$ = 1, we find that B needs only three or four of its small but heavily armed combatants. Caught in an exchange of salvoes with not more than four of the enemy, A will be out of action with many of its offense weapons unspent and wasted. Using the measure of effectiveness for littoral warfare of maximum delivered ordnance *over the combat life of the ship*, our one-ship fleet is over-weighted with striking power.

If the enemy fleet is B = 10, then one corrective action for A would be to mass four identical ships for mutual defense—in other words, to add enough cruisers to defeat the enemy attack. This would be desirable (albeit four times as expensive) if the 128-missile offensive capacity were needed for theater missile defense or Tomahawk-like strikes against strategic targets ashore.

Another correction might be to change A's balance of firepower on board. If A carries about 16 offensive missiles instead of 32, its striking power is reduced to α = 12 and it can put six of B's ships out of action. Now A can carry 48 defensive missiles capable of defending against four attackers, rather than the 32 that it carried previously.

A third corrective possibility is to out-scout and out-range the enemy. By attacking first, with an ideal distribution of fire and α = 24, each of A can deal with twelve of B. The expensiveness of this solution depends on the means of scouting and attacking selected. Using a convenient, available aircraft carrier is an inexpensive way. Purchasing a new carrier and its aircraft is an expensive way.

The principle abides: a fleet that cannot reliably attack first must mass for effective defense. If its defense cannot be made effective, then it must fight dispersed and win by out-scouting the enemy so as to avoid all attacks.

Some of the problems of a large ship can be eased by building more staying power into the vessel. This is best shown by including the possibility of leakers, which until now have been disregarded.

We have shown data on the leakage rate in the history of missile warfare at sea: one missile in three has gotten through the defenses on the average. But the *average* is not helpful because the tendency has been for the defender to be either very successful or very unsuccessful in stopping an attack. Moreover, there are no combat data yet for an Aegis cruiser, beyond its test-range performance, so historical statistics on the vessel's defenses is a matter of speculation and is debatable. Once the leakage rate becomes known, the consequences and the desirability of great staying power will be easy to show. If only one missile in ten gets through the defenses (a 90 percent defensive effectiveness), then on average the cruiser is likely to be hit by one missile while defending against ten. In that case, if *B* were to fire a total of twelve good ASCMs, it should expect to hit *A* once. If the ship could continue fighting, perhaps at reduced effectiveness, after taking two, or three, or even four hits, then the enemy would have to expend far more missiles in its attack. When leakage is a real threat, as we believe it is, a balanced warship design should have increased staying power.

Because of the cluttered environment and the reduced battle space a special concern for inshore warfare is the greater risk of catching a single ship in one's own fleet napping. There is no compelling rationale for sending large, expensive, and highly capable warships into contested coastal waters unless they are able to take several hits and continue fighting without missing a beat. It is better to fight fire with fire, using expendable, missile-carrying aircraft or small surface craft. In fact, ever since the introduction of numerous torpedo boats, coastal submarines, and minefields early in this century, contested coastal waters have been taboo for capital ships, and have become the almost exclusive province of flotillas of small, swift, lethal fast-attack craft.

A Recapitulation

Despite our emphasis on fighting in the littorals and the addition of new material to help understand missile warfare as it has been observed over the past several decades, this recapitulation has been altered only in a few details. The reader should appreciate, however, that a substantial part of a coastal fleet may be land based. Inshore operations may even be said to be missile combat in which naval vessels participate—the very epitome of joint warfare.

A warcraft with great offensive firepower and little means of defense is extremely vulnerable and creates a highly unstable tactical situation. To perform effectively, it depends on a first strike, a stealthy attack, or a better combination of scouting and weapon ranges. A warcraft with such a mix of attributes is an anomaly. Why is such a "mistake" built? Ostensibly, because designers believe that in cases when the measure of effectiveness is simple firepower, α or β, it is cost-effective to put many good shots in each craft. But that ignores the force-on-force nature of battle. A better measure of effectiveness is how much deliverable firepower it can muster over its combat life, which is a combination of offensive firepower and counterforce.

A proper analysis of deliverable firepower would still sometimes argue for massing offensive power in single platforms, simply because of the economies of scale and the low cost of adding missiles on the margin. Nevertheless, instability is a consequence of massing in this way, and the discussion above suggests the need for both technological measures (such as more defensive force, derived from such features as point defenses or chaff, as well as greater hull survivability), and tactical measures (such as plans to attack either sequentially or from many directions to confound the enemy's scouting and fire control). The combination of these would give a naval force the temporizing ability to act offensively.

The first question to answer regarding tactical configuration is how much striking power would be sufficient to eliminate the enemy threat in one blow. There is no purpose in adding more firepower for effective attack if what you have is concentrated from one or more platforms at one or more locations to meet this standard of offensive sufficiency.

The second question concerns the massing of forces, and that is answered by an analysis of defensive capabilities. Together, concentration for the offense and the possibility of massing for the defense determine the tactical disposition. Yet, these calculations are not made simply by a correlation of weight and range of firepower. Networking determines whether dispersed firepower can be concentrated offensively. Scouting networks, range- and search-plans, and, especially in littoral waters, the clutter of false targets and electronic emissions affect both offensive and defensive effectiveness. Stealthiness and other antiscouting protections also affect the final correlation.

One of the practical problems is that the correlation of force cannot be finely honed. As previous paragraphs have shown, there is a propensity in peacetime to overestimate one's own striking power. Tacticians should add some extra firepower—overkill—when they plan offensive and defensive combinations.

A tactical reserve must be a safe reserve. Withholding part of one's missile capacity for a second strike presumes that ships with that capacity will survive until they are needed. On the other hand, guaranteeing complete safety for a reserve component may require positioning it so far to the rear that it cannot influence the battle, in which case it is not a *tactical* reserve at all. (Attacking in successive waves is not withholding a reserve but a mode of offense.)

A major consequence of massing for defense is the guarantee that the enemy will be aware of the fleet and its general location. In such cases, electronic-warfare tactics should be designed not to mask the presence of the fleet, which is impossible, but to complicate the enemy's efforts to track and target the key units that constitute its striking power. In particular, commanders should not sacrifice fleet defensive firepower in order to avoid detection and tracking. Active jamming and radiating decoys are the principal tools to use to inhibit the enemy's targeting during this kind of overt operation. If the analysis shows that the fleet's active defense cannot provide enough safety to enable it to attack effectively, then the whole operation should be reevaluated. What could be worse than a plan that calls for the massing of defense and then destroys the effectiveness of the defense by an overly strict search and fire-control radiation policy? Unless the force is powerful enough to attack overtly, defensive warships such as Aegis cruisers are an electronic liability.

In the future, battles between moving forces sometimes will be fought at closer ranges because of scouting inadequacies and antiscouting effectiveness. Coastal combat is war at short range. The geography of land and ocean floor modifies the general truth that there are no flanks to attack or high ground to defend at sea. Naval forces based ashore create unique tactical combinations of sensors, missiles, and other weapons, all networked by doctrine, training, and communications. Additional possibilities for covertness and surprise out of the clutter in littoral areas add to the potential hazards. Defense is more difficult, and all ships and aircraft are proportionately more at risk.

How can a tactical commander and the staff think through the exceedingly messy tactical problems of modern littoral combat? The structure in the following section is a guide. It emphasizes scouting, C^2, and weapon range in a two-sided battle for ocean domination when a land power has the ability not merely to defend its immediate coastline but to reach far out over the ocean.

A Tactical Focus for the American Navy

Chapter 6 reviewed the changing focus of the American fleet since 1880 and concluded that in the twenty-first century the fleet's new emphasis should be on gaining access to and fighting in dangerous littoral waters. It named nine coastal regions with confined waters where hostilities may occur; all contain friendly states that the United States may wish to support. Each region has unique properties that require different combat skills. Most have narrow entrances abutted by friendly states that permit maritime interdiction of enemy shipping.

There is a difference, however, between the goals of a policy or strategy and the objectives that commanders must establish in fighting a battle. Contemporary American policy and maritime strategy emphasize preventing war if possible, or, if lethal conflict ensues, containing and terminating it without costly escalation. This policy was first adopted for strategic deterrence in recognition that widespread nuclear war would be an unmitigated evil with no winners. Some American strategists argue that the aim of war in the twenty-first century should be similar—that is, not to *win* by a traditional standard of effectiveness, such as unconditional surrender, but to aim for the more realistic outcome of avoiding the consequences of losing while containing the conflict with a negotiated settlement at the lowest possible level of violence. An apt analogy for this approach is that when two masters play chess the dominant outcome is a draw.

But the enemy has a vote in the level of violence as well. This book is not about preventing or containing war; it is about winning battles when deterrence fails. A country fights to win because a battlefield draw would be failure. The book applies the common elements of tactical success to modern deadly combat, especially in littoral waters. Although each geographic region has a unique environment, there are tactical characteristics common to all regions.

Past trends guide tactical and technological development in the U.S. Navy. Here are the trends that increasingly affect scouting, shooting, and command-and-control in modern littoral combat.

Scouting and Antiscouting

The Navy now uses unmanned aerial vehicles for detection, reporting, and targeting of enemy elements and soon will begin employing unmanned surface and subsurface scouting systems as well. Medium- or small-sized UAVs are well-suited to dangerous waters because they can be risked and lost in places where manned aircraft can be shot down. At the same time, because of the complicating clutter of islands, oil rigs, air traffic, coastal traffic, and fishing boats in such areas, tacticians on both sides must calculate what the best mix of manned and unmanned scouts would be. Some countries will use fishing boats and small vessels that resemble innocent coastal traffic to detect and report enemy presence. The Navy should factor in such approaches and achieve its own hard-to-detect scouting methods in concert with the friends whom it is protecting. The Swedish navy, for example, regards coastal traffic and other kinds of clutter as an advantage to exploit for concealment in the Baltic.

Shooting and Counterforce

Two dominant characteristics of littoral combat are shorter ranges of missile combat and the much-increased potential for surprise attack on both sides. In cluttered, confined waters the normal advantage of longer-range weapons aided by targeting with satellites and over-the-horizon radar is muted or lost. The cost of individual missiles is also more important in coastal combat because more warships and UAVs likely will be engaged, and running out of ordnance is an important consideration. In the Arab-Israeli War of 1973 the Egyptians experienced such a circumstance. After they had emptied their missile launchers without success, the small Osa and Komar missile-boats turned and fled; the Israelis gave chase and fired shorter-range Gabriel missiles at them, destroying most of the Egyptian vessels. The possibility of such sudden, short-range combat in coastal clutter suggests that warfighters should hone their gunnery skills, reminiscent of Arleigh Burke's "brace of cutlasses in the wardroom."

Near a coast, the value of manned and robotic *surface* vessels increases in relation to that of manned aircraft. Both friendly and enemy fleets can deploy large numbers of small patrol vessels carrying missiles. Remotely controlled surface vessels can remain on-station for long periods of time and carry relatively large payloads—both valuable for deterrence. The growing potential for autonomous undersea surveillance and for attack in shallow or confined seas will increase the threat to high-value nuclear submarines and other capital assets, making less expensive manned and unmanned nonnuclear submersibles all the more useful in waters such as the Yellow, Arabian, and Baltic Seas.

The fact that precise homing enables tacticians to equip smaller platforms with offensive capability has led to two recent advancements in missile warfare. One is a system called Club K, developed by the Russian armed forces, in which box launchers are carried on trucks, where they can be at least partially concealed, and can be dispersed widely. The vehicle mobility gives an attacker both maneuverability and survivability at low cost. The mobile launchers also can be used to replace or expand offensive power at sea quickly in cases where larger warships are damaged and cannot be repaired immediately; the launchers can be installed on a wide variety of vessels of varying sizes. The Club K system is being marketed by Russia for international sales, and some applications envision installing such systems in small coastal vessels or even in container ships.

A disadvantage of the concept is its very invisibility. Influence requires that in edge-of-war scenarios and crises, the deterring force must present the threatening enemy with a visible threat—a task that usually requires the presence of clearly identifiable warships. The deterring fleet also must be large enough to convince the opposition that it can endure expected losses and still press the fight. Hard-to-see armament such as mobile-launching systems do not bolster that image. Even so, smaller, less expensive missile containers with compact, reliable launch control can be installed on a variety of vessels such as littoral combat ships, frigates, joint high-speed vessels, small amphibious ships, unmanned surface vessels, or any other type of ship or boat. The second advancement, the value of which has been quantitatively measured using salvo equations by CAPT Jeffrey Cares, USNR, is to team a host ship with several offensive and defensive unmanned surface vehicles (USVs). Cares chose a littoral combat ship (LCS) as the host because it was designed to carry unmanned vessels, so it was a simple step for the LCS to take on a small set of USVs armed with missiles instead of counter-mine, counter-swarm, or antisubmarine warfare modules.[12] An LCS carrying off-board attackers armed with antiship cruise missiles might be adapted to fight in the nine geopolitical regions of primary interest to the U.S. Navy. Cares' analysis is both startling and compelling, showing how, by forcing the enemy to spread his attention among many separate units, a force of ships carrying unmanned attackers and defenders can defeat similar numbers of enemy ships. Cares demonstrates mathematically that because of the power of a numerical advantage, adding only one unmanned surface vehicle in each LCS dramatically increases combat effectiveness.

Command, Control, and C² Countermeasures

The most important change in C^2 for operations in confined waters will be a shift away from *network-centric warfare*, whose object is to connect every friendly unit and command component continuously, replacing it with a system that is harder to detect. New concepts and processes will emerge that enable tactical commanders to issue brief but adequate just-in-time commands in battle. Over the ages, signal books, once they are well-shaken-down and mature, have been a way to transmit commands to ships and aircraft via signal flags and voice-radio and to do it clearly, and *without risk of misinterpretation*. The unambiguous commands contained in a modern signal book can be sent and received in the blink of an eye.

---

12 See Cares and Dickman, *Operations Research for Unmanned Systems,* chapter 15, "Distributed Combat Power: The Application of Salvo Theory to Unmanned Systems." Cares has been a student of salvo equations for more than thirty years and applies them to enrich our understanding of why firepower distributed among many units is so advantageous. The book, not intended for mathematical beginners, includes the works of many authors who describe how to exploit unmanned vehicles for various purposes.

Command-and-control is more difficult in littoral waters because larger numbers of units must cooperate and C^2 countermeasures must confuse or confound many more enemy vessels. The Navy must plan its operations or battles in littoral waters with an eye toward cooperation and sometimes close coordination with the armed forces of the country that it is trying to support.

A new approach that could replace the more detectable system of *network-centric* operations has been termed *network-optional* warfare. A 2016 article in *Signal Magazine* describes how it could be employed in confined waters.[13] As Cares did in showing the advantages of a host ship with missile-carrying unmanned surface combatants, the *Signal Magazine* article employs an LCS as the network's hub because the vessel can carry an adaptable array of bridges, routers, and gateways in a hierarchy of protocoled layers that capitalizes on the well-developed technologies of mesh-networking. An LCS may not be the sole critical node for future development, but it is a ship that is well-suited for littoral operations.

Cyberoperations have the potential for long-range, wide-reaching, and swift effects. Their long range and wide reach mean less in tactical situations, but their swift effects can be as important in combat as they have been in peacetime and commercial application. If tacticians worldwide are alert to these differences, the experience that has been gained in cyberwarfare during peacetime will help to plan cyberattack and defense in lethal combat. Battles have been lost by abrupt degradation of control, followed by confusion and then fatal chaos. To see the effects of a loss of control, recall the confusion on both the American and Japanese sides that resulted from surprise and loss of control on the first night of the Battle of Guadalcanal, 13 November 1942.

Integrated Thinking to Attack Effectively First

For clarity, we have artificially compartmented the influence of information warfare and other fast-developing technologies on the modern battlefield. In reality, the combat activities of detect, decide, and act and their effects are interrelated and mutually reinforcing or debilitating. Moreover, the processes are united by the tactical truism that fleet battles are won by attacking effectively first. Now, however, the pace is swifter, the range of attack is longer, and in the new environment commanders must take defensive actions almost instantaneously. That said, here are some points to remember:

---

13 Bordetsky, Benson, and Hughes.

- Artificial intelligence, as a man-machine enhancing system, will help commands and staffs keep up with the revolution in data-gathering and defend themselves against the growing variety of ever-hotter new missiles.
- Unmanned vehicles open up new ways to achieve a surprise attack.
- Spies and code-breaking are not new, but cyberoperations offer new ways to intrude, either to exploit or sow confusion in the enemy's command-and-control process.
- Command-and-control facilities supported by satellites and systems may be destroyed. Whether to attack command facilities ashore may prove difficult to decide because of the possibility that that might expand a maritime war onto the land.
- The question of tactical rather than strategic deception needs more study. Whaley and Dahl both have enriched our understanding of the failure of the United States to exploit code-breaking before the Pearl Harbor attack, followed by a success six months later at the Battle of Midway; the importance of deception in temporarily freezing German divisions after the Normandy landings; and the effect of deceiving Stalin before the German invasion of Russia in World War II. The value of *tactical* deception and the means to achieve it deserves comparable study. One might start with a close examination of the Japanese naval tactics in World War II. The Imperial Japanese Navy was famous for attempting tactical deception to draw American attention away from the primary threat, but it had mixed results. Among the successful examples, the most famous was during the 1944 Battle for Leyte Gulf. A Japanese decoy force was effective in drawing Halsey away from the beachhead, opening the way for two other Imperial Navy forces to threaten the American amphibious-landing site in the central Philippines.

Littoral Campaigns: A Land-Sea-Air Interaction

Such tactical commonality is lost at the operational level of war. Each littoral region will have a different kind of campaign because the participating armed forces, the friendly nations that the United States is supporting, and the enemy that is threatening the region all have different scouting methods, logistical needs, survival tactics, and competencies.

Common to all theaters is a complicated interaction of land, sea, air, space, and cyberspace forces with tactics that cross boundaries, but it manifests itself in different ways at the different locations. The clutter of islands and neutral shipping that so often impedes littoral warfare is different in each region. The particulars also will change year to year and even season to season, so there is no practical way to describe the differences. However, the imaginary Battle of the Aegean that we shall describe in chapter 15 illustrates the kinds of challenges that might befall an operational and tactical commander in a crisis when an enemy is not deterred by naval presence.

Because such differences are so stark, it is the similarities among littoral theaters that are more easily overlooked when a tactician is developing a detailed operational plan for a particular region. One thing common to each region is that the friendly states that the United States is supporting have the potential to help by conducting their own contiguous maritime interdiction and coastal isolation campaign. Sea-denial with land-based ASCMs is as easy for friendly forces to achieve as it is for those who are menacing the region. The threat of taking away an enemy's littoral seas, resources, islands, and coastal stability may either help to forestall violent action or pave the way for de-escalation of the violence and a return to a peaceful equilibrium.

Also common to each region is the enduring role of the U.S. theater commander, guided by national policy and the Joint Chiefs of Staff, in carrying out the myriad outreach activities, basing agreements, and cooperative exercises that are associated with building stability and security in regions around the world.

Summary

Whether the new naval presence entails larger or smaller foreign policy commitments is not for a tactician to say, but past U.S. Navy forward deployments in Japan and the Mediterranean entailed commitments of forces that will be hard to exceed. What tacticians can say with confidence is that the nature of American deployments for forward presence will become even more flexible and sustainable than when aircraft carrier and amphibious task forces and nuclear submarines were deployed overseas, accompanied by large numbers of Marine Corps and Army units. U.S. presence and actions against enemy irregular operations no doubt will continue in many parts of the world, including the nine dangerous regions of primary tactical interest listed previously.[14] Maintaining safe seas for commercial shipping also will be as vital as it has been in the past.

We have encouraged the employment of salvo equations and other simple operations analysis techniques. A caution from the second edition is worth repeating. A model of battle, especially a realistic-looking computer simulation, too often can beguile users into believing that it is more than any model can ever be. No one

---

14 Baltic, Black, and Aegean Seas; eastern Mediterranean; Persian Gulf; South and East China
    Seas; Yellow Sea; and Sea of Japan.

who knows naval operations is likely to make that mistake with the mathematical models that we employ for exploratory analysis and understanding. But there is a real danger that some leaders may mistake the product of a more sophisticated naval decision-aid, augmented with the power of artificial intelligence, for an accurate predictor of battle outcomes. If the battle plan is sound, then it will succeed, even if its execution contains so many distortions that it is almost unrecognizable after the battle. Compare Nelson's simple-looking, tightly drawn battle plans for the Nile and Trafalgar with the wild, patternless appearance of the way they were executed. Combat analysis does not seek to predict the future any more than a battle plan aims to represent the reality of a conflict when it is fought. The objective of both the analysis and the operation order is to help achieve a victory. The two are not solely sufficient, but both are necessary.

Here, in summary, is the way to think of modern fleet battle tactics, not only in the critical littorals but anywhere.

- Two sides have offensive weapons, the potential advantages of which are a function of range.
- Two sides have defensive potential that takes a variety of forms.
- Each side has scouting systems, which must detect, track, and target the enemy for an effective attack.
- Each side's scouting activities may give away information that the other side will exploit.
- Each side has the potential to slow the scouting process of the enemy by using cover and deception, by distributing combat power in many units, by inducing the enemy not to radiate with his sensors, or by taking anti-scouting steps, including the destruction of enemy off-board sensors, and the jamming of his communications links.
- Each side will try to interfere with the enemy's C^2, either by direct attack on its flagship or by confounding its communications.

Ultimately the opposing C^2 processes govern all. Each commander's goal is to concentrate his firepower to achieve mission success with a focused pulse of destruction, delivered at the decisive places. Just as important as concentration is the timing of the attack. Over the years the genius of winning sea battles has not so much been knowing what to do as when to do it. This is still true. The crux of successful command is to know when to commit available attack potential to attack effectively first. Modern naval battle will be fast, destructive, and decisive. More often than not the result will be decided before the first shot is fired.

14

LOG ENTRIES

Dropping Anchor

The first thirteen chapters of this book have sought to provide naval officers with a solid introduction to the subject of fleet tactics—how the U.S. and foreign navies develop the doctrine and principles that enable them to train, practice, and go into battle, carry out the timeless maxim "attack effectively first," and succeed. The text covers the development of tactics over the years, the principles and practices that govern it, and the practical application of tactics in actual combat—including warfare in the age of missiles and advanced sensors. This chapter focuses some of the insights that have been imparted in hopes that they may provide a few safe anchorages against the storms of battle.

Fleet Tactics

Naval battle is centered on attrition, but maneuver is an indispensable part of the picture. Victory by maneuver warfare alone often works on land, but it does not succeed by itself at sea, where the tactical commander must aim for a first effective attack. The great Soviet Admiral Sergei Gorshkov referred to the importance of winning the symbolic "Battle of the First Salvo." That maxim is true enough, but grasping it is only a good beginning. Superior scouting, whose role has become more intricate in recent years, opens the door to successful attack. Information gathering by both sides has always been critical; so has attempting to impede the enemy's search efforts in an effort to stay ahead of the opposition in amassing knowledge of the battlefield. With the stunning technological advances in search-radar and computers, the capacity for information gathering has greatly expanded, and information processing has become a critical—and time-consuming—part of the attack. Communication has been streamlined and speeded up, but scouting is not complete until the vital tracking information is in the hands of the shooters. Commanders fuse scouting data to help position their forces more effectively—and to frustrate the enemy's efforts to do the same.

Neither the pace of battle nor its tension can be captured in writing or in a motion picture. Even computer war games do not communicate the urgency that hovers over such life-and-death events. Tactical success depends upon well-timed action. The goal of opposing tactical commanders is to maximize the offensive firepower that a navy actually delivers. We emphasize *delivers* as a reminder that staying power matters, especially these days, with the use of missiles, when it has become difficult to keep even a large warship in the action once it has been hit. As Russian Vice Admiral Stepan O. Makarov wrote many years ago, "A good gun causes victory, armor only postpones defeat."[1] No fleet can operate indefinitely in the face of a competitive enemy without destroying its force.

At the same time, unless the firepower is delivered, it serves no purpose. If a ship is crippled, all the unexpended ordnance in its guns, missile launchers, and magazines is out of action as well. Likewise, missiles fired at a decoy, at innocent shipping, or at a pinnacle of rock contribute nothing to the quest for victory.

Many of the characteristics that govern naval battles also have changed. The limitations on the ability of warships to operate for long periods within range of land-based weapons of comparable striking power are more severe now than they have ever been. Yet, the big advantage that warships provide over the use of ground forces—that is, greater operational mobility—is as potent as ever. The advantage of maneuverability that naval forces traditionally have offered over ground forces must be exploited to prove its worth; a ship that remains stationary merely invites attack.

There are other factors to consider. Greater weapon range and lethality have dramatically expanded the modern battlefield, but the strictures of littoral warfare threaten to cramp movement and compress inshore operations into an explosive mixture of threats—from air, land, sea, and undersea. Maritime operations now must take account of more land-based forces and the sensors they employ; indeed, sea-based forces often must team with land-based forces that are located in friendly territory. Effective cooperation—in joint and combined operations, both operational and tactical—is a modern-day imperative.

---

1   Makarov, p. 181.

A major new ambiguity that every fleet must resolve to its particular purpose concerns these contradictory choices:

- Relying on active defense—massing enough force to defeat any probable first attack by the enemy. In this scenario, a fleet must give up moving quietly in order to employ defensive weapons cooperatively.
- Relying on stealth—distributing force in an effort to make the enemy work so hard and take so long that it cannot attack effectively first. Here, the force must move quietly or it will lose the advantage of surprise.

There is no certain preference for either active defense or stealthy offense, because the tactical advantage changes with the kind of technology that is used. In either case, the choice involves trade-offs.

Fleet exercises designed to train a force for the opening salvo of a war under "rules of engagement" are the most difficult to execute. It is a mistake to overemphasize the first strike of the war in battle practice. Admiral Gorshkov's "Battle of the First Salvo" is important, but tactical doctrine must guide the whole of wartime operations, and tactics for the onset of a war are a special, difficult case.

We have shown that *firepower, scouting, and command-and-control* and their antitheses all play interlocking roles, but success comes from coordinating these processes in the face of an enemy that is trying to do the same. A good tactical plan blends its parts like a musical composition. Here are three different looks at the characteristics of fleets in combat from a different angle to the approach taken in chapter 13—weapons and sensors; planning and execution; and the relationship between fleet tactics and operations.

Weapons and Sensors

The evolution of firepower warrants deep reflection. The development of the torpedo at the beginning of the twentieth century enabled an inferior force to defeat a superior one because the new weapons delivered a highly effective *pulse of firepower* that could be delivered from many small torpedo boats or from an undetected submarine. The effect of this on tactics in World War I was astonishing. In World War II, aircraft became the means of delivering fatal "salvoes" because an air wing could reach out 200 nautical miles or more, and the effect on tactics was even more stunning. In the modern missile age, this salvo threat has achieved new status. When the "pulsed power" is a missile salvo, a weaker side that is outnumbered by as much as two to one can win—if it employs better scouting and command-and-control that enable it to "attack effectively first." Conceptually, the Battle of Midway demonstrated this conclusively.

Tactical planners who expected long-range weapon fire to be effective have been surprised to find that, for many reasons, missile-age battles can be decided at much shorter ranges. The reasons have much to do with the pace of scouting and its information processing, while the two forces stalk each other in deadly hide-and-seek on and under the narrow seas. (World War II coastal combatants fighting in the Solomons, North Sea, and Mediterranean won by employing better stalking tactics.)

If an inferior force must fight to support its national strategy, then

- A scouting edge is mandatory. Force commanders should make an estimate of the situation, and even if tactical defeat seems likely, they should concentrate on ascertaining how to take risks and inflict the most damage.
- The solution should offer hope that using the edge that is gained from scouting and deception will enable a force to attack effectively first and weaken the enemy's counterattack. Warships can be built to stay afloat and fight even after they have taken several hits from shells and bombs and more than one missile or torpedo. Big multipurpose ships in modern fleets must survive a variety of attacks and keep fighting in the open ocean. Smaller ships, which can be put out of action by one hit, must use stealth and concealment and fight in large numbers; they almost inevitably will suffer losses. With that in mind, ships and unmanned aircraft that are intended to fight in high-threat coastal areas and confined waters should be small, nimble, lightly manned, and expendable if necessary.

Because a fleet action is often decisive, a great deal of attention must be devoted to maintaining superiority. Today, mining and mine countermeasures, which are peripheral to this study and have tactics of their own, can confound a superior navy. A weaker navy is likely to rely on guerilla warfare—the use of submarines either to erode the superiority of the enemy surface fleet or to attack commerce. In both world wars, German U-boats conducted such a campaign against commercial shipping. In World War II, the Japanese strategy used submarines to weaken the U.S. Fleet until they could force the Americans into a more or less evenly matched fleet action. The next large-scale submarine campaign will be augmented by long-range aircraft or missiles. In any case, the full fleet threat calculus is now multi-domain, encompassing threats from the seabed to space, along with multi-dimensional scouting and information warfare to target an opposing fleet.

Planning and Execution

Doctrine unifies action. It influences training, technology, tactics, and objectives—and it is influenced by them as well. *Tactical* doctrine provides a framework of standard principles and procedures that govern combat. It is intended to ensure that the people who control the weapons systems in manned and unmanned ships and aircraft approach their missions from a common perspective and will be able to work together more efficiently in achieving united action. The procedures must be practical and compatible rather than theoretical and discordant. Doctrine at all levels should be specific, designed to achieve the best results from a unified team. As many have said, doctrine is like a playbook in football that can be practiced and executed with a short command structure. Yet, it also must allow room for initiative, akin to the freedom of action that is permitted a football tight-end, who can block or run to catch a pass as a play unfolds and the defense reacts.

Doctrine seeks to standardize tactics to help reduce the amount of laborious planning that is required for each military operation. In effect, it provides generic plans that units can use to practice and train with before they are assigned specific missions and operate in known locations. Modern fighting instructions help serve that purpose—without the strictures imposed by the old Royal Navy's Permanent Fighting Instructions—and ensure adaptability and flexibility in today's environment. An operation order amounts to mission-specific fighting instructions.

The more unstable the force composition is in a particular mission, the greater the need is for standardized tactics and commands. For the same reason, the more rapid the turnover rate is for tactical commanders and commanding officers, the greater the need is for personal consultation in planning and an effort to maintain tactical simplicity. The ideal, never exceeded, was Nelson's band of brothers, who knew what to do almost without signal at the Battle of the Nile and at Trafalgar. A contemporary fleet's battle network will include a signal book that standardizes tactical commands; in battle, tactical communications must be brief, unambiguous, and sparse. In future wars, the opportunity to exploit enemy signals will be potentially greater than it has been in the past.

Planning and execution are related, but they are not the same thing. One does not plan an operation while it is being executed. Rather, one executes a plan that can be altered as the operation unfolds—enabling commanders to incorporate tactical variations that can help deal with what the adversary is actually doing—the enemy has a voice. The commander must keep this plan firmly in mind. It should not depart greatly from doctrine and training or its execution will falter. Good execution may look so different from the plan that to the untrained eye there is no similarity.

Battle plans must provide for contingency operations that would take effect automatically in case the aircraft carrier, the best air-defense ship, the flagship, or a vital scouting component is put out of action. Aggregating capability in too few ships, aircraft, airfields, satellites, or communications channels, with no redundancy, is a sure way to risk defeat; the difficulties of a fleet in trouble will be compounded. Large damaged ships must be protected and escorted to safe waters. A single, perfected information network that is infected with a virus will spread its plague of confusion anywhere. A fleet whose code has been broken by the enemy cannot execute a surprise attack.

Relationships to Operations

The bare-bones conclusion that naval combat is centered on attrition alone implies that death and destruction are unavoidable—an exceedingly gloomy conclusion. But there are four factors that may mitigate that result.

First, a show of superior force is more likely to deter a naval battle than a ground battle. Neutralizing an inferior force without a fight is a common phenomenon that has been obscured in the study of tactics because history only records battles that have occurred—not those that have been averted.

Second, while modern combat forces are succeeding in destroying machines at a higher rate, the trend is accompanied by a reduction in the rate at which combat personnel are being killed or put out of action.

Third, the proportion of noncombatant personnel assigned to perform scouting, antiscouting, and logistical tasks that are not directly in harm's way is rising sharply, and may increase more rapidly with the onset of unmanned scouts in large numbers.

Finally, an encircling navy is less threatening to defending forces than an invading army. This is true when the weaker navy belongs to a continental power such as the Soviet Union. On the other hand, when a maritime nation such as Great Britain or Japan has been threatened by a powerful navy the result has been destabilizing. The growing Chinese fleet is such a threat to stability today. Mahan was right when he said that a foremost responsibility of every battle fleet commander is to concentrate forces to win sea battles. Corbett was right that campaign considerations determine whether such a concentration of force is possible. A fleet can serve its strategic purpose without engaging in a decisive battle. Many factors—the threat of a submarine campaign or the responsibility of safeguarding national interests worldwide, for example—may distract a fleet from the role of fighting a decisive battle.

Fleet actions occur when authorities are convinced that some expeditionary situation on land will eventually be intolerable if the weaker fleet does not fight.

The tactical consequence is that the superior force will be burdened with competing demands. While dealing with the enemy fleet head-on, it will simultaneously have to protect shipping, troop ships, or a beachhead. Today the reach of modern sensors and the deadliness of land-based missiles and aircraft make a fleet commander's task more difficult and make the location of an expeditionary landing site a difficult but vital choice.

Raw orders of battle do not reveal whether one combatant fleet is superior to the other. What does so is a knowledgeable comparison of prospective force, not forces, and how well that force can be delivered with timely precision. Weapon numbers and ranges, scouting capacity and C^2, and the quality of training all are variables in the equation.

Clausewitz wrote that the concern of an army without a mission is self-preservation. The same applies to a navy. Strategic submarines (SSBN) for deterrence should hide in conventional war. Amphibious forces should be out of harm's way until the coast is clear. Self-preservation has been the aim of navies that are too weak to enter into decisive battle, such as the German High Seas Fleet in World War I, when it confronted a superior British Grand Fleet.

Some uninformed commentators say there can never be another old-fashioned surface fleet action because modern weapons and sensors will drive warships under water to survive. Perhaps they have obsolete tactics and ships of earlier wars in mind. So long as nations use the surface of the ocean—and they are doing so more every year—they will maintain fleets that can control or influence the surface; and those fleets will include surface warships.

The Study of Tactics

A thesis of this book is that tactical study seeks to bring order and understanding to the chaos of battle as far as possible. Intellectually, the best way to illustrate that is to estimate the expected effectiveness of specific tactics. One such measure is an estimate of the losses that both sides are likely to sustain while accomplishing the mission, taking into account scouting plans, firepower ranges, and delivery intentions, including which side is likely to attack first or win an exchange of fire. Yet, there are two caveats here. First, although the results of these measurements are credible indicators, the chaos of battle makes it impossible to regard them as reliable predictions. Second, the measure of the losses incurred by both sides may be a proxy metric that is only indirectly linked to the mission, which itself might involve carrying out a landing or mounting a land battle with air power or missile strikes, rather than through the destruction of the enemy fleet.

In World Wars I and II, tactical thinking was done entirely by military men. Even today, although inspired ideas can come from elsewhere, working out the tactical details must occur in the fleet, and sea officers are often preoccupied with administration, weapon readiness, and engineering reliability to develop doctrine on their own. As a result, improvement in tactics requires the assistance of fleet schools and commands that should be charged with combat development and training. For airpower tactics, the Navy's famous "Top Gun" school in Fallon, Nevada, is one of these. The recently established Naval Surface and Mine War-fighting Development Center (NSMWDC) in San Diego, California, is another example, spanning surface warfare-related tactics development. NSMWDC's mission is to train junior officers in advanced tactics and doctrine synchronized across integrated air and missile defense, amphibious warfare, mine warfare, surface warfare, and anti-submarine warfare.

Analyzing historical naval battles helps today's tacticians design and calibrate the inputs for battle models and simulations. When there are no recent similar battles to examine, the most realistic substitute is to study the results of contemporary fleet exercises. Such analyses must scrutinize positions, communications, and operations tempo in detail—as rich in data as in narrative. Historical data reveal that naval weapons almost always perform significantly below what the data from peacetime experiments have led observers to expect. Why, then, does unexpectedly poor weapon performance nevertheless achieve decisive battle results?

There are three reasons:

- *Tactical*: Ineffectiveness can be advantageous if it is two-sided. At the Battle of Santiago in 1898, when gunnery failed RADM William T. Sampson, USN, commander of the Atlantic Fleet, at a range of six thousand yards, the ineffectiveness of the Spanish warships enabled him to close to one thousand yards and sink them.
- *Technological*: Modern weapons are very lethal. Even if many missiles miss their targets, a single hit can be enough to put a ship out of action.
- *Campaign-related*: History devotes itself largely to battles with great consequences. The causes of indecisive battles are just as instructive tactically.

Some people emphasize war as a science, while others view it as an art. This book emphasizes the special qualities that commanders must have, which seem to historians or journalists to be instinctive, almost like a "sixth sense." An effective leader has the human qualities that brave, wise, and inspiring leaders have displayed in the past. When these are present, the debate over whether war is an art or a science seems unimportant. Good practice is an art that grows from good theory that is more scientific. Both are necessary, but neither of them is sufficient by itself to explain the repeated successes of great tactical leaders such as Jervis, Nelson, Suffren, Togo, Spruance, and Burke.

Fiction and Forecasts

War-gaming has a long history. In the United States, "seminar" games with role-playing by human participants are a popular form to assess the strategies of potential opponents. Sometimes the game includes players of other states and groups such as the North Atlantic Treaty Organization. Strategic games are thought experiments. They explore the kinds of confrontations that tacticians believe could arise in places like the Baltic, the eastern Mediterranean, the Middle East, or the China seas.

Other war games are intended to help plan campaigns. One series of games was conducted between the world wars at the Naval War College. In that twenty-two-year period, 318 games were played with maps or on the game floor of Luce Hall in Newport, Rhode Island.[2] The games were the opposite of the thought experiments described above. At Newport, the strategic setting was assumed. The games were designed to test in more detail the various military and naval responses to the circumstances that the sponsors described. Some of them pitted the U.S. Navy against the Royal Navy—not because a war with Great Britain was regarded as likely, but because the capability, mobility, firepower, and organization that the British possessed at the time constituted the most challenging "opposition force" against which the U.S. Navy could measure itself.

For more realistic practice in campaign planning, Japan was the significant opponent—even in the 1920s, before friction arose between the Japanese and American governments. Out of 137 tactical and operational games, 127 were played against "Orange," or Japan. A 1986 article by Michael Vlahos in the *Naval War College Review* chronicles how the evolution and usefulness of these games played a key role in the development of the plans for the Navy's Pacific Ocean campaign. Because operations analysis as we know it today did not yet exist, war games were the analytical tool of choice for exploring new tactics and technologies. In retrospect, they yielded useful but imperfect insights. For example, they showed the growing importance of naval aviation, but not its coming dominance.

---

2   For an accurate summary, see Vlahos, "War gaming." Also, his *The Blue Sword* is an exhaustive study of the war games during the same period.

The prewar games emphasized a daytime battle line—which had a negative influence on the night surface tactics employed in the Solomon Islands. And they did not show the swift pace at which the close-range actions would unfold. Nevertheless, the games were valuable in exploring the size, configuration, and employment of aircraft carriers, the preferable types and mix of scout-bombers, and the importance of search plans. Vlahos records 106 purely tactical games, of which 71 were fleet actions.

Fiction writers who have attempted to predict future wars and their consequences have a checkered history. Some have amounted to blatant propaganda. A famous example was Erskine Childers' *The Riddle of the Sands*. Published in England in 1903, it was republished by the Naval Institute Press in 1991 and made into a movie. Childers creates the story of two Englishmen on holiday who sail their yacht among the islands and tidewaters along the North Sea coast of Germany. They discover a fleet of barges moored in Imperial Germany's coastal estuaries in preparation for a surprise invasion of England. Childers was obsessed with the prospect of an unexpected landing on the English coast, which he feared could overcome the feeble British army. His vivid novel drew the attention of the press, the public, and the admiralty, which was his purpose. *The Riddle of the Sands* lives on in Oxford and Cambridge student culture as mythology more attuned to modern ears than *Beowulf* or *The Iliad*. It is the best of its time. But, as Eric Grove writes in his introduction to the recent republication, "His book was far from being the only exercise in literary scaremongering at the time." Grove lists half a dozen others, including *The Great War in England in 1897*, by William Le Queux.

Similar in impact to Childers' work but intended as entertainment, is Tom Clancy's novel *Red Storm Rising*. Published in 1986, before the collapse of the Soviet Union, it describes the "real" war between NATO and the Warsaw Pact and includes some campaign moves and countermoves by the opposing sides that broke through the then-rigid boundaries of conventional Pentagon gaming and analysis. By the time the book went on sale, U.S. naval planning had become relatively stereotyped. Clancy's imaginative ideas were treated with respect and examined closely. Such works of fiction involve the thoughts and actions of the imagined participant in vivid detail. Unlike the body of science-fiction tracing from H. G. Wells' *The War of the Worlds*, some of them are relevant enough to be taken seriously by war-planners.

A recent book, *Ghost Fleet*, by Peter Singer and August Cole, rivals *Red Storm Rising* for thought-provoking insights that draw attention to creative steps that a first-class enemy could take to defeat the U.S. Navy today. The story is about a

304 ⮞ Chapter Fourteen

twenty-first-century attack on Oahu by China's People's Liberation Army Navy. Instead of bombing and neutralizing the U.S. Pacific Fleet as the Japanese did on 7 December, China conducts a surprise *invasion*. Aided by worms planted in the combat systems of American warships to incapacitate their sensors and missile systems, Chinese warships, aircraft, and missiles are able to neutralize the U.S. warships that would have defended Hawaii. Unmanned Chinese aerial vehicles, flying from innocent-looking commercial ships, then destroy American ground defenses. Their manned and unmanned ground vehicles complete the invasion and occupation.

One might question *Ghost Fleet*'s logic of China's commencing a war this way, but the surprise attack is no more a strategic folly than was Tom Clancy's initiation of a fictional World War III with a surprise Soviet attack on NATO. The thrust of the Singer and Cole book is to create a strategic setting in which they can describe modern information warfare. They identify a host of potential vulnerabilities in the American armed forces that in real life should not be ignored. They back up their descriptions of the Chinese technologies used in the book with extraordinary technological detail, validated by more than 400 endnotes supporting each of the crippling cyber, robotic, and malware attacks. On the American side the Navy initially descends into a thick fog of operational helplessness, the defenders of Hawaii are baffled and blinded, and chaos reigns throughout the United States as the Chinese shut down utilities and power systems fail from coast to coast—until Singer and Cole imaginatively describe how the United States achieves a comeback to defeat the Chinese attackers.[3]

Standing apart from fiction are what may be called *forecasts*. These can be short or long, but they omit the conversations and streams of consciousness of a novel's cast of characters. The best is Hector C. Bywater's *The Great Pacific War: A History of the American-Japanese Campaign of 1931–1933*. Bywater was a journalist and military commentator and a well-informed, insightful observer. Writing in 1925, he described the imagined events of a short, sharp conflict between the United States and Japan—a book that he said was designed to caution Japan against arousing the sleepy American giant, which had not yet begun to modernize the fleet left over after the Washington Disarmament Treaty of 1921.

The power of Bywater's argument rested entirely on the acuity of his story. It is only a slight exaggeration to say that in this single book, written sixteen years before the Japanese attack on Pearl Harbor, Bywater assembled most of the lessons that it took Naval War College gamers twenty years to deduce. He predicted

---

3 Singer and Cole.

that Japan would launch a surprise attack *before* it declared war—on the Panama Canal rather than Pearl Harbor. The book describes how closing the canal eliminates the entire Atlantic Fleet for the first two months of hostilities. Bywater foresees Japan's swift invasion of the Philippines in a landing at Lingayen Gulf, which takes place at the same time that it seizes Guam. The U.S. Asiatic Fleet is crushed at war's onset, while the Pacific Fleet, with neither cruising radius nor logistic ships, must fume in frustration.

As the war proceeds, the United States masses Marine Corps and Army troops—and transports to carry them—at Pearl Harbor while Japan stages attacks on the Aleutian Islands and along the Oregon-California coast as a distraction. Both sides attempt ambushes and both suffer from lack of scouting. Already search aircraft are a precious resource in short supply. In a temporizing move that presages the operations that the United States would conduct later at Guadalcanal, the U.S. Navy blocks a Japanese thrust to take American Samoa. Japanese invade China, and the troops become bogged down in its vastness. The American fleet, now reinforced, begins its irresistible sweep through the Central Pacific, seizing Truk atoll, which in Bywater's book is not yet the bastion that it actually would become by 1944. The climactic fleet action is in the vicinity of Yap Island. The narrative is a sort of early compression of the two great naval battles in 1944, off the Marianas in June and around Leyte Gulf in October. The Japanese in Bywater's novel, not faced with President Roosevelt's proclaimed policy of unconditional surrender, immediately sue for a negotiated, albeit humbling peace.

This book closes with an epilogue that describes an imaginary battle identical to the one in the second edition. "The Battle of Aegean" is a sound introduction to modern campaign execution. It is focused on littoral combat, information warfare, and the importance of missiles. Then the influence of new technologies such as unmanned vehicles and almost undetectable communications is evaluated to see how they might enhance a navy's performance.

This fictional "Battle of the Aegean" is intended to serve as a unifying description of modern fleet tactics, just as Nelson's Battle of the Nile served as an introduction to the six cornerstones of fleet combat, past, present, and future. It is an illustration of the dynamic processes governing naval combat today and in the future. Above all, it emphasizes the importance of skillful leadership and the training that it takes to fight and win in dangerous waters today.

15

THE BATTLE OF
THE AEGEAN

Setting the Scene

The first edition of *Fleet Tactics* closed with an imaginary narrative of a sea battle between U.S. and Soviet naval forces, viewed through the prism of the tactician. The purpose was to suggest the properties of then-new modern missile combat and suggest ways that the United States could prepare for it. "The Next Battle of the Nile," as it was known, was going to take place on the two-hundredth anniversary of Nelson's great victory of 1 August 1798. Fortunately, the fictional battle depicted between American and Soviet navies never actually took place. The tactical lessons live on, however, and the techniques needed to achieve a stunning surprise missile attack and victory against a larger fleet are still pertinent for designing tactics for today's missile-age warfare.

The Battle of the Aegean

The range of the second and third editions extends from the purely tactical to the operational level of a campaign. It was fitting in the second edition to replace the original tactical example with a more intricate campaign in which a commander had to operate in dangerous waters. In the current volume, the tactical commander from the first edition reappears, this time as the *operational* commander. His skills will be tested to the limit here. Our story line, intended to illustrate tactical simplicity amid operational intricacy, centers on the operational commander so that we can flavor the exercise with the human demands of leadership at its best. With its description of the modern tactical environment—dominated by sensors, missiles, and information operations, with undercurrents of torpedoes, mines, and amphibious operations—it is designed as a forecast. We confront our Navy hero with the kinds of operational problems and tactical situations that a naval force is likely to face when it is opposed by a respectable, integrated coastal defense that is partly ship based and partly land based. To create such a challenging adversary, we have projected onto our antagonist the capabilities of a longstanding friend of the United States and American Navy. The intent here is to emphasize that the "opponent" sees the scenario as constructed for the same purpose as the U.S. Navy played its war games against the British navy in the 1920s. The adversary is chosen not because we believe it is a likely foe but because its seaward-looking forces are a formidable test of a sea power's tactics, systems, and doctrine.

The "Battle of the Aegean," as we call it, also focuses on a *maritime* campaign in which all the physical fighting is confined to the seaward side of a coastline. The campaign is one in which any attempt to bring the whole weight of American military power to bear against the enemy homeland would be disastrously contrary to American interests, yet to allow our foe the unimpeded use of its home waters would be just as intolerable. Sea control implies the capability to carry a maritime campaign all the way to the adversary's coast.

The narrative shows the extent to which waging warfare in coastal waters requires tactics, doctrine, and combat systems that are far different from those traditionally used in a blue-water battle. By the term *combat systems*, we mean ships, aircraft, and sensors all connected for unified action through information technology and doctrine. The successful interweaving is the essence and intent of networked warfare. Our vignette also shows why an opponent who is fighting in its own waters does not need the same high technology to defend itself that the American navy would need to penetrate its coastal defenses. Doctrine for semiautonomous operations, combined with concealment and surprise, will be sufficient for an enemy to challenge our fictional hero, "Admiral Ulysses S. (Sam) Grant," to the utmost. To expand the scope—and value—of the exercise, we also equip Admiral Grant with some forces and weapons that are still being developed and are not yet a part of the American Navy.

Our imaginary vignette begins just as the version in the second edition did. New ways for the American fleet to achieve the goal of preventing our imaginary aggressor from achieving its ingenious purpose will come to mind; yet, any new technologies and tactics employed must reflect the American strategic aim, which is to avoid a war that spills over onto the land. At the end of the narrative we will suggest some new ways that may make the American operation safer and less risky; many of these are connected with information warfare and the use of unmanned systems.

The Crisis

Pondering the situation, Admiral Grant muses that before him lies living proof that operations are more intricate than tactics. His battle plan depends on reducing all considerations to a set of simple tactical actions that everyone understands well enough to carry out in the midst of the confusion and uncertainty of the impending fight. Yet, the operations now under way flow from layer upon layer of national policy and military strategy. The various parties have been drawn into battle because of a sequence of escalating events that had not been pretty for the U.S. Navy. Sam Grant would soon give the battle his full and undivided attention. For now, however, he contemplates the many-sided decisions that led to the campaign that is now rushing to its climax.

The setting embraces not just two antagonists, but three, as well as vested interests of almost every country in Europe and most in western Asia. There have been more convoluted circumstances than those that surround Grant now, he mulls, but the current outlook is sufficiently Byzantine to make it fitting that Byzantium, the capital of the ancient empire, is only a few miles across the Aegean. His mission is to cool the passions of the longtime antagonists that sit on each side of that body of water.

Grant's operational responsibility is to interpose between Turkey and Greece at this, the eleventh hour before all the dogs of war are unleashed. The United States' peace-making endeavor is down to its last chance, a chance that rests on a battle waged by his forces alone. It is the American admiral's gnawing paradox that in order to restore peace he must shed blood. That a battle will take place is certain, but its outcome is not. The U.S. Sixth Fleet, unaided, faces the entire Turkish navy and more. Yet, Grant's tacticians assert that his battle plan can succeed. With luck, skill, and staunchness, his forces will be just sufficient to the task. It will be the American Navy's greatest challenge since the Battle of Midway.

How Admiral Grant came to wear the mantle of a combat commander is itself one of those marvels of strategic intricacy. U. S. Grant is the new commander of U.S. naval forces in Europe—a post that is subordinate to the American theater commander in Europe, GEN E. F. "Famous" Grouse, USA, who was headquartered in land-locked Stuttgart, Germany. Yet, after the opening violence, Grant found himself in command and taking direction straight from the secretary of defense and in close communication with the chairman of the Joint Chiefs of Staff. The president, in his delicate calibration of the politics of violence, is committed to succeed or fail using naval force in the maritime domain alone. Employing the modest forces of the Sixth Fleet and without the full weight of American might,

Grant must bank the fires of the simmering feud between Turkey and Greece—passions that are reminiscent of the timeless hatred between the Capulets and Montagues (or, in American imagery, between the Hatfields and McCoys).

In recent months Greek zealots have fomented violence on Cyprus that has gone beyond the ability of the small United Nations peace-keeping force there to contain. A week ago Greece used the brutality as justification for deploying theater ballistic missiles to the island—missiles that could reach every vital center in Turkey in a matter of minutes. The Turkish populace was enraged. Uncharacteristically, the president and prime minister of Turkey both supported the popular anger and nurtured the swelling demand for action. The CIA believed that Turkish forces were about to put in place a strategy that they had prepared in case Greece should ever act on its threat to move missiles into Cyprus.

Turkey's minister of defense announced a quarantine to block the Greek movement to Cyprus by sea, and Turkish ships prepared to sail in force against Cyprus—all of it so conspicuously that Greece could not fail to respond. In fact, Turkey had a deeper motive. Far to the east of Greece and tucked less than 100 miles away from the Turkish mainland, Cyprus served as bait in a trap. The Greek navy, supportable only weakly by the country's air force, which would have to fly to the end of its tether, would be forced to run a deadly gauntlet. Turkish aircraft, surface warships, submarines, and land-launched missiles were poised to fight a littoral war that was heavily stacked in Turkey's favor. As the climax and conclusion of phase one in Turkey's campaign plan, Turkish commanders planned a fleet action west of Cyprus designed to reduce the Greek navy to impotence and lead to phase two, which would be centered in the Aegean Sea.

In the Aegean Sea lay the true object of Turkish ambitions. Over many years Greece and Turkey had shaped their naval forces and tactics to confront each other. Both countries believe that the outcome of a fleet encounter in the Aegean is likely to be a toss-up, perhaps even with a nod to Greece. In their own eyes, the Greeks owned (or *occupied*, as the Turks saw it) the many islands of the Dodecanese and Cyclades and expected to use missiles and armed aircraft to ambush Turkish ships and aircraft in those confined waters. But if Turkey destroyed the Greek navy first, then the islands could be isolated and all doors into the Aegean could be opened.

It had become intolerable to Ankara that with control over those islands Greece now dominated the Aegean. To the Turks, it was bad enough to suffer at the whim of a Greek government whose islands and navy could forcibly close the vital sea lane through the Aegean into the Dardanelles and Black Sea. Then,

① Greece plans to move land-launched TBMs to Cyprus

② Turkey announces intention to move major forces into Cyprus, and then

③ Crush the Greek navy

Figure 15-1. Greek Intentions and Turkish Response

in 1995, Greece had extended its territorial waters to twelve miles in accordance with the UN's Convention on the Law of the Sea of November 1994. If Greece ever enforced the terms of the UN treaty—and it had never denied itself the right to do so—by international law it would legally be entitled to control access to the Black Sea and to every port on Turkey's west coast.

Beyond that, the Greek islands influenced—in the minds of some diplomats, they actually *determined*—the demarcation of the continental shelf for the purpose of establishing underwater mineral rights. Attempts at oil exploration by Turkish-affiliated companies had led to protests from Greece charging Turkey with encroachment. Disputes involving authority over airspace and air traffic in the Aegean and the "militarization" of the Greek islands near the Turkish coast still were unresolved. From these many aggravations, the littoral waters off the west coast of Turkey took on the color of two armed camps. The final straw came when the Turkish intelligence services learned that Greece had surreptitiously introduced cruise missiles into Cos, Limnos, and Chios. From that moment the Turkish armed forces began to lay the plans now in motion to seize the islands and their missiles, as well as Samos and Lesbos. After that the government would strike the best bargain it could get in the courts of public opinion, striving for justice and for a better balance in the Aegean.

It mattered not a whit whether the Greek navy understood the Turks' two-pronged strategy to fight first at Cyprus and then in the eastern Aegean. No Greek government could survive if it abandoned Cyprus. The Greek navy would have to risk all in a single throw of the dice that clearly would be loaded in Turkey's favor. NATO leaders were appalled, for both Turkey and Greece were members of the twenty-nine-country mutual defense pact. The crisis that the other NATO nations had sought to avoid for more than fifty years suddenly was upon them, and, as frequently happened in such cases, they were helplessly divided. The United Nations was caught in irons, too, its members split between friendships on both sides of the Aegean. If there was to be an enforced peace, it would be peace brought about by American action.

American Policy Decisions

When U.S. president Rainsford C. G. Harris, a Princeton graduate and a fervent admirer of Greek and Western civilization, learned about the Turkish strategy, he was ready to intervene on the merits of the case. To him, Turkey was the aggressor, and Turkey must be stopped. At the same time, backed by the force of the Sixth Fleet, Harris must persuade Greece to defer to U.S. diplomacy—for its own good and the naval balance in the Aegean. The State Department was more even-handed. Democratic Turkey was a wedge reaching into the Asian continent. It also was a country that understood and spoke the ethos of Islam while rejecting the zealotry of Muslim theocracies. It was a strong state, struggling for stability and prosperity, that had sought and received the friendship of the United States and NATO during the years when Turkey was the easternmost outpost of the West's confrontation with the Soviet Union. Secretary of State Dan M. Tinker was sympathetic to Turkey and its people who, he thought, for years had been more than patient over the many provocations heaped upon them by the Greek Cypriot majority.

The opposing perspectives coalesced into one American action. In the view of the National Security Council (NSC), this was a maritime crisis that demanded a naval solution. For fifty years the U.S. Navy had interposed off Taiwan, the Levant, Africa, Central America, and in the South China Sea and southwest Asia. Although

Amphibious operations against Limnos, Lesbos, Chios, Samos, and Cos from Ayvalik, Cesme, Izmir, Kusadasi, and Bodrum

Figure 15-2. Turkish Strategy, Phase 2

the Navy's effect on the landward side was limited, whenever a maritime issue was at stake—as was the case now in the eastern Mediterranean—the Navy could boast unblemished success since 1949. No adversary had consummated an attack against it except by accident or with a mine.

Accordingly, the NSC proposed deploying two Aegis cruisers between Cyprus and the ports of Iskenderun and Mersin, where Turkish soldiers would soon embark for a strongly protected move to Cyprus. The American ambassador in Ankara was instructed to carry a coldly correct diplomatic note to Turkish prime minister Yusuf Bey warning that any move toward Cyprus would be viewed as a move against the United States. President Harris would publicly declare the single thing on which he and Secretary Tinker agreed—that neither Greek nor Turkish ships and aircraft would be permitted to fire upon the other, or to alter the military balance in Cyprus with missiles, troops, or anything else. To give this weight, Harris would speak with President Spiro Hatzopoulos of Greece by video teleconference to assure him that no ships would approach Cyprus without prior screening by the U.S. Navy. Hatzopoulos agreed to stand aside, but not cheerfully, for his own navy's passions had been aroused. Meanwhile, in Ankara, the interview had not gone well for the American ambassador. He could only report that his diplomatic note had met with curt dismissal by a stolid and stoic prime minister.

The Campaign Begins

Those difficult events had transpired only five days ago. As theater naval commander, Admiral Grant had been consulted, and when he heard the plan from General Grouse he ordered VADM Paul T. "Patent" Anchor, commander of the Sixth Fleet, to begin moving Aegis ships eastward immediately. On Grant's recommendation, Grouse also approved these provisions:

- Four Aegis warships rather than two would interpose off Cyprus in pairs northeast and northwest of the island.
- Three submarines would move into the same waters, unannounced and invisible.
- The carrier battle force, which comprised one CVN and four escorts, would be brought to full readiness 150 miles from Turkey, where it would have sufficient sea room for defense, but would be close enough to the interposing American warships to be able to cover them.

Meanwhile, Grant moved the three-ship Amphibious Ready Group (ARG) well to the west. The Marine Expeditionary Unit (MEU) that it carried should be protected, but all eight of his Aegis ships were committed. He considered moving the Marines ashore, but discarded the idea as impractical. Therefore he dispatched what was left—eight small *Cushing*-class corvettes that were presently tied up to a short wharf next to the Sixth Fleet flagship berth at Gaeta, Italy. As offensive ships, the 800-ton *Cushing*s were not configured for escort, but Grant wanted them under way anyway so they would be free from any interference from Italy. They would rendezvous with the three ships of the ARG and loiter in the Tyrrhenian Sea. The *Cushing*s were intended for short, swift missions, not for sustained steaming, and Grant was promised reinforcements from the Atlantic Fleet in ten days. Until then, the eight crews, sixty members each, would have to tough it out with the ARG. But the corvettes had drilled for sustained crisis operations before, and Grant was confident that CDR Charles V. Gridley, USN, the tactical commander, would keep them at the ready.[1]

On board the amphibious ships is a detachment of SEALs, experts in special warfare, for whom Grant envisioned a possible role. So he has ordered the three operative coastal patrol ships (PCs) from their base in Rota, Spain, to sea with instructions to pick up the SEALs from the amphibious vessels north of Sardinia and then head east.

Also at Rota is a 40,000-ton mother ship capable of carrying eight small Killer-Scout vessels and ten STOVL aircraft and steaming at a speed of thirty-two knots. Altogether there are thirty of the lethal 200-ton vessels, configured variously for inshore missions and tasks. Twelve of the thirty, called *Phantom*s, are armed with tactical land-attack missiles. Grant ordered the mother ship to load eight *Phantom*s in its well deck and sail eastward into the Mediterranean, with the PCs in company. (Note: Both the Killer-Scout vessels and their *Phantom* derivatives were created for this vignette.)

The Shocks

As Admiral Grant feared, the Turks were not deterred. The first attack took place on 28 July, just before midnight, during the change of the watch in the *Philippine Sea* (CG 58) Combat Information Center (CIC). It came in the form of eighteen land-, air-, and sea-launched American-made Harpoon missiles that approached from all points of the compass. The *Philippine Sea* and her consort, the USS *Porter* (DDG 78), dealt with seventeen of them, but one of the ASCMs penetrated and struck the *Philippine Sea* amidships, putting her dead in the water and out of action. The *Porter*, distracted while rendering assistance, was struck by a Harpoon in the next attack (at 0025 on 29 July), penetrating her hull and knocking out her missile battery. While the other two Aegis ships rushed to assist from sixty miles

---

1 Imaginary fourth-generation descendent of the captain of CDR George Dewey's flagship at Manila Bay in 1898.

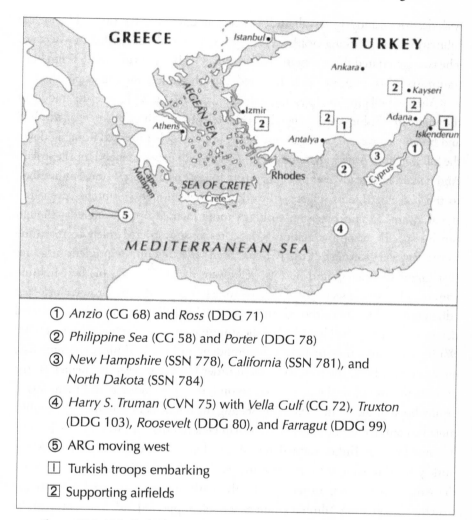

① *Anzio* (CG 68) and *Ross* (DDG 71)

② *Philippine Sea* (CG 58) and *Porter* (DDG 78)

③ *New Hampshire* (SSN 778), *California* (SSN 781), and *North Dakota* (SSN 784)

④ *Harry S. Truman* (CVN 75) with *Vella Gulf* (CG 72), *Truxton* (DDG 103), *Roosevelt* (DDG 80), and *Farragut* (DDG 99)

⑤ ARG moving west

☐ Turkish troops embarking

② Supporting airfields

Figure 15-3. U.S. Sixth Fleet Interposes

away, eight more Turkish Harpoons arrived. Five missed or were defeated by soft-kill, but two struck one ship and one hit the other, putting both out of action. At 0230 the two undamaged Aegis ships arrived from their eastern position, circled, and sweated until fleet tugs could arrive from Naples. The attacks stopped. Turkey either had no other Harpoons at the ready, was husbanding the remaining ones, or felt that the destruction was enough. In the two crippled warships there were ninety casualties.

Immediately after that, the Turks, thinking the way was clear, deployed an army brigade in five landing ship, tanks (LSTs) and two transports, heavily escorted with destroyers and frigates, all under intense air cover. But the three U.S. nuclear submarines were lurking nearby. One detected, trailed, and called in a second. The two penetrated the screen in tandem and at 0410 they sank an LST and both transports in six minutes. Seven hundred Turkish soldiers and sailors perished.

After assimilating the facts of the disaster, at 0530 on 29 July, in the middle of the night in Washington, General Grouse telephoned the chairman of the JCS and broadly conveyed a range of options in response. He proposed bringing down the full weight of American firepower on Turkey with massive air and missile strikes. And he said he already had put U.S. Army forces on full alert. Grouse subscribed to the JCS doctrine of full-spectrum dominance through comprehensive situational awareness and precision strike. A more focused option offered—though not his specific recommendation—was a response restricted solely to maritime forces. But the chairman of the JCS had been reflecting on the prudent measures that Grant had taken, and he was well aware that Grant was his best fighting admiral. He and the secretary of defense were not persuaded by Grouse's lock-step adherence to doctrine, although they remained appalled at Turkey's deep-seated determination and the bloodshed of the stunning attacks. Five hours later, at 0600 Washington time, they met with the president and received his near-immediate endorsement. First, the secretary was to order Grouse to keep his planes on the ground and troops in their barracks. Second, they concluded that if there was to be any hope of the United States forestalling the outbreak of war, then the conflict must be confined to the sea. The chairman believed that this was feasible because it would be what Turkey wanted as well. The United States somehow had to stop Turkey from moving into the Aegean—without hitting Turkish territory. Since the American role was to remain strictly maritime, they imposed a command structure designating Admiral Grant as the sole supported task force commander for the operation.

Concurrently the president and secretary of state had to move heaven and earth to bring the Turkish government to its senses. World opinion must be brought to bear, while Greece was kept on the sidelines with assurances that no Aegean island would fall to Turkey. A somewhat chastened President Harris now agreed that Turkey could be told—through the Russians perhaps—that the world would look sympathetically on its frustrations once it abandoned its intention of forcible entry into the Greek islands.

Even before the NSC meeting, the commander in chief set the wheels in motion. At 1400 Naples time on 29 July, Grant was told that his mission was to prevent Turkish forces from seizing the Greek islands—without his touching Turkish soil! In the fifteen minutes that it took the secretary of defense and chairman to outline the situation as Washington saw it, Grant formulated a solution to his knotty problem. "Does 'Turkish soil' exclude the Turkish transports in port?" he asked. The Secretary mumbled and the chairman blinked. Grant concluded that he had been given all the official sanction that he was going to get. They would have the details of his plan soon enough.

Grant immediately summons his staff, outlines his concept, and asks for a quick estimate of the situation. The staff points to the possibility that the Turks could launch an airborne invasion of the islands, but Grant rejects that; instead, he believes that if the Turks do not believe they control the coastal waters sufficiently to move safely by ship then they will not attack at all.[2]

That settled, the staff next makes the calculations for an operation order and rapidly feed it into a dynamic, geographical plot that depicts a large array of interlocking movements. By 1900 Grant has tweaked and approved the document and has disseminated it electronically to all NAVEUR ships and stations. The Joint Chiefs also receive the information and quickly digest it. USEUCOM also has it, in case the conflict escalates, and as important, for the purpose of coordinating any required support.

Enemy Moves

At 2000 the Turkish high command accelerates its timetable by issuing orders to move troops to the LSTs, LCTs, LCMs, and transports for the short run to the five Greek islands. Simultaneously, the Turkish surface fleet is ordered to close on the five ports of embarkation, in order to screen the movement and support the landings. Air Force aircraft are shifted to western Turkey and new search and covering tasks are assigned. Six modern diesel submarines move into screen stations, and minecraft, unable to match the pace, prepare to lay minefields.

At first light on 30 July, American satellites pick up evidence of Turkish troop, ship, and aircraft redeployments. By mid-morning, clues to the imminent invasion have been inserted into global command-and-control systems (GCCS) displays

---

2   This is a cavalier dismissal of a real choice, for much of the Turkish army is air-mobile. We have set it aside because we already have described what seems to be a sufficiently complicated operational situation to make the point that tactics attempt to reduce operational considerations to a simple and straightforward combat plan. Among the many American actions when an incipient air movement has been detected, one might be to insert the otherwise unemployed SEALs to perform their mischief at the airheads, which Turkey would want near its west coast for a fast turnaround.

and text. Grant has the same information in Naples that is being held in Washington. Nine destroyers and fast-attack craft will be coming down from the Dardanelles. He estimates that some of these ships carry Harpoons, but most will have shorter-range Penguin missiles that are well-suited for the cluttered waters of the northern Aegean. Although Grant cannot see them on the plot, the entire Ionian coast is blanketed with small patrol boats and fishing vessels that have been employed to supplement Turkish air reconnaissance.

The satellites show the big picture. Ten Turkish warships, clearly identified as Harpoon-shooters, will be moving west from the vicinity of Cyprus. About twenty more Turkish destroyers, frigates, and fast-attack craft are at the naval base at Aksaz on the southwest Anatolian coast, and Grant assumes all of them will be able to get under way to join the Cyprus contingent. In all, he expects to face an enemy force of 25 or more destroyers and fast-attack craft, carrying about 180 Harpoon missiles among them, coming up from the south. They will enter the Aegean on the evening of 31 July.

Even more crucial, the satellites have pinpointed the exact locations of the transports and larger amphibious ships in five ports of embarkation, Ayvalik off Lesbos, Cesme and Izmir near Chios, Kusadasi near Samos, and Bodrum adjacent to Cos. U.S. intelligence knows the exact positions of the troop ships and has passed along the precise latitude and longitude of individual targets to Grant's ships so that their crews can plug them into their missile-guidance systems.

Which missiles? They must be the small ballistic missiles carried in the *Phantoms*. These are normally used to provide tactical support for Marines or soldiers fighting ashore. Harpoons and Tomahawks are next to useless. For one thing, most of the ports are deeply embedded in the Turkish coast behind terrain that is tricky for cruise missiles to traverse. For another, Turkey will be expecting cruise missiles, and has the port defenses to take out most of them. On the other hand, the *Phantoms'* tactical ballistic missiles (TBMs) are so new that Turkey has no effective defense against them. A Navy modification of the Army's tactical weapon, the TBMs can be delivered with the greatest precision and with a time of flight of only a few minutes. From the outset, Grant has dismissed an air strike from the Sixth Fleet carrier USS *Harry S. Truman* (CVN 75), in part because he fears that an air strike would cause too much collateral damage to the port cities, and partly because the U.S. jets would face more than two hundred Turkish fighter aircraft. Instead, the Sixth Fleet's three submarines must stay in a blocking position between Turkey and Cyprus. They cannot cover all the ports in the Aegean, nor does Grant want nuclear-powered attack submarines (SSNs) tangling with Turkish mines and diesel submarines in the shallow waters of the Ionian coast.

The Tactical Plan

To deliver their TBMs, the *Phantoms* must not merely survive to reach their launch-positions within ninety miles of the targeted ports, but they must do so before the Turkish transports and LSTs get under way. Movement, even slow movement, is the friend of surface ships and foe of long-range missiles—especially in a cluttered coastal environment. Furthermore, Grant's information about where the Turkish forces are headed is not firm. The Turks have much better knowledge of the beaches and Greek defenses than Grant does. Once the transports are under way, Grant's problem will be unsolvable. That is what Grant saw instantly when the secretary and the chairman outlined his mission on the telephone, and it was why he needed their support to hit the transports in their ports where their locations were known to within a few meters.

Grant long ago had concluded that without the new *Phantoms* he would not be able to provide a maritime solution for the crisis. Eight of them, each with ten small TBMs, would be enough to neutralize nineteen transports and LSTs, ignoring the small landing craft that are too numerous to strike. The admiral estimates that if the *Phantoms* take out half or more of the nineteen large ships, then the Turks will not be able to proceed with their plan and will have to delay long enough for the full Atlantic Fleet to arrive.

Lieutenant Commander Genda, the tactical commander of the *Phantoms*, embarked in his tiny flagship, the USS *Ninja*, will target all nineteen.[3] Even though there might be a few undiscovered troop ships, Genda's orders are to shoot the works—to launch all eighty TBMs in one sudden pulse at the targets that have been located by satellite.

Although firing eighty missiles against nineteen undefendable targets may seem to be ample overkill, Grant does not expect 100 percent coverage. The missiles have bomblets that can blanket an area as large as two football fields. They are less than ideal ship-killers, but they can wreak havoc with the topsides, electronics, and bridges of each transport and probably can cause damage one deck down as well. If the transports are filled with troops, the carnage will be dreadful. Grant hopes to launch his strike before they embark. Even so, although the loss of life would seal the delay he seeks, the bloody result of such an attack would hardly be the way to soothe Turkish passion or evoke sympathy among the press and world opinion.

---

3   In his Naval Academy days Sammy (for Samurai) Genda was considered a master of creative mischief. He never would have graduated if the commandant had not persuaded the superintendent that Sammy Genda's talents would someday bring rich rewards.

The problem is moot. The attack is scheduled for the earliest possible moment. The *Phantoms'* fast carrier is slated to pass south of the Peloponnesus at 1700 on 31 July, an hour behind the *Cushings*. Since the passage will be in daylight and the weather is expected to be clear, there is a good chance that the U.S. ships may be spotted, but Grant thinks that no alarm bells will ring until the *Phantoms* actually are launched. The *Phantoms* will enter the water after dark, around 2100, just west of the Cyclades. It will take a courageous Turkish reconnaissance effort to reach across the Greek-dominated waters, along with a lot of Turkish faith in Greek restraint. An air screen from the *Harry S. Truman* (CVN 75) will be flying between the Cyclades and Dodecanese until dark in hopes of giving the Turks a false indicator of American intentions.

That said, the big hazard for the *Phantoms* is not the Turks, but the Greeks. Will the word from Athens be disseminated? Will the Greeks eschew their own reconnaissance effort? Will scores of Greek ships and aircraft and missile batteries allow unidentified ships to pass unreported and unmolested? Grant did not reveal his plan to Athens; a leak was too likely. He can afford to lose some aircraft; he will surely lose *Cushings;* he cannot afford to lose *Phantoms*.

After dark the *Phantoms* will glide through the Cyclades. Having no electro-magnetic signature, they can only be detected by human eye. Small, low in the water, and stubby (so they can fit into their mothership-carrier), they are never easy to detect, even in daylight. At night, in a state-three sea under a waning moon that will not rise until 0100, there is a good prospect that they will be able to penetrate the Cyclades unnoticed by both the Greeks and the Turks. A chance fisherman or coastal trader most likely will see dark shapes with no lights, but it will take time for the report of their mysterious presence to reach proper authorities. And no Greek or Turkish missile-seeker head can detect and home on a *Phantom;* gunfire and cutlasses are the only weapons that can be used against them. The *Phantoms* will report their movements and locations to one another with minimal detection. Genda is bemused thinking that his vessels will be almost side by side, yet are virtually invisible to each other. There will be no formation and no mutual support. Any one of them that is picked off must be abandoned, its crew of twelve left on its own.

Genda will take the *Ninja, Phantom, Ghost,* and *Furtif*[4] northeast and, after clearing the islands, run the last fifty five miles across open water—although to help suppress their wakes, the passage will look more like a tiptoe than a sprint.

---

4 In Navy tradition, warships carry names even when they cost only 60 million dollars; stealthy U.S. Air Force bombers do not, even when they cost twenty times more.

The four will take station just east of the little island of Psara and huddle almost against its coast. There they will rendezvous and await Grant's signal to launch, expected at 0400 on 1 August. Their targets are in Ayvalik, Cesme, and Izmir.

The second set of four *Phantoms* is under the senior CO, LT Stephanie Decatur, USN, embarked in the *Black Knight*. Along with the *Sting, Mist,* and *Silencioso*, this flotilla will take a more southerly route, passing slowly, quietly, and separately through the Greek islands, gathering again at its launch-point in the shadows of Dhenova north of Amorgos.[5] Its targets are in Cesme—in tandem with the northern task element—and alone in the ports of Kusadasi and Bodrum.

Everything else in the Sixth Fleet has been marshaled in support of the intended 0400 attack, but the *Cushing*s play the indispensable role. Their task, although straightforward and easy to signal, is tactically demanding, hazardous in the extreme, and best-suited to the *Cushing*s, which are the only U.S. Navy war-ships that can carry out such a mission. The eight *Cushing*s are to draw attention—and missile fire—from up to twenty-five Turkish combatants.

They Are Expendable

Earlier, Grant had ordered the eight old *Cushing*s from their berths at Gaeta to screen the three amphibious ships. Yet, once he saw that there would be fighting in the Aegean, he sent them east. There are seven of them now, because one of the corvettes broke down. Since the plan calls for them to be at the entrance to the Aegean between Crete and Kithra an hour ahead of the *Phantoms*' mother-ship, he ordered them to arrive there at 1600 on 31 July. They have 500 miles to travel, but because of Grant's foresight they have ample time. He sent them through the Strait of Messina to shorten the distance and also to *increase* the chance that the Turkish navy would know that they were coming. After all, the *Cushing*s are his bait; some—and perhaps all seven—will sacrifice themselves to draw attention from the *Phantoms*.

Years ago, at Grant's insistence when he was commander of the Sixth Fleet, twelve *Cushing*s had been homeported in the Mediterranean. They had been cru-cial in defeating the Soviet fleet in the imaginary battle that was presented in the 1986 edition of *Fleet Tactics*, which did not foresee the collapse of the Soviet Union two years later. Eight of the ten *Cushing*s still in theater have put to sea,

---

5   In her veins flows the blood of LT Stephen Decatur, the officer who, in the dead of night on 16 August 1804, cut out and burned the American frigate *Philadelphia*, which had run aground and later was captured by Tripolitanian pirates. Stephen Decatur was later killed in a duel. Since Stephanie Decatur has a temperament to match that of her ancestor, it is probably well that dueling is passé in her modern, more civilized Navy.

and seven of these are now on the way to the Aegean. Each vessel weighs 800 tons and has a crew of sixty. Their main armament consists of eight Harpoon missiles and a 76-mm gun. They have meager ASW capability, but that is irrelevant. Each carries a Lamps helicopter. They are similar to dozens of the older designs that are still in use among the world's best coastal navies. Seven will be enough to play their sacrificial role.

Commander Gridley, Grant's own choice, has been in tactical command for a year, and under his leadership the *Cushings'* commanding officers have bonded as a team; each knows what to expect from the others. The tactical execution of the upcoming operation will be Gridley's, but the tactics are an extension of a plan that Grant worked out years ago. But this time there are some additional uncertainties. The *Cushings* are obsolescent for this mission, because there is a big question whether their Harpoons will penetrate the defenses of Turkish warships. The Turks are similarly armed with their own Harpoon variant, and their navy has trained assiduously to defend itself against Harpoon attacks because the ship missiles constitute the principal threat from Greece's surface navy. The Turks' skill with and against Harpoons is an irony of American foreign military assistance, Grant muses wryly.

Gridley will pass north of Crete and will steer slowly along the coast until dark with radars on and radios blaring tactical signals to ensure that the Turks and everyone else knows where he is. Carrier aircraft scouting between the Cyclades and Dodecanese will see any Turkish formation and forestall an ambush. The aircraft will also confirm the satellite information of the enemy's composition. At dusk around 1900 Gridley will alter course radically to port, step up speed to 31 knots, and head for the little island of Anafi. At 2100 the *Cushings* will form two very ragged lines abreast of four and three corvettes. Lateral spacing between ships will be an imprecise five miles. The two lines will leapfrog alternately, on signal using laser lamps. Each line in turn will sprint ahead at thirty-five knots plus, while the other dawdles at six knots in an attempt to look like small, innocuous shipping. Near Anafi, at around 2300, they will shape a course east toward the best estimated position of the twenty-five Turkish warships.

On a rotational basis, two of their Lamps helicopters will fly south to a point near the coast of Crete, flying high with radars turned on, for what will amount to a deception within a deception. If the Turkish navy has studied the *Cushings'* tactics, it will expect them to be hugging the coast. On some other occasion, the helicopters would be crucial scouts, but tonight, with confusing contacts all around, Gridley does not expect them to add much information. He does not

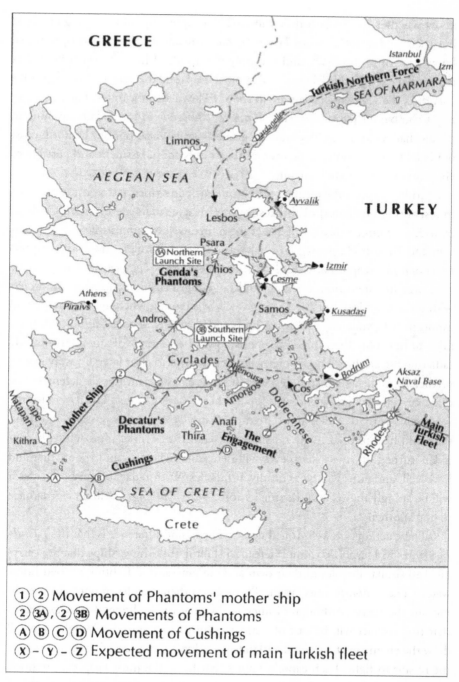

Figure 15-4. Grant's Battle Plan

① ② Movement of Phantoms' mother ship
② ③Ⓐ, ② ③Ⓑ Movements of Phantoms
Ⓐ Ⓑ Ⓒ Ⓓ Movement of Cushings
Ⓧ - Ⓨ - Ⓩ Expected movement of main Turkish fleet

324 ▷ Chapter Fifteen

know whether the Turkish fleet will have helicopters up and scouting at night, but their role is not a crucial factor, because the enemy already has operational knowledge of his presence, and it is only the details of his tactics that he wishes to conceal. If a Turkish helicopter approaches from the east to investigate his corvettes, the *Cushings'* orders are to shoot it down at eight miles. The American night combat air patrol from the *Harry S. Truman* is to intimidate anything in the air that is moving at fifty knots or greater—everywhere but off the north coast of Crete, that is. Gridley depends on the jets only for harassment and possibly to chase away enemy search aircraft.

Gridley expects the enemy's screen of Harpoon-armed fast-attack craft to be in a scouting line ahead of the destroyers. If their radars are on, then Gridley's own ships, running silent, will detect them first, well within missile range. American and Turkish Harpoons can reach seventy nautical miles, but Gridley expects to launch his weapons at a third of that because of the incipient electromagnetic duel over first detection, tracking, and targeting. Harpoons home in on targets with great precision, but the *Cushings* will be shooting where neutral traffic and innocent fishermen can end up as unintended targets. A sole *Cushing* will fire a salvo of not more than three Harpoons down the bearings of any intermittently radiating screen ship. The shooter will then attempt to clear laterally away from a predictable return salvo at high speed and to use passive antimissile defenses. The other corvettes will slow and wait for another radiating target. The reason for the weak salvo is that Gridley must attempt to survive as long as possible and drain the Turkish ships of as many missiles as he can. If the Turks approach with their radars turned off, then sharp eyes will determine who sees and shoots first and how well, and guns will be as deadly as missiles. With radars off on both sides it will be an ugly melee, and the smaller force—the *Cushings*—will do less damage to one another.

These actions are well-drilled tactics. The major difference is that the 7 *Cushings* with 56 Harpoons cannot defeat 25 skillful Turkish warships that are carrying 180 similar missiles of their own and are practiced at fighting in their home waters. The *Cushings* must, atypically, husband their missiles in hopes of stretching out the battle. Although Gridley is always wary, he hopes—even expects— that first contact will be east of Astipalaia sometime around midnight. He will draw the enemy west among the islands for as long as the surviving corvettes have the means to fight. Each captain knows that he or she must keep the attention of the Turkish force south of Amorgos, where the 4 southerly *Phantoms* will be heading.

The chief of staff reminds Grant that Gridley is going to have a fuel problem. Grant is abashed; oversights such as that can destroy the best of plans. But Gridley reports that he will arrive with enough fuel to operate wide open for perhaps three hours and his ships will not be at full throttle all the time. The ships that survive need only limp to the nearest Greek island inlet or harbor.

Grant Moves On Board

Around noon on 30 July, Grant and his battle staff depart headquarters in Naples in two tilt-rotor V-22s, leaving instructions to arrange an emergency meeting with the Greek minister of defense in Athens the next day. After landing on the *Harry S. Truman*, the designated Sixth Fleet flagship, he discusses the electronically transmitted battle plan with Vice Admiral Anchor. His old friend Patent tells Sam that he wants a bigger role, but he concedes that if the *Phantoms* fail he will have more than enough to do in dealing with some two hundred enemy aircraft. Grant plays best-of-five acey-deucey with the air wing commander, visits the chaplain, eats mid-rats with the aviators, showers, and registers a nap in the flag cabin.

At 0700 on 31 July Grant receives the satellite imagery update via GCCS. It confirms the locations and numbers of Turkish warships in motion. At 0900 he takes off in an escorted C-2 for his meeting in Athens, now set for 1300. En route the jets pass the V-22s, which also are cleared to land in Athens. On arrival, he devotes his thirty minutes with Defense Minister Giorgos Loucas to emphasize the message already transmitted from Naples. "If you please, do your utmost to tell everyone with a weapon to hold fire until a Turk tries to land on Greek soil," he tells Loucas. "Strange ships may be sighted almost anywhere. They will be American or Turkish. Please leave them be. Everything depends on every Greek soldier and sailor holding fire." Grant's plan does not actually stand or fall on Greek discipline, but if it breaks down he foresees chaos that will confound his own intentions and could open the floodgates of the war that he is trying to prevent.

At 1400 Grant's staff conspicuously boards the C-2, which takes off under a flight plan that has them bound for the carrier. Minutes later Grant departs unobserved in one of the V-22s, taking only his flag lieutenant (and communicator) and his operations officer. Grant may be the only one in his command who thinks so, but he is now firmly convinced that the battle plan will survive without him. The *Cushings* will take the crucial action, so he has arranged a stopover with them south of Cape Matapan. At 1500 Grant's hovering V-22 lowers the three NAVEUR officers to the deck of the *Cushings'* flagship, the USS *Victory* (one of the seven *Cushings* in company).

Grant's fear is not that "Ready" Gridley will be timid; just the opposite, for the tactics they had worked out were all designed to attack effectively first and win. This time, success depends on husbanding weapons so that enough *Cushing* firepower survives for an hour or more to sow confusion and draw the enemy's attention away until the *Phantoms* launch their eighty tactical ballistic missiles and they clear away to the west. Gridley has his orders, but in the flush of first battle, his passion and his killer instinct might take over. Weighing the risks like an old warhorse, Grant believes he should be at the point of attack in the *Victory.* In Naples he is superfluous. His chief of staff is the perfect campaign manager to keep Washington informed and fend off the second-guessers, and the staff does not need Grant to sort out the inevitable problems of broken parts, emergency supply, or a missed rendezvous.

In the *Victory,* Admiral Grant sits in the familiar squadron commander's station just behind the pilot and co-pilot seats. Gridley has the co-pilot's seat normally occupied by the officer of the deck (OOD). The captain, LCDR Ray Bernotti, sits at the pilot's console, which controls all operational aspects of the flagship.[6] The OOD has a fold-down seat normally occupied by the boatswain's mate of the watch, while the boatswain's mate himself stands watch on his feet, the old-fashioned way. The NAVEUR ops officer and flag lieutenant sit on campstools. It is a bit of a squeeze.

One of the terrible things about this war is that Grant is fighting an old friend. He first met and played squash with Admiral Mehmet Abdul, the present commander in chief of Turkish Naval Forces, in a port visit to Izmir when they were lieutenants. Their families grew close fifteen years ago, when Mehmet attended the Command and Staff course at the Naval War College. Later, as staff officers, they plotted and schemed over how they might coordinate a NATO operation against the Soviets in the Black Sea. The personal side of it is painful, but in addition, both friends know how the other thinks about tactics. Mehmet will know that Sam has something up his sleeve. There are not many opponents as mentally prepared to combat Grant and the Sixth Fleet as Admiral Abdul is.

Grant regrets one oversight: he might have disembarked some crew members of the *Cushings* to save lives, for not all sixty of each crew would be needed to serve the guns this night. He muses over the personal risk. If the plan fails, Grant will be relieved and court-martialed. If it succeeds, there will still be raised eyebrows

---

6 Bernotti is the great-grandnephew of Romeo Bernotti, Italy's leading writer on the tactics and operations of his day. Ray has absorbed his ancestor's penchant for mathematical analysis as well as his familiarity with operations in the Mediterranean.

because he did not manage the battle in the conventional way. If he has mis-judged the skill of Commander Gridley's captains and crews—or if he has under-estimated the enemy—then they will all be dead soon. The crews know the odds in a detached way, but they have never been in battle, and with the optimism of youth they think they are immortal.

Besides, Grant continues the thought, the *Cushings* trust me, Sam Grant, who beat the Soviets and has never lost a battle. This time, if I have assessed the battle correctly, more than half the *Cushings* will be sunk or out of action, and a quarter of these sailors—the best anywhere—will be casualties.

That is the personal side. To a combatant commander, the important opera-tional question is, "Will my plan work—and, if not, why?" If the plan fails, it will be because the *Phantoms* have also suffered severely, for there is enough overkill in their firepower that only a strange, unfortuitous event can defeat the attack. The TBMs have been tested, but never in battle. The intelligence is the best in the world, but it could have been deceived in plotting the Turkish ships. Grant's assess-ment that the troopships will still be pierside at the time of the TBM attack must be correct.

If the *Phantoms do* fail, then there will be bloody war. The rest of his Sixth Fleet, at the point of the sword, will be punished. Worse, the prestige of the United States will be in shambles, the Greeks will fight, the weakened Turks will be caught in a disaster of their own making, and the potential chaos in the eastern Mediter-ranean and in southwestern Asia will be incalculable.

All will be revealed in six hours, Grant muses. Yes, the operation will succeed because it is sound. "I didn't join this profession for its certainties," he reflects. The life is sweet, if not assured. Truly few things are safe and sure in war, yet the pieces are in place. He has assembled the forces to execute a good plan. The young commanding officers of the *Phantoms* and *Cushings* are well trained in sound doc-trine, and the ships are manned by crews able to stay up with swift and sudden warfare in these confining, confounding coastal waters.

Grant turns to the tactical commander and says,"Your weapons are free, Gridley."

Denouement

In only one aspect can the outcome of Grant's battle plan be reasonably forecast. It is that the *Phantoms* will launch their missiles on time and knock out enough Turkish amphibious capacity to fulfill the mission.

A novelist would be obligated to produce the rest of the story—the battle itself. The writer would create an aura of inevitability about the results. If Grant aspires to contemporary mores, then he must have feet of clay. He will err, but he will die a hero's death and with his honor unblemished. As far as the morals of this fable are concerned, however, Admiral Grant's life or death is irrelevant.

Grant's having put himself at the heart of the decisive tactical action will be jarring and unrealistic to some readers, but it fulfills the longstanding naval tradition that a commander leads his forces from afloat. E. B. Potter, the eminent naval historian, said that on his arrival at Pearl Harbor, Admiral Nimitz reluctantly decided that he would never be able to accompany his fleet to sea.[7] He would have to stay ashore to retain access to sensitive intelligence and have freedom to communicate up and down the chain of command. Moreover, Nimitz was going to be leading a very long campaign. Grant does not have these problems, for his short campaign must result in either one successful battle or in failure. It is fair to predict that he will succeed, partly because he is in the thick of it at the decisive point. In most contemporary circumstances, however, the fighting fleet is better served if the operational commander stays at headquarters while the tactical commander fights. Grant is almost unique because we have embodied the requisite tactical skills in him.

A novelist also would tell us whether the American fleet's tactical victory led to successful negotiation and peace restored, but this book offers the reader no assurances about that. We can only assert that the president saw his best chance, the secretary of defense and chairman of the Joint Chiefs gave the job to the best leader, and American forces contributed everything that military action could do to provide some breathing-room for negotiations.

A detailed description of the fighting would center on the *Cushings'* brave deception. The seven little combatants take on a force three times larger numerically and five times larger in displacement in order to draw some Turkish fangs. Neither side can do what every modern force armed with missiles wishes to do: stand off and deliver a decisive attack first. The battle is a purposeful melee, similar (though probably inadvertently so) to the circumstances created by RADM Dan Callaghan, USN, in his night battle of Guadalcanal on 12–13 November 1942. Callaghan lost control, but confused both sides so much that one Japanese battleship was sunk and the other retreated. He died fulfilling his mission to protect Henderson Field at the climax of the campaign.

The previous chapter discussed how to appraise the combat potential of two missile forces in opposition. If both sides are able to engage, the circumstances will be so unstable that a small change in the hit-probabilities, the distribution of fire,

---

7 Potter, "The Battle of the Coral Sea," in Sweetman, p. 244.

the defensive effectiveness, or the thwarted detection and tracking of all the enemy will create wide swings in the resulting damage. The chapter showed why this was so and that such instability is inherent in missile warfare.

As such, the only way to avoid the extreme uncertainty about the outcome of a battle is to attack effectively first. A battle of exchange will be confused and unpredictable, yet Gridley's orders from Grant are designed to *force* an exchange. Despite coherent fighting instructions, after only a few salvoes he will lose control and the result will depend on the wits, discipline, and sangfroid in each of the *Cushing*s. The same is true on the Turkish side. We have given the American side an edge in the first encounter (it is not clear whether this is reasonable), but any application of the analytical technique used in the previous chapter will conclude that the Turkish fleet can absorb an initial American success and still destroy the U.S. force.

The Turks would fight differently if their purpose were simply to sink American ships. But the Turkish tactical commander has a higher responsibility to protect the beachhead—that is to say, to secure the safety of the amphibious operation. He must also husband his forces because the Greek navy lurks just beyond the metaphorical horizon. At the operational level it is almost always the case that a victory at sea is a means and not the end, and external considerations abound.

There is another reason not to narrate the night engagement by which Gridley will empower the *Phantoms'* attack. A narrative would imply too much power in tactical analysis to trace the probable course of events and foresee the outcome in detail. For what it is worth, we expect the *Cushing*s to put an equal number of the enemy—about seven—out of action. Our forecast is that the Turkish fleet will expend about half of its 180 missiles in the confusion. The *Cushing*s should expect to put more tonnage out of action and inflict more casualties because the enemy's ships are larger. If they are skillful in the opening moves, Gridley's seven corvettes at most might hit twelve enemy warships using their fifty-six Harpoons. If the Turks are quick to react, they might lose only three or four ships.

An interesting possibility is that countermeasures against the Harpoons unexpectedly may be so successful that many ships are left untouched after both sides' missiles are used up, and the battle might conclude with gunfire. In a gunnery duel, the Turkish force has an even greater advantage. Only the possibility of widespread confusion could help the Americans to hurt and distract the Turks.

It is reasonable for Grant and Gridley to expect that when the battle is over few, if any, *Cushing*s will limp away. Applying both the history of missile combat and the quantitative analysis in chapter 13, there is no way for the American *Cushing*s to defeat the Turkish battle force that is opposing them. The uncertainty of outcome simply is not *that* great. As noted before, the Turkish fleet is quite competent, as are the coastal forces of many states when fighting in their home waters.

Gridley's *Cushings* are old, similar to smaller, aging combatants among most of the world's navies. The newness and the surprise are in the *Phantoms*. The *Phantoms*' TBMs, in combination with overhead sensors and a modern networked command-and-control system, constitute Grant's decisive combat system.

Although the circumstances of the Battle of the Aegean are unique, *every* battle in coastal waters will be unique. Many countries have well-conceived, tightly drawn, intensely practiced coastal defenses. In a more extended littoral conflict, land-based sensors, missiles, and aircraft will all be prominent. Depending on the geographical center of interest, coastal submarines and mines will be important. Based on the composition of coastal navies and their articulated strategies, small surface combatants, usually carrying missiles, will always participate. Coastal commercial vessels on the surface serving as scouts will also be important players. To reduce casualties, the U.S. Fleet must have numbers of small fighting ships that can be lost in combat without aborting a mission along a treacherous coast. It is for these reasons that in this fictional account we gave Grant the *Phantoms* and the *Cushings*. Even with all its firepower, today's American Navy cannot fight unbloodied in the home waters of states with strong coastal defenses.

Updating the Scenario

How will the new technologies that are now under development affect future American tactics in ways that were not evident almost twenty years ago when the second edition of this book was published? One obvious—and important—difference is that future commanders will be able to deploy unmanned combat aerial vehicles (UCAVs) carrying modern antiship missiles instead of the imaginary *Phantom*-class warships armed with yet-to-be-developed short-range ballistic missiles. The UCAVs would be housed in the same nondescript vessels that carried the tiny, low-observable *Phantoms*. And this time the Navy would be able to deliver several squadrons of unmanned attackers instead of the ten imaginary short takeoff, vertical landing (STOVL) aircraft that were available here. Flying low and at night, the unmanned aircraft would have a better chance of successfully carrying out a surprise attack on the four ports at which the Turkish amphibious ships were to load assault troops. In our new (future) scenario, UCAVs also will arrive faster than small surface ships, and time will be of the essence.

Another development, already in use today, is hand-launched surveillance drones such as the Puma, capable of launch and recovery from ships—large and small. Adapted from use ashore by ground forces, these small low-cost systems can provide organic surveillance extending the eyes of any ship. If the *Cushings* were so equipped in our vignette, their situational awareness of the approaching engagement would have been amplified. With these systems comes the potential for sustaining tactical awareness for longer periods without relying on own ship's radar, embarked helicopters, or external search assets. Of course, this technology is also available to the adversary, further complicating the thrust and parry of naval conflict in littoral waters.

Recently developed information warfare technology creates the ability to communicate almost without detection using a new signal book for transmitting short, unambiguous commands in milliseconds. As a result, Admiral Grant will be able to exercise a degree of control that was inconceivable twenty years ago. By exploiting information technologies, he should be able coordinate his *Cushings'* and *Phantoms'* attack or new UCAV equivalents.

The use of unmanned surface vehicles (USVs) may strengthen and enhance Grant's efforts to carry out a tactical deception, either by reducing the losses to the *Cushings* or by replacing those vessels entirely with an array of electronically noisy, deceptive USVs. Evasive vessels such as these, controlled remotely, might succeed in drawing Turkish attention and hostile fire away from the attacking *Phantoms*.

Special forces units such as Navy SEALs (for Sea, Air, and Land teams) were available in 1999, but were not used in the previous version of this vignette. In the past twenty years, however, the SEALs have expanded their competencies and techniques. Stealthy surface ships (probably not aircraft) might be ordered to insert detachments of SEALs in the vicinity of the Turkish embarkation ports, with orders to impede and delay the loading of assault forces until the *Phantoms* attack.

Modern nonnuclear submarines also are becoming more effective. They were not considered previously by the American side because they cannot transit long distances as fast as SSNs; in a crisis that boils up as swiftly as the Turkish-Greek confrontation, nonnuclear submarines would take more time to move to the scene of action. Yet, if such small, nonnuclear submarines were in the area already, they could be risked in the shallow, dangerous waters between the Turkish embarkation ports and the nearby islands that would be targets in an assault. At the same time, submarine torpedoes that sink more amphibious ships would lead to yet more Turkish casualties, and would dash the Americans' hopes of defeating the Turkish campaign with as few casualties as possible.

Although this book has discussed the use of complicated combat operations in which artificial intelligence (AI) systems quickly digest information to aid human decision-makers, the use of American AI does not seem as important in the Aegean operation as it likely would be in confronting more sophisticated enemy forces. Even so, ASCMs such as those that crippled the USS *Stark* (FFG 31) and sank the HMS *Sheffield* can be expected to be faster, hotter, and lower flying than those that were envisioned in the 1999 scenario. Perhaps coupling artificial intelligence with human decision-makers will give future Aegis ships a better chance to survive the kind of Turkish missile attack described in our current vignette—by helping U.S. commanders keep up with missile technology and diminishing reaction time.

Chapter 12 highlighted the vulnerability of space satellites. American satellites already contribute by pinpointing the Turkish amphibious ships and guiding the *Phantoms*' TBMs to their targets, but technologies already are emerging with the potential to negate or interfere with such attacks. The specific American strike tactics used in the current "Battle of the Aegean" cannot always be expected to work as well against a modern, high-end enemy that employs a full array of capabilities to contest the battlespace.

Just as the circumstances of the Battle of the Aegean are unique, every battle in any littoral waters will be different. Many nations have well-conceived, tightly drawn, intensely practiced coastal defenses. In a more extended conflict, land-based sensors, aircraft, missiles, and small autonomous aircraft will be prominent. Depending on the geographical center of interest, coastal submarines and mines may participate, conceivably augmented by autonomous undersea search-and-attack units. In turn, these will create new threats to large, high-cost submarines or multipurpose surface vessels in confined, shallow waters that are dotted with islands and shoals. Looking at the compositions of coastal navies, small, manned surface combatants, accompanied by even smaller unmanned surface vehicles, will participate. Coastal commercial vessels, including scores of fishing vessels, will serve as clandestine scouts to target easily identified large warships and deliver early warning of an aircraft attack. To reduce the casualties, the U.S. Fleet must have adequate numbers of small fighting ships and unmanned aircraft, aided by allies' scouts and attack vessels. These must be units that can be lost if need be without aborting a mission along a treacherous coast. It is for these reasons that Grant employed *Phantoms* and *Cushings* as his decisive combat units. Even with all of its firepower, the Navy cannot fight unbloodied in the home waters of states that have strong coastal defenses.

Above all, this imaginary vignette has shown the need to develop fleet tactics for modern warfare, both to defend the open ocean against enemy interdiction operations and to attack when required in confined waters characteristic of the Aegean Sea.

APPENDIX A
Terminology

The use of terms in this book is consistent with the definitions given below. Wherever possible, standard definitions from the *DoD Dictionary of Military and Associated Terms* or from standard dictionaries have been adopted or adapted.

Military terminology varies among sources and is casual in application. Even where agreement is widespread, it is impossible to apply "standard" definitions everywhere. Most dictionaries, for example, define *tactics* as an art and science. This is not general naval usage. In nautical language tactics are procedures, actions, things done or directed to be done. The science of tactics is just that—the science of tactics.

Doctrine is one of the military's most elusive words. The U.S. Navy used to avoid the problem of defining the term by ignoring it. Emphasis on joint operations since, say, 1990 has forced the Navy to take doctrine seriously, but it is premature to say that there is now agreement on the role or even the existence of Navy tactical doctrine.

One of the most common and potentially disciplining sources of military terminology is that used in physics. Even though such concepts as power, energy, pressure, and momentum cannot be as quantitative or unambiguous in the social study of men at war as it is in the study of inanimate objects, the use of these terms need not be as careless as it is in military affairs. For the purposes of this book, only *force, power,* and some of their compounds have been defined.

Special note must be made of the word *counterforce*. In the lexicon of nuclear planning, it refers to offensive attacks on enemy forces. As a prefix, *counter-* indicates opposition in direction or purposes; as an adjective, opposing or contrary; as a noun, an opposite or contrary thing; and as a verb, to oppose, offset, or nullify, to meet attacks with defensive or retaliatory steps, or to act in opposition. Thus usage with a defensive denotation seems best, despite the fact that defense against nuclear weapons has only been possible by offensive attack. We have chosen to restrict the meaning of tactical counterforce to defensive measures—that is, measures used to defeat an enemy attack in progress.

General Military Definitions

battle   a general encounter that includes combat between opposing armies, fleets, or many aircraft in order to achieve conflicting aims

combat   conflict involving the delivery of lethal force between opposing sides in a fight, action, engagement, or battle

conflict   competitive or opposing action of incompatible forces

doctrine   policies and procedures followed by forces to assist in collective action, either strategic or tactical. In a broad but acceptable sense, doctrine includes battle plans and practices for the immediate application of force.

strategy   establishes ends, ways, and means to achieve national or regional goals to protect U.S. interests. To be sure the established end is not an unattainable wish, a proper strategy includes ways (operational plans) and means (forces assigned and the tactics they employ) in order to estimate the likelihood that the end can be achieved.

tactics   the handling of forces in combat; acts of deployment, maneuver, and application of combat power. Sound tactics are procedures that employ forces to attain their full combat potential. It is not possible to define tactics or sound tactics as procedures to *win* a battle.

The Elements of Combat and Related Definitions

antiscouting   actions taken to destroy, diminish, or preclude enemy scouting effectiveness. Antiscouting includes the destruction of enemy scouts, such as shooting down a surveillance satellite or reconnaissance aircraft, deceiving enemy sensors, jamming sensors to reduce tracking or targeting effectiveness, and interfering with a scouting report.

command-and-control (C²)	the command organization, along with decisions made by and actions directed by the commander to employ force, counterforce, scouting, and antiscouting resources to accomplish an objective. C² includes the integration of scouting information, combat decisions, and the dissemination of these decisions, but it excludes acts of scouting themselves. Support for C² includes staff work, decision aids, and communications systems.
command-and-control countermeasures (C²CM)	actions taken to defeat or delay the effectiveness of the enemy's C². C²CM includes destruction, communications jamming, and the intrusion of false communications. Signals exploitation, however, is most appropriately categorized as an act of scouting.
counterforce	the capacity to reduce the effect of enemy firepower. In this book, it is the aggregate of defensive power and staying power. Although not so used here, counterforce can also include offensive attacks against enemy forces.
cover	secrecy, camouflage, or concealment to avoid attack—submergence, for example.
deception	deliberate misrepresentation of reality to gain an advantage
defensive firepower	the means of destroying attacking missiles, aircraft, or torpedoes
defensive power	the capacity to either destroy attacking weapons or defeat them by "soft-kill" methods other than shooting down
escorting	actions taken by accompanying forces to protect other forces or shipping by destroying the enemy or threatening his destruction
fighting power	a composite of force and counterforce, representing in some way the deliverable firepower over the combat life of the fighting unit. When *firepower* and *staying power* were common terms, *fighting power* incorporated both in a quantitative representation.
firepower	the material means of a fighting unit to reduce enemy forces. It is the capacity to destroy, measured in rate of delivery—as, for instance, shells per minute, or missiles in a complete salvo.
firepower kill	the elimination of an enemy force's means of delivering firepower for the duration of a battle
fleet	major forces used to gain, maintain, or dispute control of the seas. By this definition, neither amphibious forces nor ballistic-missile submarines constitute a fleet.

force   in general, the means of gaining an objective. *Military force* is the means of destroying the enemy's capacity to apply force.

forces   units that together can apply force, here defined to include not only firepower but also scouting and C^2 capabilities

maneuver   movement to achieve a tactical advantage. Maneuver can be associated with force, counterforce, scouting, or antiscouting. Ideally, maneuvers are made with all four elements in mind.

power   the rate at which force is applied against an enemy

scouting   acts of search, detection, tracking, targeting, and enemy damage assessment, including reconnaissance, surveillance, signals intelligence, and all other means of gathering information that may be used in combat. Scouting is not accomplished until the information is delivered to the commander being served.

screening   the use of forces to help protect other more valued units, accomplished by some combination of antiscouting and escorting, and often by scouting as well

search   the sensing phase of scouting. It may be active or passive or both.

sensing   roughly equivalent to *scouting*, sensing makes no assumptions about whether the sensed object is recognized (the classification step) or whether the information is delivered to the commander and assimilated into the decision process

staying power the capacity to absorb damage and continue fighting with measurable effectiveness

striking power the material means of a force to reduce enemy forces. This is a simple and unambiguous definition, but measurement of striking power can be a complicated process. The striking power of a carrier air wing can be measured by the number and category of aircraft comprising an attack, by the bombs or missiles carried, or by the estimated number of hits and damage the air wing is expected to achieve. Currently measurement of the striking power of an electronic cyberattack though important is particularly challenging to estimate.

APPENDIX B
Principles of War

···

Two compilations of principles of war are included in this appendix. They are transcribed just as they are found. The first is in then-captain Stuart Landersman's study, *Principles of Naval Warfare*, completed in 1982, when he was a member of the strategic studies group in the Center for Naval Warfare Studies at the Naval War College, Newport, Rhode Island.[1]

The second list is from Barton Whaley's study of deception and surprise, *Strategem*, completed in 1969.[2] Because Whaley is interested in the importance given to surprise by each authority, he places the principles in the order of the priority that the original authors intended or the order that Whaley believes the authors might have ranked them in the table below.

Landersman's Compilation of Principles of War

Sun Tzu	350 B.C.	Objective, unity, deception, initiative, adaptability, environment, security
Napoleon	1822	Objective, offense, mass, movement, concentration, surprise, security
Clausewitz	1830	Objective, offense, concentration, economy, mobility, surprise
Jomini	1836	Objective, maneuver, concentration, offense, deception
Mahan	1890	Objective, concentration, offense, mobility, command
Fuller	1912	Objective, mass, offense, security, surprise, movement
Foch	1918	Objective, offense, economy, freedom, disposal, security

---

1   Landersman, appendix E.
2   Whaley, pp. 122–26.

Corbett	1918	Objective, concentration, flexibility, initiative, mobility, command
U.S. Army	1921	Objective, offense, mass, economy, movement, surprise, security, simplicity, cooperation
Nimitz	1923	Concentration, time, initiative, surprise, mobility, objective, command, environment
Fuller	1924	Objective, offense, surprise, concentration, economy, security, mobility, cooperation
Liddell Hart	1925	Objective, offense, defense, mobility
Falls	1943	Objective, concentration, protection, surprise, reconnaissance, mobility
Stalin	1945	Objective, stability, morale, divisions, armament, organization
USSR	1953	Objective, surprise, speed, coordination, attack
U.S. Navy	1955	Objective, morale, simplicity, control, offensive, exploitation, mobility, concentration, economy, surprise, security, readiness
Eccles	1965	Objective, offensive, concentration, mobility, economy, cooperation, security, surprise, simplicity
Keener	1967	Objective, distribution, coordination, initiative, surprise
Mao	1967	Objective, concentration, annihilation, mobility, offense, surprise, attack, autonomy, unity, morale
U.S. Army	1968	Objective, offense, mass, economy, maneuver, unity, security, surprise, simplicity
Royal Navy	1969	Aim, morale, offense, security, surprise, concentration, economy, flexibility, cooperation, administration
Gorshkov	1976	Scope, strike, battle, interaction, maneuver, speed, time, dominance
Hayward	1976	Scope, strike, technology, mobility, coordination, readiness, concentration, reserve

Whaley's Compilation of Principles of War, c. B.C. to A.D. 1968

Theoretician	Order of Priority								
	1	2	3	4	5	6	7	8	9
Sun Tzu 4th cent. B.C.	Objective	Offensive	Surprise	Concentration	Mobility	Coordination			
Vegetius ca. 390 A.D.	Mobility	Security	Surprise	Offensive					
Saze 1757	Mobility	Morale	Security	Surprise					
Napoleon 1822	Objective	Offensive	Mass	Movement	Surprise	Security			
Clausewitz 1832	Objective	Offensive	Concentration	Economy of force	Mobility	Surprise			
Jomini 1836	Objective	Movement	Concentration	Offensive	Diversion				
P. L. MacDougall 1858	Mass	Direction	Concentration						
N. B. Forrest 1864	Mass	Direction	Rapidity	Offensive					
Fuller 1912	Objective	Mass	Offensive	Security	Surprise	Movement			
Stalin (1918–47)	Stability of the rear	Morale	Quality and quantity	Armament	Organizing ability of commanders	Surprise			
Foch 1918	Offensive	Economy of forces	Freedom of action	Free disposal of forces	Security				
C. V. F. Townshend 1920	Objective	Economy of forces	Mass	Offensive	Direction	Security			

Whaley's Compilation of Principles of War, c. B.C. to A.D. 1968 (*continued*)

U.S. War Dept., *Training Regulations*, nos. 10–5 1921	Objective	Offensive	Mass	Economy of force	Movement	Surprise	Security	Simplicity	Cooperation
Fuller 1925	Direction	Offensive	Surprise	Concentration	Distribution	Security	Mobility	Endurance	Determination
Liddell Hart 1929	Objective	Movement	Surprise	Mobility	Concentration	Security			
U.S. Command and General Staff School 1936	Offensive	Concentration	Economy of force		Surprise	Security	Cooperation		
Mao 1938	Political objective	Mobility	Offensive	Defensive	Concentration	Surprise			
U.S. Army FM 100–5 1941, 1944	Objective	Simplicity	Unity of command	Aggressive reconnaissance	Concentration of superior force	Surprise	Security		
Cyril Falls ca. 1945	Economy of force	Protection	Surprise		Maintenance of the aim				
Liddell Hart (1954–67)	Alternative objectives	Movement	Surprise						
Giap 1960	Political objective	Speed	Surprise	Morale	Security	Cooperation			
Guevara 1960	Objective	Mobility	Surprise						
Montgomery 1968	Surprise	Concentration of effort	Cooperation of all arms	Control	Simplicity	Speed of action	Initiative		
U.S. Army FM 100–5 (1962–68)	Objective	Offensive	Mass	Economy of force	Maneuver	Unity of command	Security	Simplicity	

Since both Landersman and Whaley have studied the principles of war far more extensively than we have, their lists must speak for themselves. The differences are as instructive as the similarities and are worthy of comment. They include

- The age and maturity of the author. Individuals' lists as well as organizations' lists may change over time.
- The historical period. The size of states, their forces, and their weapons affect the selection and priority of principles.
- The social milieu, especially whether it is Oriental or Occidental.
- The emphasis on tactics, strategy, or both. Nimitz deals explicitly with tactics, for example.
- The author's experience or viewpoint. Was it centered on international or revolutionary war? On major battles or guerrilla war?
- The military milieu, for example, whether the conflict takes place on land or at sea. (It seems that no author has emphasized air or amphibious warfare.)

As Whaley says, citing Henry Eccles,[3] these lists imply empirical maxims for a commander to bear in mind rather than principles denoting a primary source of wisdom, a fundamental truth, or a comprehensive law or doctrine from which others derive. They are lists of key words that together contain rich meaning. In many cases, they are interpretations of the author's intent, made either by Landersman or Whaley or by some intermediate student of the author.

Moreover, a principle properly understood is not a word but a statement that Landersman and Whaley presumed the tactician could infer from the one word. Yet, some one-word principles have changed over time or can be misunderstood. For example, *concentration*, as a guide to action, has been expressed as "concentrate superior force against the enemy at the decisive point of contact." Today, a concentrated attack can be delivered with missiles or unmanned aerial vehicles from dispersed forces, so a distinction must be made between physically massed forces from concentration of fire in time and space achieved by a dispersed disposition.

Take Nimitz, for example. As a middle-grade officer with experience in World War I behind him, he derived the principles recorded below from a slightly abbreviated transcript of his Naval War College thesis, completed in the spring of 1923. While Landersman has reduced Nimitz's conclusions to a set of representative key words, or "principles," the transcript itself is much more comprehensive, and even that is only a summary. Key words are a useful summation of a wise

---

3   Eccles, pp. 108–13.

man's deductions about the *principles* of war. Simple mathematical equations and graphical depictions are a useful summation of the *processes* of war. Landersman made much the same point in his study.

Thesis on Tactics[4]
The main and unchanging principles of warfare are:

First   To employ *all* the forces that can be made available with the utmost energy. This does not necessarily imply the offensive with its attendant advantages.

Second To concentrate superior forces against the enemy at the point of contact or where the decisive blow is to be struck.

Third   To avoid loss of time.

Fourth To follow up every advantage gained with utmost energy.

Main Principles
(a)   Attempt to surprise and deceive the enemy as to the plan of battle, and method and point of attack.

(b)   Seek to isolate a portion of the enemy battle line and crush it before it can be supported.

(c)   Maneuver on interior lines to save time, increase mobility and facilitate concentration.

(d)   Plan the battle so as to cut off retreat in case your force is stronger, or to facilitate breaking off the action if your force is the weaker.

(e)   Adhere to the plan and do not lose sight of the objective.

(f)   Modern fleets cannot be handled in single line by one officer. They must be in subdivisions, all within supporting distance of each other, with each subdivision controlled by a subordinate upon whom must be imposed authority, responsibility, and great freedom of initiative in accomplishing the end in view.

(g)   Make all practicable use of natural advantages such as wind direction, sea-state, direction of the sun, fog and reduced visibility, smoke, and smoke screens.

(h)   As a general rule, great results cannot be accomplished without a corresponding degree of risk. Efficient fleets are never *perfectly* ready for action. The leader who waits for perfection of plans, material, or training will wait in vain, and in the end will yield the victory to the one who employs the tools at hand with the greatest vigor.

---

4   Nimitz, pp. 3–4.

Bibliography

Compared with the number of books on strategy, there are very few unclassified English-language volumes that focus specifically on naval tactics. Articles on that subject in periodicals or other published research are scarce as well. Yet, comments and insights about tactics are plentiful in studies and histories of war; anthologies of sea stories; specialized books on, say, the development of aircraft carriers, radar, or naval architecture; or in books on naval operations analysis.

This bibliography contains all studies of naval tactics in English that are known to the authors. It includes books, articles, presentations, interviews, and papers that either were cited in the text or were thought especially worthwhile for research in the history, techniques, processes, combat environment, or analysis of tactics.

Abchuck, V. G., et al. *Vyendenue v Teoriu Vyraborki Reshenii (Introduction to Decision Making Theory)*. Moscow: Voyenizdat, 1972.

Albion, Robert G. *Makers of Naval Policy. 1798–1947*. Annapolis, Md.: Naval Institute Press, 1980.

Allen, CAPT Charles D., USN (Ret.). "Forecasting Future Forces." U.S. Naval Institute *Proceedings*, November 1982.

Arquilla, John. "Cyberwar Is Coming!" In *In Athena's Camp: Preparing for Conflict in the Information Age*, edited by John Arquilla and David Ronfeldt. Santa Monica, Calif.: The RAND Corporation, 1997.

———. *Dubious Battles: Aggression, Defeat, and the International System*. Washington D.C.: Crane Russak, 1992.

Bainbridge-Hoff, CDR William, USN. *Elementary Naval Tactics*. New York: John Wiley, 1894.

————. *Examples, Conclusions, and Maxims of Modern Naval Tactics.* Washington, D.C.: U.S. Government Printing Office, 1884.

Barfoot, C. B. *Crisis Response: Analysis of Historic Data.* Center for Naval Analyses representative on the London staff of the Commander in Chief, U.S. Naval Forces Europe (CINCUSNAVEUR), December 1997.

Baudry, Lieutenant Ambroise (French navy). *The Naval Battle: Studies of Tactical Factors.* London: Hughes Rees, 1914.

Beall, Thomas R. "The Development of a Naval Battle Model and Its Validation Using Historical Data." Master's thesis, U.S. Naval Postgraduate School, Monterey, Calif., 1990.

Beesly, Patrick. *Very Special Intelligence: The Story of the Admiralty's Operational Intelligence Centre, 1939–1945.* London: Hamish Hamilton, 1988; New York: Ballantine Books, 1981.

Belot, Admiral Raymond de (French navy). *The Struggle for the Mediterranean, 1939–1945.* Translated by J. A. Field. Princeton: Princeton University Press, 1951.

Bernotti, Lieutenant Romeo (Italian navy). *The Fundamentals of Naval Tactics.* Annapolis, Md.: Naval Institute Press, 1912.

Bernton, Hal. "Designed for Crew-free Sailing, Newest Military Ship Christened in Portland." *Seattle Times,* April 7, 2016, http://www.seattletimes.com/seattle-news/politics/designed-for-crew-free-sailing-newest-military-ship-christened-in-portland/.

Blackett. P. M. S. *Studies of War.* New York: Hill and Wang, 1962.

Blood, Christopher G., Richard T. Jolly, and Michael S. Odowick. "Casualty Incidence During Naval Combat Operations: A Matter of Medical Readiness." *Naval War College Review,* Autumn 1996.

Bordetsky, Alexander, Stephen Benson, and Wayne P. Hughes Jr. "Hiding Comms in Plain Sight: Mesh Networking Effects Can Conceal C² Efforts in Congested Littoral Environments." *Signal Magazine,* June 2016, pp. 42–44.

Bordetsky, Alexander, and Daniel Dolk. "A Conceptual Model for Networked Decision Support Systems." In *Proceedings of the 46th Hawaii International Conference on Systems Sciences:* IEEE Computer Security Press, 2012.

Bordetsky, Alexander, and S. Mullins. *Proceedings of the 18th International C² Research and Technology Symposium.* Washington D.C., 2013.

Borresen, Jacob. "The Seapower of the Coastal State." *Journal of Strategic Studies,* March 1994.

Brodie, Bernard. *A Layman's Guide to Naval Strategy.* Princeton: Princeton University Press, 1942.

————. *Sea Power in the Machine Age.* Princeton: Princeton University Press, 1943.

Brodie, Bernard, and Fawn Brodie. *From Crossbow to H-Bomb.* Rev. ed. Bloomington: Indiana University Press, 1973.

Brown, David. *Warship Losses of World War Two.* London: Arms and Armour Press. 1990; reprint, Annapolis, Md.: Naval Institute Press, 1995.

Brzozosky. Keith W., and Robert M. Memmesheimer. "The Application of the Souchard Ship Damage Model to World War II Ship Damage." White Oak: NSWC, 17 June 1988.

Bubke, Otto. *Clausewitz and Naval Warfare.* Bergisch Gladbach, Federal Republic of Germany: Federal Armed Forces Office for Studies and Exercises, August 1987.

Bush, Vannevar. *Modern Arms and Free Men.* New York: Simon and Schuster, 1949.

Bywater, Hector C. *The Great Pacific War: A History of the American-Japanese Campaign of 1931–33.* New York: Houghton Mifflin, 1925; reprint, with an introduction by W. H. Honan, New York: St. Martin's Press. 1991.

Callo, RADM J. F., USNR. "Finding Doctrine's Future in the Past." U.S. Naval Institute *Proceedings,* October 1996.

Callwell, Major General Sir Charles E. (British army). *Military Operations and Maritime Preponderance: Their Relations and Interdependence,* London: William Blackwood, 1905; reprint, with introduction by Colin S. Gray, Annapolis, Md.: Naval Institute Press, 1996.

Cares, Jeffrey R. and John Q. Dickman, *Operations Research for Unmanned Vehicles.* New York: John Wiley and Sons, 2016.

Castex, Admiral Raoul (French navy). *Strategic Theories.* Paris: Societe d'Editions Geographiques, Maritimes et Coloniales; reprint, translated and abridged with an introduction by Eugenia C. Kiesling, Annapolis, Md.: Naval Institute Press, 1994.

Clausewitz, Carl von. *On War.* Edited and translated by Michael Howard and Peter Paret. Princeton: Princeton University Press, 1976.

Clowes, Sir William Laird. *The Royal Navy: A History.* 7 vols. London: Sampson Low, 1897–1903.

Cohen, Eliot A. *Gulf War Air Power Survey.* 5 vols. Washington, D.C.: U.S. Government Printing Office, 1993.

Colomb, Vice Admiral Philip H. (British navy). *Naval Warfare: Its Ruling Principles and Practice Historically Treated.* 2 vols. London: W. H. Allen & Co., 1891; reprint, with introduction by Barry M. Gough, Annapolis, Md.: Naval Institute Press, 1990.

Cook, CAPT Charles, USN (Ret.). *The Battle of Cape Esperance: Encounter at Guadalcanal.* Annapolis, Md.: Naval Institute Press, 1992.

Corbett, Sir Julian S. *Some Principles of Maritime Strategy.* London: Longmans, Green, 1911; reprint, with introduction by Eric J. Grove, Annapolis, Md.: Naval Institute Press, 1988.

Crenshaw, CAPT Russell, USN (Ret.). *The Battle of Tassafaronga.* Baltimore: Nautical and Aviation Publishing Company of America, 1995.

Creswell, John. *British Admirals of the Eighteenth Century: Tactics in Battle.* Hamden, Conn.: Archon Books, 1972.

Creveld, Martin van. *Command in War.* Cambridge: Harvard University Press, 1985.

Cushman, LTG John H., USA (Ret.). *Command and Control of Theater Forces: Adequacy.* Cambridge: Harvard University Press, 1983.

Dahl, Erik J. *Intelligence and Surprise Attack: Failure and Success from Pearl Harbor to 9/11 and Beyond.* Washington D.C.: George Washington University Press, 2013.

d'Albos, Emmanuel E. A. *Death of a Navy: Japanese Naval Action in World War II.* New York: Devin-Adair, 1957.

Daniel, Donald C. *Antisubmarine Warfare and Superpower Strategic Stability.* London: Macmillan, 1985.

Daniel, Donald C., and Katherine L. Herbig, eds. *Strategic Military Deception.* New York: Pergamon Press, 1982.

Davis, Vincent. "The Politics of Innovation: Patterns in Navy Cases." *Monograph Series in World Affairs* 4, no. 3. Denver: University of Denver, 1967.

Deitchman, Seymour J. *New Technology and Military Power: General Purpose Forces for the 1980s and Beyond.* Boulder, Colo.: Westview Press, 1979.

Denning, Dorothy E. *Information Warfare and Security.* Boston: Addison-Wesley, 1999.

Deuterman, CDR P. T., USN. "The Matched Pair: A Tactical Concept." U.S. Naval Institute *Proceedings,* January 1982.

Douglas, Joseph D., Jr., and Amoretta A. Hoeber. "The Role of the U.S. Surface Navy in Nuclear War." U.S. Naval Institute *Proceedings,* January 1982.

Dull, Paul S. *A Battle History of the Imperial Japanese Navy, 1941–1945.* Annapolis, Md.: Naval Institute Press, 1978.

Dunnigan, James F. *How to Make War: A Comprehensive Guide to Modern War.* New York: Morrow, 1982.

Dupuy, COL Trevor N., USA (Ret.). *Numbers, Predictions, and War: Using History to Evaluate Combat Factors and Predict the Outcome of Battles.* Indianapolis: Hobbs-Merrill, 1979.

———. *Understanding War: History and Theory of Combat.* New York: Paragon House, 1987.

Eccles, Henry C. *Military Concepts and Philosophy.* New Brunswick, N.J.: Rutgers University Press, 1965.

Eckstein, Megan, Interview. "N99 Year-in-Review." 6 October 2016. U.S. Naval Institute, https://news.usni.org/2016/10/12/22016.

Evans, David C., and Mark R. Peattie. *Kaigun: Strategy, Tactics, and Technology in the Imperial Japanese Navy, 1887–1941.* Annapolis, Md.: Naval Institute Press, 1997.

Fioravanzo, Admiral Giuseppe (Italian navy). *A History of Naval Tactical Thought.* Translated by Arthur W. Holst. Annapolis, Md.: Naval Institute Press, 1979.

Fiske, CDR Bradley A., USN. "American Naval Policy." U.S. Naval Institute *Proceedings*, January 1905.

Fiske, RADM Bradley A., USN. *The Navy as a Fighting Machine.* New York: Scribner's, 1916; reprint, with introduction by Wayne P. Hughes Jr., Annapolis, Md.: Naval Institute Press, 1988.

Frank, Richard B. *Guadalcanal.* New York: Random House, 1990.

Friedman, Norman. *Naval Radar.* Greenwich, England: Conway Maritime Press, 1981.

———. *U.S. Aircraft Carriers: An Illustrated History.* Annapolis, Md.: Naval Institute Press, 1983.

———. *U.S. Destroyers: An Illustrated Design History.* Annapolis, Md.: Naval Institute Press, 1982.

Frost, Holloway Halstead. *The Battle of Jutland.* Annapolis, Md.: Naval Institute Press, 1936.

Fuller, J. F. C. *The Conduct of War, 1789–1961.* New Brunswick, N.J.: Rutgers University Press, 1961.

Gatchel, Theodore L. *At the Water's Edge: Defending Against the Modern Amphibious Assault.* Annapolis, Md.: Naval Institute Press, 1996.

Genda, General [*sic*] Minoru, JSDF (Ret.). "Tactical Planning in the Imperial Japanese Navy." *Naval War College Review*, October 1962.

Girrier, RADM Robert P., USN. "The Navy's Mission for UxS." Presentation, CSIS, Maritime Security Dialogue, Washington, DC, 29 January 2016, https://www.csis.org/events/navys-vision-unmanned-systems.

———. "Unmanned Systems: Enhancing Our Warfighting Capabilities Today and In the Future." *Navy Live*, 19 November 2015, http://navylive.dodlive.mil/2015/11/19/unmanned-systems-enhancing-our-warfighting-capabilities-today-and-in-the-future/.

———. "Unmanned: The New Normal." *Naval Institute Blog*, 4 August 2016, https://blog.usni.org/2016/08/04/unmanned-the-new-normal.

Gooch, John, and Amos Perlmutter. *Military Deception and Strategic Surprise.* Totowa, N.J.: Frank Cass and Co., 1982.

Gorshkov, Admiral of the Fleet S. G. (Soviet navy). *The Development of the Art of Naval Warfare.* Translated by T. A. Neely Jr., U.S. Naval Institute *Proceedings,* June 1975. First printed in *Morskoy Sbornik,* no. 12, 1974.

Green, Marjorie. "Drones, Future War—Unmanned Systems: A New Era For the U.S. Navy?" Center for International Maritime Security, July 18, 2016, http://cimsec.org/unmanned-systems-new-era-u-s-navy/26256.

Grenfell, Captain Russell (RN). *Nelson the Sailor.* New York: Macmillan, 1950.

Gretton, Sir Peter (RN). *Crisis Convoy: The Story of HX231.* Annapolis, Md.: Naval Institute Press, 1974.

Grove, Eric. *Fleet to Fleet Encounters, Tsushima, Jutland, Philippine Sea.* London: Arms and Armour Press, 1991.

Hackett, General Sir John, et al. *The Third World War: A Future History.* New York: Macmillan, 1978.

Hansen, Ib, and H. P. Gray. "Passive Protection and Ship Survivability in Years 2005–2020." David Taylor Research Center, SSPD 90–174–41. Bethesda, Md., 1990, CONFIDENTIAL.

Hazen, David C. "Nine Prejudices about Future Naval Systems." U.S. Naval Institute *Proceedings,* July 1980.

Helmbold, Robert. *Rates of Advance in Historical Land Combat Operations.* Bethesda, Md: U.S. Army Concepts Analysis Agency, 1990.

Hone, Thomas C., Norman Friedman, and Mark Mandeles. *American and British Aircraft Carrier Development, 1919–1941.* Annapolis, Md.: Naval Institute Press, 1999.

Horne, Charles. "What It Takes to Go Anytime, Anywhere." U.S. Naval Institute *Proceedings,* January 1998.

Hough, Richard A. *Dreadnought.* New York: Macmillan, 1964.

———. *The Great War at Sea, 1914–18.* Oxford: Oxford University Press, 1983.

Hughes, Terry, and John Costello. *The Battle of the Atlantic.* New York: Dial Press/James Wade, 1977.

Hughes, LCDR Wayne P., Jr., USN. "Missiles and Missions." U.S. Naval Institute *Proceedings,* December 1964.

———. "A Salvo Model of Warships in Missile Combat Used to Evaluate Their Staying Power." In *Naval Research Logistics,* March 1995, and in *Warfare Modeling,* edited by Jerome Bracken, Moshe Kress, and Richard E. Rosenthal. Alexandria, Va.: Military Operations Research Society, 1995.

———. "Speed Characteristics of the Treaty Cruisers." U.S. Naval Institute *Proceedings,* February 1953.

Hughes, CAPT Wayne P., Jr., USN (Ret.). "A Close Look at the Operational Level of War at Sea." *Naval War College Review,* Summer 2012.

Humphrey, Richard L. "Comparing Damage and Sinking Data for World War II and Recent Conflicts." Presented to the Thirteenth General Working Meeting of the Military Conflict Institute, McLean, Va., October 1992.

———. "Damage and Losses of Warships in Modern Combat." ORSA/TIMS presentation, Las Vegas, Nev., May 1990.

Huntington, Samuel P. "National Policy and the Transoceanic Navy." U.S. Naval Institute *Proceedings*, May 1954.

Hwang, John, Daniel Schuster, Kenneth Shere, and Peter Vena, eds. *Selected Analytical Concepts in Command and Control.* New York: Gordon and Breach, 1982.

Ivanov, D. A., V. P. Savel'yev, and P. V. Shemanskiy. *Osnovy Upravleniya Voyskami v Boyu (Fundamentals of Troop Control at the Tactical Level).* Moscow: Voyenizdat. Translation, Washington, D.C.: U.S. Government Printing Office, 1983.

Jameson, Rear Admiral William, RN. *The Fleet that Jack Built: Nine Men Who Made a Modern Navy.* London: Rupert Hart-Davis, 1962.

Joergensen, T. S. "U.S. Naval Operations in Littoral Waters: 2000 and Beyond." *Naval War College Review*, Spring 1998.

Kahn, David. *The Code Breakers.* New York: Macmillan, 1967.

Kelsey, CDR Robert J., (USN). "Maneuver Warfare at Sea." U.S. Naval Institute *Proceedings*, September 1982.

Kemp, Peter, ed. *The Oxford Companion to Ships and the Sea.* London: Oxford University Press, 1976.

Kennedy, Paul M. *The Rise and Fall of British Naval Mastery.* New York: Scribner's, 1976.

Kilpatrick. Charles W. *The Naval Night Battles in the Solomons.* Pompano Beach: Exposition Press of Florida, 1987.

Kisiel, Katherine. "Self-driving Warship Christened in Portland." *KATU News*, April 7, 2016, http://kval.com/outdoors/underwater-self-driving-warship-christened-in-portland.

Koopman, Bernard O. *Search and Screening: General Principles with Historical Applications.* Elmsford, N.Y.: Pergamon Press, 1980.

Lanchester, Frederick W. "Mathematics in Warfare." In *The World of Mathematics*, edited by James R. Newman. New York: Simon and Schuster, 1956.

Landersman, CAPT Stuart, USN. *Principles of Naval Warfare.* Newport, R.I.: Naval War College, 1982.

Lanza, Conrad H. *Napoleon and Modern War: His Military Maxims.* Harrisburg, Pa.: Military Service Publishing, 1943.

Lautenschläger, Karl. "Technology and the Evolution of Naval Warfare, 1851–2001." Charles H. Davis Series Spring Lecture, U.S. Naval Postgraduate

School, Monterey, Calif., April 1984. Washington, D.C.: National Academy Press, 1984.

Lehman, John. *Aircraft Carriers: The Real Choices.* Beverly Hills, Calif.: Sage, 1978.

Levert, Lee J. *Fundamentals of Naval Warfare.* New York: Macmillan, 1947.

Lewin, Ronald. *The American Magic: Codes, Ciphers, and the Defeat of Japan.* Great Britain: Hutchinson and Co., 1982; New York: Penguin Books, 1983.

———. *Ultra Goes to War.* New York: McGraw-Hill, 1978.

Lewis, Michael. *The History of the British Navy.* Baltimore: Pelican Books, 1957.

———. *The Navy of Britain: A Historical Portrait.* London: George Allen and Unwin, 1948.

Liddell Hart, B. H. *Strategy.* London: Faber and Faber, 1967; New York: Signet, 1974.

Macintyre, Donald, and Basil W. Bathe. *Man-of-War: A History of " the Combat Vessel.* New York: McGraw-Hill, 1969.

Mahan, Alfred Thayer. *The Influence of Sea Power upon History, 1660–1783.* Boston: Little, Brown, 1890.

Makarov, Vice Admiral Stepan Osipovich (Imperial Russian Navy). *Discussion of Questions in Naval Tactics,* with an introduction by CAPT Robert B. Bathurst, USN (Ret.). Annapolis, Md.: Naval Institute Press, 1990. Original translation, 1898, by LT J. B. Bernadou, USN, Office of Naval Intelligence.

Marble, ENS Frank, USN. "The Battle of the Yalu." U.S. Naval Institute *Proceedings,* Fall 1895.

McHugh, Francis J. *Fundamentals of War Gaming.* 3rd ed. Newport, R.I.: Naval War College, 1966.

McKearney, LCDR T. J., USN. "The Solomons Naval Campaign: A Paradigm for Surface Warships in Maritime Strategy." Master's thesis, U.S. Naval Postgraduate School, Monterey, Calif., 1985.

Meadors, LT Tyson B. *First Gain the Victory: Six Strategic Considerations for Naval Cyber Forces.* Prepared for and distributed by the Deputy CNO for Information Warfare and Director of Naval Intelligence, 2015.

Melhorn, Charles M. *Two-Block Fox: The Rise of the Aircraft Carriers, 1911–1929.* Annapolis, Md.: Naval Institute Press, 1974.

Miller, Edward S. *War Plan Orange: The U.S. Strategy to Defeat Japan, 1897–1945.* Annapolis, Md.: Naval Institute Press, 1991.

Mitchell, Donald W. *History of the Modern American Navy from 1883 through Pearl Harbor.* New York: Knopf, 1946.

Mordal, Jacques. *Twenty-five Centuries of Sea Warfare.* Translated by Len Ortzen. London: Souvenir Press. 1965.

Morison, Elting E. *Admiral Sims and the Modern American Navy.* Boston: Houghton Mifflin, 1942.

———. *Men, Machines, and Modern Times.* Cambridge, Mass.: MIT Press, 1966.

———. "The Navy and the Scientific Endeavor." *Science and the Future Navy: A Symposium.* Washington, D.C.: National Academy of Sciences, 1977.

Morison, Samuel Eliot. *History of United States Naval Operations in World War II.* 15 vols. Boston: Little, Brown, 1947–62.

Musashi, Miyamoto. *A Book of Five Rings.* Translated by Victor Harris. Woodstock, N.Y.: Overlook Press, 1974.

Navias, Martin S., and E. R. Hooton. *Tanker Wars: The Assault on Merchant Shipping During the Iran-Iraq Conflict, 1980–1988.* New York: I. B. Taurus, 1996.

Navy Chief of Information, Interview of RADM Robert P. Girrier, USN, Director, Unmanned Warfare Systems (OPNAV N99). CHIPS Magazine Online, 15 October 2016, http://www.doncio.navy.mil/CHIPS/ArticleDetails.aspx?ID=8294.

Nimitz, Chester W. "Thesis on Tactics." Newport, R.I.: Naval War College, 1923.

O'Hanlon, Michael E. *The Science of War: Budgeting, Military Technology, Logistics, and Combat Outcomes.* Princeton: Princeton University Press, 2009.

Osipov, M. "Vlyeyanye Chislyennosti Srazhayush-chiksya Storen Na Ix Potyera" ("The Influence of the Numerical Strength of Engaged Sides on Their Casualties"). *Voenniy Sbornik (Military Collection),* no. 6, June 1915; no. 7, July 1915; no. 8, August 1915; no. 9, September 1915; no. 10, October 1915. Translated by Robert Helmbold and Allan Rehm, U.S. Army Concepts Analysis Agency Research Paper (AA-RP-91–2), Bethesda, Md., September 1991.

Paxson, E. W., M. G. Weiner, and R. A. Wise. "Interactions between Tactics and Technology in Ground Warfare." Rand Report R-2377-ARPA. Santa Monica, Calif., January 1979.

Pemsel, Helmut. *A History of War at Sea: An Atlas and Chronology of Conflict at Sea from Earliest Times to the Present.* Translated by D. G. Smith. Annapolis, Md.: Naval Institute Press, 1975.

Polmar, Norman. *Aircraft Carriers: A Graphic History of Carrier Aviation and Its Influence on World Events.* Garden City, N.Y.: Doubleday, 1969.

Potter, Elmer B. ed. *Sea Power: A Naval History.* 2nd ed. Annapolis, Md.: Naval Institute Press, 1981.

Pratt, Fletcher. *Night Work: The Story of Task Force 39.* New York: Henry Holt, 1946.

———. *Our Navy: A History.* Garden City, N.Y.: Garden City Publishing, 1941.

Raven, Alan, and John Roberts. *British Battleships of World War II.* Annapolis, Md.: Naval Institute Press. 1976.

Reynolds, Clark G. *Command of the Sea: The History and Strategy of Maritime Empires.* New York: Morrow, 1974.

———. *The Fast Carriers: The Forging of an Air Navy.* New York: McGraw-Hill, 1968.

Richten, Eberhardt. "The Technology of Command." *Naval War College Review,* March–April 1984.

Robison, RADM Samuel S., USN, and Mary L. Robison. *A History of Naval Tactics from 1530 to 1930.* Annapolis, Md.: Naval Institute Press, 1942.

Rohwer, Jurgen. *The Critical Convoy Battles of March 1943.* Annapolis, Md.: Naval Institute Press, 1977.

Roskill, Captain Stephen W. (RN). *The War at Sea, 1939–1945.* 3 vols. London: H. M. Stationery Office, 1954–56.

———. *White Ensign: The British Navy at War, 1939–1945.* Annapolis, Md.: Naval Institute Press, 1960.

Rothstein, Hy, and Barton Whaley, eds. *The Art and Science of Military Deception.* Norwood, Mass: Artech House, 2013.

Sadkovich, James J., ed. *Reevaluating Major Naval Combatants of World* War II. New York: Greenwood Press, 1990.

Sanderson, Michael. *Sea Battles: A Reference Guide.* Middletown, Conn.: Wesleyan University Press, 1975.

Sankaran, J. "The Tactical Reach and Requirement of the Indian Navy." India: S. Rajarantum School of International Studies, October 2013.

Schulte, John C. "An Analysis of the Historical Effectiveness of Antiship Cruise Missiles in Littoral Warfare." Master's thesis, U.S. Naval Postgraduate School, Monterey, Calif., September 1994.

Secretary of State for Defence. *The Falklands Campaign: The Lessons.* London: H. M. Stationery Office, 1982.

Secretary of the Navy's Task Force Report. *South Atlantic Conflict Lessons Learned.* Washington, D.C.: Navy Department, 1983.

Sims, LCDR William S., USN. "The Inherent Qualities of All-Big-Gun, One-Caliber Battleships of High Speed, Large Displacement, and Gun Power." U.S. Naval Institute Proceedings, December 1906.

Singer, Peter W., and August Cole. *Ghost Fleet: A Novel of the Next World War.* New York: Houghton Mifflin Harcourt, 2015.

Spector, Ronald H. *Eagle Against the Sun: The American War with Japan.* New York: Free Press, 1985.

Stafford, CDR Edward P., USN. *The Big E: The Story of the USS* Enterprise. New York: Random House, 1962.

Stalbo, Vice Admiral K. "Some Issues of the Theory of the Development and Deployment of the Navy." *Morskoy Sbornik,* nos. 4 and 5, 1981.

Sternhell, Charles M., and Alan M. Thorndike. *OEG Report No. 51: Antisubmarine Warfare in World War II.* Washington, D.C.: OEG, Office of the CNO, Navy Department, 1946.

Stocker, LCDR Jeremy. "Non-Intervention: Limited Naval Operations in the Littoral Environment." *Naval War College Review,* Spring 1995.

Sweetman, Jack, ed. *Great American Naval Battles.* Annapolis, Md.: Naval Institute Press, 1998.

Talbott, J. E. "Weapon Development, War Planning and Policy: The U.S. Navy and Submarines, 1917–41." *Naval War College Review* (May-June 1984).

Tanaka, Rear Admiral Raizo (Japanese navy). "The Struggle for Guadalcanal." In *The Japanese Navy in World War 11,* edited by Raymond O'Connor. Annapolis, Md.: Naval Institute Press, 1969.

Taylor, James G. *Initial Concept of Soviet C².* Monterey, Calif.: U.S. Naval Postgraduate School, 1984.

Taylor, Theodore C. "A Basis for Tactical Thought." U.S. Naval Institute *Proceedings,* June 1982.

Tidman, Keith R. *The Operations Evaluation Group: A History of Naval Operations Analysis.* Annapolis, Md.: Naval Institute Press, 1984.

Tracy, Nicholas. *Nelson's Battles: The Art of Victory in the Age of Sail.* London: Chatham Publishing, 1996.

Tunstall, Brian. *Naval Warfare in the Age of Sail: The Evolution of Fighting Tactics, 1650–1815.* Edited by Nicholas Tracy. Annapolis, Md.: Naval Institute Press, 1990.

Tzu, Sun. *The Art of War.* Translated by Samuel B. Griffith. London: Oxford University Press, 1963.

Uhlig, Frank, Jr. *How Navies Fight: The U.S. Navy and Its Allies.* Annapolis, Md.: Naval Institute Press, 1994.

———. "How Navies Fight and Why." *Naval War College Review,* Winter 1995.

———. "Naval Tactics: Examples and Analogies." *Naval War College Review,* March-April 1981.

United States Air Force. *Dictionary of Basic Military Terms: A Soviet View.* Washington, D.C.: U.S. Government Printing Office, 1976.

United States Joint Chiefs of Staff. *Department of Defense Dictionary of Military and Associated Terms.* JCS publication I. Washington, D.C.: U.S. Government Printing Office, 1984.

Valle, J. E. "U.S. Merchant Marine Casualties." In *To Die Gallantly: The Battle of the Atlantic,* edited by T. J. Runyon and J. M. Copes. San Francisco: Westview Press, 1994.

Vego, Milan. *Soviet Naval Tactics.* Annapolis, Md.: Naval Institute Press, 1992.

Vlahos, Michael. *The Blue Sword: The Naval War College and the American Mission, 1919–1941.* Newport, R.I.: Naval War College Press, 1980.

———. "Wargaming: An Enforcer of Strategic Realism: 1919–1942." *Naval War College Review,* March-April 1986.

Washburn, Alan R. "Gross Measures of Surface-to-Surface Naval Firepower." Monterey, Calif.: U.S. Naval Postgraduate School, 1978.

Watson, Bruce W., and Peter M. Dunn, eds. *Military Lessons of the Falkland Islands War.* Boulder, Colo.: Westview Press, 1984.

Whaley, Barton. *Stratagem: Deception and Surprise in War.* Cambridge, Mass.: MIT Center for International Studies, 1969.

Wiener, Norbert. *Cybernetics.* 2nd ed. Cambridge, Mass.: MIT Press, 1961.

Willmott, H. P. *The Barrier and the Javelin: Japanese and Allied Pacific Strategies, February to June 1942.* Annapolis, Md.: Naval Institute Press, 1983.

Wilson, Henry W. *Ironclads in Action.* 2 vols. Boston: Little, Brown. 1896.

Wisecup, VADM James P. *The Network of Humans and Machines as the Next Capital Ship.* Chief of Naval Operations Strategic Studies Group 35 Final Report. Newport, R.I., 31 July 2016.

Wohlstetter, Roberta. *Pearl Harbor: Warning and Decision.* Stanford Calif: Stanford University Press, 1962.

Woodward, David. *The Russians at Sea.* London: Kimber, 1965.

Woodward, Sandy, with Patrick Robinson. *One Hundred Days: The Memoirs of the Falklands Battle Group Commander.* Annapolis, Md.: Naval Institute Press, 1992.

Wylie, RADM J. C., USN. *Military Strategy: A General Theory of Power Control.* New Brunswick, N.J.: Rutgers University Press; reprint, with introduction by John B. Hattendorf and postscript by Wylie, Annapolis. Md.: Naval Institute Press, 1989.

Ya'ari, Rear Admiral Yedidia "Didi" (Israeli navy). "A Word of Caution," originally published in the *Naval War College Review,* Spring 1995. Reprinted in the *Naval War College Review,* Summer 2014, with a comment by Wayne P. Hughes.

Index

acoustic emissions, 249

active defense, 296

Aden, Gulf of, 5

Aegean, Battle of the: American policy decisions, 311–13; confidence in battle plan, 325–27; crisis leading to, 308–11; denouncement, 327–30; enemy moves and force strength, 317–18, 329–30; fleet tactics in, 305; force strength and configuration for, 313–14, 321–22; as littoral combat narrative, 307; operational and tactical challenges in, 292, 306–7; the shocks, 314–17; tactical lessons and tactics for, 8; tactical plan, 319–25; technologies and tactics for, 307, 330–32

Aegean Sea, 135, 292n14

Aegis cruisers: Aegean battle example, 313, 314–15; massing for defense example, 282–84, 282n11; survivability of, 156, 332

aircraft: advances in range of, 5; attacks against targets at sea by land-based, 121–22; engines improvements for, 220; naval airpower development for World War II, 2, 77–80, 80n7; role in fleet operations, 78–80; scouting and antiscouting missions of, 78, 132, 186–87; speed and agility of, 172; striking power of, 336; technology development for, 24. See also bombers

aircraft carriers and naval aviation: battle to destroy carrier aircraft, 91; battle to sink, 91; daytime vs. nighttime tactics, 82–83, 83n10, 94; defensive strength and tactics, 89–91; dispersal or massing tactics, 81–82, 92–93; dual mission objectives of, 83, 94–97; early support for naval aviation, 24, 77–78; effectiveness of carrier air power, 195, 196, 262; firepower versus range comparison with naval guns, 174, 175–76; models of battle and dynamics of naval

actions with, 6, 191; net striking power and battle outcome, 84–91; offensive vs. defensive firepower, 82, 93–94, 98; overestimation and underestimations of air-strike effectiveness, 97; pulse of firepower from air wing, 84; role in Navy tactics, xxv; salvoes from air wing, 296–97; scouting effectiveness and battle outcomes, 84; screens for, 81, 91–92, 93; ship vulnerability to attacks from, 80; speed of, 194; surprise of attacks with, 28; tactical formation, 80–81, 91–92; tactical model of carrier warfare, 83–91, 97–98; tactics for, 76–80, 281; technology development for, 24; transition to, 224–25; Washington Treaty and construction of, 77; World War II success with use of, 28

air-land battle tactics, 3

airpower, 79–80, 167

American and British Aircraft Carrier Development, 1919–1941 (Hone, Friedman, and Mandeles), 2

amphibious operations, 25, 26–29, 28, 122, 123, 129

anchor, fighting at, 9–15

Anglo-Dutch wars, 39, 41, 42, 45–46, 132

anti-air warfare (AAW): carrier defenses with, 76, 79, 89, 91–92, 93–94, 98; combat life of ship and number of AAW missiles, 244; effectiveness of as counterforce, 183; prominence of as counterforce, 181; radar use in, 103; screens, 169; survivability measures against best weapons and effectiveness of second-best weapons, 182n12

antiscouting: concept and definition of, 4, 334; constants of, 212; counter-countermeasures, 188; electromagnetic technology for, 99–100; IW effects on, 248; littoral combat antiscouts, 287; missile warfare, 269; network-centric warfare, 280; process

About the Authors

CAPT Wayne P. Hughes Jr., USN (Ret.), served thirty years on active duty, commanding a minesweeper, a destroyer, and a large training command. In retirement he served more than thirty years at the Naval Postgraduate School in many teaching, research, and administrative capacities and is now dean emeritus. He received several honors from the Naval War College and the U.S. Naval Institute for his essays. Hughes is past president of the Military Operations Research Society and one of the first five fellows of the society.

RADM Robert Girrier, USN (Ret.), is founder and managing member of Strategic Navigation LLC, a consulting company. Serving more than thirty-three years in the Navy, he led the Navy staff's first-ever office for unmanned warfare systems. While on active duty he served as Deputy Commander Pacific Fleet, commanded two carrier strike groups, served as the Navy's global mine warfare commander, and commanded a forward-deployed destroyer squadron, a guided-missile destroyer, and a mine countermeasures ship. Co-author of three professional naval books, he holds master's degrees in international affairs, marine affairs, and public administration.